Jump at the Sun

Jump at the Sun

Zora Neale Hurston's Cosmic Comedy

John Lowe

University of Illinois Press   Urbana and Chicago

© 1994 by the Board of Trustees of the University of Illinois
Manufactured in the United States of America
C 5 4 3 2 1

This book is printed on acid-free paper.

Library of Congress Cataloging-in-Publication Data

Lowe, John
    Jump at the sun : Zora Neale Hurston's cosmic comedy / John Lowe.
        p.   cm.
    Includes bibliographical references (p.   ) and index.
    ISBN 0-252-02110-X (cloth : acid-free paper)
    1. Hurston, Zora Neale—Humor. 2. Humorous stories, American—
History and criticism. 3. Afro-Americans in literature.
4. Literature and folklore—United States. 5. Folklore in
literature. 6. Comic, The, in literature. I. Title.
PS3515.U789Z77   1994
813'.52—dc20   94-10586
                                                              CIP

For June Conaway Lowe

Laughter is more significant and profound than is thought. Not the laughter that is born of temporary irritability, of a bilious and morbid cast of characters, not that easy laughter serving the vain amusement and entertainment of men, but the laughter that arises in its entirety out of the bright nature of man, and arises out of it because at its bottom there lies the eternally flowing spring that is its source. . . . No: unjust are those who say that laughter perturbs. Only what is gloomy perturbs, and laughter is bright. Much would upset a man were it presented in all its nakedness. But, illuminated by the power of laughter, it already carries reconciliation into the soul. . . . But the powerful force of such laughter is not heard. Society says, "What is funny is base"; only what is uttered in a stern, tense voice is designated lofty.

—*Gogol*

American and Negro: it takes both adjectives to describe the humor. . . . This humor could not have been conceived in any other place than America by any other people than the Negro slaves and their descendants. When its *identification* with America is as fully recognized as its *identity* as Negro; when it is articulated into the corpus of American humor, as, say, Yankee (American) humor, Western (American), Irish (American) and Jewish (American) humor are articulated, the day of America's cultural maturity and of her acceptance of the moral judgments of history will not be far off.

—*Saunders Redding*

Let the people sing.

—*Zora Neale Hurston*

Contents

Acknowledgments

·

This book has a curious history. For a number of years I had been doing research on humorous American ethnic literature. I began reading the works of Jewish, Hispanic, Asian, and other hyphenated Americans after years of absorbed reading in African American literature and a growing conviction of its key role in our country's heritage. Then I started thinking about the similarities between African American and Jewish humor and how they had seemingly become the bedrock of what we call "American humor." Soon, without intending to, I was writing a study of all American ethnic laughter. At the same time, however, I was teaching more and more courses in African American literature and devoting most of my other research to that field; I kept getting excited about Zora Neale Hurston's incredible prose—especially its comic aspects, which my training in humor research made me notice and appreciate more than most people would. At scholarly conferences I kept hearing people giving papers on Hurston throw out comments about how funny her stories and novels were, but no one seemed to concentrate on that aspect of her work. Clearly, she would have to play a central role in my ethnic humor project. Before I knew it, however, Zora had conjured me with her wit and wisdom into dropping all the other writers and writing just about her.

I have no regrets. My other project has been long delayed, but my research on Hurston will make my next book better, and being under Zora's magical spell was worth any cost. I only hope my special approach will create new modes of appreciating this wonderful writer and of thinking about the humorous aspect of other African American and ethnic American writers, a very rich and revealing subject that has been almost totally ignored.

This book was written in two distinct phases. Throughout, however, the support of friends, colleagues, students, administrators, and institutions has been crucial. An excellent preparation in humor research and methods was provided via an NEH Summer Seminar, "Humor in Cross-Cultural Perspective," under the superb direction of Stanley Brandes of Berkeley's Anthropology Department in 1984. I am grateful to the Andrew W. Mellon Foundation for a year's Faculty Fellowship spent in the Afro-American Studies Department at Harvard, where I wrote the first section of this study. My ideas about Hurston were significantly strengthened through many rich conversations about her in particular, and African American literature and culture in general, with Mary Helen Washington, Nellie McKay, Carolivia Herron, Moses Nkondo, the late Nathan Huggins, and Werner Sollors, during 1985–86 and subsequent summers, when I taught courses in African American literature and southern literature at Harvard.

The first version of this book, dealing with Hurston's early career and *Their Eyes Were Watching God,* was improved by a number of helpful readers, including Rafia Zafar, Michel Fabre, Werner Sollors, and Victor Kramer.

Preparation for the second phase began with a Ford Foundation Minority Studies Fellowship at the University of Mississippi's Center for the Study of Southern Culture, which enabled me to discuss my ideas with a fine group of scholars led, in successive semesters, by Blyden Jackson and Charles Joyner. My thanks go to Bill Ferris, Charles Reagan Wilson, Anne Abadie, Maryemma Graham, and Ron Bailey for providing assistance and fellowship in Oxford. An LSU Faculty Research Grant during the summer of 1989 enabled me to begin the final chapters.

Grateful acknowledgment is made to Winifred Hurston Clark for permission to quote from Zora Neale Hurston's unpublished writings and to use a photograph of Hurston I found at the Library of Congress. An NEH Travel to Collections Grant enabled me to examine all of Hurston's original manuscripts and most of her letters, which are housed in the following collections: Alain Locke Papers, Moorland-Spingarn Research Center, Howard University, Washington, D.C.; Charles S. Johnson Papers, Special Collections, Fisk University; Department of Special Collections, University of Florida Libraries; Helen Worden Erskine Papers, Rare Book and Manuscript Library, Columbia University; James Weldon Johnson Collection, Yale Collection of American Literature, Beinecke Rare Book and Manuscript Library, Yale University; Lawrence E. Spivak Papers, Manuscript Division, Library of Congress; Manuscripts, Archives, and Rare Books Division, Schomburg Center for Research in Black Culture, the New York Public Library, Astor, Lenox, and Tilden Foundations. I would additionally like to thank the archival staffs at these institutions, especially Patricia Willis at Beinecke Library, Carmen Hurff at Florida, and most of all Esme Bahn of Howard University, who offered extraordinary assistance at a critical moment.

Scholarly writing is usually a lonely business, which explains why teaching can make the difference between an ordinary monograph and an exciting book. I have been fortunate in having motivated, intelligent, and creative students at Saint Mary's College (Notre Dame), Harvard, and LSU, who have shared my enthusiasm for Hurston and African American literature. Their papers, comments, questions, and complaints about cultures, texts, issues, and, occasionally, my teaching of them have equally enriched my work and my life.

My chairman at LSU, John R. May, offered aid at several stages, for which I am most grateful. Werner Sollors, my chairman at Harvard, provided funds for research assistance, as did the directors of Graduate Study in English at LSU, Malcolm Richardson and Jim Borck. These assistants—Carolyn Castiglione at Harvard, Deborah Wilson, Scott Johnson, and Michael Crumb at LSU—did yeoman work. Thanks also to Susan Kohler, for her generous assistance over these years.

The following friends made valuable suggestions on a variety of issues discussed in this book: Mahadev Apte, Michelle Collins, James Dormon, Ulla Dydo, Carl Freedman, Fred Hobson, Joyce Jackson, Anne Goodwyn Jones, Michelle Masse, Lawrence Mintz, Dana Nelson, James Olney, Brenda Marie Osbey, James Robert Payne, Deborah Plant, Arnold Rampersad, Mona Lisa Saloy, Keith Sandiford, Amritjit Singh, Joseph T. Skerrett, Jr., Nancy Walker, and Jerry W. Ward, Jr. The staff at Central Florida Press sent me galleys of *Zora in Florida* to read before the book was published.

The University of Illinois sent my original manuscript to two terrific readers; one remains anonymous; the other was Cheryl Wall. Among other suggestions, the first reader pushed me to give a better account of the African roots of Hurston's art. Cheryl Wall offered immensely helpful ideas about Hurston's autobiographical accounts, my stylistics, and my reading of *Seraph*. She also buoyed my spirits as I did the revisions. Karen Hewitt, my editor, has been immensely helpful and encouraging throughout. She has my heartfelt thanks. Becky Standard provided tactful and helpful copyediting.

Susan Donaldson offered a rigorous and encouraging appraisal of the *Moses* chapter. Nellie McKay provided a thoughtful, detailed, and supportive reading of my treatment of *Seraph*. Kathleen Diffley helped plan strategy and was her usual inspiring self.

While writing this book, I served on Pamela Bordelon's dissertation committee; her excellent history of the Federal Writers' Project in Florida opened up new aspects of Hurston for me. She shared her considerable research and was supportive and interested in my project.

Veronica Makowsky read every chapter as I wrote them and offered painstaking, detailed, and intelligent criticism that has made every page stronger. Her generosity, her tact, and her unfailing and cheerful support have been invaluable.

This company of saints, however, is not to be blamed for any sins I have committed herein; any fault is mine and mine alone.

Once, as a child, I remember, I asked my daddy why so many of the dedications of the books he owned were to husbands and wives. One of the benefits of writing this book was discovering the obvious answer to that childish question. I can never repay June Conaway Lowe for the sympathy, encouragement, patience, and love she supplied so abundantly during the years this project took shape. I can only marvel.

Jump at the Sun

Introduction: Co(s)mic Zora

With a few exceptions . . . black fiction has failed to produce the full, self-sustaining humorous hero, primarily because humor is out of place in what is basically a tragic literature.

    —Roger Rosenblatt

I am not tragically colored. There is no great sorrow dammed up in my soul, nor lurking behind my eyes. I do not mind at all. I do not belong to the sobbing school of Negrohood who hold that nature somehow has given them a lowdown dirty deal and whose feelings are all hurt about it. . . . No, I do not weep at the world—I am too busy sharpening my oyster knife.

    —Zora Neale Hurston

The world has finally rediscovered Zora Neale Hurston. Her books are back in print, a new wave of black women writers has claimed her as its literary ancestor, and today's generation is eagerly exploring Eatonville and its citizens. Zora must be somewhere, riding high and having the last laugh. Appropriately, when the *New York Times Book Review* published a front-page piece on Hurston a few years ago, they included a photograph of her looking out at us from the front seat of her Chevy, *laughing,* during one of her folklore collecting trips in the South (Gates, "Negro" 1). Hurston, ever wandering, ever laughing, conjures up the spirit of Esu-Elegba, the trickster Orisha of the West African crossroads, the Nigerian god who was the very personification of change and new beginnings (Ogundipe 147). Like Esu, she was a true pioneer, a woman who grew up in what was still the

Florida frontier; later she became a governess, a lady's maid, a graduate student, an anthropologist, a writer, and a legendary celebrity, but in all these and many other roles she tirelessly sought new trails to blaze. Like many writers associated with our frontier tradition, particularly in the South, she had a raucous and incredibly inventive sense of humor and delighted in mapping and executing playful, sometimes terrorizing maneuvers through every level of American life and culture. No one was too "big" for her to razz, mimic, or caricature. Marcus Garvey, Franklin Roosevelt, Alain Locke, all were fair game. She was always finding new ways to "signify" and work her narrative roots.

Be warned, though; her laughter echoes that of the similarly situated and equally African Sphinx, mysterious and profound. In guessing the riddles of her humor, we should be aware that like the Sphinx, she encodes judgments of life and death. Many of her critics, from the 1920s till today, have failed to perceive the serious issues that her humor contains and have consequently missed many aspects of her important messages. Dismissing her and her characters as simple or romantic, they underread and undervalue a profoundly serious, experimental, subversive, and therefore unsettling artist who found the complex humorous traditions of her culture worthy of presentation in their own right, but also useful in furthering her preferred method of writing by indirection.

Interestingly, her motives and her experimental method make her very much part of the modernist project to redefine the face of American culture. This protean writer often ignored canonical traditions and never wrote two novels the same way. Like the protomodernist Melville, she ceaselessly reinvented her modes of narration and her style, always searching for new forms as her varied interests took her into ever-new directions.

Hurston relished these new paths partly because of her profoundly democratic impatience with banal narrative methods she found bankrupt, especially in "proper" fiction's disdain for humorous narration and style; she knew that humor could be a corrective to any tendency toward sentimental, romantic, or egoistic approaches to culture: "My sense of humor will always stand in the way of my seeing myself, my family, my race or my nation as the whole intent of the universe. When I see what we really are like, I know that God is too great an artist for we folks on my side of the creek to be all of His best works. Some of His finest touches are among us, without doubt, but some more of His masterpieces are among those folks who live over the creek" ("How" 281). Her comments form an intriguing parallel to

James Joyce's oft-quoted idea that detachment is central to the artist's perspective toward life and link her project more closely to modernism than many might suspect.

But we would be wrong to assume that Hurston's identification with "the folk" always operated along racial lines. Her authorial voices were many and diverse and testify to the protean aspect of her personality and aesthetic. She tells us of being transfixed by the voices she heard in Greek, Roman, and Norse myths as a child and of thrilling to the ballads of the British Isles (*Dust Tracks* 53). Her last book may be about white characters, but they speak in the Cracker bush-country cadences of inland Florida, and we have no reason to think that Hurston saw a strict separation between their utterances and those of the community that produced her.

Paradoxically, despite her preference for a literature of indirection, Hurston understood, even at the beginning of her career, that in one respect, subterfuge of a basic type would not work; her effort to speak to her fellow African Americans while simultaneously reaching across the racial boundary to white readers had to be done in her own voice. The careful, measured cadences of Du Bois's talented tenth were not for her. In this sense alone she altered the terms of black-white literary discourse, for she accepted the modernist shift in stance from a presentation aimed at sincerity to one that expressed authenticity. For many years, this meant to her the voice of the folk, or alternately, the folk-generated, educated voice of Hurston, the omniscient narrator, a voice, in all its modulations, concerned with creating what Henry Louis Gates, Jr., has rightfully termed "the speakerly text," a book that seeks to communicate in the voice(s) of the culture that produced it (Gates, *Signifying* 181).

Hurston as Griot: The African Comic Tradition

Now the Negro adds his new act to the unfolding human comedy. There is seriousness in this comedy act and we who laugh about it are neither nihilists nor clowns. We are, rather, men afflicted with the passionate faith that man can be better than he is and with the equally passionate conviction that honest laughter underscores the need to close the gap between human aspirations and human performances. This is not to say that the Negro will save modern society, only that he is a part of it.

—*Louis E. Lomax*

As Houston Baker has recently noted, Hurston tells stories herself but also narrates tales that stem from the deepest spiritual beliefs of an oral culture. "Rather than an engaging lay narrator, she is a spiritual

griot seeking her authority in doctrines and practices that have ancient spiritual roots" (*Workings* 94). Baker's observation takes on added significance when we recall that Africans felt the spoken word had
mystical power, so much so that it symbolized the interconnection of
all peoples and things in the universe.

This belief crossed the Atlantic; in spite of the terrors of the middle passage, Africans brought their spirituality and an exuberant humorous tradition to the shores of the United States in the seventeenth
century and have been adding new resources to their comic arsenals
ever since. A history of this tradition would be a very long book indeed and lies beyond the scope of this volume; nevertheless, Hurston's career eventually involved virtually every aspect of African American humor and has much to tell us about its history.[1]

To find that history, one must turn to Africa; unfortunately, most
scholars of African culture have neglected humor, even though it is
ubiquitous in all societies. Isidore Okpewho has commented on the
tendency of somber Western Africanists to look for religion or world-
view at the expense of what he calls the "basic play interest" of African artists. He wryly points to analyses of African art that discuss
phallic or erotic aspects of objects, but only in conjunction with initiation or fertility rites, ignoring the obvious humorous intent of many
pieces. The bowdlerization of anthologies of African folklore, which
rarely include the uproarious ribaldry of the African villages, also
amuses him (2). The sociological and linguistic articles that have
treated this area are often more concerned with a joke's structure or
its social underpinnings than with examining the pleasure it creates.

Africans themselves assume humor exists everywhere, even in the
highest levels of existence. In Yoruba belief, two of the principal gods
are comic figures. The supreme god, Oludumare, instructs Obatala,
the god of laughter, to create the earth, but the latter gets drunk on
palm wine and, as a result, botches the job, producing, among other
things, albinos and hunchbacks (Awoonor 71ff.). Esu-Elegba, in many
ways the most important deity, operates as agent between God and
humans, thereby playing the same role as the trickster does around
the world, particularly coyote and raven of the North American Indians but also Brer Rabbit and his cronies.[2] Like most of them, Esu,
famous for his ravenous appetite (especially for sex), his wandering,
his vanity, and his unpredictability, delights in transgressing boundaries of all types. He and all other African tricksters, including the
Signifying Monkey and Anancy the spider, figure in endlessly varied
plots and possess a playful unpredictability (Edwards 156). Often, as

an African American toast suggests, a trickster starts trouble just for the sake of it:

> Deep down in the jungle so they say
> There's a signifying motherfucker down the way.
> There hadn't been no disturbin' in the jungle for quite a bit,
> For up jumped the monkey in the tree one day and laughed,
> "I guess I'll start some shit."
>
> (cited in Levine 378)

Trickster traditions were still very much part of African American folklore when Hurston began collecting, even though the stories were undergoing substantial change. Hurston was also well aware of the trickster's position in world folklore from her studies at Columbia and used all versions of these stories in her work.[3] Tales of Esu, Anancy, and the Signifying Monkey and other narrative performances had been disseminated in Africa by griots, a term popularized in the United States by Alex Haley's phenomenally successful book *Roots*. Today "griot" has become shorthand in Eurocentric culture for describing oral historians, whereas in Africa the term is applied to many types of African performers, most often paid praise singers, either for royalty or rich citizens. Most praise singers are men, although many Yoruba oriki (praise poetry) singers are women (see Barber).

A more accurate term for such a performer might be "African poet/musician." In most of West Africa, particularly where Islam predominates, griots sing or play instruments in addition to telling their tales. Hurston played on these talents in her writing, for many of her key figures are musicians: both John and Lucy in *Jonah's Gourd Vine*, Tea Cake in *Their Eyes Were Watching God*, Miriam in *Moses, Man of the Mountain*, and Arvay and Kenny in *Seraph on the Suwanee*. Hurston herself produced several musicals and acted and sang in them on occasion. She delighted in singing work songs and blues lyrics to all types of audiences; recordings of her performing are available from the Library of Congress.

As much as she tried to be a griot, their dances and gestures were more difficult to approximate in print. She understood dance quite well, however, and apparently choreographed musical numbers for her shows, such as *The Great Day*, and sometimes performed in them as well. Later, she would made some keen observations on dances she saw in the Caribbean while researching *Tell My Horse*. Ultimately, she found ways to work the communication of the body in motion in her written work. In her fiction, all movement, even mere walking, receives loving attention. For instance, she compares the roundabout, here-and-there walk Pheoby employs in going to Janie's at the start of *Their Eyes* to the walk of a chicken, an expanding metaphor that eventually pays off in several ways. A griot would probably act this out physically. Hurston very often, in fact, will hold back descriptive, Jamesian passages written to indicate the character's unconscious thought in favor of telling movements, gestures, and coded exclamations, a narrative pattern with African antecedents.

Most griots inherit their role from fathers or uncles, who train them. Griots have to know hundreds of songs and the history of tribes or families back as far as seven generations. Most importantly, perhaps, they absolutely must know the ritual songs that summon spirits and appease ancestors. For we should not forget the griots' profound link with the spiritual realm; in some ways these conjurors of words seem to be ancestors of conjure men and women in the United States, who were frequently known for their storytelling abilities too, like Kitty Brown of New Orleans, whom Hurston immortalized in the last chapter of *Mules and Men.*

Brown, like the griots before her, told and retold a repertoire of stories; similarly, Hurston was constantly recycling her materials and frequently told a tale over again with a different ending or different tone, as in the several versions of Cal'line's story, originally told in "The Eatonville Anthology." Again, the griot, though usually telling a preset story, relates it according to mood and the nature of the audience. His ability to "change his words" augurs well for his ultimate success (Ba and Kestellot 5).

Clearly, there are multiple points of reference between the griot's roles and Hurston's characters too; many of them excel at storytelling, are well-informed about both kin and nonkin relationships and histories in the community, and use remarkably effective performative skills in discourse. Griots must be masters of dramatic form and convention; audiences expect them to impersonate animals and to employ mime and colorful dialogue. The bards will frequently comically link everyday local objects, customs, geography, and flora and fauna into the tale to bring it closer to the experiences of their audiences, often personifying physical objects or phenomena. Hurston's Moses, as divine messenger of the gods, frequently does this, as in his speech involving references to a still or in making Balaam's ass talk. Throughout Hurston's work, we see inanimate objects, animals, and forces of nature animated and personified, often in a comic manner, beginning with her awkward but interesting sketch "Magnolia Flower," which is narrated by a river to a brook, and extending onward through folk proverbs and idioms to the talking buzzards of *Their Eyes* and the philosopher lizard of *Moses*.

Griot Figures and Comic Performance

Oral narrative in Africa was usually meant for entertainment first and only secondarily for edification. A griot's presentation was often tantamount to the performance of a play, with the griot acting out all the roles. Accordingly, multivocality was a prized commodity, one much in keeping with Mikhail Bakhtin's concepts of the dialogic imagination and multivocal texts. An anthropologist who studied the griots of the Ivory Coast was amazed at their ability to masterfully act out the various roles and voices in complex narratives (Finnegan, *Oral* 502). Indeed, this attention to performing style sometimes comes at the expense of content. At times the narrator, even of the more important African tales, will sacrifice religious elements to the playful aspects of the performance (Okpewho 2).

Audiences dictate this, as bards are expected to lard their tales with humor. Much of this is calculatedly bawdy and "delivered with sensuality or roguish mischief." Moreover, in Africa, even serious themes are frequently described with their humorous elements emphasized; a terrible decapitation may be described as "his two shoulders became inseparable friends" (Okpewho 203, 205). Even in performances of African epics, it seems, the griot is more intent on keeping the audience's interest than in maintaining a stately, dignified tone. Thus the insertion of humor—particularly at unexpected moments—has the effect of jolting the audience into fixed attention.

Similarly, the griot frequently makes use of sudden exclamations, which are often comic, for the same effect. Hurston concludes many of her short pieces that way, as in "The Book of Harlem," which ends with "Selah!" She was similarly careful to insert the punctuating exclamation "Ha!" at the end of lines in John Pearson's great sermon in *Jonah*. This has the effect of creating an essential element in oral narrative, the "sense of moment" (Okpewho 221).

Nor are griots harmless; their tales may be contemporary and thus include gossip and excoriating, witty commentary. Or they may embark on a general and devastating satire of the entire marketplace community. As Paul Oliver notes, the griot's knowledge and thus power create the opportunity for de facto blackmail. The audience will frequently fear being the target of a griot's humor, but will attend a performance so as to catch the latest news about others (46, 47).

Griots were often called upon to perform at special events because even serious rituals often have comic dimensions, especially among the Yoruba, Igbo, Ewe, and Fon peoples. One of the most important, the Yoruba mask dance for the Egun (a group of men who communicate with the dead) aims to amuse, even when performed at funerals. Many mask dances employ mime and satire. Chinua Achebe tells us the typical griot often was present to praise clients' ancestors, especially at weddings, circumcisions, and funerals (Morell 44–45; cf. Oliver 47). Hurston similarly employs ritualistic feasts, dances, and communal gatherings, which privilege what Bakhtin called the discourse of the public square, always a rich source of ribaldry and laughter.

As we see, the griot of West Arica is an ambivalent figure. Although people delight in his trickery, gossip, humor, and manipulation, they are suspicious of his fitting of his own words to old songs and fear his tendency to lunge out at victims in the audience. Crowds are amused, however, when stingy patrons are prodded into generosity by a griot's satiric treatment, a public form of blackmail. Like the griots, Hurston excelled at manipulating patrons, and her letters are perhaps the best available proof of that, in their mixture of humor, flattery, and hidden motives.

In all cultures, humor originates from rupture, surprise, and unexpected juxtapositions. Thus the comic performer walks a narrow line between pleasurable surprise and uncomfortable shocks. The danger of this maneuvering between boundaries makes her act all the more magnetic. And indeed, this ambiguity made griots a caste apart in West Africa. Burying a griot with more respected citizens would be viewed as a desecration. According to Oliver, griot remains were frequently inserted into the trunks of baobab tree cavities, where they would putrefy (47).

What an irony, therefore, that Zora Neale Hurston, master of all the griot arts, was indeed buried "apart," in an unmarked grave. Was it her irreverence, her refusal to "go along," be it with the talented tenth, smug white elitists, or black revolutionaries that consigned her to such a fate? Like the griot, she knew all the stories, but retranslated them for new audiences, "changing her words" a bit too much for some, perhaps.

Changing the Joke/Slipping the Yoke: African American Humor

Once in the New World, enslaved Africans retold traditional African stories, but refigured them with North American animals. They also focused more on the animals' "mother wit" than any presumed link with gods; as many skeptical slave tales indicated, "de Lawd" was not that helpful when "de Massa" elected to play god. Trickery of all sorts seemed not only permissible, but advisable, in the face of the horrors of slavery. Accordingly, many of the animal fables, even those of the child-pleasing Uncle Remus, concluded with the wily Rabbit causing the violent and painful death of larger animals, who represented the slaveowners.

When the weak but sly animals found human form, it was in the shape and signifying, comic voice of the crafty servant John, a figure who prompted one of Hurston's most memorable and suggestive essays, "High John de Conquer," which she published in the midst of 1943 as a way to give the war-torn nation hope. "We have given the rest of the nation song and laughter. Maybe now, in this terrible struggle, we can give something else—the source and soul of our laughter and song. We offer you our hope-bringer, High John de Conquer" (542). Hurston brilliantly forces her readers to think of themselves, like blacks, as under the oppression of an Old Massa: "When the lash fell on a slave in Alabama . . . somebody in the saddened quarters would feel like laughing and say, 'Now, High John de Conquer, Old Massa couldn't get the best of *him*'" (543). John could outwit Ole Massa and Big Missy, or the Devil himself, and after slavery it was the Landlord who got needled.

John, however, frequently gets tricked himself, as were his predecessors the Signifying Monkey, Anancy, and Brer Rabbit. His foibles, and theirs, must be seen as part of the self-reflexive aspect of African American humor, which was a perhaps inevitable result of the coded nature of the humor slaves crafted to use in the presence of whites. This important tradition Langston Hughes labeled "Jokes Negroes Tell on Themselves" and may best be exemplified by a classic joke about how blacks came to be black. The Lord calls everybody to come wash in the River of Life. "The Negroes lingered and loitered along the way, dallied and played, and took their own good time getting down to the river. When they got there, the other folks had used up all the water and had emerged whiter than snow." With no water left, the "Negroes found only . . . mud. . . . They waded. . . . They bent down and put the palms of their hands in the mud. By that time, even the mud was used up. There, to this day, nothing is light about Negroes except the palms of their hands and the soles of their feet. Late, always late" (Hughes, "Jokes" 23). The joke mocks both blackness and "colored people" time and closely resembles the self-reflexive jokes told by Jews among themselves.[4] As Hughes notes, such humor stems from "frustration and the laughter with which these sallies are greeted, for all its loudness, is a desperate laughter. White people often do not understand such humor at all" (22). A sociologist found that middle-class blacks liked black self-reflexive jokes better than their lower-class black counterparts and concluded that they conceived of these jokes as corrective and directed at lower-class blacks (Middleton). Similarly, poor southern whites frequently tell derogatory jokes about "rednecks," assuming they're not in that category or in need of such correction.

As self-reflexive jokes suggest, it should not be supposed that African American humor always comes off as heroic, creative, and exuberant. Like that of all other cultures, it can be cruel, stereotypical, sexist, and exploitive. Jokes exist within the culture that ridicule other members of the diaspora, such as West Indians (L. Brown); many others disparage women, particularly "black black" women, a subject that receives prominent treatment and scorn in Hurston's *Their Eyes* and more personally, *Dust Tracks*. There she wryly points to the hypocrisy present in raucous laughter generated at the expense of black black women: "If it was so honorable and glorious to be black, why was it the yellow-skinned people among us had so much prestige?" (226). Some jokes poke fun at "down-home" or uneducated brothers and sisters; some put down members of other ethnic groups. Black minstrels, for instance, offered comic and derogatory impersonations of Indians, while the Irish and Jews were not spared either. In cities, today as in the past, one finds Italians, Mexicans, American Indians, and the Chinese being needled by black quipsters (Levine 301, 305, 306), and this company has lately expanded to include Asian merchants, particularly Koreans.

During the terrible decades before and after the turn of the century (the "nadir" of black experience in the United States), animal tales also gave way to images of heroic badmen, such as Stackolee, Railroad Bill, and John Hardy, who form a breed apart from High John. But all these figures develop out of oppression. As Jessie Fauset put it later, "The remarkable thing about this gift of ours [humor] is that it has its rise, I am convinced, in the very woes which beset us. Just as a person driven by great sorrow may finally go into an orgy of laughter, just so an oppressed and too hard driven people breaks over into compensating laughter and merriment. It is our emotional salvation" (166). We may thus view these superheroes as a response to the growing despair of African Americans, as agents of the law denied them justice. Mingling elements of the conjuror and the trickster, this type personifies the "bad nigger" who is anathema to whites for breaking their laws and conventions. Jack Johnson, the championship fighter who had a white mistress, was hated anyway, but his booming laughter became the very sign of his outrageous status as the nation's premiere "Bad Nigger" (Wiggins 35). To African Americans, however, "bad niggers," whether they be mythical like Stacko-lee or flesh and blood like Johnson, represent heroic struggle against injustice and incarnate the rebellion African Americans feel but may not act out without severe punishment.

Not surprisingly, each of these heroes is also a masterful comic wordsmith who can "talk that talk" with the best of them. The exaggerated, obscene boasting of the "Great McDaddy" offers a typical example: "'I've got a tombstone disposition, graveyard mind. I know I'm a bad motherfucker, that's why I don't mind dying'" (Dance, *Shuckin'* 224). Sally Ann Ferguson has suggestively outlined how Hurston may have made use of these figures in *Their Eyes,* and an even better earlier example comes in the definitely "bad" title figure of the short story "Spunk," whose boasting, wife-stealing, and outrageous manner seem to lead to his inglorious death on a sawmill blade.

The "toast" constitutes the genre setting par excellence for the "bad nigger" tradition and has African antecedents. That continent's poets sometimes became known for their self-praise ("boasts"), which in many ways were mini-autobiographies; this was practiced often, for instance, by the Shonas in Zimbabwe (Opland 32).

A long narrative poem created from the oral traditions of the culture, the African American toast receives braggadocio performances, usually on the street, in bars, or in poolrooms. The toaster seeks both audience involvement and approval, and as Bruce Jackson keenly observes, "That is one of the major differences between written poetry and folk poetry: with written poetry, the audience makes its judgment after the fact; with folk poetry, the audience's judgment is part of the fact" (ix). Toasting does not function in Hurston's writing except in tangential ways, but the "braggadocio" of characters such as Slemmons, Amy Crittenden, Ned Crittenden, John Pearson, Jody Starks, and Big Sweet has the "flavor" of it, as Hurston does herself, especially when she shifts into her co(s)mic mode in *Dust Tracks.*

The shift from animal fables and High John stories to toasts and Stackolee or McDaddy tales was a major event in African American culture and was accompanied by an increase in verbal dueling conventions and, again, has African parallels. In East Africa, for example, poets may duel for a court or association, singing ritual insults. The contestant who attracts more partisans among the spectators wins (Finnegan, *Oral* 103). In the United States, this rich verbal culture produced terms such as signifying, sounding, the dozens, woofing, bookooing, loud-talking, and marking. All of them eventually found their way into American literature and into Hurston's writing, although sometimes in diluted, censored form in characters such as Big

Sweet, Sam and Lige of Joe Clarke's front porch, and Moses and Aaron.

In terms of the printed word, however, authentic African American humor did not loom large on the national literary horizon until the invention of mass printing and increased magazine and newspaper circulation. Hurston knew her work had to correct both racist stories and images in American popular magazines such as *Puck* and *Judge;* the latter, a "paper for the family and fireside," was said to be "satirical without being malicious, and humorous without being vulgar" (cited in Dormon, "Ethnic" 490). Both periodicals were filled with nasty ethnic cartoons, and the other popular entertainments of the late nineteenth century were similarly offensive, picturing blacks with big noses, thick lips, and idiotic or leering expressions. Africans were sketched in grass skirts with bones in their noses, dancing around a missionary who's in their dinner pot cooking. Other ethnic groups fared the same. James Dormon finds implicit rationalization and justification for harsh Indian policies, for instance, in the caricatures of Indians as savage beasts ("Ethnic" 494–95). Nineteenth-century American newspapers were rife with both ethnic caricatures and ethnic spokespersons and columns, especially in the major cities where indigenous Americans eagerly sought out information about their new, if properly distanced, neighbors. African American and other ethnic communities set up their own newspapers to counter these images, to bolster group confidence and identity, and to achieve the paradoxical and somewhat opposed goals of assisting readers in the "Americanization" process, while ministering to their nostalgia for vanishing folkways, be they from the American South or the south of Europe.

The twentieth century brought phonograph records, then radio and cinema to the people, and all three forms continued and developed racial stereotypes, as in Al Jolson's blackface songs, "Amos and Andy," and the various mammies, pickaninnies, and Steppin' Fetchits that Hollywood cranked out.[5] One of the major results of the new technology for African Americans was the national dissemination of the blues, the great musical tradition that had evolved out of the field songs, the black church, and the spirituals. The music struck a responsive chord in white Americans and forced an awareness of the suggestive, coded lyrics. Black writers were quick to recognize the possibilities of using blues forms and narrative techniques in their writing, and much of this tradition was sly, ironic, or simply comic. The blues contained a lot of pain, but sweetened by wry, sometimes raunchy humor, especially in the suggestive lyrics of the blues queens Bessie Smith, Clara Smith, Mamie Smith, Ida Cox, and, of course, Ma Rainey.

Indeed, Hurston could be said to be a great blues singer, and Paul Oliver has suggested that parallels exist between the attitudes of the West African savannah communities toward the griot and those African Americans have had toward blues singers. Like griots, blues artists provide laughter and entertainment and frequently offer devastating signification on people and events. But also like griots, Oliver notes, blues performers can be considered lazy, unreliable, immoral, and untrustworthy, partly because of their nomadic tendencies. Overt obscenities in private performances or double entendres in public ones also link the two schools. Although blues are popularly conceived to be laments of victims, they are at the same time yearnings for, and expressions of, freedom and of the intent to expand freedom. It makes sense, therefore, that many of the songs, however tragic in content, get expressed humorously and playfully, for the style liberates the content. Rejected and abused lovers voice their pain, but also signify, sometimes wickedly, on their mates, who get tried and convicted in the course of the song.[6]

Blues performers' subsequent recordings illustrated the suggestive and comic aspect of the blues, such as these by Charles "Cow Cow" Davenport:

> I ain't no iceman: I ain't no iceman's son
> But I can keep you cool: until the iceman comes.
> I ain't no wood chopper: I ain't no wood chopper's son
> But babe I can chop your kindling: until the wood chopper comes.
> Baby I ain't no stove man: I ain't no stove man's son
> But I can keep you heated up: babe until the stove man comes.
> Baby I ain't no butcher: and I ain't no butcher's son
> But I can furnish you plenty of meat: baby until the butcher comes.
> I ain't no milkman: I ain't no milkman's son
> But I can furnish you plenty of cream: baby until that milkman comes.
>
> (1938; Taft 70)

Similarly, Ida Cox in "Southern Woman's Blues" vows to go back to the sunny South, "where I can get my hambone boiled / These northern men: are about to let my poor hambone spoil" (1925; Taft 67). Or Ma Rainey:

> Lord, I'm just jealous: jealous as I can be.
> Got a range in my kitchen: cooks nice and brown
> All I need is my man: to turn my damper down.
>
> (1924; Taft 220)

Ragtime, the blues, gospel, and jazz began to percolate in the great cities of the North as the great migration began. One of the most important results was the extraordinary concentration of black talent that began to cluster "up in Harlem" after World War I.

Hurston was hardly the only literary cutup in her Harlem crowd. Langston Hughes, her longtime pal, was one of the funniest writers in American history, and when those two got together things started cooking. Their friend Wallace Thurman had a wicked wit tempered by more than a little bile; his roman à clef, *Infants of the Spring*, skewered everybody in the movement, including him. Rudolph Fisher's inventive stories frequently bubbled with humor, as did his Harlem send-up *The Walls of Jericho* (1928), a masterfully ironic comedy of manners. Claude McKay created wonderful comedy in *Home to Harlem* (1928), while more refined and ironic humor found its way into Nella Larsen's slim novels.

The wickedest writer of all was George Schuyler, whose brilliant satire *Black No More* (1931) tells the story of Dr. Crookman's discovery and exploitation of a process that makes blacks white. In his clever essay "Our Greatest Gift to America" he claims, "Descendents of convicts, serfs, and half-wits, with the rest have been buoyed up and greatly exalted by being constantly assured of their superiority to all other races and their equality with each other. On the stages of a thousand music halls, they have had their vanity tickled by blackface performers parading the idiocies of mythical black roustabouts and rustics. Between belly-cracking guffaws they have secretly congratulated themselves on the fact that they are not like these buffoons" (124). Poets, too, used rollicking humor, especially Langston Hughes and Sterling Brown, whose *Southern Road* (1932) contributed the hilarious but evocative character of Slim Greer to American literary lore.

Why was so much humorous literature created "uptown" in the twenties? As Ernest Gaines has noted, "Humor and joking are part of change" (Gaudet and Wooton 22), and change was the order of the day in Harlem; people coming, people going, customs changing, all pointed to the development of what was called "The New Negro." This demanded a change as well in literary expression, especially since the people, as usual, were ahead of the artists in coining new idioms, words, and rituals.[7]

Humor, the Literature of Indirection, and the Minstrel's Mask

As Deborah Plant demonstrates, the indirect mode of presentation characterizes the oral tradition generally, and African cultures in

particular. To prove her point, she cites Oyekan Owomoyela, who has outlined proverbs' role in Yoruba communication, which generally prefers "circuitousness and opacity." Plant notes this tendency in the United States has extended to the tradition of linguistic masking, so evident also in folktales, sayings, jokes, proverbs, and parables (167).[8]

Proverbs offer one of the best examples of indirection in African and African American discourse. Their usefulness has been demonstrated, particularly in African child-rearing practices. Proverbs speak from folk wisdom, and when cited, shift the locus of instruction from the parent involved to the people, along with the "guilt" or responsibility for parenting. Similarly, in African legal proceedings, proverbs play a central role similar to that played by legal precedent in Western courtrooms. Successful lawyers are frequently known for their skillful application of proverbs, a valuable legal commodity (Arewa and Dundes 70).

Hurston dramatizes the use of proverbs in everyday life throughout her fiction, and the issues of advice and judgment, in all their forms, never move very far from the surface of the narrative: "'Ignorance is de hawse dat wisdom rides'" (*Jonah* 128); "'Jump at de sun and eben if yuh miss it, yuh can't help grabbin' holt uh de moon'" (95); "'Unless you see de fur, a mink skin ain't no different from a coon hide'" (*Their Eyes* 19). The voice of "Mouth Almighty," the folk in deliberation and judgment, reverberates in her narrative, as the community watches and comments on an individual character's actions. Its discussion frequently takes on the quality of a legal proceeding, as proverbs provide a center for the discourse, along with signs, markers, and precedents from the cultural past. Virtually all of them are memorable to the oral culture because of their clever constructions, which frequently turn on a witticism, such as Hurston's favorite, "hitting a straight lick with a crooked stick." Proverbs, because of their ambiguity and multivalent constitution, function as "crooked sticks" that are used to "lick" home a point of comic correction.

Humor and Representation

I know that I cannot accept responsibility for thirteen million people. Every tub must sit on its own bottom regardless.

—*Zora Neale Hurston*

Humor, however, does not necessarily operate in a positive manner, and various ethnic groups have always used humor to cast aspersions on others, particularly through stereotyping. Many of the stereotypes of African Americans that existed in Hurston's day unfortunately remain with us even today, albeit in muted form. During the nineteenth century and the early twentieth, however, they constituted a veritable staple of American culture. This mode of racial representation very directly presented black people as naive, childlike, and just plain stupid. Surveys of this tradition in the United States show how pervasive such patterns were at every level of society and how they were related to general patterns of oppression applied to other ethnic groups and often to women of all races.[9]

The nineteenth century's appetite for "Negro" folktales and folk humor proved insatiable, especially after the Civil War, when new cultural modes were sought to deal with white psychological fears caused by emancipation. Collections of "negro humor," plantation tradition short stories and novels, and, above all, the minstrel show and popular stage productions solidified the image of the "comic darkie."

These stereotypes began in Europe, in English plays such as George Colman's *Inkle and Yarico* (1787), which, although somewhat sympathetic to the slave's plight, presented grinning, singing, dialect-talking "darkies" to the public. American imitations soon appeared; and then, in the early 1820s, Thomas Dartmouth (Jim Crow Rice), a white performer, observed an old black man singing and dancing in Louisville and created a blackface act around the song "Jump Jim Crow." Rice's amazing success quickly spawned imitations, ritualized such songs and acts, and encouraged the collection of comic "negro stories." A collector could be an abolitionist or a southern planter; a reader could be a western miner or a Boston housewife. We should exercise caution, however, in dismissing the comic anthologies, for many of them (sometimes inadvertently) contained subversive humor and genuine contributions by black people, in addition to the racist material.[10] "Negro humor" of this type was good business; during Hurston's lifetime (even as late as the fifties), anthologies of racist jokes were still being written, bought, laughed over, and accepted as accurate renditions of African American humor under titles such as *Chocolate Drops from the South* (1932).

How was this stereotype generally depicted? Paradoxically, it provided doubled images, damning African Americans no matter what approach was taken. To choose but one example, they were often said to be lazy; on other occasions, however, they were dumb enough to "work like a nigger." Similarly doubled labels were stupid but crafty, humble but scheming, cowardly but reckless, innocent but lascivious.

The most basic all-purpose comic stereotype, however, sketched in the caricature of a slow, childish, lascivious, always happy, full of rhythm, lover of chicken and watermelon who just loved to cut the buck and the wing to keep the white folks happy.

American minstrel shows growing out of an elaboration of Rice's act kept this image alive with white actors in burnt-cork makeup. These entertainments complemented down-home-on-the-plantation stereotypes with a new one depicting the gaudy African dandy of New York's Broadway, "Jim Dandy."[11] As Nathan Huggins has demonstrated, these "types" were anything but simple and had little basis in African American culture. The rough, plain-talking, "country" Jim Crow figure was obviously an avatar of white culture's backwoods and riverboat characters and, I would add, of "Brother Jonathan"/"Uncle Sam" figures. "Jim Dandy," by contrast, effeminate, urban, and fast-talking, was Yankee Doodle's parallel and, in comic opposition to Jim Crow, provided a smiling mask for the deep struggle between U.S. pastoral romanticism and onrushing urban industrialization. In another avatar he became "Zip Coon," a crafty urbanite who frequently preyed on greenhorns come to the city from "down home."

Dualities were, in fact, the staple of minstrelsy and signifiers of the genre's ambivalence and fluidity. Black on white disguise, later complicated by blacks acting out whites acting the part of blacks, was accompanied by males dressed as females as well. Minstrelsy often gets dismissed as a vile phenomenon of American popular culture, but its long-lasting popularity was partly due to its constantly evolving nature, its ambiguities, and its invitation into the world of the ethnic "Other." Nathan Huggins suggests that although the shows certainly stereotyped blacks, they also created characters that spoke to white yearnings for freedom and irresponsibility, an alternative approach to life that blacks have always mirrored for whites. As Huggins succinctly puts it, "That tautness of fear and self-doubt could be released in explosions of laughter once one saw that the fool—the animal, the corruption one feared most—was nothing more than a prancing darky on a stage." Huggins brilliantly demonstrates, moreover, that such portrayals by blacks, Jews, or Italians of their own stereotypes on stage could please members of those ethnic groups too, for both the actor and the audience would pride themselves on being above the "type" presented of the ignorant "darky"/"schlimiel"/"dago" (254, 259).

Finally, minstrelsy also included "straight" love songs for both sexes, and handsome leading men became "matinee idols"; serious themes such as poverty, family, and race were dealt with under the mask of shrewd folk proverbs, riddles, and idiom so the shows went beyond both humor and stereotype at times (Stowe and Grimsted 82–86). Over the years, the humor gained in subtlety, and the standard sets featuring cotton patches, cabins, and riverboats gave way to fancy society parties and Broadway pleasure palaces (H. Adams 14). Further, the subtlety of the humor coupled with the rollicking music of the shows allowed for the evolution of the blues. A kind of traveling vaudeville perpetuated by troupes from the Rabbit Foot Minstrel Tours and the Theatre Owners' Booking Association circuit allowed performers to move away from minstrelsy and blackface toward more positive modes of representation. Minstrelsy and this new form of vaudeville gave black performers a chance to break into the American entertainment circuit and provided early careers for stars of later eras, such as Ernest Hogan, the ragtime and musical comedy composer; Bert Williams, the musical comedy star; W. C. Handy, the bluesman; Dewey "Pigmeat" Markham, the comedian; and the blues queens Ma Rainey and Bessie Smith (Toll 228). Virtually all of these artists found ways to work around stereotypes and to insert truly authentic African American art forms. Hurston is no exception to this tradition.

Complementing this realm of theatrical entertainment, a literary synthesis of the ersatz images of African Americans and their actual cultural traditions began when Joel Chandler Harris began publishing his Uncle Remus tales. These stories followed those played by stereotypical black supporting characters in "high" white culture stories in novels by writers such as James Fenimore Cooper, William Gilmore Simms, Edgar Allan Poe, John Pendleton Kennedy, and Harriet Beecher Stowe. The coded nature of African American mythology so evident in the minstrelsy humor of black performers also characterizes Brer Rabbit tales. Harris tirelessly collected and edited these and other classic African American animal tales from the 1870s to his death in 1905. But his racist frame story, wherein a desexualized old black man tells the stories to his mistress's little blond son, caters to stereotype and has always led unwary readers to reductive and simply wrong readings of the tales themselves; their charming surface images and boisterous humor mask core narratives of terror, trickery, and violence and a different, crueler, and more ironic level of laughter.[12]

At the turn of the century, the black writer Charles Chesnutt would try to counter the image of Uncle Remus by writing a new form of plantation tradition fiction featuring credible and admirable black characters, but his books were vastly outsold by those of his white contemporary, Thomas Nelson Page, who brought the art of depicting the "oldtime darkey" to its most genteel peak in stories such as "Marse Chan" and "Meh' Lady." Outright racist writers such as Thomas Dixon, in books like *The Leopard's Spots* (1902) and *The Clansman* (1905), villified emancipated blacks as rapist apes. Popular magazines and newspapers added to the image as well; even the *New York Times* depicted black men as "Brutes" or "Sambos," replete with all the vicious stereotypes (Boskin, "'Black'" 174).[13]

Sadly, even fine African American poets, such as Paul Lawrence Dunbar, felt they had to cater to this tradition and set most of their dialect-driven poems on bucolic plantations. Commenting on this overall pattern of comic representation in 1925, Jessie Fauset, Hurston's Harlem Renaissance contemporary, perceptively noted, "The medium through which this unique and intensely dramatic gift [the gift of laughter] might be offered has been so befogged and misted by popular preconception that the great gift, though divined, is as yet not clearly seen" (161).

Minstrelsy's legacy had an even greater "fogging" effect in the theater and in popular music. The gifted black comedians Bert Williams and George Walker not only wore burnt cork in their early days; when they and other black artists began acting in black musical comedies (the first was *A Trip to Coontown* in 1899–99), they were singing lyrics such as

> As certain and sure as Holy Writ,
> And not a coon's exempt from it,
> Four things you'll always find together,
> Regardless of condition of sun and moon—
> A watermelon, a razor, a chicken and a coon!
> (Dormon 456)

During the "coon song" craze of the 1890s that Williams and Walker were part of, urban blacks were spotlighted, especially their vicious way with a razor.[14] The visual semiotics of American advertising placed images from the tradition before the public daily; from Currier and Ives prints to cereal boxes, grinning darkies were everywhere.

Even when authentic material such as the spirituals became the vogue, black performers felt they had to wear the mask in other ways, especially in talking about themselves. Sheppard's Colored Jubilee Singers swore they had "no pretensions as to musical abilities, they being unable to read or write" and claimed their leader had been the slave of Robert E. Lee; other groups transformed spirituals into comic, stereotypical songs, such as "Carve That Possum" (Toll 236–38).

This kind of posturing continued up into Hurston's heyday. Hall Johnson, a choral leader also under the thumb of Hurston's white patron Charlotte Mason, sent "Godmother," as she liked to be called, a brochure for his singers which read, "If you hear them, you, too, will be unable to resist the wonderful emotional appeal of this touching and delightful music, the charming naive humor of the old-time slave and the genuine beauty of these wonderful Negro voices."[15] Before judging Johnson and his predecessors too harshly for catering to white stereotypes, we should remember Paul Laurence Dunbar's famous lines:

> We wear the mask that grins and lies,
> It hides our cheek and shades our eyes—
> This debt we pay to human guile:
> With torn and bleeding hearts we smile,
> And mouth with myriad subtleties.
>
> (Dunbar 486)

Hurston, in her dealings with Godmother, wore the mask too, as the servile and flattering letters she sent Mason reveal. She could see how such a pose could pay off in the workplace for others as well; in an undated and unpublished short story, "The Conversion of Sam," Hurston describes the value the title character has for his white employer: "Besides being a good worker, Sam radiated good humor wherever he happened to be, and his witticisms kept the men about him in a cheerful mood and made good workers out of them too" (8).

The price of wearing the mask was heavy, and sometimes there were no rewards. It was often expected by white slaveowners and, later, bosses as a marker of docility and gratitude. John Killens made this powerfully clear in a section of his novel *Youngblood* (1954), where a brutal white foreman unmercifully hounds Joe Youngblood for refusing to sing and laugh while performing backbreaking work: "'Can't understand you at all. Don't never sing or laugh or grin. Make me think you ain't happy. A nigger ain't supposed to look straight faced all the time'" (44–45).

Some might castigate Hurston for her pandering to Godmother and attitudes like those manifest in "Sam" and praise Killens for his in *Youngblood*. But we should be cautious in judging a humor and a cultural situation that still had the motivation of the legendary High John de Conquer. It facilitated African Americans' *survival*.

Hurston, like so many other great writers in the African American tradition, in the body of her work attempts to provide outsiders with an inside view of the culture she so loved. But she knew to do so would take cunning masking stratagems and enticing devices, and humor was chief among them in terms of its ability to promote human understanding.[16] "Cuttin' the monkey for the white folks" sometimes seemed worth it. As Janie says in *Their Eyes*, "'Tain't no use in me telling you somethin' unless Ah give you de understandin' to go 'long wid it. Unless you see de fur, a mink skin ain't no different from a coon hide'" (19). For Hurston, her culture was mink, not coon, and humor, masked and unmasked, frequently expressed in such utterances, helped her show the world the difference.

On the other hand, humor within the group, when the mask was off, could sting as well. Throughout her life, Hurston was well aware of the envy and malice of others and how it could find a shape and form in aggressive, mocking, "Mouth Almighty" humor. The lowest point of her life came in 1948 when she was accused of molesting a young boy and the black press took it up as truth, trashing her and quoting knowingly from the just-published *Seraph on the Suwanee*, whose hero, presumed to be speaking for Hurston, demands a "'knowing and a doing'" love. She could have well said, as Pheoby does of Janie's critics in Eatonville, "'So long as they get a name to gnaw on they don't care whose it is, and what about, 'specially if they can make it sound like evil'" (*Their Eyes* 17).

We know that Hurston, throughout her career, understood the way the humorist's mask, frequently consisting only of dialect or folk-inspired language, could soften the impact of even devastating criticism, as she reveals in a 1945 article, "Crazy for This Democracy," daringly written shortly after victory over Japan. Exposing the hollow promises made to thousands of black servicemen as they fought for what she calls the "Arse and All" of democracy, parodying Roosevelt's grandiose expression, she dons the mask of Will Rogers, whom she tellingly quotes: "All I know is what I see by the papers. . . . It seems like now, I do not know geography as well as I ought to. . . . I thought when they said Atlantic Charter, that meant me and everybody in Africa and Asia and everywhere. But it seems like the Atlantic is an ocean that does not touch anywhere but North America and Europe" (45). In the best traditions of that old bluff, countrified brother Jonathan, a caustic Hurston signifies on FDR: "Maybe, I need to go out and buy me a dictionary. . . . Maybe I mistook a British pronunciation for a plain American word. Did F.D.R., aristocrat from Groton and Harvard, using the British language say 'arse-and-all' of Democracy when I thought he said plain arsenal?" (45). Typically, she keeps re-figuring the phrase, also using "Ass-and-all" and "Ass-and-all-he-has" to emphasize the economic motivations of worldwide racism. By the end of the essay, Hurston's artful significations on American political hypocrisy make us re-read her title as "Crazy *from* This Democracy." Her ringing call for "complete repeal of All Jim Crow Laws in the United States, once and for all, and right now" (48), however, minces no words.

Hurston knew it would be useless to cater to people's desires regarding their literary presentation, for as she remarked at one time, in a different context, "It is no longer profitable, with few exceptions, to ask people what they think, for you will be told what they wish, instead" (*Dust Tracks* 337). Proof of her comment comes from Nick Aaron Ford, professor at a black college in the 1930s, who persuaded a friend traveling with him to go down some narrow country roads in search of Zora Neale Hurston. They found her, and Ford asked her why she did not write directly about the race issue. "'I was writing a novel and not a treatise on sociology,'" Zora exclaimed. "'There is where many Negro novelists make their mistakes. They confuse art with sociology'" (96). Later he started thinking about what that meant. For one thing, it freed Hurston to zero in on her own people, a project Sinclair Lewis had been actuating for some time, to great acclaim and profit. Why, thought Ford, could not a black writer do something similar without getting severe criticism from within the race? He decided it was because African Americans had always been the jester for other Americans. "Is it surprising, then, that he should look askance at any member of his own race who could be so unkind as to wound him where he is weakest, and to join hands with his enemies who delight in heaping abuse upon his already bowed head?" (98). Ford finally decided that "if the Negro is to rise in the estimation of the world, he must be continuously presented in a more favorable light even in fiction. . . . His virtues must be stressed. He must cease to be portrayed as the clown of the human family, and be represented in his normal activities as an ordinary American citizen." He felt Hurston's *Jonah* to be a failure because she didn't make John Buddy into "another Ben Hur, bursting the unjust shackles that had bound him to a rotten social order" (99).

As William A. Stewart has pointed out, much of the "racial uplift literature" of the late nineteenth century had precisely this attitude about the representation of black speech itself, and yet "it inadvertently accepts the idea that distinctively Negro speech is evidence of low intellectual ability. As a result, much of it admonishes people not to use nonstandard dialect forms. Obviously this doesn't do any good, because one simply can't tell a person to just stop speaking the way he does speak" (127).

This issue cropped up over and over during Hurston's career in African American culture as a whole. The issue of dialect proved a particularly knotty problem and was being raised as late as 1971. Henry D. Spaulding, compiling the *Encyclopedia of Black Folklore and Humor*, wrote in the preface of his original plan to clean up the dialect he found in the primary documents "to avoid offense to the militant young generation of today, and because I realize that dialect has all too often been used to cloak innate prejudice." Fortunately, Spaulding did no such thing, and indeed, states, "Dialect, and its descendant, black English, are offered here without apology—indeed, with a deep sense of pride" (xii–xiii).

Karla Holloway has eloquently demonstrated Hurston's achievement in challenging the perjorative view of dialect writing that prevailed in her time: "She was preserving a language that linguists saw as an attempt at English, broken or truncated, or otherwise disabled from full reflective and cognitive power. . . . She had a powerful myth to supersede. But Hurston never abandoned the poetry of her folk" (114). This is especially evident in the magnificent poetry of lines such as John's, commenting on his silence in court: "'Ah didn't want de white folks tuh hear 'bout nothin' lak dat. . . . Dey's some strings on our harp fuh us tuh play on and sing all tuh ourselves'" (*Jonah* 169).

Strikingly, this "show the race's best face" attitude was present even in the militant, nationalist phase of the sixties and seventies, and it is still with us, as a recent discussion among more than a hundred black artists, scholars, and actors prior to the 1991 Broadway staging of the Hurston–Langston Hughes play *Mule Bone* demonstrates. After a group reading of the play, a majority of those present voted that it should not be produced because it was uncomfortably close to racial stereotypes (Short 72). Fortunately, the play went ahead anyway. As Henry Louis Gates, Jr., commented, "For a people who seem to care so much about their public image, you would think blacks would spend more energy creating the conditions for the sort of theater and art they want, rather than worrying about how they are perceived by the larger society. But many black people still seem to believe that the images of themselves projected on television, film and stage must be policed and monitored from within. Such convictions are difficult—even painful—to change" ("Debate" 5). Gates goes on, however, to sympathize with the naysayers, for he knows they are troubled by the long racist tradition, centered in minstrelsy and vaudeville, of bogus representations of black humor.

Defining Humor in a Modernist World

We would understand Hurston's relation to the more playful and experimental aspects of modernism better if we had a much needed discussion of the central role humor played in that movement, especially among ethnic authors, such as Pietro Di Donato, Henry Roth, or Jean Toomer. Until recently these writers have rarely been included in studies of modernism but played key roles and were as innovative in fiction as Duke Ellington and Aaron Douglas were in music and art.

Modernism coincided—indeed, was partially created by—Freud's emergence in the Western intellectual tradition with his revolutionary concepts of human identity. We tend to forget that Freud, in addition to founding psychoanalysis, also provided the first scientific basis for the study of humor in his groundbreaking 1905 work *Jokes and Their Relation to the Unconscious,* only five years after *The Interpretation of Dreams* appeared.

Since that publication, many theorists have claimed no definitive theory of humor may be formulated. Paul McGhee, a psychologist, flatly states, "It is preposterous at this point to try to explain cognitive, social, motivational, and physiological aspects of humor within a single system" (41). Still, this hasn't stopped any number of scholars from trying, and most begin with Freud, who demonstrated how jokes work as a social process. His basic definition of humor might be reduced to a play upon form, especially in the yoking together of dissimilar concepts, objects, or words. This play frequently relies on inversion of opposites, a central operation in American and African American "democratic humor," and one Hurston often employed. Freud's reduction of joke technique to the three basic operations of condensation, multiple use of the same material, and double meanings has relevance to all people, but especially overlaps in African American culture with the pithiness and piquancy of African American proverbs and idioms; marked use of repetitions; and coded, doubled, and indirect discourse.

Freud felt that at times a joke's content could be completely secondary to its form, which in many ways cannot be separated from its delivery. Indeed, the performance/form may be the message, the central component of the joke, and in both African and African American humor, this frequently is the case. But in all comic scenarios, jokes have a social context, require an audience, and constitute a basic form of communication. Freud goes much further in his analysis by noting that jokes strip away pretense and disguise, revealing the truth, and are therefore frequently obscene, aggressive, and hostile. They may alternately or simultaneously be cynical, critical, blasphemous, and skeptical.

Freud's 1905 treatise has consequently often been interpreted as proof that humor is basically aggressive. But he also agreed with previous critics that "playful judgement, the coupling of dissimilar things, contrasting ideas, 'sense in nonsense', the succession of bewilderment and enlightenment, the bringing forward of what is hidden, and the peculiar brevity [or condensation] of wit" are basic considerations (14). He further claimed that jokes can create pleasure even when they aren't "comic," when they challenge oppressors by indicating an alternative, or by creating sources of pleasure denied by censorship (96). Furthermore, his 1928 follow-up essay "Humour" credits that faculty with more positive aspects:

> Humour has in it a *liberating* element. But it has also something fine and elevating, which is lacking in the other two ways of deriving pleasure from intellectual activity. . . . It refuses to be hurt by the arrows of reality or to be compelled to suffer. It insists that it is impervious to wounds dealt by the outside world, in fact, that these are merely occasions for affording it pleasure. . . . Humour is not resigned; it is rebellious. It signifies the triumph not only of the ego, but also of the pleasure-principle, which is strong enough to assert itself here in the face of the adverse real circumstances. (1–6)

These latter observations have important implications for analysts of African American humor, for they centrally situate the creation of pleasure, address the concepts of oppression by the dominant culture, posit humor's role in creative subversion (indeed, in revolution), and suggest Freud would object to a reduction of his theory to "humor is aggression."

This matter of aggression in humor deserves further attention; Mary Douglas has offered a very useful elaboration of the role of aggression in the comic, in a differentiation of Bergson's and Freud's influential formulations of humor. For Bergson, a man who slips and falls on a banana peel makes us laugh because in losing his bodily control, he becomes a helpless automaton; Freud, Douglas suggests, would find the event humorous because for a split second, the stiff man has moved with the "swiftness of a gazelle, as if a new form of life had been hidden there." Douglas claims that the actual thing both Bergson and Freud notice is the humor that results when something formal gets attacked by something informal, "an upsurge of life for Bergson, of libido for Freud. The common denominator underlying both approaches is the joke seen as an attack on control" ("Social" 364).

As these theories suggest, humor has great political and social potential for democratic cultures and processes. In much of this study, I will be relying on Bakhtin's theory of humor as "uncrowning," which more strongly posits an ideological role for humor. Freud, Bergson, and Douglas too seem to have the same basic understanding of the fundamental mechanism at play, whatever the ultimate meaning of the humorous event or utterance appears to be.

Correlatively, American social theorists have naturally related Freud's implications to the structures and modulations of democracy. In a provocative statement, David Riesman commented about ethnic roles in popular American entertainment, where blacks traditionally played a major role in comedies, in all media: "Now obviously the fact that Jews and Negroes could climb, and even avoid the ethnic affronts, most easily in the arts and entertainments, put them in a good position of leadership when the larger society itself shifted to embrace consumption values. Thus ethnics liberate the majority. Increasingly, America's play patterns may suffer from the lack of a customary though under-recognized stimulus and elan when there are no more immigrants or people close to immigrant culture" (323–24n2). It follows that literature written with the intent of realizing these ends would possess a rather peculiar sense of the traditional aspects of literary discourse.

Many of Hurston's characters dream grand dreams, and this forms a subject in many other classic works in the African American canon. Freud makes several comparisons between "dream-work" and "joke-work"; an entire chapter in *Jokes* links the two activities and suggests that humor plays a central role in identity formation, particularly as both dream-work and joke-work ponder the absurdities of life and frequently combine opposites in condensed, nonsensical ways in an attempt to reconcile differences (28). Both endeavors provide, to use an African American expression, "a way out of no way," one within the unconscious itself, the other in social intercourse.

Paul Ricoeur, in his study of Freud, has noted the parallels between the displacement that occurs in dreams and jokes and how both phenomena are marked by condensation, distortion, hidden meanings, and codes (168). Freud's method thus permits a superimposition of dream-work, creative work, joke-work, and art interpretation, all important enterprises in a study of African American humor and in the process of social struggle that helped engender it. The condensation and displacement of joke-work and dream-work find expression in classical rhetoric in the ideas of metaphor (condensation) and metonymy (displacement); hence the significantly metaphorical nature of African American literature and its high incidence of metonymy.

Mahadev Apte, in his influential *Humor and Laughter,* has offered a contemporary definition of humor, albeit one based upon Freud's foundation. Apte explains humor as, first, a cognitive, often unconscious experience that involves mentally refiguring reality and resulting in mirth; second, the outside factors that trigger such a response; third, the pleasure consequently derived; and fourth, the external manifestations of the process, usually smiling and laughing (14). This definition helpfully factors in the body, always a key signifier of the comic in Hurston's narratives.

But how can we tell when something in literature is meant to be funny? Many of Hurston's characters laugh, shriek, dance, and snicker, just to name a few responses, when something seems funny. Other responses can be more subtle. Hurston's often sardonic authorial voice, rising above and lacing through the action, offers another indicator that something funny's going on. My reading of African and African American humorous folklore and traditions has also helped me to see humor in things our age would ignore, as has my investigation of the larger American cultural context of the twenties and thirties. Finally, however, at times I have simply relied on my own judgment.

Humor, Primitivism, and Modernism

Harlem is vicious
modernism. BangClash.
Vicious the way it's made.
Can you stand such beauty.
So violent and transforming.
  —*Amiri Baraka*

It has become a commonplace to say that no culture can know itself without the invention of the "Other." It follows that a reexamination of the self thus means an adjustment of the mirror, a "refiguration" of the "Other." The explosion of modernism in the United States after World War I led to renewed interest in African American culture, especially after the appropriation of African art forms by the European aesthetes. Marianna Torgovnick has recently charted the often fantastic global creation of the primitive, a process that in many ways has never ended. She focuses on Edgar Rice

Burroughs, D. H. Lawrence, Joseph Conrad, Sigmund Freud, Bronislaw Malinowski, and, nearer our own time, Margaret Mead. For Torgovnick, primitivism functions as "a place to project feelings about the present and to draw blueprints for the future" (244), and doing this "brings us back to ourselves, which we reveal in the act of defining the Other" (11).[17]

In the popular realm, the concept has traditionally involved a nostalgic return to a tropical and erotically charged Eden, where complicated codes and modes of perception are dissolved in a kind of prelapsarian pastoral. As Torgovnick states, Western societies assumed that "the primitive is prior to the civilized and can be subordinated by it" (197). Moreover, Americans came to feel that the primitive was still with them, in the form of Native Americans and blacks. It is no accident that Zora Neale Hurston's white benefactor, Charlotte Mason, had subsidized research in Native American culture before turning to her new self-styled role of "Godmother of the Primitives," patron of the tyros of Harlem. To more casual fanciers of the primitives, "Indians" lacked the cachet of blacks, for the former were, to the mind of whites, neither as sensual, musical, nor humorous as the latter. There was a long tradition of considering the Indian as stoic, silent, humorless (the "noble savage" syndrome), while minstrelsy had for decades provided Americans with the image of the grinning darkie. White intellectuals like Mason and Carl Van Vechten, who were probably both sincere and trendy, were appalled by the minstrel tradition, recognizing it as a white travesty of genuinely "primitive" culture. They and others like them solved the problem by returning black peoples to their supposed points of origin in primitive art. This return to the "authenticity of the jungle" was easy enough, at least symbolically, especially in the hot jazz nightclubs up in Harlem where tropical, angular, vibrantly hued artwork by Aaron Douglas and other "primitivist" painters set an appropriately exotic scene.[18] Dancing the black bottom to the jazzy rhythms of a "hot" band in black district speakeasies was more convenient and much more appealing than traveling the so-called "Beads and Feathers" route to the desert West, only to sit around a smoky campfire listening to "monotonous tom-toms" and watching "shuffling" circle dances.

It was the heyday of black comedians as well; new Broadway shows featured black comic duos such as Flournoy Miller and Aubrey Lyles of 1921's trail-blazing black hit comedy *Shuffle Along*. This musical, set during an election in a black southern town, in many ways prefigured Hurston's Eatonville locales, but with minstrel touches. Characters spoke in malapropisms and were heavily involved in petty fraud. Unfortunately, this racist mode of depiction was part of the show's legacy as well, for audiences and producers wanted more of the same throughout the twenties. A musical like *Put and Take* (1921), which tried to provide more sophistication with a northern locale, was critically damned. What made *Shuffle Along* sensational was a dazzling cast (Florence Mills, Josephine Baker, Paul Robeson, and Adelaide Hall were in the chorus), fantastic dancing, and, most of all, music by Eubie Blake and Noble Sissle, including the classics "Love Will Find a Way" and "I'm Just Wild about Harry." Other imitative shows followed; in the next three years, nine black musicals written by and starring black acts opened on Broadway, and black composers began to be hired to write music for white shows (Woll 72–74). *Runnin' Wild* (1923) gave the decade its theme song, "Charston," and a dance and also featured Miller and Lyles's comedy acts, praised because they were "utterly spontaneous and unstudied" (cited in Woll 88). While intellectuals like Van Vechten and Mason wanted their dosage of primitivism straight from the source, the public seemed happier with these debased forms. The shows continued to trouble many African Americans, however, because the humor still depended in part on minstrel traditions. Alain Locke complained that Negro dramatic art had to depart from white images of black characters; writers had to have the "courage to be original, to break with established dramatic convention of all sorts . . . to develop its own idiom, to put itself into new moulds; in short, to be experimental" ("Stage" 116).

Situated plumb in the middle of all this, Hurston was consequently attempting to demonstrate the glories of African American humor at a time when its false image had once again taken America by storm, and not just on stage. *Amos 'n' Andy* was the most popular radio show in the twenties and thirties and as Melvin Ely's study demonstrates, combined new breakthrough representations of African Americans (eventually leading to the television version, with its all-black cast), alongside negative and stereotypical portrayals.[19]

Why were white Americans, intellectuals and lowbrows alike, so suddenly interested in "Negro" art and amusements after World War I? The perceived insularity and down-home, rural wit and wisdom of the black cosmos made it seem as though African Americans had somehow preserved a unified community with a coherent and "happy" view of the world, a world that to white eyes seemed increasingly bewildering, technological, sterile, and forbidding. This view was epitomized in Eliot's coldly elegant *The Waste Land* (1922), but also in Sinclair Lewis's popular *Babbitt,* published the same year, a comic masterpiece that similarly expressed the cri de coeur of a prosperous but enervated middle-class. The transatlantic literary stage was set for simplistic comparisons between white and black consciousness, often expressed flamboyantly in books like Ronald Firbank's *Prancing Nigger* (1924) and Carl Van Vechten's *Nigger Heaven* (1926), in highly sensationalized depictions of black characters. Although W. E. B. Du Bois and Godmother Mason hated Van Vechten's book, Hurston and Langston Hughes agreed that their friend had written a great novel, one that found a way to insert Negro themes into white America's discourse. Godmother loathed the book because it was ersatz primitivism, but she and her two protégés loved Claude McKay's *Home to Harlem* (1928), which corrected many of Van Vechten's errors of presentation but duplicated his interest in showing sensational aspects of black urban life.

Hurston herself was a life-long friend of Van Vechten and seemed to have believed in the idea of the primitive, but on her own terms. In her essay "How It Feels to Be Colored Me," which in many ways demolishes the concept of race altogether, she rejoices in her primitive essence. Describing a visit to a Harlem club with a white friend brings out some paradoxically fevered prose:

> This orchestra grows rambunctious, rears on its hind legs and attacks the tonal veil with primitive fury, rending it, clawing it until it breaks through to the jungle beyond. I follow those heathen—follow them exultingly. I dance wildly inside myself; I yell within, I whoop; I shake my assegai above my head, I hurl it true to the mark *yeeeoww!* I am in the jungle and living in the jungle way. My face is painted red and yellow and my body is painted blue. My pulse is throbbing like a war drum. I want to slaughter something—give pain, give death to what, I do not know. But the piece ends. . . . I creep back slowly to the veneer we call civilization with the last tone and find the white friend sitting motionless in his seat, smoking calmly. "Good music they have here," he remarks, drumming the table with his fingertips. . . . He is far away and I see him but dimly across the ocean and the continent that have fallen between us. He is so pale with his whiteness then and I am *So* colored. (154)

This clever narration obviously lets Hurston have it both ways. Unlike Helga Crane, who in a similar passage in Nella Larsen's *Quicksand* (1928) loses the veneer of civilization in actual fevered dance, Hurston figures her "jungleization" mentally, in controlled, literate prose, and includes the ability to return instantly to civilized discourse the second the music stops. Moreover, the "rending of the veil" relates to breaking taboos, both the "white" veil of the temple in Jerusalem and an analogue to the "black" veil Du Bois associates with African American double consciousness. Thus one may be simultaneously sophisticated and primitive, but only if one is "colored," which here becomes a social construct rather than a racial one, as the rest of the essay makes clear.

This paradigmatic scene from "How It Feels to Be Colored Me" has important implications for understanding the Afrocentric yet modernist devices Hurston wanted to use to appeal to her audience. As she filters these sensory perceptions through her intellect, thus making them "meaningful," both to herself and others, she has satisfied John Dewey's modernist formulation, one that had equal meaning for science and the arts, the dual realms of Hurston's vocation as artist and anthropologist: "A well-conducted scientific inquiry discovers as it tests, and proves as it explores; it does so in virtue of a method which combines both functions. And conversation, drama, [the] novel, and architectural construction, if there is an ordered experience, reach a stage that at once records and sums up the value of what precedes, and evokes and prophesies what is to come. Every closure is an awakening, and every awakening settles something" (Dewey 169).

But what about the origin of Dewey's experiments? Surely another necessary ingredient would be the willingness of the investigator to launch out into new directions, to be fearless, creative, even playful in order to plumb the unknown. It was typical of Hurston to challenge norms and to take risks in general, but that was the actually pragmatic pattern of African American communal humor from the start. Albert Murray has asserted that it is precisely "play and playfulness that is indispensable to the creative process. Play in the sense of competition. Play in the sense of chance-taking. Play in the sense of make-believe and play also in the sense of vertigo or getting high. Play also in the direction of simple amusement as in children's games, and play in the direction of gratuitous difficulty as in increasing the number of jacks you can catch" ("Regional" 4).

There were other aspects of Hurston's playfulness/fearlessness. As should already be clear, she was always inserting herself into white worlds through various means. A black southerner, she joins the continuing war against northern persecution of all southerners. As an Ivy League–educated social scientist she functions as a detached observer of the scenes she describes, yet remains a "native." A woman, Hurston considers herself perfectly capable of speaking for all women, including white women, as she does in her final novel. Raised as a Christian, but also a skeptical scholar, she speaks authoritatively about the Bible people only think they know. But perhaps most importantly, as a black American with an intimate and scientifically informed knowledge of the construction of both black and white American worlds, Hurston enjoys a unique perspective. She offers, in her own person, as expressed in her multivocal, performing, explaining, bridge-building, comic language, access, intimacy, entertainment, education, and connection, something Harlem nightclubs offered too.[20]

Let me twist the lens one turn further; Torgovnick has been struck by the way in which Western discourse of the primitive inevitably begins to overlap the tropes it uses for the female and the colonized. As she puts it, "The dance of the colonizer and the colonized, becomes sexual politics, the dance of male and female" (17). We have remarked on Hurston and Larsen's choice of a dancing female to symbolize the primitive. This figure, in fact, exists as a constant referent in most discourses of primitivism and appears repeatedly in the literature of the Harlem Renaissance, especially in works by male writers. Langston Hughes's "Jazzonia" is merely the most famous of his many poems employing this figure, and a dancing woman occupies the center of "Theater," a key piece in Jean Toomer's brilliant modernist masterwork, *Cane*. But above all, Claude McKay's poem "Harlem Dancer" became virtually the signature piece of the era. A woman dancing in a nightclub seems to have the "voice of blended flutes," while she herself becomes "a proudly swaying palm." In the conclusion, McKay encapsulates the lure and the falsity of cheap primitivism, while nevertheless focusing on his figure's mystery:

> The wine-flushed, bold-eyed boys, and even the girls,
> Devoured her shape with eager, passionate gaze;
> But looking at her falsely-smiling face,
> I knew her self was not in that strange place.
>
> (741)

Hurston's figuration on this trope seems even more impressive when we recognize the ironic contrast between McKay's dancer's wan smile and Hurston's wicked comic send-up of the tradition.

I hardly need to go over the European fascination with African art—particularly sculpture—that revolutionized representation in general for Picasso, Braque, Brancusi, and many others, a process that continued into Hurston's own time as this school of artists had their own effect in turn on world art.[21] In a a revealing analysis of the French artist Dubuffet's concept of the primitive, the art historian Kirk Varnedoe makes some distinctions I should like to apply to Hurston. He argues that in Dubuffet's "primitivizing" art of the forties and fifties, he "sought to fuse the untempered physical and emotive aggressivity he sensed in tribal objects with the unpoliced force found in the graffiti and in the trashiness of the modern city. He held that the Primitive spirit was recoverable within Western culture, not via the 'dead language' of a desiccated high humanism, but in the marginal and the vernacular, the "language spoken in the street" (637). For Varnedoe, this links Dubuffet with Gauguin, who similarly sought what Varnedoe calls the "most significant residue of the Primitive, and thus the greatest power of creation," first in the peasants of Brittany and then in the South Sea Islanders of the Pacific (637). Hurston too, like Dubuffet, Gauguin, Varnedoe, and, above all, Bakhtin, recognized that in the marginalized culture the "Other"—in this case, African American life—one could find once again those mythic, energizing creative forces. This seems implicit both in "How It Feels" and in the ending of her early short story "Drenched in Light." Hurston understood the primitive the way Dubuffet did, as a complex, brash art that frequently caricatured, deformed, and fetishized representations of the human. Like him, she rejected an art that sought out the primitive merely to justify an interest in abstract form and a simplification of aesthetics. It was Hurston's genius, in her fiction, her essays, and in her life itself, to demonstrate that folk culture was anything but simple, anything but serene.[22]

In my exploration of all these issues, I shall demonstrate the many performing roles Hurston took on in her life and her art to facilitate the delivery of her many messages. Her overall stance makes her into a Virgil to take her readers on a tour of what they think are the "lower depths" and scramble their notions of what Heaven and Hell, the Devil and God are. Perfectly suited to play this role, she often casts herself as explicator of the places she shows. This becomes obvious in *Moses,* where she translates the Bible back to its Afro-Asiatic roots, but also in her repeated appendage of "glossaries" to various texts, a natural outgrowth of adding brief translations of idiomatic terms discovered in her folklore-gathering trips in her letters to Godmother. The roles of guide and translator always imply her equality with the reader, and frequently, as in the Harlem nightclub incident, superiority. Her mocking tone, comic detachment, and amused reaction to her friend's take on the "scene" offer wry commentary on how Hurston could create comedy out of the vogue for the "primitive," even while marketing it.[23]

More importantly, in her fiction, Hurston gives us the ability to read so-called "primitive" humor this way, on its several levels, illuminating its profundity and its connection to the deeper being of the people who created it, as well as to the meaning of our current lives. But she was also at the time offering up a reflection to her people of a magnificent culture that few of them could see whole. As an old African proverb states, "No people should be hungry for their own image."

Co(s)mic Zora

Hurston does not always speak in a comic mode. She also summons up a poetic diction and imagery that sweeps us into the firmament of the cosmos, as in this memorable passage: "Janie saw her life like a great tree in leaf with the things suffered, things enjoyed, things done and undone. Dawn and doom was in the branches" (*Their Eyes* 20). Such moments came from Hurston's search for horizon, which began in the dreams of her youth. Many of them found a focus in the classical myths she read and in the folktales of her people, which often had a similarly cosmic dimension. Still, she pondered the differences as well, in notably cosmic form:

> Why did the Norse tales strike so deeply into my soul? I do not know, but they did. I seemed to remember seeing Thor swing his mighty short-handled hammer as he sped across the sky in rumbling thunder, lightning flashing from the tread of his steeds and the wheels of his chariot. The great and good Odin, who went down to the well of knowledge to drink, and was told that the price of a drink from that fountain was an eye. Odin drank deeply, then plucked out one eye without a murmur and handed it to the grizzly keeper, and walked away. That held majesty for me. (*Dust Tracks* 53)

Later in her life, she would fashion a rhetoric to deal in a cosmic way with a new set of gods, when she encountered the ancient African mysteries of hoodoo. Describing one of the dreams she had during her rites of initiation, she writes: "In one, I strode across the heavens with lightning flashing from under my feet, and grumbling thunder following in my wake" (*Dust Tracks* 91).

She would use this imagery to project herself into the future as well:

> I know that nothing is destructible; things merely change forms. When the consciousness we know as life ceases, I know that I shall still be part and parcel of the world. I was a part before the sun rolled into shape and burst forth in the glory of change. I was, when the earth was hurled out from its fiery rim. I shall return with the earth to Father Sun, and still exist in substance when the sun has lost its fire, and disintegrated

in infinity to perhaps become a part of the whirling rubble in space . . . what need of denominations and creeds. The wide belt of the universe has no need for finger-rings. I am one with the infinite and need no other assurance. (*Dust Tracks* 279)

Returning to the sun meant creation but also filial adherence to her mother's encomium "Jump at de sun."

Frequently, Hurston found the cosmic in biblical allusion. She had grown up reciting from the "great book" in her father's church, and in many ways developed what we might call a biblical imagination. The titles of all her novels have a biblical/sacral aura: *Jonah, Moses,* and *Seraph* all use biblical nouns; *Their Eyes* features God himself. But notice also that all four titles link God/sacral writ and the Earth; Jonah finds representation as a man and a vine, but both are motivated and developed by God; Moses meets God on the mountain; the angel or "seraph" descends to the Suwanee; earthly eyes are raised to God. All four, too, are comedic structures, linking the holy and the human in a reverberation of laughter that simultaneously evokes the sacred and the profane. Hurston instinctively understood the enobling effect her unique cosmic imagery could have on narrative that frequently highlighted "leveling humor" and sometimes gritty folk life. Hurston's co(s)mic prose would play a useful function, creating a kind of systolic movement to her books, like the beating of a great heart.

Methodology and Theory

A single theory sufficient both to analyze and to explain all types of joking relationships in human cultures everywhere, however, may be much less insightful than theories tailored specifically to individual cultures. A single broad theory would also be contrary to the holistic principle inherent in the understanding of individual societies and cultures and emphasized by the disciplinary perspective.

—*Mahadev Apte*

Taking Mahadev Apte's words seriously, I have attempted in this book to use theory drawn from many disciplines that nevertheless concentrates on African American humor. On the other hand, there are always times when insights gained from other cultures seem relevant, if they are consonant with the reality within the context of the black text. Collecting and using this wide range of interdisciplinary, multicultural tools has been my response to Henry Louis Gates, Jr.'s challenging call to critics of black literary traditions in the opening essay of *Black Literature and Literary Theory:* "We . . . owe it to those traditions to bring to bear upon their readings any 'tool' which helps us to elucidate, which enables us to see more clearly, the complexities of figuration peculiar to our literary traditions. Close reading of any critical complexion is what this volume advocates; there can be no compromise here" (4).

Accordingly, my study makes extensive use of plot, partly because this is the nature of close reading, but also because an understanding of the humor embedded in a text requires full knowledge of the context that generated it. It also seems to me that critics of ethnic literature have recently been leaping over this important step in what used to be a gradual uncovering of an author's canon. It is fashionable today to write multiple-author studies, which of course operates against extended readings of any author's texts, and even when monographs appear, they are frequently theoretical/ideological mediations circling above and around the text and the author. This is not to say that such studies are not necessary; but in the past, they followed close textual analyses, which laid a foundation. Cleanth Brooks, Olga Vickery, and Michael Millgate, for example, provided close readings of Faulkner that facilitated more theoretical, abstract interpretations, such as John Matthews's or Warwick Wadlington's. African American writers deserve this kind of attention as well, particularly since this type of exercise demonstrates, and generates, the kind of new critical approaches we must have to understand the cultural origins and differences of these texts. Our critical blindnesses have effaced their greatness for too long.

Additionally, I wrote this study for all of Hurston's many admirers, not just those in the academy. I share John Wideman's concern about the growing inaccessibility of scholarly work for the general public and ask, with him, "At what point do our words become an irrelevance to the people who nurtured us, whose lives we sought to touch and celebrate when we embarked on a quest for knowledge?" (3). Craig Werner has recently proposed one possible antidote to this problem: we should attempt to construct bridges between diverse vocabularies; this has been one of my goals ("Recent Books" 130).

Sources for Hurston's work have also intrigued me, and some of my speculations here are just that. We know very little about Hurston's reading, but we can name a fairly extensive list of books that she read and appreciated that are mentioned in her works. I have discovered a little-known mini-autobiography that Hurston apparently co-wrote for a 1942 biographical dictionary, wherein she named her favorite authors: Anatole France, Maxim Gorky, George Bernard Shaw, Victor Hugo, Mark Twain, Charles Dickens, Robert Nathan,

Willa Cather, Irvin S. Cobb, Anne Lindbergh, the Chinese philosophers, and Sinclair Lewis. One notices the many comic geniuses on her list, some of them, like Nathan and Cobb, now largely forgotten. We might understand the absence of any black writers by analogy with what follows this list: "I read every bit of Irish folk material that I can get hold of" (Kunitz and Haycraft 695). As this remark indicates, the folk tradition functioned as her prime source. We are able to amplify Hurston's list by the references she makes to books in letters and in some of her fiction and essays. Despite this, however, with the exception of the Bible, very little overt proof exists that she used the work of other writers to strengthen her own. In this book I have tried to show her extremely camouflaged use of some authors wherever possible.

I frequently focus on what I call the "cosmic" aspect of Hurston's aesthetic, but some of the areas that I examine might simultaneously be considered "mythic" ground. The term "myth," however, has been configured for us by centuries of European history and culture and codified by recent myth-shamans such as Joseph Campbell. While various observations of earlier myth-school critics and scholars obviously have value in dealing with certain black writers, caution must be used in applying a white construct onto a black aesthetic. For this reason, I have chosen not to employ many literary terms derived from myth, such as *picaro,* though Hurston herself and many of her characters plainly "wander," or any of the terms favored by Northrop Frye in his *Anatomy of Criticism,* though many of his figures, such as the *eiron,* could be fitted into my discussion of Hurston's humor. My work here seeks at all times to allow a generous latitude for African-derived literary figures and conventions. I favor social science approaches to culture and language over the traditional literary types, as befits Hurston's training as a social scientist, but also because of the truly innovative work that has been done by scholars in these fields in humor research over the past three decades.

On the other hand, in my examination of the comic, I have relied extensively on the critical insights of Mikhail Bakhtin. One might legitimately ask what his work has to do with Hurston. Is Bakhtin not a "Eurocentric" critic? Shouldn't we be using "Afrocentric" approaches to her work?

Yes and no. Bakhtin feels the greatest example of carnival was found in the common people, especially in Roman Saturnalia. We know that Hurston was keenly interested in Roman myth and used it extensively in her books. Her studies at Columbia certainly involved an intense study of myth, which was considered part of training in folklore. But Bakhtin's interest in myth never lies with the gods but rather with the common people's concept and use of them. His perceptions about folk humor are frequently just as useful for understanding African American, and sometimes African, humorous conventions, as for Europeans. What he called "carnivalization" has many analogues in both African and African American culture. Moreover, his perspective was shaped by his precarious position as an intellectual in the Stalinist Soviet Union. He was constantly in danger of imprisonment and often went hungry. His insatiable desire for knowledge, pioneering spirit, passion for the folk, and boisterous—dare we say bodacious?—sense of humor make him in many ways an ideal colleague for Hurston. His lifespan, 1895–1975, approximates hers, and like her his country had had a system of slavery that ended at virtually the same time; Alexander II freed the serfs in 1861. Oppression, however, continued in many ways there and here, especially, perhaps, for those like Bakhtin, after the Russian Revolution.

Bakhtin and Hurston had three major consuming interests in common: the folk and their culture, the novel, and humor's role in human relations and language. Both writers saw that what Bakhtin would call the "carnivalization of language" enabled ordinary people to subvert the formal language of the state, to puncture its pretensions, and to pull off the pompous disguises elite culture draped around its mechanisms of power and prestige. As Bakhtin put it, "Carnival forms, transposed into the language of literature, became a *powerful means* for comprehending life in art, they became a special language whose words and forms possess an extraordinary capacity for *symbolic* generalization, that is, for *generalization in depth*. Many essential sides of life, or more precisely its *layers* (and often the most profound), can be located, comprehended, and expressed only with the help of this language" (*Dostoyevsky* 157).

Although parallels must be carefully made, some African societies have also featured special holidays of comic license, when groups or individuals are permitted free humorous expression; no person, high or low, has immunity from their barbs. As such, these seasons of liberty are akin to the European carnival tradition, particularly paschal laughter, when communicants were permitted to conduct mock, blasphemous rituals in the churches themselves, even targeting priests in suggestive and outrageous ways.

Parody has always occupied a central position in African American humor. Slaves brought their masters and mistresses down to their level by mocking virtually every pronouncement they made. If they could use a white preacher's text to do so, so much the better, especially sermons that included biblical texts on obedience. Many folk rhymes were created in this mode. A takeoff on the Lord's Prayer read

> "Our Fadder, Which are in Heaben!"—
> White man owe me leben and pay me seben.
> "D'y Kingdom come! D'y Will be done!"—
> An' if I hadn't tuck dat, I wouldn' git none.
>
> (Talley 122)

White hymns were parodied as well. "Reign, Master Jesus Reign," could thus become

> Oh rain! Oh rain! Oh rain, "good" Mosser!
> Rain, Mosser, rain! Rain hard!
> Rain flour an' lard an' a big hog head
> Down in my back yard.
>
> (Talley 122)

These slave parodies not only level masters through humor—their blasphemous appropriation of God-like powers becomes noted and mocked as well.

It is fascinating to compare this African-derived phenomenon with the European tradition of "parodia sacra" developed in the Middle Ages, where sacred texts and rituals were blasphemously parodied as part of carnival. As Bakhtin notes, parody forces "the creation of a *decrowning double*" (*Dostoyevsky* 127), and there was "no genre, no text, no prayer, no saying that did not receive its parodic equivalent" (*Dialogic* 74). At the same time, we must remember Mary Douglas's observation that a joke works, at bottom, as an "anti-rite," in that a joking connection of opposites destroys hierarchy and order ("Jokes" 102). Among themselves, the same was true for American slaves. Gilbert Osofsky has eloquently commented on the way that the humor of slave oral traditions was used "to keep men sane under the most trying of human conditions" (47).

Bakhtin points out that virtually every one of Dostoyevsky's heroes has several parodic doubles, and we find the same in Hurston. In Jonah, for instance, the Reverend John Pearson finds a comic echo early in the book in Mehaley's beau, Pomp, and later in Rev. Felton Cosy and Deacon Harris. Janie's parodic double in *Their Eyes* is Annie Tyler, while Tea Cake's is Who Flung. Moses' becomes Aaron, and in *Seraph* Arvay's is Larraine. But rhetorical genres get parodied as well, as in the famous mock religious service Jody conducts over the dead mule's carcass in *Their Eyes*, to name only one of many examples in Hurston's oeuvre. Bakhtin calls this the speech of the public square; in Hurston's Eatonville, it flourishes on Joe Clarke's store porch.

We must be careful to observe some caveats while comparing the very different Afrocentric and Eurocentric comic conventions. Bakhtin lived in large cities and received his knowledge of the folk from literature and city marketplaces, rather than in rural communities. He thus always thought of folk language as a counterforce to the rigidities of Soviet government, custom, and stiff utterances. Hurston, by contrast, because of her folk background, was more interested in the dialogics of the folk culture itself, *in situ*. Despite this basic difference, both writers identify and target monological figures, inside and outside various groups, skewering them with folk humor and utterance.

I have been inspired to do this work by those who preceded me in the study of African American humor. We all owe a great debt to indefatigable artists, collectors, and scholars such as Langston Hughes, Harold Courlander, J. Mason Brewer, Alain Locke, Richard Dorson, Arthur Huff Fauset, Thomas Talley, E. C. L. Adams, James Weldon Johnson, Roger Abrahams, Thomas Kochman, Philip Sterling, Claudia Mitchell-Kernan, Lawrence Levine, Alan Dundes, Daryl Dance, Charles Nichols, Linda Goss, and many others, who have gathered together and preserved precious documents from our literary past. Their brilliant commentary and reverent feeling for the material have been equal blessings for us all.

Finally, I would like to turn to Ralph Ellison. Zora surely would have approved of this literary cousin, who commented so tellingly on a subject very close to her: "Given the persistence of racial violence and the unavailability of legal protections, I asked myself, what else *was* there to sustain our will to persevere but laughter? And could it be that there was a subtle triumph hidden in such laughter that I had missed, but one which still was more affirmative than raw anger? A secret, hard-earned wisdom?" (*Invisible Man* xv–xvi). As Zora would no doubt have proclaimed, "Selah!"

Notes

1. Mel Watkins, however, has written just such a study, *On the Real Side*, which expands brief but valuable efforts by earlier critics to limn the contours of an extremely rich vein. His book appeared too recently, however, to be considered here. African American humor has chiefly been recorded and preserved by folklorists. Two fine books that frequently comment on African American humor are Sterling Brown's neglected *The Negro in Amer-*

ican Fiction and *Negro Poetry and Drama* (both 1937). There are many fine articles on African American humor (particularly those by Hurston's contemporaries Sterling Brown, Jessie Fauset, and Langston Hughes), but only a few longer studies. The most influential of the latter have been William Schechter's *The History of Negro Humor in America* (1970), a somewhat dated but still valuable treatment; the many articles and books of Roger D. Abrahams (particularly *Deep Down in the Jungle* and *Positively Black*); Charles H. Nichols's brief but rich survey (1978); and the superlative fifth chapter of Lawrence Levine's *Black Culture and Black Consciousness*, "Black Laughter" (1977). The best thing about Levine's analysis is the inclusion of dozens of illustrative jokes and anecdotes, many of them hilarious. He groups them around rubrics such as ritual insults, absurdist humor, unmasking humor, corrective humor, and self-reflexive humor. Others deal with all types of sexual behavior and many glory in the stereotype of the "black stud" popular in white culture. Perhaps most remarkably, Levine presents jokes that deal humorously with lynching and racial violence, which he links to Freud's "triumph of narcissism" theory, where rebellious humor signifies a victory of the ego, a syndrome we frequently term "gallows humor" (343). Unfortunately, Levine doesn't link his discussion to African American literature very often, but to be sure, that would have been a book in itself.

Many articles deal with joking traditions and linguistic patterns in African American culture, and many have been written by folklorists. Few literary critics have addressed humor in African American literary texts, possibly because humor analysis isn't "serious work" and therefore compromises the integrity of the investigator. This problem, I hardly need to add, exists in all fields of humor research and makes it very difficult to fund scholarly investigations of humor.

2. For two important studies of African American tricksters, see Edwards and Roberts. The African roots of the tradition have recently been enumerated in section 1 of Gates's *The Signifying Monkey*. A short overview of the trickster tradition in general may be found in Abrahams's "Trickster, the Outrageous Hero." A basic study, although based in Native American culture, is Paul Radin's *The Trickster* (1956).

3. Lawrence Levine provides an excellent discussion of the trickster tradition in African American culture and charts the changes that were taking place in it in the early twentieth century (370–86).

A biographical paradigm exists for Hurston's appreciation of trickster stratagems. We now know, thanks to Cheryl Wall, that Hurston pulled a fantastic trick on the world by pretending to be ten years younger than she actually was. Census records reveal that she was born on January 7, 1891, rather than January 1, 3, or 7, 1901 or 1903 (Hurston could be fickle about her fictions). This means, among other things, that she was actually thirty-four when she entered Barnard College, though people around her thought she was in her early twenties (Hemenway, *Zora* 9). The Hurston family Bible, however, lists the date of her birth as January 15, 1891 (Bordelon, "New Tracks" 8).

4. For treatments of self-reflexive ethnic humor, see Davies, 121–24; Apte, 136–37. The standard treatment of Jewish humor in general may be found in Reik's *Jewish Wit*.

5. The best books on black stereotyping, racist, and authentic African American humor in the movies are Daniel Leab's *From Sambo to Superspade* and Donald Bogle's *Toms, Coons, Mulattoes, Mammies, and Bucks;* also see Thomas Cripps, "The Death of Rastus: The Negro in American Films since 1945."

6. Even the catalogues were funny; OKEH Records had the following teaser for Victoria Spivey's latest disk: "G'wan, Spivey, you tell 'em, girl, you're wicked with them shake down Blues. Be yourself! We mean you've got low-down patter in a lazy creepy drawl. Hey! Hey! . . . they rock 'em from the ground up with an easin', pleasin', teasin' feelin'. The Blues Pleasure Imps are struttin' fast in every song listed. . . . Oh hear the horns quiver in wild delight. Ask your Okeh Dealer to play them for you. . . . What's a good man gonna do . . . so many pleasin' mammas easin' him with sweet Blues. Just ask to hear them all" (Harrison 58).

7. One good example was the "rent party," which quickly developed its own protocol. According to Ira DeA. Reid, the custom came from southern cities, where parties were given to raise money to help a family pay the rent. They were also, he claims, "a wild form of commercialized recreation in its primary stages" and "humor was the counterpart of their irony" (144). Invitations were printed, and often they were headed with comic expressions taken from the blues: "Leaving Me Papa, It's Hard to Do Because Mama Done Put That Thing on You" or "You Don't Get Nothing for Being an Angel Child, So You Might as Well Get Real Busy and Real Wild," especially at parties featuring musicians such as "Kid Professor, the father of the Piano" (146).

8. This phenomenon fits in with Hurston's observations about the secretive nature of much of African American humor, but also with Arthur Koestler's theory of humor's bisociation, which he describes as the perception of a situation or idea in two different frames of reference. "The event in which the two intersect is made to vibrate on two different wave lengths as it were" (35). I would add the qualification that the *humor* in all these genres, not just in jokes, forms a metacategory of indirection all its own that deserves detailed analysis.

I would like to thank Deborah Plant for generously sharing her work with me. Her project makes extensive connections between African oral traditions and the forms they took in the United States.

9. See Wittke; Huggins; Ostendorf; Dormon, "Ethnic" and "Shaping"; and especially Boskin, "'Black.'"

10. In 1914, a typical collection was published in Louisville by Marion F. Harmon, *Negro Wit and Humor*. It offers folklore, folk songs, "race peculiarities," "race history," and a sugary introduction that claims race relations "except in aggravated cases" are "peaceable and pleasant." "Splendid" colleges have been built for blacks, and the author sadly predicts, "the ex-slave will soon be no more, and to preserve the quaintness, the wit and humor of the 'Old

Time Darkey,' this book has been brought into existence" (6). The book also contains several dialect poems by African American poets, including Joseph S. Cotter and Paul Laurence Dunbar, many of them loaded with stereotypes.

11. A cogent discussion of Rice and his career may be found in Dormon's "The Strange Career of Jim Crow Rice." The standard work on minstrelsy for many years, and still valuable, is Wittke; more recent explorations include Boskin (*Sambo*), Huggins, Ostendorf, Toll, and Lott. Toll's book-length study of minstrelsy contains much valuable information but is somewhat flawed in its documentation and mode of presentation. For a critique and correction of Toll, consult Stowe and Grimsted. Lott's important book-length study, *Love and Theft: Blackface Minstrelsy and the American Working Class* (Oxford, 1993), appeared too late to be considered here.

12. Robert Hemenway's introduction to the new Penguin edition of *Uncle Remus* offers a sensible and valuable assessment of Harris and his achievement.

13. Bruce Jackson's *The Negro and His Folklore* anthologizes much of this material and offers some subtle assessments of origins, their forms, and their effects.

14. For a thorough discussion of the coon song phenomenon see Dormon, "Shaping."

15. Brochure advertising the Hall Johnson Negro Choir, Hall Johnson Folder, Charlotte Mason Papers, Moorland-Spingarn Research Center, Howard University Library, Washington, D.C.

16. Hortense Powdermaker's classic essay "The Channeling of Negro Aggression by the Cultural Process" describes the cultural dimensions of the mask and suggests that much more than overt aggression is part of the hostility behind it. She relates much intrarace conflict and crime to frustration over the inability to vent hostility on whites and finds a correlative release of this tension through interrace wit and humor. Interestingly, Powdermaker, as early as 1943, made a cross-cultural connection between Theodor Reik's analysis of Jewish masochistic humor and a similar phenomenon among African Americans, something she sees heightened in the latter group through a smug sense of irony traceable to the black church. Since black suffering and white power-mongering will receive appropriate rewards in Heaven and Hell (and thus reverse, I would add, roles, thereby creating humorous inversion), pain has a paradoxical psychological benefit. For a related syndrome, see my discussion of Coser's observations of hospital humor in chapter 5.

17. Unfortunately, Torgovnick does not consider the substantial roles played by primitivism in African American literary discourse and in fact offers surprisingly little analysis of the African and Asian art that figures so largely in her study. The major emphasis is on white male artists who purvey images of the primitive and the effect of their aesthetic production on Western intellectuals and consumers. Still, her work offers many exciting points of departure for future scholars. The subject of the intersection of modernism, primitivism, the avant-garde, and black literary discourse during the twenties and beyond is an important and neglected subject that I

cannot pursue further here. We have had some promising initial discussions of the subject lately in Houston Baker's *Modernism and the Harlem Renaissance,* Michael Berube's study of Melvin Tolson and Thomas Pynchon, and Werner Sollors's *Beyond Ethnicity,* but what we need is a book that surveys the subject in depth, one that factors in humor's contribution to all these fields. The title of James De Jongh's *Vicious Modernism* is misleading. De Jongh offers an ambitious survey of Harlem's literature from the twenties to the seventies, including works in Spanish, but does not provide a sustained discussion of modernism, modernist aesthetics, or a definition of black modernism.

18. As the flood of African studies scholarship in the past few decades demonstrates, Douglas and other black artists of the twenties and thirties had rather hazy ideas of African culture, but many of the Harlem writers, painters, and sculptors nevertheless embraced the notion of a primitivist ethos. At the same time, the lack of a clear, traceable connection was achingly felt and understood. As Countee Cullen memorably phrased it:

> What is Africa to me:
> Copper sun, a scarlet sea,
> Jungle star and jungle track,
> . . . .
> *One three centuries removed*
> *From the scenes his fathers loved*
> *Spicy grove and banyan tree,*
> *What is Africa to me?*
>
> (250)

19. One of the more interesting aspects of Ely's book is his documentation of black support of the show, which gradually deteriorated in the fifties and sixties when the introduction of minstrelsy-derived characters such as the Kingfish, Sapphire, Lightnin', and the shyster lawyer Calhoun tended to cancel out the more humane characterizations of Amos and Andy. Ely persuasively argues that the program's appeal lay not in its racial humor but rather in its depictions of values shared by many Americans during this period. Ely's book falls short, however, by failing to measure the show's humor against the standard of contemporary comic creations by African Americans.

20. The key role played by nightclubs in general and Harlem night spots in particular is discussed cogently in Lewis Ehrenberg's lively study *Steppin' Out.*

21. See Torgovnick, especially part 2, "Making Primitive Objects High Art," for a trenchant synopsis.

22. Many of the concepts I have discussed here, including those of sincerity and authenticity, are probed in Daniel Singal's excellent article on the rise of modernism, which, among other things, discusses the many links between primitivism and modernism. For a classic refutation of the notion that the literatures and cultures of primitive peoples are simple, consult Paul Radin's "The Literature of Primitive Peoples."

23. Ralph Linton asserts that the "primitive" artist aims to "present his

subject as he and his society think of it, not as he sees it. The development of convention for this not only saves labor but also facilitates communication between the artist and his audience." He calls this quality "an indifference to naturalism" (48). An artist thus expresses herself not only as *she* feels, but as her *community* feels. This takes us into the realm of what Henry Louis Gates, Jr., calls the "speakerly text," one that annuls the separation between the voice of the artist and her community.

White intellectuals were slow in understanding all this, thinking the art forms expressed naivete because of their conventional qualities. As Linton states, in an arresting example, an Arapaho Indian showed him a moccasin he had made that was beaded like others, except for one oblong shape, which symbolized that in his youth he had been a great warrior and a man of pride and furious temper but he had now become so gentle that he would not injure even a worm." Thus the moccasin to him conveys the "poignancy of old age," while a white person would only see a "bit of beadwork" (51).

Part 1  Sunrise

Some folk is born wid they feet on de sun and they kin seek out de inside meanin' of words.

    —*Mules and Men*

ONE

"Cast in Yo' Nets Right Here": Finding a Comic Voice

For while I had structured my short stories out of familiar experiences and possessed concrete images of my characters and their backgrounds, now I was confronted by nothing more substantial than a taunting, disembodied voice. . . . I was in the process of plotting a novel based on the war then in progress. . . . I was most annoyed to have my efforts interrupted by an ironic, down-home voice that struck me as being as irreverent as a honky-tonk trumpet blasting through a performance, say of Britten's War Requiem.
—*Ralph Ellison*

Cast down your bucket where you are.
—*Booker T. Washington*

For many years, Hurston wandered from job to job, city to city, first as a lady's maid with a Gilbert and Sullivan company, and then on her own. Everywhere she worked, however, she made a place for herself—even in a Washington barbershop—through her infectious humor and her inexhaustible fund of stories. Eventually, she put these gifts to academic use, initially in her studies at Morgan Academy. Her work for the Howard literary magazine, the *Stylus*, enabled her to put her oral tradition and repertoire into print. Right from the start, she was determined to create a new art form based on the African American cultural tradition. This resolve strengthened and took on a new form after she decided to become a folklorist, while studying with Ruth Benedict and Franz Boas at Columbia. But Zora was getting a second education in literary bohemianism, Harlem style, at the same time, through her joyous participation in the "New Negro" movement, a seminal American literary episode that had ambivalent consequences for Hurston and her subsequent reputation.

The years of wandering that followed Hurston's mother's death finally brought Zora to Harlem, and at a propitious moment, poised to plunge her nets into the currents of the Harlem Renaissance. Significantly, Robert Hemenway begins his biography of Hurston at this critical juncture,[1] picturing her arrival in the city in January 1925 with $1.50 in her purse, without a job or friends, "but filled with 'a lot of hope,'" carrying a bag of manuscripts, and with "the map of Florida on her tongue" (*Zora* 9).

Although Hurston plays a leading role in the various accounts of this age of the "New Negro," she was only part of the Harlem literati for a few years; she looms larger in histories of the period because she represents many of the movement's best qualities. Surprisingly, only a few writers in the group were actually from the South. Thus Zora brought a special resonance to the movement, for her "down-home" qualities meshed rather well with the new interest in the so-called "primitive," a word that had much more of a cachet in the 1920s. Moreover, her rapidly reappearing works now reveal her as one of the most original, exuberant, and productive writers the group produced. Still, she would quite probably be surprised to hear herself mentioned as one of the more important figures of the Harlem Renaissance; she devotes all of one paragraph to this renowned literary event in *Dust Tracks* (168). Others who knew her in the twenties have frequently noted Hurston's contagious sense of fun, her dramatic appearance, and her store of folktales, anecdotes, and jokes; all this made her a favorite at the fabled Harlem "rent" parties, salons, and gab fests.

So Hurston's presence during the Renaissance was definitely noted; why, then, did so many scholarly studies, biographies, autobiographies by other Renaissance celebrities, and literary histories fail to do justice to her work and worth? More centrally, considering Hurston's vast current popularity, some might be puzzled; why did earlier readers eventually turn away from this supremely gifted artist? These two questions are intricately related, for the seeds of Hurston's rejection were paradoxically sown just as she was initially reaching an audience. In *Their Eyes Were Watching God*, Hurston would create a central figure, Janie, mythically modeled on the Roman god Janus; his doubled aspect would be a signifier for Hurston's literary reputation throughout her career.

Although Zora Neale Hurston suffered some outrageous slings and arrows for being born black and female, as many critics have noted, she also was silenced for her outrageous sense of humor, something blacks and women were permitted only when it took the most passive forms. Her brand of ethnic humor became associated with the negative sense of the word "primitive." In the midst of the decade when the "Negro" was in vogue a raging controversy erupted over the publication of Van Vechten's *Nigger Heaven* in 1926. The fallout from this firestorm over the issue of representation had many consequences; one was that the humor of the black folk, always fraught with stereotypes, suddenly became even more of a minefield for writers, and Hurston found herself with no clear path.

Humor was a basic, continuing component in her work; to her, laughter was a way to show one's love for life; an indirect mode useful in saying the unsayable and in negotiating differences; a wonderful teaching tool and thus a way to bridge the distances between rural and urban, black and white, rich and poor, man and woman, author and reader. Consequently, humor played a crucial role in her initial reception by, and later relations with, the other members of the Harlem Renaissance; in her sense of folklore and its functions; in the anthropological definitions of culture she formulated, which grew out of her training as a professional folklorist; and in her ever-changing and increasingly complex fiction, including her masterworks *Their Eyes Were Watching God* and *Moses, Man of the Mountain*.

Eventually, however, this at first refreshing quality came to seem, for some, embarrassingly close to white stereotypes of blacks. According to Walter Lippmann's classic definition, a stereotype constitutes a set of mental pictures formulated by human beings to describe the world beyond their reach; these pictures are at least partially culturally determined. Lippmann stresses that stereotypes are factually incorrect products of a faulty reasoning process and that they tend to persist despite new knowledge and education. An analogue for a stereotype might also be a reflection in a funhouse mirror. Depending on one's position before the mirror, the image reflected may be slightly or terribly distorted, but it is usually still recognizable.

Alain Locke, one of the elder leaders of the Renaissance and one of Hurston's mentors, touched on these matters in one of his own contributions to *The New Negro* in 1925: "The elder generation of Negro writers expressed itself in . . . guarded idealization. . . . 'Be representative': put the better foot foremost, was the underlying mood. But writers like Rudolph Fisher, Zora Hurston . . . take their material objectively with detached artistic vision; they have no thought of their racy folk types as typical of anything but themselves or of their being taken or mistaken as racially representative" (50). Locke seems to implicitly deny here that rural blacks are representative of the race. Gradually, this stance began to affect the literati's view of Hurston herself; at first charmed by her wit and appearance, they began to have reservations about her "seriousness." Sherley Anne Williams offers a sensible explanation of how this concept developed and proliferated in literary history:

> For a long time she was remembered more as a character of the Renais-sance than as one of the most serious and gifted artists to emerge during this period. She was a notable tale-teller, mimic, and wit, confident to the point of brashness (some might even say beyond), who refused to con-form to conventional notions of ladylike behavior and middle-class de-corum. To one of her contemporaries, she was the first black nationalist; to another, a handkerchief-head Uncle Tom. . . . To Alice Walker and others of our generation, Zora was a woman bent on discovering and defining herself, a woman who spoke her own mind. (ix–x)

Women very rarely are permitted to publicly take on a comic's role, in any society. The traditional effort to place normative restrictions on women has sought the model "good girl": "Chaste, gentle, gracious, ingenuous, good, clean, kind, virtuous, noncontroversial, and above suspicion and reproach" (Fox 807). Virtually all of these communal goals for women are antithetical to the qualities associated with the hu-morist; it therefore comes as no surprise that women around the world rarely engage in the verbal dueling or ritual insult sessions common among males or that the many tricksters in world folklore are over-whelmingly male. This prejudice goes so deep that in some cultures women who laugh freely in public are considered wanton.[2] In Ameri-can society, moreover, many believe women generally are unable to tell jokes "correctly" in any case. A female folklorist discovered that even in all-female gatherings, women "consistently began and ended with apologies: for speaking, for the content of their speech, for speaking too long."[3] If a female humorist seems offensive, she can only become more so if she somehow uses this stance to obtain money.

Much of the long-term damage to Hurston along these lines came from Wallace Thurman's roman à clef of the Harlem Renaissance, *Infants of the Spring*. Thurman, a sharp-tongued, bitter, but brilliant man, almost certainly felt a kind of rivalry toward Hurston, one of his collaborators on the short-lived periodical *Fire!!* Left holding the finan-cial bag when the magazine failed, he had to resent Hurston's ability to get fellowships and loans from wealthy white women. His caricature of her, the figure of Sweetie May Carr, a leading light of "Niggerati Manor," severely damaged Hurston's literary image:

Sweetie May was a short story writer, more noted for her ribald wit and personal effervescence than for any actual literary work. She was a great favorite among those whites who went in for Negro prodigies. Mainly because she lived up to their conception of what a typical Negro should be. It seldom occurred to any of her patrons that she did this with tongue in cheek. Given a paleface audience, Sweetie May would launch forth into a saga of the little all-colored Mississippi town where she claimed to have been born. Her repertoire of tales was earthy, vulgar and funny. Her darkies always smiled through their tears. . . . Sweetie May was a master of southern dialect, and an able raconteur, but she was too indifferent to literary creation to transfer to paper that which she told so well. The intricacies of writing bored her, and her written work was for the most part turgid and unpolished. But Sweetie May knew her white folks. . . . "It's like this," she had told Raymond. "I have to eat. I also wish to finish my education. Being a Negro writer these days is a racket and I'm going to make the most of it while it lasts. Sure I cut the fool. But I enjoy it, too. . . . Thank God for this Negro literary renaissance! Long may it flourish!" (229–30)

Thurman's portrait had an element of truth in it; Hurston was interested at this point in finding patrons, and other aspiring artists thought this translated into "cuttin' the monkey for the white folks." Sweetie's coldly selfish pose, however, runs counter to Hurston's nature, as does the idea that she cared nothing for her craft.

Larry Neal's assessment of Hurston's role during the Renaissance, written a few years before the corrective of Hemenway's biography, shows how lingering the effect of reports like this were. Although he begins by stating that her reputation was perhaps hurt by the "complexity of her personality and the controversy that attended her career," he carries on the tradition by repeating all the old stories and making the old charges. "Miss Hurston," Neal claims, was "very bold and outspoken, an attractive woman who had learned how to survive with native wit." Moreover, "Zora could often be an inveterate romantic. . . . The historical oppression that we now associate with Southern black life was not a central aspect of her experience. . . . She was no political radical. She was, instead, a belligerent individualist who was decidedly unpredictable and perhaps a little inconsistent" (11–24).

Thus we see a woman who was presumed dangerous because she didn't direct all that "belligerence" at the proper target, racial oppression; the unstated assumption is that it can therefore only be released in one direction: at black men. Further, by locating her in the South, but subtracting the "hardening" of racial oppression, Hurston becomes saddled with all the negative baggage that label applies, without its only perceived merit, the ability to say "been in the fire so long." Neal also accuses her, as others had before, of being "opportunistic" because she had been Fannie Hurst's secretary and Carl Van Vechten's friend. He then quotes Langston Hughes's oft-cited dig at her, which blithely fails to mention that Hughes himself was the benefactor of the very same white patron.

Indeed, Hughes's celebrated falling-out with Hurston over the ownership and proposed production of their co-written play, *Mule Bone*, had much to do with their status as veritable sibling rivals for Godmother's favors, a factor that certainly had an impact on Hurston's troubled relationship with Alain Locke, another Mason protégé. Both men would first support and then attack her.

In his autobiography Hughes recalls her this way:

> In her youth, she was always getting scholarships and things from wealthy white people, some of whom simply paid her just to sit around and represent the Negro race for them, she did it in such a racy fashion. She was full of side-splitting anecdotes, humorous tales, and tragicomic stories, remembered out of her life in the South as the daughter of a traveling minister of God. She could make you laugh one moment and cry the next. To many of her white friends, no doubt, she was a perfect "darkie," in the nice meaning they give the term—that is a naive, childlike, sweet, humorous, and highly colored Negro. (*Big Sea* 239)

Hughes's remarks are revealing; he mentions Hurston's ability to make people laugh, her rural background, and implies a connection between them. He also infers that someone who is funny and from the South therefore comes off as naive, childlike, *humorous,* as if it were a package deal.

Later, in a letter to Van Vechten discussing the *Mule Bone* controversy, he would similarly remark, "Girls are funny creatures," a putdown along gender lines that parallels the above racial ones. Hughes, having arrived in Harlem from Cleveland and Washington, here seems to share his contemporaries' stereotypes of the South, southern blacks, and women, including the "nice girl" image.[4] He no doubt could have felt this way about Hurston at the time they met; later, however, he made her world his own by touring the South with Hurston and making an intense study of black folklore. Indeed, he became the leading anthologist of black folk culture, compiling collections of humor and folklore, and his character Jesse B. Semple, in some ways his greatest creation, has much in common with Hurston's folk. By the time he wrote *The Big Sea* (1940), then, there was no excuse for this kind of portrayal except jealously and hurt.

Alain Locke played a doubled role with Hurston, as she did with him. As sibling rivals for Godmother's affection and money, they had to pretend to like each other but each frequently covertly, and sometimes overtly, worked against the other's standing. Locke involved himself repeatedly in Godmother's deliberations over Hurston's allowance, and once wrote a letter to Mason suggesting she cut Zora off for a time, for her own good: "If Zora isn't doing creative work, she should for the time being do some bread and butter work. These young folks really don't know what rare advantages they have had."[5] In light of these comments and activities, Locke's later, somewhat negative review of *Their Eyes* must be viewed suspiciously.

Using Locke, Hughes, Thurman, and other males as expert "eye-witnesses" to Hurston's participation in the movement became the pattern for many male commentators on the Harlem Renaissance.[6] Larry Neal asserts that Hurston commercially popularized black culture via a calculated pandering to white stereotypes of blacks. He is appalled to hear a story about Zora hosting a racially mixed party wearing a red bandana, and, he adds pejoratively, "Aunt Jemima style," obviously forgetting that many other people besides Aunt Jemima wore and wear kerchiefs, especially in the South. Worst of all, she served her guests "something like collard greens and pigs' feet" (23).

As much as Neal spied Hurston playing out stereotypes in her life, others found them lurking in her work, which had been so heavily influenced by the Eatonville milieu of her childhood and her anthropological studies and fieldwork. Her work also came hard on the heels of Van Vechten's *Nigger Heaven* (1926). His well-meaning but mistaken emphasis on the exotic, the violent, and the sensual led him, and many readers and subsequent writers, back to the old stereotypes and caused quite a few black writers and leaders to eschew anything that smacked of the "primitive." It was difficult for many of these people, when confronted with Zora Neale Hurston's comic folk figures, not to see parallel lines of development. Even though she dealt, for the most part, with positive elements of folk culture, they only saw stereotypes; the baby had to go out with the bathwater.

Unfortunately, Hurston's critics have failed to understand that stereotypes may also be positive, favorable, even overvalued (Vinacke 229–43). Julian Mason reminds that though it is popular to bemoan the use of stereotypes, literary production would be impossible without them, and in fact, there are "good" and "bad" attributes to composite stereotypical images that we selectively use and discard, respectively. "Where would Aesop have been without stereotypes, and where would we be without his stereotypes? The answer in each case is, 'Much poorer.'"

Mason points to the constant use of stereotypes in the Bible, especially in Jesus' parables, where the good samaritan, the prodigal son, and others provide a starting point for discussion. For Mason, stereotyping becomes wrong "only when it distorts or misrepresents more than it provides a useful distillation or even occasionally an essence" (63, 70).

We should also remember that not many Americans of this era, black or white, really understood the true greatness of black folk culture, which had never been included in American history and literature courses, themselves relatively new fields at this time, when the folk expression "If it's white, it's right" held great sway with the black bourgeoisie. Hurston was one of the first writers or scientists to assess the riches of black folk culture and map its contours. Even Alain Locke at one time scorned the spirituals, although he changed his mind with a vengeance when they became the vogue. It was presumed that dealing with rural people was demeaning to the race; the representation issue was vehemently argued again and again, with figures like Du Bois demanding that the "talented tenth" lead their people artistically with properly genteel (which in many cases meant "white derived") models. Jesse Fauset and Nella Larsen were much more to this school's taste than the bodacious Hurston.

This line of argument has arisen again recently, even from scholars of African American literature, who often tend to be northern raised or northern trained. They sometimes judge interest in southern black folk exemplary of "romantic pastoralism," a particularly onerous category for those with a Marxist bent. Hurston gets judged harshly for not writing about the misery of northern slum dwellers, for not being, in other words, Richard Wright or James Baldwin. Northern blacks, according to this argument, are more "representative" of black culture in the thirties and forties.[7] This claim ignores the fact that Hurston really did not know northern black areas that well, always thought of herself as a southerner, hated cold climates, and returned to Florida whenever she could. Her few pieces set in Harlem suffer by comparison with her Florida works.

Crayon Enlargements of Life: Hurston's Method of Representation

Although the ideology of the argument against Hurston today is quite different, the crux of the matter—representation—is still the same. Hurston chose to portray the people she knew in their daily lives, rather than in dramatic and violent confrontations with white society. The way she accomplished this with humor drawn from her own observations may readily be seen through a brief examination of her autobiography.

Dust Tracks never bores the reader, largely because the book, in celebrating Zora Neale Hurston, also salutes the culture that made her. She lards the text with humor, both as structure and adornment. Hurston uses comic expressions, jokes, an entire collection of humorous effects to amplify, underline, and sharpen the points she makes, part of her attempt to provide what she called "crayon enlargements of life." Deceptively delightful words such as these often contain a serious meaning, just as the slave folktales did. Hurston skillfully trims and fits folk sayings into integral parts of her narrative; on the first page, for instance, she describes her hometown by saying, "Eatonville is what you might call hitting a straight lick with a crooked stick. The town . . . is a by-product of something else" (3). This type of description becomes more pungent when she combines these materials with her own imaginative coinages, as in the following description of her father's family: "Regular hand-to-mouth folks. Didn't own pots to pee in, nor beds to push 'em under. . . . No more to 'em than the stuffings out of a zero" (13). This utterance alone gives proof to Hurston's assertion that the Negro's greatest contribution to the language was the use of metaphor and simile, the use of the double descriptive, and the use of verbal nouns ("Characteristics" 40). It also reveals the way such tools can be used to revitalize language by working simultaneously in the comic mode.

Additionally, this metaphoric and frequently hyperbolic language may be combined with a comically ironic presentation of the discrepancy between appearance and reality in daily biracial life, as in this account of what happened when white visitors came to observe at Hurston's black elementary school: "We were threatened with a prompt and bloody death if we cut one caper while the visitors were present. We always sang a spiritual, led by Mr. Calhoun himself. Mrs. Calhoun always stood in the back, with a palmetto switch in her hand as a squelcher. We were all little angels for the duration, because we'd better be. She would cut her eyes and give us a glare that meant trouble, then turn her face towards the visitors and beam as much as to say it was a great privilege and pleasure to teach lovely children like us" (46–47). The description amuses, partly because of the language and tropes, also partly because (along with the narrator and the black teacher) we know the realities hidden from the white visitors.

The biggest gap, however, that the young Zora has to bridge stretches between her fictional/imaginary world and her real one: "My soul was with the gods and my body in the village. People just would not

act like gods. Stew beef, fried fat-back and morning grits were no am-
brosia from Valhalla. Raking back yards and carrying out chamber-pots,
were not the tasks of Thor" (56). This momentary distaste for the real
world is dispelled, however, when Zora becomes initiated into black
adult coded language on the porch of Joe Clarke's store, where the
males of Eatonville congregate to swap gossip and have a "lying session"—straining against each other in telling folktales. The young Zora
gets a sense of the connection between the real and the imaginary,
since the tales are based on real people and events. "I would hear an
occasional scrap of gossip in what to me was adult double talk, but
which I understood at times. There would be, for instance, sly references to the physical condition of women, irregular love affairs, brags
on male potency. . . . It did not take me long to know what was meant
when a girl was spoken of as 'ruint' or 'bigged'" (62). She was also hearing the double talk of animal tales, black interpretations of the Bible,
and "tall tales." Soon she was making up her own "lies" and getting
roundly chastised for it by her grandmother, surely a prototype for
Nanny in *Their Eyes,* who even utters a malapropism that nevertheless
hits the nail on the head, one of Hurston's favorite devices: "'I bet if I
lay my hands on her she'll stop it. I vominates a lying tongue'" (72).
Further clashes with authority receive similarly comic treatment: "I just
had to talk back at established authority and that established authority hated backtalk worse than barbed-wire pie" (95).

Before long, Zora Neale began to see a way to be *rewarded* for her
saucy imagination. Leaving home quite early, she became a governess
and soon discovered she could get out of housework by entertaining
the children with humorous stories; as a lady's maid for a northern
Gilbert and Sullivan company, she found out that she had a gift:

> I was a Southerner, and had the map of Dixie on my tongue. . . . It was
> not that my grammar was bad, it was the idioms. They did not know of
> the way an average Southern child, white or black, is raised on simile
> and invective. They know how to call names. It is an every day affair to
> hear somebody called a mullet-headed, mule-eared, wall-eyed, hog-
> nosed, 'gator-faced, shad-mouthed, screw-necked, goat-bellied, puzzle-
> gutted, camel-backed, butt-sprung, battle-hammed, knock-kneed, razor-
> legged, box-ankled, shovel-footed, unmated so-and-so! . . . They can tell
> you in simile exactly how you walk and smell. They can furnish a pic-
> ture gallery of your ancestors, and a notion of what your children will
> be like. What ought to happen to you is full of images and flavor. Since
> that stratum of the Southern population is not given to book-reading,
> they take their comparisons right out of the barnyard and the woods.
> When they get through with you, you and your whole family look like
> an acre of totem-poles. (135–36)

This passage provides a deeper understanding of Hurston's comic dimensions and her conception of communal humor. It shows her awareness of the comic possibilities of accent, idiom, dialect, inflection, simile, invective, the tall tale, the boast, and comic anthropomorphism; more importantly, it suggests an awareness of signifying, specifying, woofing, loud-talking, bookooing, the toast, the dozens, and marking, all key elements in both Afro-American culture and her fiction. Finally, it offers eloquent proof of her oft-repeated assertion that African American culture was highly pictoral, with stacks of invective functioning like the layers of a Northwest totem pole.

Of all of these comic possibilities, signifying dominates humorous conventions in black culture. The most readily understandable definition comes from Geneva Smitherman, who shows that this process involves the verbal art of insult, frequently with no harm intended:

> A speaker humorously puts down, talks about, needles—that is, signifies on—the listener. Sometimes signifyin (also siggin) is done to make a point, sometimes it's just for fun. This type of folk expression in the oral tradition has the status of a customary ritual that's accepted at face value. That is to say, nobody who's signified on is supposed to take it to heart. It is a culturally approved method of talking about somebody— usually through verbal indirection. Since the signifier employs humor, it makes the put-down easier to swallow and gives the recipient a socially acceptable way out. That is, if they can't come back with no bad signification of they own, they can just laugh along with the group. (118–19)

Smitherman further lists signifying's eight characteristics: indirection or circumlocution; use of metaphorical-imagistic language rooted in daily life; humor and irony; rhythmic fluidity and sound; teaching but not preaching; direction toward someone present; punning; and use of the unexpected (121). Hurston at one point says it just means to show off (*Mules* 133n4).[8]

Hurston's best example of signifying may be found in the relationship between the leading characters in *Mule Bone,* Jim Weston, a guitarist, and Dave Carter, a dancer, a duo that performs for pay, frequently for white audiences. Their comic rivalry over Daisy Blunt becomes exponentially expanded in the development of the play as the rival Methodist and Baptist churches they respectively belong to meet for a battle.[9]

Signification series were favorites of Hurston's, and she devoted many pages of *Mules and Men* to the genre. Essentially a form of signifying in a series of statements, it involves a situation where people swap, and try to top, each other's insults. A typical exchange from *Mules* will illustrate: "'Man, he's too ugly. If a spell of sickness ever tried to slip up on him, he'd skeer it into a three weeks' spasm.' 'He ain't so ugly. . . . Ah seen a man so ugly till he could get behind a jimpson weed and hatch monkies.' 'Ah seen a man so ugly till they had to spread a sheet over his head at night so sleep could slip up on him.' 'Those men y'll been talkin' 'bout wasn't ugly at all. Those was pretty men. Ah knowed one so ugly till you could throw him in the Mississippi river and skim ugly for six months'" (73). Between these remarks the narrator comments: "Everybody laughed and moved closer together" and "they laughed some more," signaling humor's ability to promote intimacy and also demonstrating the comic momentum that such an escalating exchange is designed to achieve. At the end of the sequence, we think the last joke has "capped" the exchange, for a character says, "'Give Cliff de little dog. . . . He done tole the biggest lie,'" but Joe Martin "caps" the "cap" itself: "'He ain't lyin'. . . . Ah knowed dat same man. He didn't die—he jus' uglied away.'"

Like signification, woofing, a mode frequently used in courtship rituals, offers what I shall be calling a mode of indirection, where speakers may "talk around" a subject by the use of humor. Specifying is another form of signifying that goes one step further, so that it really "gits down" on the victim, much like Hurston's remembered name-calling.

Toasts are traditional long poems taken from the oral tradition. The speaker relies on braggadocio for approval and for engaging listeners (Kochman, "Ethnography" 159). Toasts frequently employ obscenities that are sometimes offered in short rhymed stanzas. This also characterizes exchanges in the dozens, as in the following:

> I hate to talk about your mother,
> She's a good old soul.
> She's got a ten-ton pussy
> And a rubber asshole.
> She got hair on her pussy
> That sweep the floor.
> She got knobs on her titties.
> That open the door.
> (Abrahams, "Playing" 300)

The dozens forms a variant of what I shall be calling verbal dueling, where oral combatants exchange what are usually escalating insults; as such, the dozens practically constitutes a kind of rite for groups of adolescent boys. The dozens may be initiated by the introductory trigger phrase "Yo' mamma" and is followed by some sort of insult, usually sexual, directed at her. The invitation may be refused by saying, "Hey man, I don't play in the family," "I don't play under clothes," or simply, "I don't play." All the target's female relatives are fair game, and male relatives may be dragged in too. The person who "wins" "caps" the exchange. Alternately, but rarely, the game ends in physical violence, but resorting to fists instead of words constitutes "bad form."

The dozens goes under the name of "sounding" in some northern cities, especially New York and Philadelphia. There sounding identifies the verbal leader of the group, the person who excels at all the oral games of the culture. Such a champion usually has memorized traditional responses, but perhaps more importantly, excels at spontaneous creation. A "sounding" situation is generally signalled when A taunts B before an audience with a ritual insult that all involved know isn't true, such as, "Your father got such long teeth they growin' out his behind" (Labov 106).

Hurston defines several terms in *Mules and Men* herself, such as "bookooing" as "loud talking, bullying, woofing," and "woofing" as "aimless talking."[10] But her major means of introducing her white audience to this part of black culture was to let some of her characters play dumb. She often set the scene as in this passage from *Mules and Men:* "I heard somebody, a woman's voice 'specifying' up this line of houses from where I lived and asked who it was. 'Dat's Big Sweet' my landlady told me. 'She got her foot up on somebody. Ain't she specifying?' She was really giving the particulars. She was giving a 'reading,' a word borrowed from fortune-tellers. She was giving her opponent lurid data and bringing him up to date on his ancestry, his looks, smell, gait, clothes, and his route through Hell in the hereafter" (*Dust Tracks* 186). Hurston, supposedly an innocent, then asks what it means to "put your foot" up on a person, which allows her to reveal to her unknowing audience that this is to play the dozens (187).

These and other masterful devices allowed Hurston to interpret and use her culture in her work. She had always known about these verbal genres, but her training at Barnard and Columbia had given her the "spy glass" she needed to reconceptualize her culture, which had heretofore fit her "like a tight chemise. I couldn't see it for wearing it" (*Mules* 3). Hurston had finally returned home and to a realization that this was where she wanted and needed to be if her writing and her soul were to receive the nourishment both needed. By casting her nets down, not in Harlem, but in Eatonville, Hurston came into her own as a writer. Like Faulkner, she needed to write from her own local culture to achieve her greatest potential.

One of the stories she collected in *Mules and Men,* which significantly came from the Bible, underlines this point and offers a comic parable as a signification on Hurston as well. It seems Christ is walking along the ocean with his disciples and tells them all to pick up a rock. All do but lazy Peter, who contents himself with a pebble. Then Christ tells them to "'Cast in yo' nets right here'" and their efforts are rewarded with many fish. Christ turns the rocks into bread, but Peter's pebble produces hardly a "moufful." The next time they take a walk, with similar instructions from Christ, Peter lugs a huge rock along. Christ admires it so much that he says, "'Why Peter, dis is a fine rock you got here! It's a noble rock! And Peter, on dis rock Ah'm gointer build my church.'" Peter replies, "'Naw you ain't neither. You won't build no church house on *dis* rock. You gointer turn dis rock into bread.' Christ knowed dat Peter meant dat thing." The Lord then turns the stone into bread and feeds five thousand, building his church instead on the glued-together rocks of the other eleven disciples. The moral is "that's how come de Christian churches is split up into so many different kinds—cause it's built on pieced up rock" (*Mules* 29–30).

By casting her own nets down in Eatonville, Hurston found nourishment for her writing. Moreover, Hurston's decision to build the church of her fiction on the rock of black folk culture, divided and fractious though it might be, truly gave her, and us, bread.

Climbin' to the Pulpit: The Short Fiction, 1921–33

The brother in black puts a laugh in every vacant place in his mind. His laugh has a hundred meanings. It may mean amusement, anger, grief, bewilderment, chagrin, curiosity, simple pleasure or any other of the known or undefined emotions.

—*Mules and Men*

Hurston's literary career began in 1921, when Howard University's *Stylus* published her short story "John Redding Goes to Sea." The tale features an ambitious, yearning central figure in a rural setting, whose wish to go to sea is opposed by the tradition-bound women in his family. In some ways the story seems derivative; the wailing, clutching mother curiously resembles old Nora in Synge's *Riders to the Sea*. But the tale prefigures Hurston's later work in that it presents male-female conflicts, a plethora of local-color touches, and references to conjuring and superstition. One misses Hurston's fully developed use of dialect, mature mastery of metaphor, and distinctive, humor-laden voice. The narrative succeeds, however, in depicting a warm relationship between a black father and son (which Hurston would reprise in *Moses*) and achieves an aura of irony. The only joker in the story is nature, "Ole Massa," for John gets his wish to go to sea when a storm knocks him off a bridge and his dead body sweeps downriver atop a pine tree.

By contrast, "Drenched in Light" (1924) demonstrates all the qualities that were lacking in "John Redding," perhaps because Hurston here begins to use materials from her own experience. This and her subsequent short stories are definitely responses to a call voiced in the same year by William Stanley Braithwaite, who was disturbed by the short fiction black writers had been producing: "Most every one of these stories is written in a tone of condescension. . . . Many of these writers live in the South or are from the South. Presumably they are well acquainted with the Negro, but it is a remarkable fact that they almost never tell us anything vital about him, about the real human being in the black man's skin. . . . Always the Negro is interpreted in the terms of the white man. White man psychology is applied and it is no wonder that the result often shows the Negro in a ludicrous light" (24). Hurston's "Drenched in Light" would seem to be more an answer to a prayer than a mere response to this plea.

In this story Zora is able to provide a deep profile of a family while fictionally righting some wrongs left over from her childhood. On the death of her mother, Zora was looked after for a time by her maternal grandmother, whose caretaking went against her granddaughter's natural behavior. John Hurston, Zora's father, never favored her. According to *Dust Tracks* he later married a woman who hated his children and sent them all away (although recent information suggests the stepmother was in fact admired and respected by some of Zora's siblings [Bordelon 12–13]). The central character of "Drenched in Light," Isie Watts, clearly resembles the young Zora. Considered a "limb of Satan" by her wizened grandmother, Isie spends long hours, as Hurston did (see *Dust Tracks* 36, 45) hanging on the gatepost, looking down the beckoning and shining shell road toward the horizon. She cannot be bothered raking the yard, impudently turns cartwheels to spite Granny, and gives the puppy a bath in the family's dishpan. Forced to sit down at last, she slouches till "she all but sat on her backbone. 'Now look atcher,' Grandma screamed. 'Put yo knees together, an' git up offen yo' backbone! Lawd, yo know dis hellion is gwine make me stomp huh insides out'" (371). The proper English of the narrator intrudes, with interpretation, quaint terms, and a translation: "Now there are certain things that Grandma Potts felt no one of this female persuasion should do—one was to sit with the knees separated, 'settin' brazen' she called it—another was whistling, another playing with boys, neither must a lady cross her legs" (371). Isie charms us, but we can see what a nightmare she would be to actually raise. The extremity of Granny's language, dialect, and salty folk expressions, coupled with her wizened age, make her an extremely comic character.

Isie further displays her impish and impulsive nature when, egged on by her brother, she attempts to shave the straggling whiskers on the sleeping Granny's chin. The old woman awakes "to behold the business face of Isis and the razor-clutching hand. Her jaw dropped and Grandma, forgetting years and rheumatism, bolted from the chair and fled the house, screaming" (372). Hurston also moves away from this mainly autobiographical tale by taking on society in this scene, which uses and explodes a negative stereotype, that of the black man killing a woman with a razor, by substituting a humorous old granny and an impish little girl.

We see a number of new elements in this story, including a more sophisticated use of dialect and metaphor, more individualized characters, and, most importantly, a buoyant exuberance and energy that emanate from a stronger release of Hurston's comic imagination. The story ironically prophesies the major criticism Hurston would attract in the twenties, for Isie escapes punishment and in fact wins rewards because of her pranks and comic artistry. Knowing her actions will bring on a whipping, Isie steals Granny's red shawl and thereby equips herself for attendance at a barbecue, where she amuses everyone with her antics and "gypsy" dancing. A white woman traveling through with her obviously bored and boring husband becomes entranced; she eventually stops Granny from whipping Isie, pays for the ruined tablecloth, and carries the child off to their hotel to dance for her: "'I want brightness and this Isis is joy itself, why she's drenched in light!'" (374).

"Drenched in Light" also begins Hurston's focus upon joking relationships, a complex subject that would increasingly appear in her creations. Radcliffe-Brown, working with African cultures, describes a joking relationship as one "between two persons in which one is by custom permitted, and in some instances required, to tease or make fun of the other, who in turn is required to take no offense" (105). Various African cultures developed these systems of exchange specifically to remedy relationships that had historically failed in communication, so that "each of the persons is safe in what would otherwise be hostile territory" (107). Usually these systems exist between a man and his wife's siblings, between cross-cousins (for example, mother's brother and sister's son), or between grandparents and grandchildren.[11]

Joking relationships among African Americans, while usually not as complicated as their African sources, also function as mechanisms whereby overt conflict is avoided, both in rural and urban settings; humor thereby not only instills civility (even when on the surface it appears rude) but can also signal a friendly attitude while maintaining distance. Ulf Hannerz offers the example of a man passing another man he knows who wants liquor money; the former preserves their cordial relationship without giving in by saying, "'Too late, you can't take it to the bank today anyhow'" (66). A more general form of this relationship might be seen in football rivalries of universities; University of Tennessee fans, for instance, regularly show up at Vanderbilt games in Nashville carrying toilet seats and toilet paper to illustrate their nickname for the Vanderbilt Commodores, "Commode-doors." Everyone takes it good-naturedly, as part of an agreed-upon comic ritual, a process certainly preferable to fighting.

Hurston's fictions are filled with models of joking relationships, but also with ones that are transgressive. In African American culture, a grandmother such as the one here would ordinarily command respect, and any young girl like Isie who acted this "womanish" (prematurely "bodacious"), would likely be punished; conversely, in certain African societies, her comic stance toward her grandmother would be *required*. Isie and her grandmother amuse us partly because Isie seems fiendishly intent on establishing an improper joking relationship with her grandmother, a sentiment the elder figure adamantly refuses to recognize, so much so that her rigidity becomes a source of humor.[12]

Isie's impropriety, her "spunk," her courage, her humor, and, above all, her creativity shows us what Zora was then. But Isie's formal recognition, first by a crowd of her "people" and then by an appreciative white woman, Helen, who knows "folkart" when she sees it, shows us what Zora wanted to be. This rich woman with her beautiful dresses and the gold shoes with the blue bottoms listens attentively to Isie's story of really being a princess and of her make-believe trips to the horizon. Helen not only provides an accurate portrayal of Godmother Mason before her entrance into Hurston's life but she also prefigures the white audience that Hurston wanted. Zora knew by the time she wrote this story that there was a deep need for fiction like hers among both white and black cultures, and she was determined to fill it.

And also by the time she wrote this story she had planted the seeds of themes and characters that would later flourish in her novels. Isie, her father, and Granny would all reappear in *Jonah*. Helen looks "hungrily" ahead as she says, "'I want a little of her sunshine to soak into my soul. I need it'" (374). Here we find the first mention of Hurston's life-long identification with the sun. Helen's "hungry" listening also prefigures Pheoby, who responds to Isie/Janie/Zora's "call" from a vibrant, creative culture that still has its soul. Hemenway considers the tale evidence of Hurston's considerable thought about her identity as she began to function in the Harlem literary scene (*Zora* 11). This kind of comic autobiographical shorthand, a recreation and correction of her past, was practiced again and again by Hurston.

Hurston was by no means secure in her craft, however. "Magnolia Flower" (1925), a relatively humorless and awkwardly handled tale about Indians and blacks in frontier Florida, offers little appeal. Its mode of narration, however, fascinates; Hurston creates a call-and-response session between a silly brook and a mighty river, as the former recalls the events of the story proper, a preview of both the mode of narration used in *Their Eyes* between Pheoby and Janie and that novel's surreal scene with the talking buzzards.

"Spunk," Hurston's award-winning 1925 story, deals with a romantic triangle between Spunk, a macho sawmill worker, the sexy Lena, and her cowardly older husband, Joe. Significantly, the community plays an important role in this story by using cruel humor to goad Joe into seeking revenge. He attacks Spunk from behind with a razor and is killed. Spunk, convinced that Joe has returned from the dead as a black bobcat to haunt him, loses his customary aplomb and is killed by the circular saw. The story shows Hurston's mastery of dialect proceeding, but it also introduces the concept of communal humor as an instrument of torture, and the ending chills with its irony: "The women ate heartily of the funeral baked meats and wondered who would be Lena's next. The men whispered coarse conjectures between guzzles of whiskey" (173).

"The Eatonville Anthology" (1926) offers a series of fourteen short sketches, somewhat like snapshots; some are only one paragraph. They economically and masterfully describe colorful events and characters in Hurston's hometown. This piece, although much more amusing and detailed than the melodramatic "Spunk," has no central narrative line, but nevertheless signals a real advance in Hurston's craft, merging elements of fiction, folklore, and humor in an economic narrative shorthand. Most of all, the sketches interrelate, as Hurston has the characters repeat themes and motifs, enabling us to retrospectively reread and more fully understand sketches with our growing knowledge, joyously received, of a folk culture.

The first sketch, "The Pleading Woman," pictures a wife who begs merchants for scraps of food, pretending her husband doesn't provide for her: "'Hits uh SHAME! Tony don't fee-ee-eee-ed me!'" (177). The episode was so successful that Hurston reprised it for *Their Eyes*. Other sketches describe Becky, who has eleven children of assorted colors and sizes but has never been married; Old Man Anderson, terrified when he hears a train coming, functions as a forerunner of John Buddy's country-bumpkin amazement at seeing his first train in *Jonah*.

Coon Taylor, who appears later in *Jonah,* never steals, but "if he saw a chicken or a watermelon or muskmelon or anything like that that he wanted he'd take it" (180). Then there's Mrs. Clarke, a prototype for Janie in *Their Eyes,* who works in her husband's store and gets beaten and yelled at for her pains. But she has her small revenge: "She shouts in Church every Sunday and shakes the hand of fellowship with everybody in the Church with her eyes closed, but somehow always misses her husband" (181).

The "bones" of *Mule Bone* are here as well, for "The Head of the Nail" details the life of Daisy Taylor, the town vamp, who in a much prettier incarnation, under the name of Daisy Blunt, becomes the heroine of that play. Here, Daisy Taylor pins down the "little bushy patches" of her hair with shingle nails and flirts with married men because the only two single men are uninterested. Her affair with Crooms and the enmity it inspires in Mrs. Crooms seems a likely source for the Delia-Sykes-Bertha triangle in Hurston's later story "Sweat."

Bertha there is largely silent, but Daisy here is more vocal, especially when warned that Laura was coming down the road. "'Who? Me! Ah don't keer whut Laura Crooms think. If she ain't a heavy hip-ted Mama enough to keep him, she don't need to come crying to me,'" and she makes "goo-goo" eyes at Laura and taunts her repeatedly (185).

Finally, in a replay of a scene from Hurston's mother's life, Laura knocks Daisy into a ditch with an axe handle. Lige Moseley, a store porch regular, gets the penultimate laugh: "'I was just looking to see if Laura had been lucky enough to hit one of those nails on the head and drive it in.'" But Hurston saves the last laugh for herself, intoning deadpan as narrator, "Before a week was up, Daisy moved to Orlando. There in a wider sphere, perhaps, her talents as a vamp were appreciated" (185). This story, along with "Muttsy" and some portions of "Sweat," begins Hurston's focus on female rivalry, one of her most important examples of female humor and a theme she would return to again and again. The story also functions as a parable about the need to protect the family unit and thus provides a good illustration of her willingness to overlook rather appalling violence for the sake of a laugh if it encases a moral, another constant in her work.

Those who accuse Hurston of romanticism might find support in "Double-Shuffle," whose clear nostalgia emerges in the first line: "Back in the good old days before the World War, things were very simple in Eatonville" (182). Indeed, Heiner Bus claims that Hurston reconstructs a lost world, a "communal life before the distortions through acculturation claimed their toll." He sees Hurston as part of a larger group of writers who are trying to navigate between the shoals of those who

condemn small towns and let their pasts disappear and those who ro-
manticize the past. In this project of "reconstruction, documentation,
and re-interpretation, of making the past useful," she thus resembles
Anderson, Masters, Lewis, Steinbeck, Wilder, and Faulkner (73–74). I
would add, however, that unlike most of these white men (with the
major exception of Faulkner, and with a nod to Lewis and Steinbeck),
Hurston sees the role of humor in culture as much more central, and
the "reconstructive" history Bus claims she is writing relies heavily on
comic expression to convey what he terms the "spirit" and the "sense
of community" (77).

Back then, the narrator tells us, people did the grand march instead
of the fox trot, for comically pious reasons: "By rural canons dancing
is wicked, but one is not held to have danced until the feet have been
crossed. Feet don't get crossed when one grand marches" (182). She
also gets uncomfortably close to stereotype here: "Sweating bodies,
laughing mouths, grotesque faces, feet drumming fiercely," as they sing
"Great big nigger, black as tar / Trying tuh git tuh hebben on uh 'lec-
tric car," but the line itself provides an astute comment on the threat
of materialism to human values (182).

Other verses quoted signify on both "black" and "yaller" gals and
the preacher, suggesting the comic aspect this figure has always presented to the black community, an issue Hurston would explore at
great length in *Jonah*. Here, it's in a comic nutshell:

> Would not marry uh preacher
> Tell yuh de reason why
> Every time he comes tuh town
> He makes de chicken fly.
>   (183)

The verse purposefully and ingenuously makes the word "chicken"
ambiguous, thereby suggesting the preacher's reputation for eating the
best pieces of the chicken when invited to dinner, but also his covert
sexual appetite, as "chicken" also means woman. Hurston underlines
this by following the song with men sticking their arms out to the ladies: "You lak chicken? Well, then take a wing" (183).

Sketch eight consists of two jokes. 'Lige reports that Sewall, who
moves around a lot, has gotten his chickens so accustomed to this that
when he comes out into his backyard they lie down "and cross their
legs, ready to be tied up again," thus overlapping with the double entendres of "Double Shuffle."

In some ways the most interesting sketch, because of its similar but
more overt resemblance to events in *Jonah*, is "Pants and Cal'line."

Cal'line and Michael Potts are Hurston's actual aunt and uncle, whose story is also told in *Dust Tracks* (25). They also, however, prefigure Lucy and John Pearson in *Jonah,* especially in John's fondness for other women. The tempter featured here, Delphine, also appears in *Jonah.* The town watches and gossips, amusing themselves in speculation over whether and how Cal'line will respond to Delphine's threat to her marriage, performing the usual comic choral function they play in all of Hurston's Eatonville narratives. The plot thickens when Mitch/John says Cal'line better stay put or he'll use his "African soup-bone" (translated for the reader by Hurston as "arm" in an early manifestation of her delight in the role of cultural and linguistic intermediary). When Cal'line glimpses her husband scurrying to hide a shoebox, she reads this "sign" instantly, and Hurston cleverly confines her reaction to one word: "So!" (186). While Michael bathes and dresses, Cal'line keeps on ironing, but as soon as he leaves the house she follows him, in one of his old hats, with the axe, as a blood red moon dips toward the horizon. The porch sitters see both go by and start laughing and placing bets.

But here Hurston shocks us; instead of providing a comic denouement, she ends the story with Joe Clarke lighting the lamp against the total darkness. Why? Hemenway, noting the completion of the tale in *Dust Tracks,* suggests a printing error was made at the *Messenger* office and the last part got left out (69). If Hurston *herself* abbreviated it here, perhaps she wished to indicate that despite the humor of the sketches, they often mask tragedy and pain. She may also have been unwilling to go further with this tale from her own family at this early stage in her career.

The last sketch, a charming, untitled animal *fabliau,* differs dramatically from the others. Very like a tale by Joel Chandler Harris, it details the rivalry of Mr. Dog and Mr. Rabbit over Miss Nancy Coon. During the courting ritual, Mr. Dog poses the question by asking, "'Which would you ruther be—a lark flyin' or a dove asettin''"; Hurston would use this particular scene in a more serious way in *Jonah's Gourd Vine,* when John proposes to Lucy. Mr. Dog complains to his rival about his lack of a good singing voice, whereupon trickster Mr. Rabbit says he has a solution he has used before on Sis Lark and Sis Mockingbird—just stick out your tongue. The foolish Mr. Dog complies; the rabbit cuts part of it off and scampers away. The story thus explains the continuing enmity of the dog for the rabbit and employs the courtship theme, which we will see again in "Muttsy"; the rivalry of the two males for the female would also be used and vastly expanded in *Mule Bone,* where one character, as here, has a good voice.

Most importantly, however, this tale throws all the other stories into contrast and demonstrates the origin of their folk ethos, thereby lifting the local into the mythic. It also suggests that the other stories may someday evolve to this level, for as Hurston stated in "Characteristics of Negro Expression," "Negro folklore is not a thing of the past. It is still in the making" (27).[13]

Despite the relative successes of these early stories, all of them differentiated Zora Neale Hurston from her equally successful Harlem Renaissance colleagues in a peculiar way; not only was she from the South but she chose to write about the South from the insight of a native. Only Jean Toomer had thus far written about the South so masterfully in his magnificent *Cane* in 1923, but he did so from the perspective of an outsider.

Hurston's one attempt to write about the Harlem scene, while she was actually in it, was "Muttsy" (1926). It represents Hurston's comic genius just beginning to simmer and shows particular development of her use of signifying. The plot rather sentimentally details the arrival in New York of a timid "down-home" greenhorn, Pinkie, from Eatonville, Florida. In some ways this might be Hurston as her white patrons and male contemporaries would be comfortable seeing her. If Hurston intended Pinkie to represent her, she certainly creates a coy version of the real thing. But like her heroine, Hurston "had no home to which *she* could return" (247). Pinkie's pathetic qualities seem to stem from either Hurston's nostalgic self-pity or a comic signification on the same or both. Hurston was no greenhorn when she moved to New York, however, having lived and traveled on her own for years, including many spent in Baltimore and Washington.

Pinkie unfortunately finds lodgings at the disreputable Ma Turner's place, a combination speakeasy and whorehouse, after being spotted at the ferry landing and given directions by Bluefront, Ma's sleazy scout. The situation of an innocent landing in a brothel, a classic in comic literature, appears in Roman comedies as early as Plautus's *The Menaechmi*. In American fiction, perhaps its greatest analogue appears in Faulkner's 1931 *Sanctuary*, where the hick Snopes boys cruise the streets of Memphis looking for a bordello, not knowing they just registered as lodgers at Miss Reba's whorehouse.

Pinkie's folk-derived name signifies not only her light skin but also her baby-like innocence, both sexual and cultural, the latter suggested by her ignorance of big-city slang: "She hung her head, embarrassed that she did not understand their mode of speech" (248). Ma's hapless husband, a down-home type relegated by Ma to a corner, takes an interest in Pinkie and tries to give her lessons, both in things she already knows, such as how to eat a fish, straight out of Eatonville lore, and things she does not know, such as how a whore (which he assumes she's interested in becoming) should sit: "'Don't set dataway,' he ejaculated. 'Yo' back bone ain't no ram rod. Kinda scooch down on the for'ard edge uh de chear lak dis.' (He demonstrated by 'scooching' forward so far that he was almost sitting on his shoulder blades)" (247). Obviously, this broad body comedy provides a lesson in "settin' brazen," the opposite of that taught Isie by Granny in "Drenched in Light," and a good example of Hurston's endless delight in refiguring her materials. Hurston excels in setting the smoky, crowded, frenetic scene, expressive of the rich melange of cultures the area had become, demonstrated here by the interbraiding of southern and northern black dialect and idiom, the special lingos of Harlem hustling and gambling, and the resultant comic linguistic snafus. Hurston, like all great comic writers, delights in chaotic scenes and gleefully milks them for all they are worth:

> Some more men and women knocked and were admitted after the same furtive peering out through the nearest crack of the door. Ma carried them all back to the kitchen and Pinkie heard the clink of glasses and much loud laughter. . . . A very black man sat on the piano stool playing as only a Negro can with hands, stamping with his feet and the rest of his body keeping time. "Ahm gointer make me a graveyard of mah own. . . ." Everyone . . . was shaking shimmies to music, rolling eyes heavenward as they picked imaginary grapes out of the air, or drinking. (247)

The setup seems ideal for comedy in several ways. Pinkie's bewilderment enables Hurston, as foxy narrator, to enlighten equally "uneducated" readers through that of a central character they can love but patronize.

Caricature, always a staple in Harlem short stories, which had already established a set of Harlem "types" for the general public, permits broad comic sketching. Hurston had no doubt learned much about this by studying stories in *The New Negro*, such as Rudolph Fisher's "City of Refuge," which showed a master at work. Caricature was always a strength for Hurston too, but her use of it placed her dangerously close to stereotypes at times as well.

In many ways, Hurston was replicating staples of immigrant comic literature, where the clash of differing customs, dress, and language are basic humorous ingredients, as in Abraham Cahan's classic *Yekl*, a tale of the Jewish ghetto, or Mario Puzo's more recent *The Fortunate Pilgrim*, an Italian-American tragicomedy. Many ethnic literatures detailed the plucking of ignorant immigrants by con artists who waited for them at the boat landings, as Bluefront does here.

Hurston cannot take the genre very far, however, for she's operating in a very short short story. The abundant possibilities for the humor of initiation aren't realized, for Pinkie does not really change but rather forces others to do so. Her virginity survives intact until the end of the story when the title character, a gambler, unable to seduce her, rather improbably marries her and gives up his wild life to become a stevedore, an opportunity for Hurston to capitalize on her knowledge of the docks.[14] "Muttsy" seems more notable for its southern materials, as seen in the characterizations of Pinkie and Pa Turner, and the folk-derived humor that most of the characters share than for its Harlem touches.[15] Robert Bone has judged "Muttsy" to be "hopelessly incompetent" (144). Bone errs in this reading, for the story certainly has strengths, even if its raucous and quite rich comic virtues are ultimately undercut by the sentimental plot line.[16]

Hurston's comic gifts, simmering in "Muttsy," came to a boil with *Fire!!* the magazine issued by the "New Negro" group in 1926. "Sweat," the more gripping of her two contributions, details the grim story of hardworking Delia Jones and her no-good, philandering husband, also a devotee of practical jokes. Hurston cleverly turns this aspect of her villain into a structural device, for the entire story turns on the idea of jokes and joking. She begins with one of Sykes's cruel jokes: he throws his "long, round, limp and black" bullwhip around Delia's shoulders as she sorts the wash she must do for white folk in order to support herself (197). Sykes's prank, motivated by Delia's abnormal fear of snakes, begins the sexual imagery that makes the story more complex. Is Delia's fear of the explicitly phallic nature of the snakes a sign of her innate fear of sex or, more likely, a fear that has been beaten into her? What has caused Sykes to seek the beds of other women? The story raises but never really answers these questions, yet suggests Sykes cannot stand his wife's supporting them by washing the soiled sheets, towels, and undergarments of white folks. Lillie Howard thinks that "whether [Delia] needs Sykes at all is questionable and perhaps he senses this and looks elsewhere for someone who does need him" (260–62). On the other hand, Delia reflects that she "had brought love to the union and he had brought a longing after the flesh" (199). Only two months into the marriage he beats her. Why?[17]

In any case, Sykes's laughter at his wife and her fears fill the story; he continually slaps his leg and doubles over with merriment at the expense of the "big fool" he married fifteen years ago. Clearly, his insults deflect attention away from the "big fool" he knows he appears to be in the community, as he has never held a steady job himself and depends on Delia for his livelihood. Hurston in this story seems to be developing gender-specific forms of humor, which will be extremely important in *Jonah, Their Eyes,* and *Seraph.*

We may thus notice a difference in the rhetoric employed here. Delia too, although grimly serious in her defiance of Sykes, uses the deadly comic signifying language of female rivalry; referring to her husband's mistress, she states, "'That ole snaggle-toothed black woman you runnin' with aint comin' heah to pile up on *mah* sweat and blood. You aint paid for nothin' on this place, and Ah'm gointer stay right heah till Ah'm toted out foot foremost'" (199). Later, alone, Delia takes comfort in folk wisdom: "'Oh well, whatever goes over the Devil's back, is got to come under his belly. Sometime or ruther, Sykes, like everybody else, is gointer reap his sowing'" (199).

The appearance of the communal comic chorus in the personages of the loiterers on Joe Clarke's porch constitutes another significant development in Hurston's craft. When Delia passes by with her pony cart delivering clothes, they render the community's sense of pity for her and contempt toward Sykes, especially regarding his new mistress: "'How Syke kin stommuck dat big black greasy Mogul he's layin' roun' wid, gits me. Ah swear dat eight-rock couldn't kiss a sardine can Ah done throwed out de back do' 'way las' yeah'" (200). The men's humor rises a notch as they wryly observe that Sykes has always preferred heavy lovers over the thin Delia. Hurston signifies here on jokes in the black community about some men's preference for hefty women. A classic blues expression goes: "Big fat momma wid de meat shakin' on huh bones / Evah time she wiggles, skinny woman los' huh home" (Hughes and Bontemps 384). The last line should particularly intrigue readers of "Sweat," for Sykes's plot is designed not so much to kill Delia but to secure her property.

Significantly, all of the men on the porch continually chew cane, but they do not throw the knots as usual, which creates a foundation for the extended natural metaphor that Clarke, their leader, uses to summarize the inversion of the story they are actually helping us to read.

> "Taint no law on earth dat kin make a man behave decent if it aint in 'im. There's plenty men dat takes a wife lak dey do a joint uh sugar-cane. It's round, juicy an' sweet when dey gits it. Buts dey squeeze an' grind, squeeze an' grind an' wring tell dey wring every drop uh pleasure dat's in 'em out. When dey's satisfied dat dey is wrung dry, dey treats 'em jes lak dey do a cane-chew. Dey throws 'em away. Dey knows whut dey is doin' while dey is at it, an' hates theirselves fuh it but they keeps on hangin' after huh tell she's empty. Den dey hates huh fuh bein' a cane-chew an' in de way." (201)

This casually brilliant rendering of a tragic truth provides a double irony for readers who know all of Hurston's work, for this same Joe Clarke emerges as a wife-beater himself in "The Eatonville Anthology" and becomes the model for Jody Starks in *Their Eyes,* who treats Janie like a mule he owns. Furthermore, the liquid squeezed out, the receptacle discarded, mirrors the title figuration of a woman's sweat and her weary body.

Normally comic expressions can be used to deadly effect as well. In the heat of August's "Dog Days!" (202), the "maddog" Sykes plays his ultimate and cruelest joke to drive Delia from the house that he has promised to Bertha. He keeps a caged rattlesnake on the porch, knowing Delia fears even earthworms. When she asks him to kill the rattler, he replies with a comically coined word and devastating irony: "'Doan ast me tuh do nothin' fuh yuh. Goin' roun' tryin' tuh be so damn asterperious. Naw, Ah aint gonna kill it. Ah think uh damn sight mo' uh him dan you! Dat's a nice snake an' anybody doan lak 'im kin jes' hit de grit'" (203). When Delia's fury overflows into courage, she tells Sykes, "'Ah hates yuh lak uh suck-egg dog'" (204), and, of course, the imagery seems right, for Sykes's gender is usually associated with dogs, and a "suck-egg" dog would be a predator of women, egg bearers. Hurston would later use the egg and snake symbolism to characterize the couple in *Jonah.*

When Sykes replies with insults about her looks, she replies in kind, joining a verbal duel that finally silences him: "'Yo' ole black hide don't look lak nothin' tuh me, but uh passle uh wrinkled up rubber, wid yo' big ole yeahs flappin' on each side lak uh paih uh buzzard wings. Don't think Ah'm gointuh be run 'way fum mah house neither. Ah'm goin' tuh de white folks bout *you,* mah young man; de very nex' time you lay yo' han's on me. Mah cup is done run ovah'" (204). Delia here effectively "caps" Joe by verbally emasculating him, in a doubled way. The "wrinkled rubber" seems obvious enough, but the buzzard reference varies her refrain that he is not man enough to support her; he just preys on her. This speech has much in common with Janie's silencing of Joe in the great scene in *Their Eyes,* but our pleasure in "Sweat" at Sykes's punishment is compromised by the ambiguity of our response throughout the story. Certainly, we feel for Delia, but the emasculation of the black man by a racist, capitalist society is on Hurston's mind here too, and Delia's threat to bring the white folks, whose laundry she washes, down on Joe, partially mitigates our natural inclinations to champion Delia; so does her tendency to taunt Joe about the fact that she brings home the bacon. Delia's Christian righteousness, evident in the scene when she returns from a "Love Feast" at church, also seems challenged by her failure to seek help for Sykes after he has been bitten by the snake at the end of the story and by her deliberate showing herself to him so he will know she knows what he attempted and that there is no hope for him.

This climax occurs when Joe, trapped in the dark bedroom with the snake he left in Delia's basket, jumps in terror onto the bed, where he thinks he'll be safe; the snake, of course, lies coiled there. In Tennessee Williams's *Cat on a Hot Tin Roof,* Big Mama, advising her daughter-in-law, Maggie, pats the bed she is sitting on and tells her that all the big problems in marriages can ultimately be traced *here;* Hurston, at least in this story, would seem to agree. The final joke on Sykes is that his obsession with male, phallic power, and the way he misuses it in his marriage, finally kills him, in a doubly figurative and dreadfully comic way.

What made this story special? For one thing, it was written after Hurston had been collecting black folklore for several years in the South and returned to live in Eatonville. When writing this story, she seemed to have learned how intertwined comedy and tragedy were in folk culture and also how the comic was embedded in the cosmic. These relationships are always manifest in her best work, like "The Gilded Six-Bits."

The story concerns a young married couple, Missie May and Joe Banks, who create a clean, sunny, happy home out of ordinary ingredients: "Yard raked so that the strokes of the rake would make a pattern. Fresh newspaper cut in fancy edge on the kitchen shelves" (208). Although Hurston did not choose to emphasize it, the patterned dirt yard and the bottles stuck along the walk are African survivalisms, the latter connected with providing lodging places for the spirits of the ancestors, a type of communal art form that has been described and analyzed by Robert Farris Thompson, Robert L. Hall, and others. The creativity of these expressions, the only thing emphasized in the story itself, nevertheless has little to do with the white world and suggests a self-sufficiency and authenticity that seems vital to racial health in Hurston's fiction. The first line's repetitions emphasize this: "It was a Negro yard around a Negro house in a Negro settlement," and even though the inhabitants are dependent on the fertilizer factory where Joe works, "there was something happy about the place" (208).

Why? Because the Bankses keep their relationship fresh and lively through elaborate games, jokes, and rituals. Each payday Joe hides and throws money through the doorway; Missie May pretends to be mad and gives chase, which results in a comic tumble. They speak in hyperbolic but culturally specific terms to express ordinary facts: "'Ah could eat up camp meetin', back off 'ssociation, and drink Jurdan dry'" (210). Hurston describes their dinner lovingly and deliciously, in an effort to portray the healthy satisfaction of appetite that the marriage represents: "Very little talk . . . but that consisted of banter that pretended to deny affection but in reality flaunted it" (210). This is a wonderful example of communication by indirection and humor, one that foreshadows the marriage of Janie and Tea Cake.

The twin themes of sexuality and cleanliness are merged in the opening interior image, as we voyeuristically watch Missie May bathe herself and admire her black beauty. The theme of washing becomes metaphysical after her adultery, when she knows better than to think that she can wash herself clean like a cat, with its tongue, although this phrase won't be used until *Jonah*. Missie May learns that expiation must be earned through deeds, not talk.

The tragicomedy stage becomes set for her adultery when Joe mentions the proprietor of the new ice-cream store, Mr. Otis D. Slemmons, a pompous imposter just arrived from the North who apparently has many gold teeth and plenty of money. Missie May expresses her contempt through folksy food imagery: "'Aw, he don't look no better in his clothes than you do in yourn. He got a puzzlegut on 'im and he so chuckle-headed, he got a pone behind his neck. . . . His mouf is cut cross-ways, ain't it? Well, he kin lie jes' lak anybody else. . . . A wouldn't give 'im a wink if de sheriff wuz after 'im'" (211). The passage indicates Missie May discerns more than the reader might think, also demonstrated by the way she "talks that talk," in signifying judgment. Appropriately, and ironically, she bases her "reading" of Slemmons on a glimpse she caught of him when she was purchasing a box of *lye*.

Hurston creates a little physical comedy too; while Missie May dresses, Joe, who admires Slemmons's "puzzle-gut" as a sign of prosperity, tries to make his "stomach punch out like Slemmons' middle. He tried the rolling swagger of the stranger, but found that his tall bone-and-muscle stride fitted ill with it" (212).[18]

Later we find that Joe admires Slemmons for his verbal ability as well; he quotes him as saying, "'Who is dat broad wid de forte shake?'" Hurston creates broad humor here, for as in "Muttsy," a broad with a "forty" shake would be a prostitute who charged forty dollars a night. Ma Turner in that story, her husband tells Pinkie rather proudly, and thus pathetically, was once called "Forty-dollars-Kate": "'She didn't lose no time wid dem dat didn't have it'" (246). Pinkie, however, like Joe here, naively doesn't understand, and comic innocence in both stories gets underlined by reader-author irony, especially when Joe tells Missie that Slemmons found her to be "'jes' thirty-eight and two. Yessuh, she's forte!'" Joe's remark of appreciation, however, ironically predicts Slemmons's ultimate effect: "'Ain't he killin'?'" (212).

Hurston then transforms the story with tragicomic irony. Slemmons succeeds in seducing Missie May one night while her husband toils at the G. and G. fertilizer plant. Joe unexpectedly comes home; it seems the acid supply at the fertilizer plant has run out, but an abundance of acidic marital bitterness awaits him at home. Although he always carefully washes himself before joining Missie May at table and later in the bed, she has brought defilement to the bed and the marriage. We readers know, however (and surely Joe does too, eventually) that he had much to do with it in his oft-expressed yearning for money and power.

In the dramatic scene of discovery, Joe strikes a match and strides into the bedroom; he thus ironically puts to the lie his earlier assertion, "'Ah can't hold no light to Otis D. Slemmons'" (211). Joe's stunned reaction to what he sees? He laughs before punching his rival out and grabbing his gold watch chain. Although a callous reader might feel Joe laughs at the undeniably funny image Hurston paints of the lumbering Slemmons "fighting with his breeches in his frantic desire to get them on" or Hurston's sexual innuendo as she describes "the intruder in his helpless condition—half in and half out of his pants," we know Joe cannot be amused (214). In black culture, laughing does not necessarily occur as a response to a joke or something funny; it can mean a strong point has been made (Smitherman 106). Pearl Stone has the same reaction when Janie walks back into town in *Their Eyes*.[19]

Hurston balances the tragicomedy, however, with the cosmic in a beautiful expression she had taken from an African American sermon: "The great belt on the wheel of Time slipped and eternity stood still" (213). This moment, however, for all its pain, proves liberating, for Joe and Missie May understand now how wrong they were to yearn for the gold Slemmons represented. The link between historical slavery and the ideology of consumerism emerges clearly in the piece of broken chain Joe has grabbed along with the gilded coin.

Joe's laugh, however, is a last one in more ways than one; although the marriage continues, the absence of laughter and banter reflects its changed state. After a long period of abstinence, Joe returns to Missie May's bed and leaves her the gold watch chain and its attached coin, which she discovers to be a gilded half dollar, thereby laying bare the extended joke of Slemmons's imposture. Further, in its doubling of the whore's traditional "two-bits," it offers her wages for sleeping with both men. Insulted, she leaves, she thinks forever, but in a stereotypical scene, she meets her mother-in-law, speaks briefly, and returns. "Never would she admit defeat to that woman who prayed for it nightly" (216)—another example of Hurston's interest in depicting the various ironies of female rivalry.

Months later, when Missie delivers a son that is "'de spittin' image'" of Joe, everyone, including the reader, breathes a sigh of relief, especially Joe's formerly suspicious mother, who confesses her previous doubts in a rush of folk-warmed euphemisms: "'And you know Ah'm mighty proud son, cause Ah never thought well of you marryin' Missie May cause her ma used tuh fan her foot round right smart and Ah been mighty skeered dat Missie May wuz gointer git misput on her road'" (217). All of this richly metaphorical language lends a great deal of humor and interest to the story, yet never intrudes as it sometimes does in the more sprawling pages of *Jonah;* moreover, although Hurston creates the impression of a natural spontaneity, the metaphors actually work in a system of reference. For example, the rather refined "road" euphemism used by Joe's mother had been employed by Missie earlier, when she speculated to Joe that they might discover some gold, like Slemmons's: "'Us might find some gon' long de road some time,'" for indeed, her misbehavior in the "road" with Slemmons obtains the gold. Similarly, the real breakdown at the fertilizer plant works beautifully to set up the cosmic slippage of a belt at God's "factory," which seemingly "deals in shit" on occasion too, obviously on the command of the Cosmic Joker.

The various levels of the comic in the final pages once again conceal the cosmic. Joe's forgiveness floods forth after the birth of his son. As he buys a load of candy kisses with Slemmons's gilded coin, transforming a token of shame and stain into a staple of love and nourishment, he furnishes the story's key symbol, which expresses the magical ability of charity, love, and forgiveness to render the polluted pure and testifies to the way deeds, not words, can indeed "wash" away sin. Hurston plays the scene for laughs at first, however. Joe boasts about the way he outsmarted Slemmons to the callous white clerk, leaving out, of course, the real details. The clerk remarks to his next customer, a white, "'Wisht I could be like these darkies. Laughin' all the time. Nothin' worries 'em'" (218), signaling his failure to read Joe as a human, but rather as a type, little suspecting the pain that underlies Joe's brave laughter.

This harks back to another misreading. In a startling move, Hurston takes us into Slemmons's mind just after Joe laughs when discovering him and Missie May: "He considered a surprise attack upon the big clown that stood there laughing like a chessy cat" (214). His link with the clerk is unmistakable. Slemmons, who represents the corruption of folk values by a sojourn in the materialistic North, has lost his ability to truly "see" his own people, as he has acquired the con artist's values.

The story ends when Joe resumes the ritual of throwing money on the porch, accompanied by Missie May's game reply: "'Joe Banks, Ah hear you chinkin' money in mah do'way. You wait till Ah got mah strength back and Ah'm gointer fix you for dat'" (218). The barometer of laughter thus signals the return of joy, and therefore health, to the marriage, one presumably stronger because of the testing it has received.

After reading this story, Lippincott called on Hurston for a novel, and she responded by writing a remarkable book, *Jonah's Gourd Vine*, which, like this beautiful and funny story, would center on the concept of marriage. The belts of time seem to have worked exceedingly well at this point for Hurston, for as "The Gilded Six-Bits" testifies, she had reached a new maturity in both her form and content, and she had never been closer to an understanding of the way humor provided, as the spiritual says, the "wheel within the wheel" of folk culture, an always spinning mechanism that would never fail her.

Notes

1. Ironically, although he begins his biography with this moment, Hemenway has recently joined the critical trend toward discounting the very idea of a Harlem Renaissance. Most critics are taking this tack because labeling the literary period this way needlessly circumscribes a much wider rebirth of literary activity (there were lively black literary communities trying out new modes of writing in Chicago, Philadelphia, and Washington during the period, for instance). Hemenway claims her career has been "distorted" because of her identification as a Harlem writer, since most of her work appeared in the thirties ("Personal" 32). If you extend the period to 1940 and the publication of *Native Son*, as many do, you have a much more appropriate endpoint for the Harlem Renaissance. Many of the so-called Harlem writers did their best work in the thirties, particularly the novelists.

2. This is discussed by Lakoff 56; see also Kalcik 56.

3. For a thorough and penetrating analysis of female humor, a subject that only recently has attracted scholarly attention, see Nancy Walker's *A Very Serious Thing*, and also chapter 2, "Sexual Inequality in Humor," in Mahadev Apte's *Humor and Laughter* 67–81.

4. Hurston was well aware of how all southerners, both black and white, were stereotyped, and she railed against it throughout her life. A letter to her friend Mary Holland ascribes her being fired from an Air Force job to both her Ivy League credentials and her southern, not black, identity. She details how she and white southerners were victims of what Hurston calls "a sly latter-day Reconstruction program of crying down southerners, of putting in mostly poorly educated northerners before prepared southerners. . . . So I made a point of keeping everybody in mind that I was a Floridian, the implication being that as far south as I came from, I stood there the best educated

and most cultivated person among them. . . . This intimidation and low-rating of southerners . . . can readily be traced to all this lurid literature showing us to be practically uncivilized and under-privileged down here. I don't mean Negroes. *All* southerners. Ignorant Northerners not only expect us to eat missionaries, but eat them raw" (June 27, 1957, Hurston Collection, Rare Books and Manuscripts, University of Florida Library, Gainesville). This clever letter also makes the point that all southerners are alike by applying what is usually an image of primitive natives (eating a missionary) to whites as well.

5. Alain Locke to Charlotte Mason, June 9, 1931, Alain Locke Papers, Moorland-Spingarn Research Center, Howard University Library, Washington, D.C.

6. Hurston's early male critics in the academy, who based many of their objections to her on the testimony of Hughes, Thurman, Sterling Brown, Richard Wright, and other male writers included Nathan Huggins, Darwin Turner, and Larry Neal; their critiques of Hurston have been rebutted by several feminist critics, including Mary Helen Washington ("Zora") and Lorraine Bethel.

7. See in particular Hazel Carby's "The Politics of Fiction, Anthropology, and the Folk," where this argument is given its fullest articulation. Carby, organizing her essay around political imperatives, seems to privilege the writings of Langston Hughes, and especially Richard Wright, over Hurston. She charges Hurston with "privileging the nostalgic" and of "displacing" the all-important conflict of class with Eatonville "as the center of her representation of the rural folk" (78). This leads to Carby's harshest charge, that Hurston is guilty of a "romantic" and "colonial imagination." Carby also insists that Janie's ownership of a home "permeates" the novel with "a bourgeois discourse that differentiates her from the folk as community." Finally, Carby argues that Janie's pulling in of the horizon at the end is "an assertion of autonomy" that exists only for "pleasure of the self," one that "displaces the folk as community utterly and irrevocably" (87). I have come to different conclusions.

8. A more formal and often-used definition is provided by Claudia Mitchell-Kernan, who states that signification is "the recognition and attribution of some implicit content or function, which is potentially obscured by the surface content or function. The obscurity may lie in the relative difficulty it poses for interpreting (1) the meaning or message the speaker is adjudged as intending to convey; (2) the addressee—the person or persons to whom the message is directed; (3) the goal, orientation or intent of the speaker. A precondition for the application of the term *signifying* to some speech act is the assumption that the meaning decoded was consciously and purposely formulated at the encoding stage. In reference to function the same condition must hold" (314). See also Kochman, "Speech," 155.

9. The 1991 Broadway production of *Mule Bone* amply demonstrated the use of signifying gesture, tone, song, dance, verbal duelling, and many other conventions of African American humor.

10. For complete discussions of these and related terms in black humor, see Smitherman, Mitchell-Kernan, Doilard, Kochman, and especially Abra-

hams's "Playing the Dozens" and his revision of that piece ("The Negro Stereotype").

11. In particular, joking relationships have been investigated among the
Buissi along the Congo (Jacobson-Widding), the Mossi of Volta (Hammond),
and the North American Chippewa (Miller).

12. As Mahadev Apte has demonstrated, joking relationships within a nu-
clear family are rare because the kin ties are too close. The most common form,
in fact, would be between grandparents and grandchildren; this is true, however, only when the grandparents are not responsible for the children's moral
upbringing, and this doesn't seem to be the case here. Apte's chapter on joking relationships is the most exhaustive treatment of a complex subject (46–66).

13. This point has been brilliantly demonstrated by Daryl Dance in *Long Gone*.

14. Although how she got to know this world remains unclear, know it she
did, for Fannie Hurst was introduced to the life there by Hurston on some of
their travels through New York's "lower depths," with Hurston playing Virgil
to Hurst's Dante (Hurst 21).

15. Hurston would later master Harlem material in "Story in Harlem Slang"
(1942), which proved so delightful on the stage in 1990 as part of the evening
of plays based on her short stories.

16. A companion piece to "Muttsy" is Hurston's "The Conversion of Sam."
Stella, a "greenhorn" from Virginia, gets a job as a waitress at Jim's sleazy restaurant, where Sam, a genial local ne'er-do-well, falls in love with her. Inspired,
he gets a job, marries Stella, settles down, and prospers, but the envious Bluefront and Fewclothes (both characters in "Muttsy") pull him down into the
gutter again. He reforms for good at story's end after Stella is injured while
searching for him. Although "The Conversion of Sam" has some good moments, its sentimentalism and lip service to white values (expressed by Jim's
"Good Ole Massa" employer) contrast with the opposite values of "Muttsy,"
which also, and above all, demonstrates the comic creativity and richness of
black speech.

17. The theme of love that sours shortly after marriage was the subject of
Lizzie Miles's popular twenties blues song about a washerwoman who supports
her philandering husband:

> I hate a man like you, don't like the things you do,
> When I met you, I thought you was right,
> You married me and stayed out the first night.
> . . . .
> Walkin' around with a switch and a rod, shootin' dice, always playing cards,
> While I bring a pan from the white folks' yard.
> . . . .
> Eatin' and drinkin', sittin' at the inn,
> Grinnin' in my face and winkin' at my friends.
> When my back is turned you're like a rooster at a hen,
> Oh, I hate a man like you.
>
> (cited in Harrison 87)

Miles was performing in New York clubs when Hurston wrote "Sweat," so the latter could have heard the song, although there were many like it.

18. The 1990 New York stage production of the story made very effective physical comedy from this moment.

19. This connection of laughter to revenge is even more interesting when linked to Africa. The Yoruba god Ogun is the powerful god of fire, hunting, war, and iron, but he is also the god of laughter and debauchery. His laugh, however, can be terrible, for he is also the god of revenge, and a Yoruba *ijala* (a hunting poem) warns, "Ogun's laughter is no joke" (Awoonor 94).

Part 2 ✴ Sun's Up

Way over there, where the sun rises a day ahead
of time, they say that Heaven arms with love and
laughter those it does not wish to see destroyed.
He who carries his breath in his sword must perish.

   —"High John de Conquer"

TWO

In the Words of Our Father:
The Sacred and Sorrowful Humor
of Jonah's Gourd Vine

The novel's roots must ultimately be sought in folklore.
        —*Bakhtin*

From long looking I have concluded that my people are not the monkey-see-mon-key-do of folk-lore, nor yet the shining geniuses of the platform. The monkey stories have grown out of a certain exaggeration of qualities plus the will to laugh at one's self which is common to all people. Add to that our will to laugh, even if it must be off-key, and you have the answer. The shining negro hero of the platform is another expression of making your own sunshine to warm yourself by. It too is common to all races. So knowing negroes to be human, I see the real us somewhere between the two pictures—part hero, part clown, just like the rest of the world. We gloom like night, and break like day. Selah.
        —*Zora Neale Hurston*

J onah's Gourd Vine was Zora Neale Hurston's first published book, but she had written *Mules and Men,* her collection of African American folktales, before the novel, even though it would not appear until 1935. *Mules* reads like a novel, for it achieves coherence and narrative flow through the device Hurston developed of featuring her own role as collector. The author/character thus offers us centuries of folk wisdom via a proscribed set of experiences the narrator has with various rural folk during the fixed term of collecting the tales.

Mules and Men begins in a personal way, with "I was glad when somebody told me, 'You may go and collect Negro folk-lore.'" Who was the someone who charged Hurston? Since she dedicated the book to Mrs. Osgood P. Mason, the white patron who financed the trip, we think of her, but Franz Boas, her teacher at Columbia, may be as likely—or maybe Hurston wanted to honor both and thus doubled the reference through its lack of specificity, a clever ruse, one that no doubt amused her. But more importantly, the first line signifies on God, in that it parodies the first line of Psalm 122, "I was glad when they said unto me, Let us go into the house of the Lord." David, the king, speaks of the temple in Jerusalem; Zora, High Priestess of Folklore, speaks of her own holy of holies, folk culture. Biblical signifying became addictive for Hurston, leading to many short pieces and finally to two novels, *Moses* and the unpublished "Herod the Great"; the process of appropriating, mimicking, reshaping, and parodying "sacral" utterances—those of preachers, prophets, and God himself—began on a large scale in *Jonah*. But more importantly, Hurston began her novelistic career by appropriating the voice of her *earthly* father, the preacher John Hurston.

Preaching and the Word

Bakhtin and Hurston, as even the brief epigraphs above suggest, obviously agree that the novel's roots must ultimately be sought in folk culture, "the word" generated from vox populi. All four of Hurston's published novels, even one set in biblical Egypt and Sinai, are firmly rooted in the black southern folk world. She would surely have agreed with Bakhtin that in "that broadest and richest of realms, the common people's creative culture of laughter," one may find the authentic folk roots of multivocal narrative (*Dialogic* 20). The people's endless desire to democratize culture produces a never-ending stream of parody and devastating yet cheerful laughter. And yet this laughter does not erase; it merely levels and thereby sets up the possibility of new creativity.

Clearly, Hurston always thought of the Bible as a folk history, with the cantankerous Hebrew people constantly engaged in pigheaded and glorious rebellion against the god who chose them. She began a large-scale investigation of the possibilities of these insights in her first novel, whose central character individualizes the constant struggle between a rebellious, sensual people and God. The actual writing of the book came about unexpectedly. Hurston was rather surprised when a publisher at Lippincott, impressed by one of her short stories, "The Gilded Six-Bits," asked if she had a novel for them. "Why yes," she said, knowing she didn't. Speedily manufacturing one from scratch meant going to two sets of material she knew better than any other: her family's history and the folklore she had written into the manuscript of the then-unpublished *Mules*. She might have seen merit in embarking on this project for another reason; there was a ready market for tales involving philandering ministers. Sinclair Lewis had proved that with his runaway 1927 bestseller *Elmer Gantry*, a serious satire of American religious hypocrisy featuring a womanizing minister. Hurston claimed Lewis was one of her favorite authors, so she may have read the book (Kunitz and Haycraft 695). There was also the example of Marc Connelley's Broadway sensation, *Green Pastures* (1930); its success had demonstrated Americans' interest in black religion.

In a matter of months, Hurston had written a book studied from life, which documented her father's rise from an "across the creek nigger" to his marriage with the talented and intelligent Lucy Potts, his further ascent under her guidance to minister and state Baptist official, and his decline and fall, occasioned by constant adultery and philandering, before, during, and after his marriages to Lucy, Hattie, and Sally.

As the manuscript title page indicates, the novel was originally called "Big Nigger." Hurston may have had second thoughts, however, after remembering the brouhaha that ensued over Carl Van Vechten's *Nigger Heaven*. "Big Nigger," however, would have signaled a double message to the black audience, for they would realize the term meant one thing to whites (someone uppity or to be feared) and another to blacks. Although the first meaning would refer to someone in the upper range of class structure within the race (obviously the main reference Hurston had in mind),[1] it is also very close in meaning to "bad nigger," which Daryl Dance tells us from its beginning has had positive connotations to certain black people and negative connotations to white people. Its earliest meaning was a man who fought against the system, and sexual prowess constitutes one of his signifiers. However, the "bad nigger" has been defined as a man working out his hostility to his mother, who raised him to suppress his masculinity in an effort to equip him with the mask he needs to confront white racist society (Dance, *Shuckin'* 225). Moreover, many "bad niggers" confine their courage to dealings with black people (Brearly 583), as John largely does. John, as we see early on, loves his mother, seems virtually fearless, even before whites, and appears to love women, though he surely undervalues them in his overt focus on their bodies. On the other hand, his first wife, Lucy, becomes a mother figure for him, gives him detailed instructions about how to handle his ministry, and in her loving forgiveness of his sins simultaneously creates a never-ending source of guilt. His infidelity in some ways seems a rebellion against both her authority and her charity, which forms an analogue with that of the church he serves. Indeed, much of the book's effect depends on conveying very serious subjects such as these through a basically comic style, and that mode of approach characterizes virtually all of Hurston's writing.

"Big Nigger" also resonates as a title via the theme of envy. John's enemies in the book are always trying to "pull him down" and "chop him down" by punishing his pride, as does Jonah's gourd vine, but also by exercising their jealousy. Obviously, Hurston's own ability to rouse the envy of others had to be on her mind here, and she tells us in *Dust Tracks* how it was said when she was a baby that she was "growing like a gourd vine" (30). Another oedipal figuration emerges here, for Hurston also discloses that she and her siblings used to call their father "Big Nigger" behind his back because of his "well-cut broadcloth, Stetson hats, hand-made alligator-skin shoes and walking stick" (114).

This theme of "big niggers" being cut down to size by the community would be addressed years later by Richard Wright in *The Long Dream* (1958), when Professor Butler gives Fish advice via a folk rhyme, upon his setting out in the world:

> Big niggers have little niggers upon their back to bite 'em.
> And little niggers have lesser niggers, and so on *ad infinitum*.
> *And* the big niggers themselves, in turn, have bigger niggers to go on;
> While these again have bigger still, and bigger still, and so on.

Butler comments, "The white folks are on top of us, and our own folks are on top of our folks, and God help the black man at the bottom" (208).

One of the ways to avoid being on the bottom, as Hurston's book demonstrates, was to mount the pulpit. Accordingly, *Jonah* begins Hurston's lifelong intense examination of her inherited religion, a subject she devotes an entire chapter to in her autobiography. We would do well, therefore, to begin there to see how she conflated the issues of religion, humor, and ethnic identity. Written tongue in cheek, in a saucy tone, the chapter nevertheless presents a profoundly serious restatement of the enduring questions a would-be believer asks about God and the church. The following is typical: "Neither could I understand the passionate declarations of love for a being that nobody could see. Your family, your puppy and the new bull-calf, yes. But a spirit away off who found fault with everybody all the time, that was more than I could fathom" (*Dust* 268).

In fact, Hurston treats the church in this deceptively offhand way throughout her memoirs: "I tumbled right into the Missionary Baptist Church when I was born" (266). Her accounts of revival meetings are fondly mocking, as in her rendition of the "little jokes" told about some of the testimony; a deacon says that

> Sister Seeny ought to know better than to be worrying God about moving the sun for her. She asked him to move de tree to convince her, and He done it. Then she took and asked Him to move a star for her and He done it. But when she kept on worrying Him about moving the sun, He took and told her, says, "I don't mind moving that tree for you, and I don't mind moving a star just to pacify your mind, because I got plenty of *them*. I aint got but one sun, Seeny, and I aint going to be shoving it around to please you. . . . If you can't believe without me moving my sun for you, you can just go right on to Hell." (275)

Hurston also renders a comic vision of Christian history, where Constantine uses his "good points—one of them being a sword—and a seasoned army" to win converts. "In Rome, where Christians had been looked upon as rather indifferent lion-bait at best, among other things as keepers of virgins in their homes for no real good to the virgins, Christianity mounted" (276). These anecdotes help us see that Hurston understood black religious culture to be markedly different from white versions, especially in the constant joking about the most sacred things, including God himself. This stance appears repeatedly in *Jonah,* partly because Hurston was indifferent to creeds herself: "I am one with the infinite and need no other assurance" (279).

Still, why would Hurston relate religion and humor like this throughout her career? Can such apparently opposed subjects be related? Hurston recognized what recent social science suggests; a parallel between religion and humor exists because, as Mahadev Apte states, "Both allow humans to dispose of much that seems unpredicted, capricious, and out of place in life; that mythology bridges the gap between the psychological and cognitive aspects of religion by the use of humor, and that the religious values of humor are important and if they are lost or forgotten, then religion is thereby deprived of one of its principal techniques for meeting life's defeats" (233).

Hurston knew too that her central subject, the black preacher, inspired both veneration and joking traditions in the black community. Black parishioners have always accepted the fact that their leader functions as God's anointed in the pulpit and as an ordinary human being the rest of the time, and as Henry Spaulding notes, any excesses or posturing will be quickly targeted by a congregation's wits (161). Hurston probably also liked to poke her own fun at preachers because her father was one. She gained ample ammunition from her life but even more from the many tales and jokes she collected. Louisiana blacks had a verse that went "I wouldn't trust a preacher out o' my sight, / Say I wouldn't trust a preacher out o' my sight, / 'Cause they believes in doin' too many things far in de night" (Levine 327). A traditional song quotes a preacher on this subject:

> I know I've got religion,
> I know I was called to teach,
> Pay no 'tention to what I do,
> Just practice what I preach.
> (Johnson 149)

As Gerald Davis reminds us, "preacher" stories often "turn on his supposed gluttony, lust, avarice, and ironically, his malapropisms," despite the fact that this figure operates centrally in the formulation of African American cultural forms (xiv). Or as a parishioner in South Carolina stated in a more earthy way: "Dey holler, 'God, Jesus' an' 'Lord,' an' talk 'bout heaven an' Sunday atter dey done preach, an' you better pray or you'll burn in hell, den dey will eat up all de grub you kin put on you' table, set down an' go to pickin' dey teet' an' lookin' at you' baby gal. Don't tell me 'bout no preachers" (E. Adams 259).[2] Hurston in fact had already set several preacher stories in the play she wrote with Langston Hughes, *Mule Bone*, as in the exchange Lindsay and Walter have about a Baptist picnic. Walter claims, "Only chicken I seen was a half a chicken yo' pastor musta tried to swaller whole cause he was choked stiff as a board when I come long . . . wid de whole deacon's board beating him in de back, trying to knock it out his throat" (61).

The manuscript of *Jonah* includes a dedication, which was not published: "To the first and only real Negro poets in America—the preachers, who bring barbaric splendor of word and song into the very camp of the mockers. Go Gator, and muddy the water." The addition of this comic folkloric sign-off (which gives approval and encouragement) signifies Hurston's view of black preaching as a folk art form and also indicates that she saw her father's story as metaphoric of a larger experience. Indeed, in a letter to James Weldon Johnson, she said that John Pearson was "a Negro preacher who is neither funny nor an imitation Puritan ram-rod in pants. Just the human being and poet that he must be to succeed in a Negro pulpit. I do not speak of those among us who have been tampered with and consequently have gone Presbyterian or Episcopal. I mean the common run of us who love magnificence, beauty, poetry and color so much that there can never be too much of it. . . . I see a preacher as a man outside of the pulpit and so far as I am concerned he should be free to follow his bent as other men. He becomes the voice of the spirit when he ascends the rostrum."[3] We also remember that Hurston, as an anthropologist, was well aware of the interplay of these concepts in non-Western cultures, particularly in Africa, and with the exception of Melville Herskovits, the great anthropologist and exponent of African cultural survivals in the United States, no one at the time saw more Africanisms in black American culture than she did.[4]

And John indeed develops into a cosmic poet, saving himself several times from disgrace by mapping the heavens and the earth for his parishioners with his golden tongue. On the other hand, he often becomes the target of playful, approving, but also aggressive and envious humor, as his shifting status in the communities he passes through causes joy, envy, and efforts to "crown" and also "uncrown" him, to use Bakhtin's formulation. Accordingly, as a man who "talks that talk" without parallel, he excels as a master of comic discourse himself. Thus Hurston's encomium against John being "funny or a Puritan ram-rod" should be balanced against her actual treatment of the character and her pronouncement that black characters, like all others, should occupy a place between the clown and the hero.

Still, her presentation of John as preacher does in fact strip away a comic dimension that actually was associated with pulpit activity itself. Most studies of black sermons mention jokes or humorous comments that preachers employ to ensure that their sermons keep the audience's attention; as one parishioner put it, "He [her minister] has a lovely deliverance . . . and he'll keep you laughing and yet he says, 'I'm not telling this for you to laugh,' but when he gets through with a parable, you're able to see the thing that he's trying to present to you" (Davis xi). Hurston's relative tentativeness about both the depiction of her father and the danger of dealing with stereotypes about black preachers perhaps made her make this division rather strict; by contrast, she certainly relaxes the boundary between humor and pulpit religion significantly in *Moses*. She also no doubt wanted to avoid the stereotypical minstrel-type humor of the vastly popular and relatively contemporaneous play and movie *Green Pastures*, which she detested.

Here, however, we see a remarkable parallel between the two halves of John's soul, in that the sacred side—serious, mystical, poetic, formal—and the secular side—folkloric, comic, sensual, and all too human and thus understandable—find common ground in the elements that both the preacher and the man that "talks that talk" both have to have. Each must be able to speak spontaneously, deriving a "reading" of sacred and secular "texts" from a deeply personal recreation of the same. The Christian Bible, spirituals, gospel songs, and daily events that are employed in the black sermon find their secular counterparts in folktales, tall tales, work songs, toasts, marking, signifying, and the blues. We might usefully think of these two identities/voices/roles in musical terms as well, as spirituals and blues.

Moreover, both of John's roles overlap with those of the African griot, who keeps the community's culture alive through narration and music. William Wiggins has championed the black preacher as the master storyteller of African American culture, one who constantly utilizes the three "scripts" of personal experience, retellings of biblical stories, and jokes. Wiggins points out that the community expects the minister to be able to comfort the bereaved with a droll story about the deceased or to spice his remarks at weddings, baptisms, and public social events with jokes. Wiggins cites the Reverend Ralph Abernathy's humorous descriptions of the white stereotypes "Miss Ann" and "Mister Charlie" at tense civil rights meetings as comic energizers of the movement (209–10).

Joyce Jackson adds that the performance styles of African griots and black American folk preachers are quite similar, and in the retelling of both personal and biblical narratives, preachers, like their predecessors, deal with "heroic material and draw upon a particular wellspring of imagery which is usually fitted into a metrical pattern." Both act as mediators between the folk and those in power. Moreover, the three stages of training of each vocation are similar: listening to the griot/pastor and attempting to echo him (John's "marking" of sermons when he works in a tie-camp); involvement with performances as an apprentice (in John's case, as in many, singing in the choir or offering inspired prayers from the audience); developing both repertoire and individual style in the official role/pulpit (Jackson 207–8). I would add that the rhythmic element, which becomes sharpened because of John's experience in the tie-camp, is also part of the griot's wares, for in West Africa (particularly among the Limba of Sierra Leone), the storyteller must be expert at speaking, singing, and drumming (Finneman 74). We might also note that the key mediating figure in folktales, the trickster, also has much in common in terms of narration and the use of humor with the griot and the folk concept (and sometimes the reality) of the black preacher.

In yet another sacral/social/scientific authorial role, Hurston functions in this book as chronicler of her culture. Setting down its quotidian markers Hurston preserved and told, providing both substance and spirit. In this respect, documenting what she knew to be a rapidly changing culture, she performs the activity of some griots, a function not unlike that of the preacher. Ministers receive calls to preach; only rarely do they inherit a pastorate. A griot, however, frequently inherits his father's role, and as a sacral/social/scientific teller of tales—and, most significantly, her father's tale—Hurston signifies that she alone of her siblings has been bequeathed the prophetic/narrative mantle and voice.

Furthermore, Hurston's personal development of a novelistic voice, through her father, no doubt helped her rehearse the processes of female empowerment in *Their Eyes*. Anne Goodwyn Jones has recently theorized that Hurston in that book accomplishes as author what Nanny wants to do. Nanny's greatest wish was to preach a great sermon about a woman's voice, and Hurston, through the novel, does just that (87). I would go further to suggest that this impulse shapes the entire contour of Hurston's career, actually beginning even earlier in short stories and drama, but unfolding as a *modus operandi* in *Jonah*.

Even during childhood, Hurston's reach for patriarchal authority was manifest. She had imaginary playmates formed from objects such as Miss Cornshuck, but prominently including Reverend Doorknob, who presumably preached righteous ways to Sis and her friend, a soapbar named "Mr. Smellsweet," and officiated at the imaginary funerals and weddings Hurston staged (see *Dust Tracks*). Male ministers have confirmed similar childhood activities. A Bishop Cleveland claimed that preachers aren't called, but are rather born, and remembered that "me and my sister and other kids would play church, and I'd always be the preacher. And I'd get in the wagon and preach. . . . And I'd feel it just like I do now" (Davis ix).[5]

Finally, telling her father's story meant not only appropriating his voice, but *becoming* that voice. Doing so meant working through her personal problems with her father, a powerful man whose relationship with his second daughter had always been, at the least, problematic. *Jonah* thus constituted a personal odyssey into her patriarchal origins and legacy and a coming to terms with both. This in many ways echoes James Baldwin's purpose in writing both *Go Tell It on the Mountain* and his play *The Amen Corner*. He described the latter in the following way: "I was thinking not only, not merely, about the terrifying desolation of my private life but about the great burdens carried by my father. I was old enough by now, at last, to recognize the nature of the dues he had paid, old enough to wonder if I could possibly have paid them, old enough, at last, at last, to know that I had loved him and had wanted him to love me. I could see that the nature of the battle we had fought had been dictated by the fact that our temperaments were so fatally the same; neither of us could bend" (*Go Tell* xvi). Like Baldwin, Hurston was coming to terms with her affinities with her father, a process of discovery that continued in her autobiography. There, her mother becomes alarmed at Zora's tendency to wander, saying someone had sprinkled "travel dust" around the doorstep on the child's birthday. Hurston wonders why her mother never saw the connection to John Hurston, "who didn't have a thing on his mind but this town and the next one. That should have given her a sort of hint. Some children are just bound to take after their fathers in spite of women's prayers" (*Dust Tracks* 32).

In a related way, this process would also empower her as a female writer, permitting her to employ some of the sacrosanct traditions of the black male oral tradition in fiction, especially the figuration of serious issues in comic and coded discourse and the invitation to "expand on a text" of the black minister. On this subject, Toni Morrison has said that black literature should "try deliberately to make you stand up and make you feel something profoundly in the same way that a black preacher requires his congregation to speak, to join him in the sermon, to stand up and to weep and to cry and to accede or to change and to modify—to expand on the sermon that is being delivered" ("Rootedness" 341). The very title, *Jonah's Gourd Vine*, indicates this, as it lists a "text," something that a preacher must always address, a passage from the Bible, in this case that portion of Jonah where the reluctant prophet has repented his flight from God, gone to Nineveh, and prophesied the destruction of the city. The people repent and God spares them, causing Jonah's anger at thus becoming a false prophet. He sits on a hill to watch the city's fate, and God causes a gourd vine to grow over him, sheltering him from the sun. God also, however, prepares a worm that eats the vine away, exposing Jonah yet again and enraging him. God rebukes his servant for pitying the vine but not the people of Nineveh.[6]

Hurston comically sexualizes this fable, but with profoundly serious implications. Although many readings of the basic metaphor seem possible, the most obvious one pertains to John's sexuality (the worm) destroying Lucy, his career, and the spreading comfort his voice gives his parishioners (all versions of the grapevine). This central trope expands in power through parallelism; very early in the book John sees a train for the first time and becomes transfixed by it. The figure of the train, in its power and thrust, develops into a symbol of both John's potent rhetoric and his sexuality, merging in the surge and roll of his magnificent "train" sermon. The locomotive therefore operates as one of the most important unifying symbols in the book; it functions to signify John just as the pear tree signifies Janie in *Their Eyes*.

Significantly, Hurston introduces this theme in an initiation scene, when John leaves his rural home to seek work on the Pearson plantation and spies the train in a hamlet railroad station. Communal laughter results as the townspeople laugh boisterously over the bumpkin's amazement; the engineer's calculated blast on the horn makes John jump and causes more amusement. Significantly, John hears the train saying something, but he can't understand it. The scene emblematizes an old set of jokes told by citified blacks about rural lads who see trains huffing and puffing in the station for the first time, only to remark something like "Po' thing sho is thirsty." John, however, instinctively responds to its threatening power: "The engine's very sides seemed to expand and contract like a fiery-lunged monster" (16), introducing rather overtly the sexual symbolism of the black train that will be identified with John throughout the book and that will kill him.[7]

The phallic metaphor here gets paralleled by one of Hurston's many uses of snake symbols. She makes John's courtship of Lucy heroic by having him kill a huge moccasin that lives under the footbridge, a monster made mythical by Lucy's assertion that this "'ole devil . . . been right dere skeerin' folks since befo' Ah wuz borned'" (34). But they both know the snake's mate must be near; the victory could be momentary. And indeed, the parallel "serpent" under the "high road" symbolized here emerges in John's sexual philandering, the "worm" that cuts down this "Jonah's Gourd Vine," as one of John's enemies dubs him.[8]

As an extension of the aptness of the train imagery for both John and the black pulpit in general, a markedly sexual quality often emerges in the structure of the black sermon, in that the minister and the people, striving together in call-and-response mode, aim toward a spiritual climax. The audience's shouts, comments, and general "getting happy" all work toward this moment. Rhythm and timing are especially important as the moment comes closer. As Joyce Jackson notes, most preachers evoke this by using some form of intonation, "variously referred to as 'moaning,' 'hollering,' 'shouting,' 'chanting,' 'grunting' or any one of several other terms, especially in the inspirational climaxes of their sermons" (213). Grace Sims Holt adds that the rich language is calculated to raise the church sisters into a state of "fainting, sweating, groaning, and simulating a mass orgasm," and indeed, "the preacher's ability to arouse an erotic response is an index of his success and vitality" (327–28). Thus John's duality—his earthy sexuality and his spirit-filled voice—precisely and ironically makes him such a success in the pulpit.

We may trace this pattern in John's delivery of his famous "dry bones" sermon, a response he gives to a rival preacher whom the congregation may install in place of John.[9] The theme of most variants of this standard is that of the second chance, of how God can take dry bones and make them live. John's powerful sermon proves this, for his adulteries have made him "dry" too. The sermon also refers, of course, to a sinning people, who has need of renewal, provided for in the restoration of the covenant. In many ways, John's wandering from Lucy/church parallels that of the idol-craving Hebrews, and thus combines the story of a sinning individual with that of a sinning people, both watched and judged by an angry god. In some ways, writing this novel not only recapitulated a sorrowful past for Hurston but also represented a powerful rehearsal for *Moses*, which traces a similar pattern of redemption/sin, redemption/sin, but with an emphasis on the society rather than the individual.

John's "dry bones" sermon seems to recharge him as well as his parishioners: "He brought his hearers to such a frenzy that it never subsided until two Deacons seized the preacher by the arms and reverently set him down"; Sister Hall gloats, "'Dat's uh preachin' piece uh plunder'" (158). Taking over the pulpit from John, Rev. Felton Cozy, John's rival, advertises himself as a "race man" and proceeds to examine black-white relationships. "After five minutes . . . Sister Boger whispered to Sister Pindar, 'Ah ain't heard whut de tex' wuz.' 'Me neither.'" Reverend Cozy's litany of the accomplishments of black men, including the claim that Christ was black, gets interrupted by his revealing need to order the parishioners to say "'Amen.' Don't let uh man preach hisself tuh death and y'll set dere lak uh bump on uh log and won't he'p 'im out. Say 'Amen'!!" (159). When Deacon Harris asks the sisters how they liked Cozy's sermon, Sister Boger makes "an indecent sound with her lips: 'Dat wan't no sermon. Dat wuz uh lecture.' 'Dat's all whut it wuz,' Sister Watson agreed and switched on off" (159). These comically scornful physical gestures beautifully underline the difference between the merely intellectual and the sublimely spiritual. As C. Eric Lincoln and Lawrence H. Mamiya show, failure to achieve spiritual ecstasy often results in polite compliments of "good talk" or "good lecture," and not the ultimate "You *preached* today!" (6).[10]

Hurston clearly wished to emphasize the power and mystery of John's voice and no doubt understood that early religion and many contemporary world religions required this sort of catharsis in their ceremonies. It has frequently been observed that the black church has always functioned as the communal theater in the community, working toward catharsis; but going beyond Greek drama and more anemic religions, the congregations sought not just emptying of emotions but "an enduring fellowship with God in which the formal worship service provided the occasion for particular periods of intimacy" (Lincoln and Mamiya 6). With this understood, it would be surprising if pulpit performances did *not* contain a somewhat sexual structure. Clearly, Hurston suggests that the very thing that makes John a powerful servant of God causes his downfall, first in the personal realm, but ultimately in the church as well.

This issue of text and address necessarily, however, raises the matter of racial difference. White-dominated society seeks to create a boundary between the body and the soul, the sexual and the sacred, and Hurston was writing for that audience. Accordingly, she may have decided to make the division between John's discourse in the pulpit and in the wider community more dramatic than it had been in her own father's life. In *Jonah*, then, the overwhelming saturation of the man of words's discourse with humor may be differentiated from the narrative world of the preacher by the general absence of this quality in the pulpit—or at least in the sermon—even though this differentiation would not be as strict in actual practice.[11]

The Verbal Duel and Marriage

A close reading of the first chapter, which deals largely with John's parents, will facilitate an initial understanding of how Hurston loads virtually every line of the book with grave meaning rendered through comically inventive folk language. The troubled relationship of John's parents finds expression this way, although they themselves obviously feel pain as they invent novel ways of signification. Their marital verbal dueling sets a pattern that will be repeated later, first in the loving give-and-take teasing of John and Lucy's courtship, then later in the darkening discourse of their marriage, for John appears to be the doomed inheritor of patriarchal postures.

The ominous first line of the chapter sets an appropriate mood; like the dueling couple, God seems at play, but with weapons that can do deep injury: "God was grumbling his thunder and playing the zigzag lightning thru his fingers." But Amy, John's mother, quickly tames the deity through her domestic observation, which not only brings

God down to earth but feminizes him, in the manner of Edward Taylor's classic poems from the colonial American period "Housewifery" and "The Creation"; she declares, "Ole Massa gwinter scrub floors tuhday," thus making God "Ole Massa" over all humankind, but cleverly subverting that too, in the image of God on his knees scrubbing floors, which a slave woman would do. Like Amy, Hurston obviously seeks the intimacy that humor always creates by bringing its subject closer, as a bridge between oppositions and characters, and personally, between the painful distance separating the author and her father. What she and Amy do with God the father in the first scene will be done with John the father throughout the book.

The idea of judgment also looms large, as represented by the fiery thunderbolt; it becomes coupled with washing/cleansing aspects of both water and fire, which in fact are dominant images throughout the novel, echoing the powerful neo-Puritan motif established by Booker T. Washington's immensely influential *Up from Slavery*, which Hurston seems to have known well. She mentions Washington regularly, and approvingly, throughout her books. John Hurston, like his fictional counterpart John Pearson, grew up near Notasulga, Alabama, which is in Macon County, Alabama, about ten miles from Tuskegee, and Zora was born there too. The institute would thus quite naturally loom large in Hurston family legend. Moreover, Washington's emphasis on washing, rebirth, cleanliness—most memorably when he has to clean a room completely to prove his worthiness to enter Hampton Institute—fits quite well in a story about John the Baptist in modern dress, for John serves a Baptist church, as did Hurston's father. To maintain pastoral control and piety, however, one must constantly publicly "wash" one's soul clean, as John attempts to do in this story. Although Lucy later claims that John can't wash himself clean from sin, like a cat, with his tongue, the church's doctrine permits precisely that, forgiving John over and again after his movingly poetic and confessional sermons.

This comment of Lucy's, when coupled with Amy's observation about the lightning, causes one to remember that fire (lightning) can "wash" too, in its power to purify. But purification can be punitive; Amy threatens her husband, John's stepfather, who has picked on John: "'Ah'll wash yo' tub uh 'gator guts and dat quick'" (3). Ned, obsessed with the "stain" on his honor represented by Amy's half-white son, claims, "'Ah feed 'im and clothes 'im but Ah ain't tuh do nothin' tuh dat lil' yaller god cep'n wash 'im up.'" But Amy remarks on John's obedience and humility, "'Yet and still you always washin' his face wid his color and tellin' 'im he's uh bastard.'" Here washing becomes rather a staining, its opposite. Hurston extends her metaphors in this discussion. Ned, who thinks Amy likes the "Gold" colored John because she is "color-struck," signifies on the term (a point presumably proved for Ned by her affair with a white man). "Washing" takes on new meaning when Amy reminds Ned of his original feeling about her son during courting: "'You washed 'im up jes' lak he wuz gold den. You jes took tuh buckin' 'im since you been hangin' round sich ez Beasley and Mimms'"—two white men (3). In some ways we properly hesitate to term this powerful scene comic, but the sarcasm and creativity involved in formulating thoughts in unexpected ways make this conversation kin to the verbal duel, albeit a very bitter one.

A more positive manifestation of humor comes when John boisterously enters and ruptures the parental narrative: "The children came leaping in, racing and tumbling in tense, laughing competition" (2). Despite the games and joking, however, the humor in this first chapter emerges largely through aggression, centering on the angry relationship between Amy Crittenden and Ned Crittenden, one strongly proleptive of James Baldwin's characters Gabriel Grimes and Elizabeth Grimes of *Go Tell It on the Mountain*—for in both narratives the husband serves as surrogate father to his wife's son by another man—and in Ned's case, the other man was a white man. It also sets the paradigm of the woman who shelters a son, like Jonah's gourd vine, from male punishment/persecution.

Ned uses hyperbolic language, claiming that for Amy, this son is a "'li'l' yaller God.'" Amy's reply to this combines a number of folk expressions: "'Dat's uh big ole resurrection lie, Ned. Uh slew-foot, dragleg lie at dat, and Ah dare yuh tuh hit me too. Yo know Ahm uh fightin' dawg and mah hide is worth money. Hit me if you dare!'" (2–3). Amy here not only challenges Ned to linguistic and physical combat; she also suggests he's already proven his inability in the verbal realm with a "slew-foot, dragleg lie." We perceive the violent nature of this marriage largely because of Ned's intolerance of Amy's independence and her resultant predilection for "changing words," which includes creative signification: "'Don't you change so many words wid me, 'oman! Ah'll knock yuh dead ez Hector. Shet yo' mouf!' 'Ah change jes' ez many words ez Ah durn please! Ahm three times seben and uh button. Ah knows whut's de matter wid *you*. Youse mad cause Beasley done took dem two bales uh cotton us made las' yeah. . . . Don't you lak it, don't you take it, heah mah collar come and you shake it!'" (5–6).[12] Amy goes on in a harangue that insults Ned's inability to support his family, echoing in many ways the marital situation in Hurston's story "Sweat." Knocking him as "dead as Hector" brings in the classical heritage of the South, which has crossed over into black language, and implicitly casts Ned on a losing side. We also see here a clear prefiguration of male characters in Alice Walker's novels, as well as a foremother of those men's female opponents. Ned especially suggests Celie's presumed father in *The Color Purple* in that he binds John over to Cap'n Mimms, "'dat everybody knowed wuz de wust [overseer] in southern Alabama. He done whipped niggers nigh tuh death'" (7).

Clearly, these skilled protagonists' joking relationship goes back years, but seems based in nursed grudges rather than affection or respect. Significantly, Hurston presents Alf Pearson, a white plantation owner and judge, as John's probable biological father. Pearson becomes John's employer and, in many respects, mentor. As a result of Pearson's original refusal to acknowledge and provide for his son, Ned, acting as stepfather, has theoretically taken on that burden, but his abuse of not only John but also of Amy belies that claim. Ned's binding of John over to Mimms thus replicates not only the historical analogue of slaveowners who sold their own children but the more immediate situation with Pearson. John, however, tells his brother Zeke, "'Ah jes' ez soon be under Mimms ez pappy. One 'bout ez bad as tother. . . . Dis ain't slavery time and Ah got two good footses hung onto me'" (8).

Hurston exposes this joking assertion, however, as false, for in a powerful scene with oedipal implications, Ned's brutal attack on Amy finally causes John to strike his stepfather. This presents a more complicated version of the familiar family romance, for old-time patterns of color hierarchy within the race (imposed by white standards) and their resultant historical patterns receive a brilliant rehearsal through Ned. Ordering John, "dat punkin-colored bastard," "dat half-white youngun" out of the house, Ned asserts, "'Yaller niggers ain't no good nohow. . . . Dese white folks orta know and dey say dese half-white niggers got de worst part uh bofe de white and de black folks'" (9). Earlier, he had jealously compared John's supposedly pampered state with that of house servants: "'John is de house-nigger. Ole Marsa always kep' de yaller niggers in de house and give 'em uh job totin' silver dishes and goblets tuh de table. Us black niggers is de ones s'posed tuh ketch de wind and de weather'" (4). Hurston projects the implications further through extending the skein of signification, rehearsing the tangled snarl of race and class that demarks the relationship between plantation house servants and poor rural whites, as Amy comments,

"Is mo' yaller folks on de chain-gang dan black? Naw! Is dey harder tuh learn? Naw! Do dey work and have things lak other folks? Yas. Naw dese po' white folks . . . jealous. . . . Ole Marse got de yaller nigger totin' his silver cup and eatin' Berksher hawg ham outa his kitchin when po' white trash scabblin' 'round in de piney woods huntin' up uh razor back. Yaller nigger settin' up drivin' de carriage and de po' white folks go tuh step out de road and leave 'im pass by. And den agin de po' white man got daughters dat don't never eben smell de kitchin at the big house and all dem yaller chillun got mammas, and no black gal ain't never been up tuh de big house and dragged Marse Nobody out. Humph! Talkin' after po' white trash! If Ah wuz ez least ez dey is, Ah speck Ah'd fret mahself tuh death." (10)

We notice how effortlessly Hurston manages to insert quite a bit of social history here, history that significantly helps to explain both immediate and later issues of the narrative, and she does it through folk humorous narrative, albeit a frequently cruel one. Amy mockingly accuses Ned of mimicking the poor whites he associates with: "'Monkey see, monkey do,'" and indeed, his absurd statements sometimes seem right out of Klan folders. "'De brother in black don't fret tuh death. White man fret and worry and kill hisself. Colored folks fret uh li'l' while and gwan tuh sleep. 'Nother thing . . . Hagar's chillun don't faint neither when dey fall out, dey jes have uh hard old fit'" (10). Amy answers this charge, comic in its absurdity, in kind: "'Dass awright. Niggers gwine faint too. May not come in yo' time and it may not come in mine, but way after while, us people is gwine faint jes' lak white folks,'" using a triviality to sugarcoat the presentation of a hard and hopeful truth. Hurston here signifies on the racist stereotype that Ned and Amy apparently believe; they don't seem to understand the comic aspects that Hurston obviously wishes to employ.[13]

These opening scenes thus provide the context for John's departure for a new life, but also place his origins in the liminally vexed state of the post-slavery black generation. Hurston's insistence about placing characters between the hero and the clown suggests the divided state of John's life and consciousness throughout the book. Caught initially between the legacies of slavery and freedom, body and soul, black and white, father and mother, then trying to choose between "nat'ul man" and priest, hedonistic pleasure and familial responsibility, John's ambiguities doom him to torment and irresolution. Despite the tragic potential, which ultimately finds realization, the ironic aspect of his situation combined with the abundant folk humor endemic to his setting makes the book a tragicomedy.

The Comedy of Initiation and Liminality

John leaves, telling his mother he accepts his exile: "'Ah ever wanted tuh cross over'" (10). In a moving tableau, under a black and starry sky, Amy accompanies John to the creek, reminding him he was born over there. He promises to make money and come back for her, thereby echoing once again slave paradigms. Crossing over to the birthland and ironic reunion with his father creates a parallel to the Israelites returning to their ancestral home and a new covenant with their heavenly father and also of "coming through" religion. As such, these moments suggest what Van Gennep calls "rites of passage," which involve three phases: separation, margin or liminality, and aggregation. The middle period, characteristically and markedly free of both the past and future realms, frequently is situated in a neutral territory in nature, ordinarily deserts, marshes, and, most commonly, forests (18).[14] Such motifs find several echoes in spirituals.

In a scene we see again in her setting of the Moses story, Hurston cosmically describes John's "crossing over" the creek into relative freedom in allegorical, almost magical detail. The scene fits well with Van Gennep's description of the liminal phase: the creek "thunders" like the machinery of fate as he stands "on the foot-log, half way across the Big Creek where maybe people laughed and maybe people had lots of daughters" (12). The laughter of youth and courtship will replace the "ugly laughter" of Ned and Amy's troubled household, one dominated by mimicry of patriarchal oppression. Clearly, John will use laughter as a barometer of a people's emotional health.

John stays in this position while the moon rises and then, later, the sun. Thus in this epiphany of freedom, suspended over the rushing boundary of freedom and bondage that cosmically doubles as the water of life, John purposely suspends himself for a time in the liminal state, enjoying the moment of transition, but also postponing his actual crossing till the parallel crossing of the new sun in its path in the sky. John's crossing also takes the form of baptism and symbolic rebirth, while bearing a nascent and predictive sexual quality as well, as he crosses first with his clothes held high then recrosses and swims across yet again, nude and free of burden. In this amazingly full paragraph, Hurston gives John and the reader the sun, the moon, and the stars of freedom and identity, cosmic markers of the sacral and predictive moment we share with him. As Victor Turner's seminal work on liminality indicates, initiates frequently are stripped to demonstrate that as "liminal beings they have no status, property, insignia, secular clothing indicating rank or role, position in a kinship system" and their condition represents a "moment in and out of time," one simultaneously "in and out of secular social structure." For in the social aspect of liminality, the initiate participates in an alternative to structured, hierarchical society, one that Turner terms a state of "communitas," where "liminality implies that the high could not be high unless the low existed, and he who is high must experience what it is like to be low" (95). Hurston had of course gone through her own rites of liminality, especially in her hoodoo initiation, spending three days in a passive state, nude, on a snakeskin (see *Mules* 192–215, esp. 192).

Social scenes of meetings and initiations soon follow the creek scene, for Hurston invariably establishes the intimacy of relationships and their consequential role in the development and complication of personal identity with humor. For instance, John's vision of "laughing daughters" finds fulfillment as soon as he crosses the real and symbolic boundary of the creek into a new identity; children erupt from a school "shouting and laughing," and the first one of them to address him, Lucy Potts, "a leader," looks him over boldly and exclaims, "'Well, folks! Where you reckon dis big yaller beestung nigger come from?' Everybody laughed. He felt ashamed of his bare feet for the first time in his life" (13–14). The laughter proves infectious and community creating, for when Lucy looks into his eyes and laughs, "All the others laughed. John laughed too." Lucy further informs John he's mistaken to ask for "Marse Alf Pearson": "'Don't y'all folkses over de creek know slavery time is over? 'Tain't no mo' Marse Alf, no Marse Charlie, nor Marse Tom neither. . . . We been born since freedom. We calls 'em Mister'" (14).

This little girl later becomes his wife; their relationship significantly starts in laughter, and communal and corrective laughter at that ("Seemed as if she had caught him doing something nasty") (14). The something "nasty" registers too, for John's embarrassment partly stems from the fact that although Lucy speaks first and he notices her first, he sees another, more mature girl behind her virtually at the same time, who "had breasts, must be around fourteen," and in fact this one "came walking out hippily from behind the other, challenging John to another appraisal of her person" (14). This saucy scene prefigures the tragedy of the book, for over and over again, a woman emerges from behind Lucy's back to tempt her man. This "Jezebel," Phrony, becomes the first woman John has sex with after meeting Lucy and prefigures many to come.

This mythical scene is similarly employed in *Their Eyes* and *Moses*. All feature the entry of the hero from a journey of rebirth into a strange culture and a greeting from a woman at the well who offers water. The typescene appears to be a constant in black culture; indeed, in *Their Eyes,* when Janie and Jody enter Eatonville, the other men criticize Tony Taylor's welcoming speech because he doesn't include a reference to Isaac and Rebecca, prototypes of the woman/well imagery (68). In *Moses* Zipporah appears along with a number of women, just as Lucy does here. In *Jonah,* the school signifies the well; book learning and folk wisdom are "water." Like Zipporah, Lucy directs John/Moses to the house of his new "father," but Jethro here is Alf Pearson, who probably actually *is* John's father.

The train scene, another initiation, this one phallic, tellingly precedes one of patriarchal recognition, the meeting between John and Alf Pearson, who is nearby. After a long look, Alf says, "'What a fine stud! Why boy, you would have brought five thousand dollars on the block in slavery time! Your face looks sort of familiar but I can't place you. What's your name?'" (17). We laugh at the joke on Pearson, but we wince as well at the equally ironic and immediate translation of a human being, his own son, into financial and breeding terms, which seems to be a postbellum hangover of slave owning. Pearson immediately hires John as a coachman; he drives home Pearson's "cream-colored" buggy, which underlines his mulatto status.

Whether Pearson knows of John's lineage remains somewhat ambiguous, but he seems bursting with pride over his new "hand," and he recounts the circumstances of John's birth and Amy's subsequent marriage to "some stray darky" quite clearly.[15] This parodic recognition scene precedes a more touching one, as Aunt Pheemy, John's hostess, acknowledges her grandson: "'Ahm yo' granny! Yo' nable string is buried under dat air chanyberry tree,'" thus linking him to her not only through blood and memory but through reference to sacred and traditional African ritual as well.[16]

Yet another powerful link to slave times emerges when Pearson volunteers to bring some of his white son's outgrown clothing down to John at the quarters rather than have him come up to the house to get them. Later, we learn that Mrs. Pearson objects to John driving her carriage because he is too big. Could it be that she detects a resemblance to her husband? We never know, but the parallels to slavery's narratives seem unmistakable.[17] We note as well that later, when John has outgrown Pearson's white son's clothes, the father begins to give John his own cast-off garments. This coincides with Pearson's delegation of major plantation duties to this black son because of the esthete white son's continuing study in Paris. Hurston surely means to signify on a biblical theme here, where the elder son's blessing passes to the younger, but only in a cruelly meager and mocking way.

A further link to slave times is in the scene where John and Lucy go into the school after their initial meeting. The ugly side of humor comes to the fore, for the teacher, Lucy's uncle, tyrannically likes to make students squirm. He humiliates John and demands a complete name. John says, "'Mama, she name me Two-Eye John,'" and the class rings with laughter, but not Lucy's. When the students learn John has no last name, however, all are silent; the teacher gives him Pearson as a last name since he was born on Pearson's place. Ironically, this really *should* be his name, but this incident goes deeper, for renaming scenes like this one are enacted over and again in slave narratives when agents of northern education and civilization provide new names for newly freed slaves.

Moreover, when John meets Alf, he says Amy chose the name "'Two-Eye John from a preachin' she heered'" (17). Clearly, then, John should be read as a text himself, one to be studied and considered as representative, for of course the appropriation of Amy's body by Marse Alf was chapter and verse in the blasphemous text of slavery. The name "Two-Eye" has much meaning, however, for it suggests the soul/body split that torments John throughout the book and the doublings of meaning that Hurston folds in at virtually every level, including the forward and backward perspectives present at the point of liminality. Typologically, John the Baptist fits John Pearson as a Baptist minister, but John the Evangelist works even better, since the saint of Patmos operated as God's instrument, filled with his visions and telling others. He has traditionally been associated with the sense of revelation, final judgments, mystery, and the cosmic, hence seeing the future with one eye and the present with the other.[18]

This theme of splits, borders, and liminality continues throughout the novel, but one final example will suffice to show how it applies not only to individuals but also to families and groups. The major shift of scene in the novel (from Alabama to Florida) occurs well into John and Lucy's marriage, and as the family's major moment of initiation, Hurston characteristically presents it through humorous conventions. They arrive in Eatonville in a "wagon full of laughter and shouts of questions" (108). Without any real introduction, Hurston has the men on Joe Clarke's porch appear to comment on Lucy's merits and to joke with John about taking her away from him. Their friendly jibes are in reality compliments, but John takes care to maintain the proper boundaries to the verbal play. When one says, "'You might up and die uh she might quit yuh and git uh sho nuff husband, and den she

could switch uh mean Miss Johnson in dat big house on Mars Hill.'"
John's reply, "half in earnest" to the "general laughter," is "'Less squat
dat rabbit and jump uhnother one.'" But Joe Clarke senses the tone
things are taking and intervenes: "'Aw, he jes' jokin' yuh, Pearson. . . .
I God, you takin' it serious'" (110). Clearly, the community's jocular
remarks ironically reverse the situation that actually exists, and even
the suggestion of such a thing infuriates John.

The Humor of Female Rivalry

In the early scenes set on the Pearson plantation, Hurston takes advantage of the slack time in the farm's routines to have the young
folks meet and initiate newcomer John; they play folk games, replete
with songs, verses, and sayings, most of them witty. In the midst of
them, Phrony mentions Lucy, who can run extremely fast. Phrony
piques John's interest further by disclosing that the Potts are "big
niggers." Since we know of John's ambition and that the original title of the book was "Big Nigger," we immediately see the way in which
he thinks of a shortcut up the social ladder through Lucy. Meanwhile,
however, we are introduced to a recurring comic subject, female rivalry over John; Phrony's plans to snare him are foiled as Mehaley,
her former friend, verbally duels with her after a tryst in the haystack
with John. Phrony asks for her comb back after seeing them together, and Mehaley replies,

> "You kin git yo' ole stink hair comb any time. Ah'll be glad tuh git it
> outa mah house. Mama tol me not tuh comb wid it 'cause she skeered
> Ah'd git boogers in mah haid."
> "Youse uh lie! Ah ain't got no boogers in mah haid, and if you'
> mamy say so she's uh liar right long wid you! She ain't so bad ez she
> make out. Ah'll stand on yo' toes and tell yuh so."
> "Git back outa mah face, Phrony. Ah don't play de dozens!" (24)

This humorous and somewhat ritualistic exchange has a serious un-
dertone to it, as the reference to the dozens should make clear, for
if a player strays from fictional statements about one's female relatives to one that might be true, violence looms as a possibility, and
indeed, the two girls start to fight immediately. They exchange more
words and some body language humor too: Mehaley taunts Phrony,
saying, "'Ah'll betcha Alabama wid uh fence 'round it he won't never hide wid yuh no mo'.' . . . Mehaley preened herself akimbo and
rotated her hips insolently" (25).[19]

There are malapropisms and coinages galore here. John praises

Lucy's brains, obviously a major factor in her victory over her female rivals: "'Take Lucy Potts for instink. She's almost uh 'fessor now. . . . Dey say she kin spell eve'y word in Lippincott's Blue-back Speller. . . . Dey tell me she can spell compresstibility, and when huh git dat fur 'taint much mo' fuhther fur yuh tuh go'" (27). To get as much humor as possible out of these lines, Hurston pulls out all of her many tricks. Hyperbole gets linked to dialect ("almost uh 'fessor now"); the disastrous rendering of "compresstibility," funny alone, gets coupled with John's obvious feeling he's used the right word. Thus we have reader-author irony at the character's expense. On the other hand, the clever constructions of the duelists offsets any sense of superiority we might have.

When John comes home for Christmas and Lucy's birthday, Mehaley gets her friends to go to Macedony Church with her, though all three belong to Shiloh. "'Less go slur dat li'l' narrer-contracted Potts gal,' she urged. . . . 'She fool wid me tuhday Ah means tuh beat her 'til she rope lak okra, an en agin Ah'll stomp her 'til she slack lak lime'" (67). Her signifying body-slurring fury stems in part from issues of class and elitism; she accuses John at one point of wanting more than "quarter niggers" like her, thereby providing an echo of themes raised by Ned earlier in his campaign against John.

John in passing points out something uncanny to Mehaley—that Lucy's birthday is December 31, while his is January 1. Remarkably, the Hurston family Bible reveals these were the actual birthdays of Lucy and John Hurston (Bordelon 7). Zora Hurston, who sometimes listed her own birthdate as January 1, was keenly aware of the two faces of Janus associated with these dates and the concept of the double they represent. Here, the duality becomes emblematic in another sense, for Mehaley represents the avatar of all the other women John will dally with; they stand for the new, the forbidden, the uncharted, while Lucy signifies the traditional, the tried, the true, home and hearth. This gets stressed when Mehaley and Lucy first become rivals for John's love, in a scene that secondarily focuses on male violence toward women. An irate John discovers Mehaley has erased her hated rival Lucy's name from Aunt Pheemy's chimney, where John had carved it. As the phallic chimney suggests, the locus for this signature has much to do with John's male pride in his romantic prowess, but also in his gathering powers of expression, for the signature forms a tribute to Lucy's teaching abilities as well; Hurston specifically tells us that inscribing it "proved his new power to communicate his thoughts" (32). John assumes another man defaced it: "'Ahm jes' ez hot ez Tucker when de mule kicked his mammy, and any man dat tell me tuh mah face dat he done it he got tuh smell mah fist.'" But when it turns out Mehaley did it, the punishment becomes God-like and more severe: "'Ah feel lak Ah could take and lam her wid lightnin'.'" The appropriately named Bully urges him on, saying, "'Ah'd beat her jes' ez long ez she last. Anyhow she takin' de under currents on you.'" John, however, clearly has heard the comic story "Why Women Always Take Advantage of Men" and devined its serious message, for he replies, "'Uh man is crazy tuh do dat—when he know he got tuh submit hisself tuh 'em'" (51).

Although as readers we disapprove of John's many infidelities, we need to remember that time and time again women throw themselves at him, suggesting that Hurston wants us to recognize that women have sexual drives as well, that they too can choose to exercise choice and go out seeking partners, and that men, just like women, may be viewed as sexual objects. On the other hand, some of these women, particularly Mehaley, seem to genuinely love John.

We consequently feel for Mehaley as she puts John's hand on her heart and in a comic but heartbreaking speech declares, "'My heart is rearin' and pitchin' fur you lak uh mule in uh tin stable. . . . You so pretty and you ain't color-struck lak uh whole heap uh bright-skin people . . . hug me till mah dress fit tight'" (52). The fade-out here, as elsewhere in the book, indicates a sexual encounter, one followed the day after by the sight of John comically signifying his repentance by reinscribing Lucy's name in huge letters across the chimney.

The Humor of Courtship

From the beginning of their relationship, Lucy frequently greets John with comic folk rhymes, a device used more in this book than in any other work of Hurston's: "'Hello yuhself, want uh piece uh cawn bread look on de shelf.'" She translates this for John and the reader into "'Whyn't *you* come tuh school too?'" (15).

Although John enjoys the favors of at least five girls, he pines for Lucy and asks her to help him learn to speak pieces. He offends her, however, by using the word "bottom" in a folk expression, even though he's referring to a chair's bottom, not hers. He realizes the "nasty" nature of much of his store of folk humor, especially sayings such as "Some love collards, some love kale / But I loves uh gal wid us short skirt tail" (33). Nasty or not, Hurston (presumably with a careful eye on the censor) plugs the text liberally with comically flirtatious sayings and songs such as these.

The humorous folk adages John and Lucy send each other in lover's notes reveal the way courtship can function as learning, particularly in the true meaning of words usually taken for granted: "Dere Lucy: Whin you pass a mule tied to a tree / Ring his tail and think of me. Your sugger-lump, John." Lucy replies, "Long as the vine grow 'round the stump / You are my dolling sugar lump. Mama whipped me last night, because Bud told her we was talking to each other. Your sweet heart, LUCY ANN" (52–53). John's note is comic but hardly romantic (especially the reference to a mule's ass), till the salutation, where the sweetness appears apart from him and in a "lump." Lucy, on the other hand, summons up the natural world of growth in her imagery (which runs counter to Mehaley's violent conjuration of a mule kicking down a building) and also the book's title. As long as John's rampant sexuality gets trimmed back to conform with her spreading, sheltering vine, they will be lovers. She also adds a personal touch in referring to her family's persecution of her, which tells us of her willingness to suffer for love. Finally, her salutation gives us "sweet heart" in two words rather than one, providing a powerful human "cap" to John's insufficient "sugar lump."

John's attempt to initiate himself into the fellowship of the Potts family doesn't succeed, however, for Lucy's mother, Emmeline, never accepts him. Mehaley's comic venom finds a match in this character, who clearly resents her husband's preference for Lucy. In many ways her actions are parallel to those of Lucy's rivals; she appears determined to marry her daughter to Archie Mimms, for elitist and class reasons.

John's often awkward courtship of Lucy offers Hurston an abundant source of bittersweet humor that touches all who were once teenage sweethearts. When they are on the porch in two separate but close chairs, Emmeline bursts in: "'Lucy! Whut you doin' settin' on top uh dat boy?' 'Ah ain't settin' on top of 'im. Uh milk cow could git between us.' 'Don't you back talk *me*. How come you ain't movin'? Mah orders is five feet apart. . . . Heifer! Move dat chear 'way from dat boy!'" When her husband calls her down, she prays to God: "'Lawd You know it 'tain't right fuh boys and gals tuh be settin' on top one 'nother; and Lawd You know You said You'd strike disobedient chillen dead in dey tracks, and Lawd make mine humble and obedient, and tuh serve Thee and walk in Thy ways and please tuh make 'em set five feet apart'" (73–74). Her husband punctures this holy balloon quickly: "'Aw Emmeline, dat prayer uh yourn ain't got out de house; it's bumblin' 'round 'mong de rafters right now and dat's fur as it'll ever git'" (74).

The combination of awkward animal imagery with the genteel

rules of courtship, the use of exaggeration throughout ("settin' on top one 'nother"), and the revealing self-serving prayer that comically combines the cosmic with the trivial and personal get presented in an economical and effective way through Hurston's brilliant use of folk dialogue, punctuated by appropriate and consistent epithets ("Heifer!") and comic repetition ("five feet apart").

Nor does Emmeline relax her vigilance inside the house. Eagle-eyed and sharp-tongued, she seats herself in the parlor to stand watch, even after John has "kept company" with Lucy for a year. Yet when Mrs. Potts snatches a school slate from John's hand after he has sneaked a message on it in chalk, Hurston's comic sketching of the scene bears a poignant underlying portrait as well: "Emmeline's hand flew out like a cat's paw and grabbed the slate. She looked on both sides and saw no writing, then she opened it and looked hard at the message. . . . Emmeline couldn't read a word and she was afraid that no one would read it correctly for her, but one thing she was sure of, she could erase as well as the world's greatest professor" (72). Here we have a telling comment on Emmeline's impoverished past, but also a critique of her resistance to knowledge and creativity.

Mrs. Potts and Lucy have another quarrel about the maternal plan to marry Lucy to the older and prosperous Archie Mimms. This conversation, like others they have, constitutes a verbal duel that flies outside the normally permitted joking relationships between mothers and daughters and in itself offers evidence of Lucy's new maturity and the linguistic ability that signifies her worth. When Emmeline signifies on John as "'uh nigger dat ain't hardly got changin clothes. . . . He aint got uh chamber pot tuh his name nor uh bed tuh push it under,'" Lucy's countering caricature of Mimms prefigures Janie's reaction to Logan Killicks in *Their Eyes:* "'He is so ole, too. Ah looked at 'im good last big meetin'. His knees is sprung and his head is blossomin' fuh de grave. Ah don't want no ole spring-leg husband.'" When Emmeline mentions Mimms's mules, Lucy "caps" the conversation: "'Whut Ah keer how many mules he got paid fuh? Ah ain't speckin' tuh live wid no mules. You tryin' to kill me with talk. Don't keer whut yuh say. Ahm gointer marry John dis night, God bein' mah helper'" (77).

Also, this Mimms could possibly be either a crossracial relative or even the black son of the cruel former overseer mentioned in chapter 1, where Amy challenges Ned's plan to "sell" John to Mimms, thus establishing a parallelism between the appalling willingness of former slaves, Ned and Mrs. Potts, to imprison their children in reconstructed versions of slavery, indenture and marriage, respectively.

Emmeline, in her plans for her daughter and in her general inability to comprehend the true nature of freedom, obviously suggests Nanny, in *Their Eyes,* and in some ways receives a sympathetic presentation. In many aspects a comic figure, her rejection of knowledge and a new approach to the future makes her tragic. Embedded within the often comic mother-daughter duel, we find a profoundly serious dialogue over the merits of property, youth, security, and love, one that also represents the generation gap between those born in slavery and their progeny, born free. Furthermore, this mother-daughter sparring forms a female counterpart and parallel to the father-son discourse/duels between John and his stepfather, Ned. Finally, we also recognize that the sharp words exchanged here cut the bonds that must fall with the marriage ceremony in any case. As Hurston varies the image subsequently, "Her [Lucy's] family, her world that had been like a shell about her all her life was torn away and she felt cold and naked. The aisle seemed long, long! But it was like climbing up the stairs to glory" (79). Lucy gets a scene of initiation/rebirth equivalent to John's earlier ones, one with an ironic connection to Langston Hughes's magnificent poetic tribute to black motherhood, "Mother to Son," and its evocation of the life of black mothers as "no crystal stair." The reference to the "shell" around Lucy fits the pattern of female "egg" images repeatedly connected with her, in contrast with the snake/train metaphors used with John.

Earlier, in one of the most moving scenes in the book, John meets Lucy secretly and tries to secure a declaration of the love he knows she feels by asking her, "'Are you a flying lark or a setting dove?'" (75). Robert Hemenway's famous analysis of this scene concentrates on translating the folk codes and rituals embedded in what might seem to be a simple and straightforward presentation, demonstrating that John's question presents "a ritualistic opening to a courting formula that existed among slaves in the nineteenth century" ("Flying" 135). This tableau has its comic dimensions as well, which buttress the mechanisms noted by Hemenway. Lucy greets John at their tree by teasing: "'Ah see you fixin' tuh make soap. . . . Ah see yuh got yo' bones piled up.' She pointed to his crossed legs and they both laughed immoderately." Often, however, both of them find it impossible to verbalize the real text of their interests. John first finds recourse to a coded reference to an illness, a something that "'boils up lak syrup in de summer time.'" Eventually, unable to say what he wishes, he throws the burden on Lucy: "'You know whuss de matter wid me—but ack lak you dumb tuh de fack.' Lucy suddenly lost her fluency of speech" (75).

This embarrassing failure of language to cover pressing human needs finds its answer, as it does time and time again in Hurston's work, in the remedy of folk myth, speech, and narrative. "'Whut Ah wants tuh know is, which would you ruther be, if you had yo' ruthers—uh lark uh flyin', uh uh dove uh settin'?'" As Hemenway notes, this reference translates, but only if you know a setting dove represents a woman with a mate while the flying lark signifies one who is free ("Flying" 136). I would add that the "settin' dove" image extends the female "egg" imagery associated with Lucy and relates it to initiation. Further, it poignantly testifies to Leopold Sedar Senghor's observation: "Black voices, being undomesticated by the school, reveal all the nuances of ideas steeped in feeling; drawing freely from the unlimited dictionary of nature, they borrow her sonorous expressions, from the lucid songs of doves to the dark bursts of thunder" (cited in Okpewho 243).

Meanwhile, Lucy has been seeking release in the attempted tying of a lover's knot, another physical message drawn from the folk; her success steers the conversation forward, for doubly building on the metaphor of the knot, John proposes tying one with her that won't come undone till Judgment Day and appeals for her to "'look me in de eye Lucy. Kiss me and loose me so Ah kin talk'" (76), yet another reference to the knowledge theme associated with her.

Folk religion then becomes the text: "'Lucy, Ah looked up intuh Heben and Ah seen you among de angels right 'round de throne, and when Ah seen *you*, mah heart swole up and put wings on mah shoulders, and Ah 'gin tuh fly 'round too, but Ah never would uh knowed yo' name if ole Gab'ull hadn't uh whispered it tuh me'" (76).[20] Daryl Dance, in her anthology of contemporary black folklore, presents "I Raised Hell While I Was There," wherein a black man goes to Heaven and shows off his new wings by doing fancy and reckless flying, eventually upsetting the table, causing his ejection: "Well, they put me out, but HEY! HEY! I raised hell while I was there" (13–14). Although there are other variations on this story, Hurston likely had this one in mind, for the ultimate implications here parallel those of the more central Jonah myth; the exercise of inappropriate individual freedom may have serious consequences. John's reckless philandering dooms his "heavenly" relationship with Lucy, and eventually he overturns the "table" of their domestic harmony. One could argue, indeed, that his infidelity hastens and foreshadows her death, particularly after he slaps her. More significantly, as the shepherd of his pastoral flock, John's sins upset Christ's table of communion as well.

Significantly, John's earlier initiation at the creek recalls baptism, as befits his male and spiritual namesake, while Lucy's initiation rite seems specifically female (the egg imagery). From this point on, Lucy's maturity grows in paradoxical tandem with John's dependency; she becomes the "Church Mother" by in effect becoming his. This extends the initiation into knowledge theme that took a differing form in the courtship episodes.

Hurston does not conclude her presentation of courtship and marriage here. Mehaley, finally giving up on luring John from Lucy, accepts Pomp's offer of marriage. In the comic simplicity of his proposal to Mehaley, "'Whenever you needs somebody tuh do uh man's part Ah'll be 'round dere walkin' heavy over de floor'" (82), we see the antithesis of John and Lucy's complex courtship, and in Mehaley's folk marriage ceremony we are allowed what we were denied in terms of Lucy and John's bare-bones ceremony, namely the rituals and folk traditions connected with black rural weddings. Pomp's failure to show up keeps Mehaley, relatively unconcerned, in her work-clothes: "'Humph! Y'all think Ahm gwine put mah trunk on mah back and de tray on mah head, and dat man don't never come? Naw indeed! Ah ain't gwine tuh dress tuh marry no man 'til unless he be's in de house.'" And her comic unconcern finds a match in Duke, who offers, "'He jus' keepin' colored folks time. When white folks say eight o'clock dey mean eight o'clock. When uh colored person say eight o'clock, dat jes' mean uh hour ago. He'll be heah in plenty time'" (82). This scene has a serious component, however, for as Mehaley suggests, the time appears less important than the event. The African predisposition to natural rather than artificial time receives expression here. As Daniel and Smitherman state, "What matters is not the exact, abstract time of the month or day, but one's participation in a wedding or harvest during a given period of the year or season. Being on time has to do with participating in the fulfillment of an activity that is vital to the sustenance of a basic rhythm, rather than with appearing on the scene at, say, 'twelve o'clock sharp.' The key is not to be 'on time' but 'in time,'" and Pomp and Mehaley seem to understand this (32).

When the groom appears at nine, late because he had to borrow wedding clothes, the parallelism with John and Lucy continues with a quarrel between Mehaley's parents as to who will perform the ceremony, her father or the minister summoned by her mother. "'Ah don't keer if you *is* her pappy,' the mother stated, 'you ain't nothin' but uh stump-knocker and Ah wants dis done real. Youse standin' in uh sho 'nuff preacher's light. G'wan set down and leave Elder Wheeler hitch 'em right. You can't read, no-how. . . . If us wuz down in de swamp whar us couldn't git no preacher, you'd do, but here de pastor is. You ain't nothin' but uh jack-leg. Go set in de chimbley corner and be quiet'" (83). The argument, based in class, yet admits exceptions and once again contains the poignant reminder of the widespread illiteracy of this generation, born in slavery, underlined by the father's stubborn assertion, "'Dis de fust one uh mah chillun tuh jump over de broomstick and Ah means tuh tie de knot mah own self,'" and he does. Comically, the preacher and the father argue so long, however, that Pomp has taken off his painful borrowed shoes. He tells Mehaley, "'Now Ah can't git 'em back on. Dat don't make uh bit uh diff'rence. You goin' tuh see mah bare foots uh whole head after dis'" (83), a gently disguised sexual joke. The father pompously holds an almanac taken off the wall in front of him as he conducts the service, pretending he knows how to read. After the ceremony, unknown voices urge Pomp to "'bus' her rat in de mouf'" (84), and women and men take the bride and groom off separately for ritual washing.

This comic tableau tends to suggest Hurston working the classical mode of pairing a "royal couple" with a "peasant couple," even though, as we know, all four lovers are from the folk. As in Shakespeare's comedies, particularly *Twelfth Night,* with its rustic lovers in counterpoint to the pair more nobly born, John and Lucy stand higher because of their education, but also Lucy's pedigree, since her family members are termed "Big Niggers." As Nella Larsen's Helga Crane ruefully reflects in *Quicksand,* "Negro society . . . was as complicated and as rigid in its ramifications as the highest strata of white society. If you couldn't prove your ancestry and connections, you were tolerated, but you didn't 'belong'" (8). The fact that the Pottses, while well-off, are several social levels below Helga, makes Emmeline's pretentions even more absurd. Still, the Pottses obviously stand in contrast to Mehaley and her family circle.

At the same time, Hurston typically refuses to leave these figures as stereotypes; that night Mehaley gets out of bed for snuff and breaks into heartbroken sobs to find the women who washed her got suds into the snuff box, obviously a situation that emblematizes her broken dream of John, the real cause of her tears.

Male Humor, the Power of Language, and the Training of the Man of Words

The oedipal struggle of John and his foster father comes to a climax in physical and verbal fashion, a deadly serious duel, one nonetheless structured and punctuated by comic modes of speaking and maneuvering. The crux of the matter seems to be illiterate Ned's displeasure over his hated stepson's acquiring power through language by learning to read and write. John's other paternal figure, Pearson, offers another reading of "gittin' biggety"; he takes vicarious pride in John's sexual appeal and appetites, seeing a repetition of his own fondly remembered youthful womanizing, and no doubt a contrast to his white son, who is "studying" in Paris.

After warning John from courting Duke's wife, Exie, Pearson seems hugely amused to learn that she in fact has been pursuing John. "'Get along you rascal you! You're a walking orgasm. A living exultation.' 'Whut's dat, Mist' Alf?' 'Oh never mind about that. Keep up with the pigs'" (50). Although Alf does not mean it that way, Hurston surely slips in an ironic author-reader joke here, as we see all too clearly that Pearson, for all his pride in John, looks at him essentially as less than a man, as a "stud"—and his sexual exploits do little more than enable him to "keep up with the pigs" and the other animals in gargantuan sexual appetite. As in Rabelais and comic writers before and after him, excessive appetite will always have a comic perspective. Still, he tells John, "'Don't steal and don't get too biggety and you'll get along'" (42). We note, as well, that "beget" is embedded in "biggety," giving it a punning and sexual dimension, one in keeping with what proves to be John's fatal flaw.

When John goes home for a visit, Amy cries with joy and pride to learn he can read and resolves that all her children will win this prize as well. But after this resolution she is confronted by Ned again, who like Huck's Papp Finn rails against book larnin': "'Whut fur? So dey kin lay in de peni'ten'ry? Dat's all dese book-learnt niggers do—fill up de jails and chain-gangs. . . . All dey need tuh learn is how tuh swing uh hoe and turn a furrer. Ah ain't rubbed de hair offa mah haid 'gin no college walls and Ah got good sense. Day ain't goin' tuh no school effen Ah got anythin' tuh say 'bout it. Jes' be turnin' 'em fools!'" (28). He of course repeats Papp's error of revealing his own ignorance, becoming a character who causes ironic smugness in the author-reader relationship. On a deeper level, however, we might agree with him, for the "uppity" black did indeed frequently wind up on the chain gang or lynched.

Interestingly, Ned, in a variation of Pearson's warning, accuses John of getting "powerful biggety" since he's been on the Pearson place. Ned assumes sexual maturity has played a role in John's insolence, which clearly adds to the oedipal equation. He complains to Amy that John "'must smell hisself—done got so mannish. Some fast 'omanish gal is grinnin' in his face and he tries tuh git sides hisself'" (45). The humor of his complaint comes from the folk expression for puberty (or sometimes, mere precocity), both male and female ("smell hisself," "mannish," and "actin' 'omanish"). Ned's greatest objection, however, seems to be to book learning, rather than sexual knowledge.

A demonstration of the correctness of Ned's perception that an expanded knowledge of words equals power emerges when John seeks oedipal release in the abusive linguistic conventions of black speech. Rebelling on the sly, he comically signifies on his stepfather, abusing a burnt-off trunk of a tree as surrogate:[21]

> "And you, you ole battle-hammed, slew-foot, box-ankled nubbin, you! You ain't nothin' and ain't got nothin' but whut God give uh billy-goat, and then round tryin' tuh hell-hack folks! Tryin' tuh kill somebody wid talk, but if you wants tuh fight,—dat's de very corn Ah wants tuh grind. You come grab me now and Ah be yuh Ah'll stop *you* from suckin' eggs. Hit me now! G'wan hit me! Bet Ah'll break uh egg in yuh! Youse all parts of uh pig! You done got me jus' ez hot ez July jam, and Ah ain't got no mo' use fuh yuh than Ah is for mah baby shirt. Youse mah race but you sho ain't mah taste. Jus' you break uh breath wid me, and Ahm goin' tuh be jus' too chastisin'. Ah'm just lak uh old shoe—soft when yuh rain on me and cool me off, and hard when yuh shine on me and git me hot. Tuh keep from killin' uh sorry somethin' like yuh, Ahm goin' way from heah. Ahm goin' tuh Zar, and dat's on de other side of far, and when you see me agin Ahm gointer be somebody. Mah li'l finger will be bigger than yo' waist. Don't you part yo' lips tuh me no mo' jes' ez long ez heben is happy—do Ah'll put somethin' on yuh dat lye soap won't take off. You ain't nothin' but uh big ole pan of fell bread. Now dat's de word wid de bark on it." (47)

This rich assembly of folk epithets offers evidence of the wide-ranging directions of classic signification (especially bestial references) and utilizes metaphors drawn from the domestic realm. Ominously, in terms of future events, John equates pigs, women, and children in an effort to feminize and thus symbolically castrate the father figure. Indeed, John verbalizes his desire to *kill* the father, thus expanding the more innocent claim that he has no more need for a baby shirt into parricide.

The threat "Ah'll put somethin' on yuh dat lye soap won't take off" returns us to Ned's early claim that John represents a stain that won't wash clean. His continuing rejection, however, finds more than a match in John's final "signification" on him; "Youse mah race but you sho ain't mah taste," a common enough expression, here points significantly to Ned's apparent blackness in skin only, for he has bought into the patterns of patriarchal oppression.

In setting this comic peroration after Ned's musings on language and education, is Hurston saying that book learning can strengthen verbal ability in folk speech as well? John's "signifying" may be a masterpiece in idiomatic vernacular, but he never speaks this well, this confidently, or this creatively before his school days. Still, his words here, however masterfully orchestrated, belong exclusively to the folk tradition. In any case, the reflections in this section of both John's fathers on his growing powers deepen the book's concerns with patriarchy, coming of age, and the oedipal struggle; further illustrate the meaning of the original title; and are of a piece with the overall themes of knowledge, sexuality, and power.

Meanwhile, the supposedly world-wise "'omanish" creature Ned correctly imagines John loves, Lucy, sends creative love notes, sent from "Sweet Notasulga, Chocklit Alabama Date of kisses, month of love," that say things such as "Sugar is sweet, and lard is greasy, you love me, don't be uneasy" (45), hardly the words of a femme fatale. For John, however, she combines the power of sexuality and the power of language and knowledge.

At the other pole of male humor, we find John a man among men, linguistically speaking, in a number of situations. Before his marriage, John's initial appearance in a tie-camp where he seeks work causes alarm, for the men are gaming and think he's white, a "buckra" (59). Once again, John's first contact with a key group begins in laughter: "'Ha, ha! Y'all thought Ah wuz white, didn't yuh?'" (59). Here and elsewhere in her work, Hurston demonstrates how humor can provide access to a group, particularly of workers. Mahadev Apte has pointed to the way joking relationships are used to initiate new members into work groups; conversely, carrying on joking without including the newcomer constitutes ostracism. Thus joking relationships and joking may serve to screen prospective members of groups and to maintain or redefine boundaries (Apte 55).

And in fact, after John's initial joking, "everyone laughed except Coon Tyler," who proves to be hostile to John's inclusion. The men say not to mind Coon, that he's just "funnin'," which makes Coon even madder: "'Y'all know Ah don't joke and Ah don't stand no jokin'. 'Tain't nothin' in de drug store'll kill yuh quick ez me'" (60). Obviously, Coon does practice humor, but an ugly, aggressive sort, one that operates against the idea of community, unlike John's. His variant of sounding, or verbal insult, includes traditional components, such as provocation, goading, and taunting, but lacks any pleasurable element, and indeed, ends in violence.

Coon's name suggests Hurston was signifying on the Coon Song craze, where stereotypical comic images of blacks were proffered in vaudeville skits, frequently written and performed by black performers such as Bert Williams and George Walker, sometimes in blackface. An obverse image of the basic grinning darkie stereotype was the "toughest," "meanest," or "bully" coon, a stereotyped image that had much in common with the "bad nigger" figure. The 1904 song "I'm the Toughest, Toughest Coon" included the lyrics,

> I'm the toughest, toughest coon that walks the street;
> You may search the wide, wide world, my equal never meet;
> I got a razor in my boot, I got a gun with which to shoot,
> I'm the toughest, toughest coon that walks the street.
> (Dormon, "Shaping" 461)

Ignoring Coon, John quickly acquires two guides; one, an old man named Ezeriah Hill, provides needed advice, despite the fact that he's known by "de lady people" as Uncle Dump. Perhaps Hurston offers a joke here; "dumped" by the women, and thus free of the entanglements of sex, he's become wise. In any case, Uncle Dump becomes yet another father figure for John, a mentor much like Moses' Mentu in Hurston's later novel. The other guide, a younger man, complements and yet paradoxically and humorously contradicts Uncle Dump. Called Do-Dirty "because of his supposed popularity with and his double-crossing of women," he teaches John lessons in town vice (60). We see here and in a similar camp in Florida how this backwoods world of men gives John linguistic training in the two realms of his future life, womanizing and preaching, as he also learns to "mark" preachers during this time. He thus learns to "talk sweet" like the minister, using decorum and formality; to "talk broad" like the male workers, employing joking and license; and presumably, to "talk bad," or obscenely, about women and sexuality, an activity Hurston can only suggest because of the censorship of her day.[22]

In a prefiguration of Tea Cake in *Their Eyes*, John quickly becomes the favorite of the camp, partly because of his athletic abilities, but also for his gift for "telling lies" (stories), another example of how verbal ability equals power. He also wins respect with his first fight, occasioned when Coon steals the bread John had cooked for his visiting brother Zeke. Although John's "funnin'" with the men has truly been in fun, Coon's laugh now constitutes what Moses will call an "ugly laugh." "'Ah et yo' damn bread. Don't you lak it, don't yuh take it, heah mah collar, come and shake it,'" offering a male-versus-male use of a slave-days taunt that Amy used earlier in the book against Ned. In yet another indication that words can yield power, the narrator tells us John's courage has been heightened by a message from Lucy, and he expresses it comically: "'Nex' time he fool wid me, Ah bet Ah'll try mah bes' tuh salivate 'im. He try tuh be uh tush hawg—puttin' out his brags everywhere'" (63), and indeed, the verbal sparring, which the term "salivate" suggests, eventually leads to John's thrashing of Coon.

Later, after John's marital infidelities have forced him to leave Alabama (and for a time, Lucy and his family), his job on a Florida railroad crew parallels this earlier passage and also allows Hurston to effortlessly insert her research on the folk culture of railroad camps that forms such a key part of *Mules and Men,* including the work songs. Spiking has a submerged sexual joke, for as the men drive the spikes home they sing a song that calls their wives' names.

Hurston also initiates us and John to the world of marking and his subsequent career as a preacher at the railroad camp, when he mimicks the sermon of a preacher for the men. "'You kin marks folks,'" said Blue. "'Dass jes' lak dat preacher fuh de world. Pity you ain't preachin' yo'self,'" which leads to the suggestion that John go to the newly formed all-black town nearby to observe and then mark the eccentric Methodist preacher there (107).

This picture of John developing his pulpit style complements the earlier comic scenes portraying him and Lucy as lovestruck choir members. A character comments on Lucy's extraordinary musicality (akin to her verbal gifts) saying she "'kin sing all de notes—de square ones, de round ones, de triangles'" (27), providing a wonderfully amusing illustration of what Hurston called the race's tendency to think hieroglyphically.[23] More importantly, however, the choir practice presents Hurston with a comic opportunity as she describes the various voices in conflict with each other, finally narrowing it down to Lucy as a hunter and her brother Bud as her prey: "Bud growled away in the bass but Lucy treed him and held him growling in discomfiture out upon a limb until the end of the piece cut him down" (53). Extending the metaphors, John owns the most successful bass voice, and Lucy exercises the winning treble. In their marriage, the high notes will mostly be hers, while the low ones come from him. Both, however, want to lead.

Hurston also employs the singing sessions as prophecy. In a scene significantly set at the school closing ceremonies, John and Lucy sing a comic duet: "It was the gestures that counted and everybody agreed that John was perfect as the philandering soldier of the piece and that Lucy was just right as the over-eager maid. They had to sing it over twice" (37). These are their fated roles, and they will indeed be repetitive.

Most importantly, however, for John's later role in the pulpit, his singing ability is established; "John began to have a place of his own in the minds of folks, more than he realized" (37). African American preachers are deemed superior when they are masters of all aspects of their calling, and a good singing voice and the ability to use it in sermons constitute valuable commodities, especially in Baptist denominations.[24] Indeed, many successful ministers have singing careers as well (Rosenberg 63).

Thus John's involvement with the poetry of the sermon mode begins in parody, in a folk setting, the comic realm of self-expression that shapes his daily intercourse with others, inaugurating John as what Roger Abrahams calls "the man of words," whose performances are "typified by his willingness to entertain and instruct anywhere and anytime" but who also attempts to "amuse and dazzle" ("Rapping" 135).[25] Hurston, too, in a contrasting way, discussed the creative aspects of black speech, linking the man on the street and the preacher, in "Characteristics of Negro Expression." This important essay, which appeared in the same year as *Jonah*, features Hurston's comments on the way "every phase of Negro life is highly dramatized" and "acted out"; "No little moment passes unadorned." Applying all of this to the black sermon, the preacher creates "prose poetry. The supplication is forgotten in the frenzy of creation. The beauty of the Old Testament does not exceed that of a Negro prayer" (41). These patterns are made possible by an innate gift for mimicry, which accepts the basics of English; everything becomes transformed, however, as the black speaker makes it *his* tongue through creative embellishment, which frequently involves the key traits of angularity and asymmetry. Hurston, however, carefully forestalls an interpretation of "mimicry" into "monkey see, monkey do"; no, it is "an art in itself. If it is not, then all art must fall by the same blow that strikes it down" (43).

Obviously, all these "characteristics" apply to John, who by these terms, as both a "man of words" in the secular realm and a "poetic preacher," operates as a consummate artist. And indeed, that artistic aspect feeds into his other self, the lover, for as Hurston adds, "Love-making and fighting in all their branches are high arts" ("Characteristics" 44).

As the book develops, John's performative utterances divide into these two streams, both profoundly poetic—the humorous expression of everyday life and serious poetics of the pulpit, modes of address that become emblematic of his fractured soul. As a vessel of God periodically touched with divine afflatus, John refers backward to the heroic, often illiterate slave preachers, who found a way to sustain and support their people even as suspicious masters listened in to make sure the "servants, obey your masters" line was privileged. Intent on conversion, the primary goal of evangelical Protestantism, he perforce occupies himself in a kind of leveling—and indeed, the oft-vaunted African American devotion to religion must be partially linked to this impulse, which was in some ways even more marked in slave days, when black ministers could sometimes become heads of mixed or even predominately white churches, and when acceptance of the white religion also obviously meant a level field for sinners, regardless of color.[26] Leveling sermons of course find their public counterpart in John's proficiency in leveling humor, a staple of the African American tradition; "God and the Devil are paired, and are treated no more reverently than Rockefeller and Ford. . . . They talk and act like good-natured stevedores or mill-hands" ("Characteristics" 42). John Pearson in this regard resembles the heroic human trickster Jack, aka High John de Conquer, who tricks everyone, even God, with his cunning humor.

We may take the meaning of John's parallel talents further; his role in the public realm bifurcates when he runs for mayor, using male humor to make his "big voice" heard politically with the choral group of men communed on Joe Clarke's porch. John's puffed-up pride leads him to declare for the office right to the face of the incumbent, Sam Mosely, in an extended verbal duel.[27] "'You and Clarke ain't had nobody tuh run against, but dis time big Moose done come down from de mountain. Ahm goin' tuh run you so hard 'til they can't tell yo' run-down shoe from yo' wore out sock.'" Joe Clarke comments on the rivalry implicit in even the best of male friendships, like this one: "'I God . . . Ah never seen two sworn buddies dat tries tuh out do on 'nother lak y'all do. You so think 'til one can't turn 'thout de other one, yet and still you always buckin' 'ginst each other'" (113), a sexuality-as-power theme that dominates *Mule Bone* as well, where the best friends Jim and Dave duel linguistically and musically over the affections of Daisy.

Characteristically, the post-election analysis on the porch mixes humor, biblical legend, and practical lore. Walter Thomas, explaining Sam's loss to John, says, "'Yo' morals is clean ez uh fish—and he been in bathin' all his life, but youse too dry fuh de mayor business. Jes' lak it 'twuz wid Saul and David'" (114), thus doubling our original biblical typology that presented the New Testament anti-type of John the Baptist. The Old Testament type for John now becomes David, a man who was king, but one who was corrupted by womanizing, in particular with Bathsheba.[28] And we note as well that the comic explanation once again presents us with the theme of sin/washing/ purification, which prepares us for some expected news. For of course John's travels across the state to preach at revivals place sexual temptation before him, and he falls yet again.

These scenes and others, however, show John maturing his various voices. The two public realms would interact in any case, for his overall performance as a preacher depends not only on his relatively formal rhetorical ability in the pulpit but also on his corresponding creativity, freely mixed with folk expression, in daily conversation with his parishioners. Here the humor largely missing from sermons is a necessary and, indeed, expected ingredient. Proficiency in humorous folk idiom, which would be known as slang in an urban setting, gives the communal leader a constant sense, as Abrahams puts it, of "newness, vitality, and pleasurable aggressiveness" ("Rapping" 139), factors naturally associated with sexual identity as well.

John's life after Lucy's death declines sadly; her ability to help him channel his "natchul" energies into his sermons has gone with her, but his friend, Deacon Hambo, stoutly supports him at every juncture. This bluff widower employs his camaraderie and skill at signifying to make John do right and to steer him away from temptation, as when Hambo comes with other men to criticize Hattie's evil ways, or when, at the end of the book, he describes another siren, Ora Patton: "'Jes' ez fresh ez dishwater. . . . She's after yo' money. . . . I seen her pass here eve'y few minutes—switchin' it and lookin' back at it. . . . Her egg-bag ain't gonna rest easy 'til she git nex' tuh yuh. . . . Ah wouldn't give uh bitch uh bone if she treed uh terrapin'" (196). If you read Hambo, as some readers might, as replacing Lucy, in the traditional American literary tradition of comrades being more supportive than women, he fails to measure up to her standard; for John chooses to walk away from his church after his disastrous years with his new wife, Hattie, lead to public recriminations and disgrace.

Hattie, however, clearly sees Hambo as a rival for John's allegiance. She marvels that John lets his friend chide him so vividly: "'Thought you tole me dat Hambo wuz yo' bosom friend?' 'He is, Hattie. Ah don't pay his rough talk no mind'" (139). And indeed, when John quietly leaves Hambo's house after a brief visit back to Eatonville without saying good-bye but leaving ten dollars and some new night-shirts as gifts, Hambo's true nature is revealed, first in comic invective but then in human gestures that speak to Hurston's ability to portray male friendship: "'Well de hen-fired son-of-a-gun done slipped off and never tole me good bye again! Bet de wop-sided, holler-headed—thought Ah wuz gointer cry, but he's uh slew-footed liar!' Whereupon Hambo cried over the stove as he fried his sow-bosom and made a flour hoe-cake. Then he found he couldn't eat. Frog in his throat or something so that even his coffee choked him" (200).

Hambo enjoys a special joking relationship with John; his "rough talk" is characteristic of the playful insults of male contemporaries, one based on the personal friendship and cordiality of the two "pals." In Africa, among peoples such as the Gusii of Kenya, such men likely underwent ritual initiation together, and in fact are expected to insult each other. A Gusii expression goes "Those who abuse one another and are not angry are those who love one another" (Mayer 34). In Hurston's novel, Hambo's generational link to John combines with the brotherhood of the church and its extended community to form a similar bond.

Marriage as Sorrow's Kitchen

Hurston recorded the story in *Mules* of how man and woman, as equals, were always fighting to draws until God granted man extra strength. Woman, on the advice of the Devil, asks God for three keys he has near him, which the Devil shows her are those to the kitchen, the bedroom, and the cradle. As the teller, Mathilda, comments, "'You men is still braggin' 'bout yo' strength and de women is sittin' on de keys and lettin' you blow off till she git ready to put de bridle on you'" (33–38).[29] We note how the conflict between John and Lucy after they move to Florida elaborates on this theme and also rehearses the marital tragicomedy of *Their Eyes; Jonah*, however, focuses on language's important role in establishing male predominance in marriage, as John's lies grow bolder and more numerous. Lucy's goodness seems to prevent her from truly signifying on John, although she gets enough licks in to make him mad enough to slap her on her deathbed. Still, he doesn't really win; he just pretends to himself that he does.

It would be hard to deny Lucy a spiritual victory in this duel of wills, in any case, for as her name, which means "light" suggests, she becomes linked throughout the book with the church. The forgiveness of the congregation John serves clearly parallels and magnifies Lucy's tolerance; Lucy and the church become virtually interchangeable.

The first years of their marriage, spent in Alabama, pass by in one sentence, with the casual announcement by Hurston of the birth of their third child. But John hasn't changed, and we learn this from Alf Pearson, who now takes on the role of the watchful god Lucy frequently calls on: "'Well, John, you'd better keep Big 'Oman out of that Commissary after dark. Aha! You didn't think I knew, did you? Well, I know a lot of things that would surprise folks. You better clean yourself up.' . . . The hand of John's heart reached out and clutched on fear. Alf Pearson returned to work, chuckling. Two days later Big 'Oman was gone" (85). "Big 'Oman" appearing in the commissary suggests the generic nature of John's concept of all women except Lucy. They're commodities casually taken off the shelf of life to be used as needed. In his reaction to this liaison, Pearson takes on the role of not only an all-seeing and punitive god but a rather indifferent one who finds amusement in the foibles of one of his "creatures," this time his own son. His detached observation of John's rise and fall could be seen as Hurston's devilish signification on God's treatment of Christ. Whether John fears Lucy's finding out or more severe displeasure on Pearson's part or both we aren't told, but in their secular-patriarchal and spiritual-matriarchal functions in his life, they in any case form a sort of parental couple.

This relatively comic scene with Pearson sets the stage for a more dramatic "act of God" when John, returning home from an assignation with Big 'Oman, tries to cross a flooded river and is knocked unconscious when the bridge is struck by one of the logs afloat in a river "full of water and red as judgment" (86). The cosmic scene strongly recalls the trial by water episode in Faulkner's *As I Lay Dying* (1930); in another passage in that novel, Reverend Whitfield significantly muddies himself from the waist down, as he fords a dangerously swollen river while simultaneously thinking about his adultery with Addie. More importantly, Hurston here extends the "washing" references to a near-fatal baptism into repentance that merges quite obviously with the catastrophic, and almost final, purgation of flood. The scene begs to be read in conjunction with John's eventual and fatal encounter with a train as well. In terms of plot, it precipitates John's emergence as an expert at prayer, for he offers an eloquent thanksgiving for deliverance at church and thereby gains the notice of the deacons. This quite serious moment deepens our sense of John's later "calling," which at first seems suspect.

The intensity of the pattern of rising repentance and crashing fall back into sin soon takes on a new configuration. John hangs out at jooks with a woman named Delphine when Lucy struggles to give birth to their fourth child, neglecting his family to the point that they have no money or food. Her brother tells Lucy folks think John will leave her this time and that Delphine is "'strowing 'it herself all over Macon County and laffin' at yuh'" (90), alerting us to the "ugly laugh" of public ridicule that John's affairs cause for his family. John's absence here fits a recurring pattern, his habit of running away from his problems, typified by his flight to the arms of another woman when his favorite daughter, Isis, seems to be dying. Hurston employs devastating understatement to render her verdict: "When he returned a week later and found his daughter feebly recovering, he was glad. He bought Lucy a new dress and a pineapple" (117). Although Isis plays a small role in this book, we should note that Zora's double creates a sly bit of revenge on Hurston's sister Sarah, who was actually her father's decided favorite (see *Dust Tracks* 98–99).

Hurston's sympathies frequently lie with John in the first part of the book, but here, in the middle portion, until Lucy dies, they are with her. Lucy, taking John's infidelities to God, begs eloquently, but not without a touch of comic pluck: "'Lawd lemme quit feedin' on heart meat lak Ah do. Dis baby [Isis] goin' tuh be too fractious tuh live. . . . Lawd, if Ah meet dat woman [Hattie] in heben, you got tuh gimme time tuh fight uh while. Jus' ruin dis baby's temper 'fo' it git tuh dis world. 'Tain't mah fault, Lawd, Ahm jus' ez clean ez yo' robes'" (114).

John's affairs always result in his repentance, and Lucy typically signifies her forgiveness, after her painful delivery of Isis, by joking. John, expressing his pride in his first daughter, declares, "'Dis chile it almost big as her [Lucy]. She so little Ah hafta shake de sheets tuh find her in de bed.' She slapped him feebly. 'Ain't you got no better sense dan tuh set in uh man's lap and box his jaws? He's liable tuh let yuh fall thru his legs'" (93). Ultimately, however, John cannot abide this mother love; Martha in Edward Albee's *Who's Afraid of Virginia Woolf*—also a tragedy in comic form—similarly indicts the husband she loves for forgiving her: "'Whom I will not forgive for . . . having seen me and having said: yes; this will do; who has made the hideous, the hurting, the insulting mistake of loving me and must be punished for it'" (191). Apparently, forgiveness may not be forgiven. If we understand that forgiveness inevitably gives the person bestowing it power, we may understand John's ultimate resentment of it better.

Hurston does not neglect to show John's ironic double standard regarding infidelity. After men in Eatonville kid around about taking Lucy from him, he will not permit any joking about the matter from Lucy; when she teases, "'If you tired uh me, jus' leave me. Another man over de fence waitin fuh yo' job,'" John, who has his gun with him, lays down the law: "'Lemme tell you somethin' right now, and it ain't two, don't you never tell me no mo' whut you jus tole me, 'cause if you do, Ahm gon' tuh kill yuh jes' ez sho ez gun is iron'" (110). This rather appalling act of dominance and hypocrisy nevertheless stems from his deep love for Lucy and has sources in the community's double standard of sexuality. The other men's admiration of her has to be on his mind too. He rethinks his life and announces he's been called to preach by God. This "call" links up with his earlier "marking" of preachers he had heard and makes us believe that John's "call" has come from personal necessity rather than from God. And in fact, Hurston quotes men who tell jokes about bogus calls in *Mules and Men,* including one tale where a man receives "the call" from a mule (22–24).[30]

But the people, it seems, view John as God's instrument. In a few sentences, we see Reverend Pearson's swift rise through a number of churches, each larger than the next. Lucy increasingly becomes his counsel, as when she introduces the original title of the book: "'Jus' you handle yo' members right and youse goin' tuh be uh sho 'nuff big nigger'" (112). Although Lucy probably doesn't realize it, the punning joke is that if John restrains *his* member he'll be able to maintain his success.

Lucy's wisdom bears the mark of authenticity because of the folk language that frames it and the modes of authority she embeds within it. Warning John of pampering the deacons, she says,

> "Much up de young folks and you got somebody tuh strain wid dem ole rams when dey git dey habits on. You lissen tuh me. Ah hauled de mud tuh make ole Cuffy. Ah know whuts in 'im. Don't syndicate wid none of 'em, do dey'll put yo' business in de street. . . . Friend wid few. Everybody grin in yo' face don't love yuh. Anybody kin look and see and tell uh snake trail when dey come cross it but nobody kin tell which way he wuz goin' lessen he seen de snake. You keep outa sight, and in dat way, you won't give nobody uh stick tuh crack yo' head wid." (112)

The passage demonstrates humor's warmth and power for good but also warns against its use by enemies, thereby commenting on laughter's power and ambivalent use in folk culture. It also underlines the competitive verbal element—John as the "young ram" butting heads/ tongues with the elders.

The young ram, we note, also wars with his elders primarily for sexual access to the ewes. The animal imagery shifts in the references to snakes, perhaps an accommodation to the fact that John can't control his sexuality but he can surely hide it. In the parallel to the Edenic relationship of God, Adam, and the snake, Lucy emerges as the deity.

Most importantly, however, the passage shows us, and perhaps John too, that in many ways, except for her sex, the most likely candidate for the pulpit is Lucy, both in terms of spiritual sincerity and everyday wit and shrewdness. Her verbal ability as a schoolgirl receives prominent mention. In fact, a few critics have nominated Lucy as Hurston's real interest in the novel, but this would seem to ignore the facts of the novel's sources, the circumstances of its composition, and the simple point that John dominates virtually every page, while Lucy dies well before the conclusion.[31] Still, in her potential for the pulpit we can easily relate her to the woman preacher Baby Suggs in Toni Morrison's *Beloved,* who urges her parishioners to "love your heart. For this is the prize" (89). But despite his sex, John actually has more in common than Lucy does with Baby Suggs as preacher, for both are clearly filled with God's presence, becoming rhetorical instruments for the divine afflatus, something Hurston never suggests Lucy has. A parallel situation develops in Hurston's *Moses,* where the title figure and his sister Miriam are both hoodoo doctors; only males, however, may speak for God and actually lead the people. In both novels, Hurston's linkage of male sexual potency and power with effective preaching, while hardly palatable with contemporary concepts of female preaching, cannot be ignored.

We also remember that Lucy mothers many children whose father displays little interest in them. For that matter, however, neither does their authorial creator; Hurston in this regard closely resembles her Harlem Renaissance contemporary Nella Larsen. In her *Quicksand,* the central figure Helga Crane, like Lucy, winds up married to a rural southern preacher and saddled with a houseful of children. In neither case do the childless authors give the children any real roles to play; indeed, Larsen doesn't even name them. Both books, however, demonstrate that the maternal role frequently subtracts substantially from a woman's potential for creative expression, in life and in everyday utterance.

Finally, while there can be no doubt about Lucy's goodness and saintlike power, and her desperate external maneuvering to keep John on track and her family functioning, we find no *internal* struggle in her character; the narrative interest, what Faulkner called "the human heart in conflict with itself," lies in John. A woman does stand at the center of the book and between the lines lies a woman who manipulates her male surrogate and appropriates his voice—Hurston herself.

Still we agree with the men who collectively tease John, agreeing with Mosely that he's a "'wife-made man. . . . If me and him wuz tuh swap wives Ah'd go past 'im so fast you'd think it wuz de A.C.L. [the Atlantic Coast Line Railroad] passin' uh gopher'" (113).

When a terminally ill Lucy confronts John with his affair with Hattie, he rails against lying folks "'so expert on mindin' folks business dat dey kin look at de smoke comin' out yo' chimbley and tell yuh whut yuh cookin','" he uses humor as a shield and a diversion, but ironically harks back to the real chimney where he carved his undying love for Lucy. Our admiration for her increases when she provides her wrong-doer with good advice as to how to wriggle free of the closing accusations: "'Don't you go 'round dat church mealy-moufin 'round dem deacons and nobody else. Don't you break uh breath on de subjick. Face 'em out, and if dey wants tuh handle yuh in conference, go dere totin' uh high head and Ah'll be right dere 'long side of yuh'" (120).

After John heads off rebellion at a church committee meeting, things look better,[32] but Lucy knows John's enemies have not given up; she advises him to discard the traditional Passover supper/communion sermon in favor of a self-condemning piece that nevertheless recounts his good acts. And indeed John preaches a brilliant sermon that reminds his flock that he is just a simple man who functions as the Lord's mouthpiece, one with seven "younguns" at home, which testifies to the fact that he's a "natchel" man. This subtle approach situates the children as visible and acceptable signs of his sexual appetite, which he knows preys on his parishioners' minds, but with more negative manifestations. His appeal to the parishioners as his "children in Christ" links them with his "natchel younguns" too, in one family. Saying he doesn't always remember things, he appears to compliment them on their memories as they sit on their porches "passin' nations thew yo' mouf" along with him, asking them to try to remember his good deeds over the years. In powerful language, he admits his hands may not be worthy any longer (the cleanliness theme again) to serve communion, and he shuts the book and makes to step down, but "strong hands were there to thrust him back. The church surged up, a weeping wave about him. Deacons Hambo and Harris were the first to lay hands upon him. . . . He was roughly, lovingly forced back into his throne-like seat" (123). Hurston's magnificent, cosmic writing in this scene makes us feel the power of John's presence and his link to holy passion and ritual. And in moments like this, notably devoid of humor, Hurston forces us to consider the role of the instrument of God; is a flawed servant perhaps more effective than one wholly clean? The biblical Jonah was such a man; conversely, Lucy, should she mount the pulpit, would certainly be "clean." Do the ends (spiritual elevation and salvation of the parishioners) justify the means (the "unclean" agent)?

Hurston brilliantly juxtaposes this powerfully ceremonial climax, ending in the "ritual sacrifice of a God" rather than that of the minister, with a following chapter, where we accompany Lucy's chief rival Hattie on a visit to a conjure woman. In her ominous and eerily described "hut," An' Dangie takes Hattie's money and gives her a charm and a recipe for a magical procedure, promising to keep "de bitter bone" in her mouth to protect Hattie as she works the spell. In the scene's remarkably dramatic conclusion, which bears resemblance to several in *Mules* and *Tell My Horse*, we see the old woman creep to the altar, where she dresses candles with war water and the coffin in red, saying, "'Now fight! Fight and fuss 'til you part.' When all was done at the altar she rubbed her hands and forehead with war powder, put the catbone in her mouth, and laid herself down in the red coffin facing the altar and went into the spirit" (126).

As readers attendant at both these "services," our natural question becomes, "Whose God is stronger?" This portion of the book becomes more gripping after reading Hurston's 1925 unpublished story "Black Death," wherein the narrator tells of the bloody flux that Old Man Morgan, the conjurer, placed on Lucy Potts, suggesting as this novel does that Hurston believed her mother's death was preceded and perhaps precipitated by hoodoo practices.

The next scene offers the most painful moment in the book. Lucy, lying dying of consumption, has to rouse herself to chide John, so careless now that he leaves letters from Hattie around for the children to read. He accuses her of being a "hold-back," a whiner, and a complainer, and finally slaps her, an act that seems worse than all his secret philandering.[33] The scene offers a repetition of an earlier one, when Lucy's own brother took the bed from under her as she lay ill. John's consistent betrayal of his bride, whose name means light itself, runs parallel to his betrayal of his church, for as Christ the bridegroom marries the church, so must the preacher. Lucy's prophecy chills him: "'Youse in de majority now, but God sho don't love ugly,'" and he feels "like Nebuchadnezer in his exile" (129). This likely refers to Nebuchadnezer II, King of Babylon, who attacks Palestine and enslaves the Hebrews, ending Judah's period of independence, but more importantly, curtails the Davidic line of kings. Since John was earlier compared with David, this line has resonance, for it indicates that our current figure has "killed" the spreading dreams of the younger man, thereby fitting a complicated set of biblical narratives together, for at this juncture John's slap becomes the equivalent to the worm that destroys Jonah's gourd vine. The vine stands for Lucy and her "sheltering shade," which in turn may be seen as what John claims she tries to be and he doesn't need: a "'guardzeen'" (116, 128).

In several ways, John's repetition of this phrase and his very infidelities suggest a pattern, one ordinarily associated with the social development of adolescent boys who lack fathers. John forces his li'l' bit wife to act more like his mother, and his refusal to admit she has this power causes their problems to expand exponentially, a poisonous growth directly at odds with the sheltering foliage of Lucy's love. Indeed, John admits as much just before he slaps her: "'Ah don't need you no mo' nor nothing you got tuh say, Ahm uh man grown'" (128).

When Lucy lies dying, Hurston employs the details of her own mother's death, as one may readily see by reading chapter 6 of *Dust Tracks.* There Hurston gives us one of the most wrenching yet beautifully written death scenes in our literature, comparable to the passing of Old Gant in Thomas Wolfe's *Of Time and the River.* Even while facing death, Lucy seems to be thinking of John, for she asks Isis to turn to the twenty-sixth chapter of Acts for her, wherein Paul recounts the story of his conversion on the road to Damascus for Agrippa. There one reads the Lord's call, and Paul's response: "But rise, and stand upon thy feet; for I have appeared unto thee for this purpose, to make thee a minister and a witness both of these things which thou hast seen, and of those things . . . which I will appear unto thee. . . . To open their eyes, and to turn them from darkness to light. . . . Whereupon, O king Agrippa, I was not disobedient unto the heavenly vision." Does this passage refer only to Lucy's constant attempt to shape John into God's perfect minister or does it perhaps reflect her own desire to "preach it" through John, since communal standards dictate her sideline stance? Clearly, she has repeatedly issued the "call," hoping to find in John the right "response."

In any case, Lucy preaches a vital sermon to Isie, her "heart's child":

> "'Member tuh git all de education you kin. Dat's de onliest way you kin keep out from under people's feet. You always strain tuh be de bell cow, never be de tail uh nothin'. Do de best you kin, honey, 'cause

neither yo' paw nor dese older chillun is goin' tuh be bothered too
much wid yuh, but you goin' tuh git' long. Mark mah words. You got
de spunk, but mah po' li'l' sandy-haired chile goin' suffer uh lot 'fo'
she git tuh de place she kin 'fend fuh herself. And Isie, honey, stop
cryin' and lissen tuh me. Don't you love nobody better'n you do yo'self.
Do, you'll be dying befo' yo' time is out." (130)

This profoundly moving speech concerns gaining and keeping power through language; it also seems, however, to deny supreme value
to the totally giving, loving "service" Lucy has seemed to give uncom-
plainingly to John throughout the book, favoring instead self-love and
development. One could even say she seems to be assigning her over-
abundant love for John responsibility for her death. As these words
are used to describe Hurston herself rather than her mother in *Dust
Tracks,* we see a combination of Hurston and her mother in Lucy.[34]

Lucy's deathwatch finds punctuation through her intermittent
observation of a spider's progress down the wall. Here Hurston recreates the trickster Anancy, presumed in West African culture (especially among the Yoruba) to be the creator of all people. In the
American South, the spider could mean a visitor is coming, with the
color of the spider indicative of the visitor's (Ellis 258). Here the
spider announces the impending visit of death. Or is it God? Once
again the trickster deity appears as a joker, this time asleep at the
wheel—for Lucy in her suffering finally calls out to the evening sun
to tell the Lord she's waiting, and the narrator comments, "And God
awoke at last and nodded his head" (132).

As Hurston's mother gave her, Lucy gives Isie instructions to prevent mourners from taking the pillow from under her head or cov-
ering the clock and looking glass when she dies. As in *Dust Tracks,*
Lucy and her child are overruled by the adults present, and Lucy tells
Mrs. Clarke, a neighbor worried about Lucy's soul, "'Don't worry
'bout me, Sister Clarke. Ah done been in sorrow's kitchen and Ah
done licked out all de pots. Ah done died in grief and been buried
in de bitter waters, and Ah done rose agin from de dead lak Lazarus.
Nothin' kin touch mah soul no mo','" a speech that echoes Hurston's
own comments in the autobiography, rather than her mother's.
(131).

The deathwatch the community performs as Lucy dies conforms
to African practices. In both cultures, the dying person looking toward the wall signifies a "bad death." One also had to lie completely
flat—thus the removal of the pillow (Creel 84–86). Hurston mentions
some of these practices in *Mules:* "The spirit newly released from the
body is likely to be destructive. This is why a cloth is thrown over the

face of a clock in the death chamber and the looking glass is covered over. The clock will never run again, nor will the mirror ever cast any more reflections if they are not covered so that the spirit cannot see them" (236). Hurston identifies these and other customs with the Ewe-speaking peoples of West Africa. All of the funeral practices are designed to keep the spirits of the dead pacified and quiet, for they have the power to walk the earth and terrify the living. And indeed, the night of Lucy's death, a great wind shakes the house and sets the dogs howling, "and John huddled beneath his bed-covers shaking and afraid" (133), clearly believing both in his guilt and the walking-abroad of a vengeful Lucy. But the next day, "the hot blood in John's veins made him deny kinship with any rider of the pale white horse of death" (135), a clear reference to the book of Revelation, which provides much of the cosmic imagery of the novel. In this section of the Bible, the figure called "Faithful and True," a description that perfectly suits Lucy, rides a white steed (Rev. 19, 11). The power of this sequence comes partly through a diminishment of the comic and a corresponding expansion of the cosmic.

Communal Humor: Festive and Corrective

To a certain extent, this pattern increasingly dominates the remainder of the book. After Lucy's death, her memory haunts John's life, pointing to what he has lost and casting an elegiac mood over even the most comically engaging scenes. But then in a sense, the entire book may be read as a pastoral elegy; Hurston's provision of so many communal scenes suggests an interest in memorializing a way of life that was passing away forever. Where else in our literature is there a more accurate and beautiful portrait of rural black communities, their homes, their habits, their dress, and their rituals and celebrations? Jean Toomer's *Cane*, consciously conceived as a "swan song" of a vanishing culture, had perhaps suggested this approach to Hurston when it became a touchstone for the Harlem Renaissance. We could assign this aspect of Hurston's authorial program the historian's function, and as noted, the minister's role in the community (which Hurston as author appropriates to herself), equates with one aspect of some griots. Thus we have Hurston, the griot/preacher/anthropologist making the "dry bones" of history come alive with vivid folk portraiture, much of it touched with the enlivening breath of folk humor. In this concluding portion the novel proceeds from the personal to the communal, opening out into a cosmic conclusion.

Some of the book's most memorable effects come from descriptions of domestic scenes, like the Pottses' farm and drawing room; from our attendance at choir practice; or from celebrations, like a school commencement. One example will suffice. The hog roast and festive dance that follows the cotton harvest reveals Hurston's wonderful ability to dramatize illustrations of folk culture in general and festive humor in particular. The celebration, for blacks only, unites friends from three plantations. Everyone contributes: "Some brought 'likker.' Some crocus sacks of yellow yam potatoes, and bushels of peanuts to roast, and the biggest syrup-kettle at Pearson's canemill was full of chicken perleau. . . . Old Purlee Kimball was stirring it with a shovel" (29). This passage emphasizes the gigantic, the bursting, the monumental, but also personifies the traditional and the wisdom of age in the person of Old Purlee.

Bully, the emcee, gnawing on a giant hog rib, comically calls out, "'Stop de music. Don't vip another vop 'til Ah says so. Hog head, hog bosom, hog hips and every kind of hog there ever wuz is ready! . . . De chickens is cacklin' in de rice and dey say "Come git it wilst iss fittin 'cause t'morrer it may be frost-bitten!"'" (29). He stops the Western instruments and calls for clapping only, prompting one of Hurston's anthropological minilectures on the drum, "the instrument . . . brought to America in their skins . . . the voice of Kata-Kumba, the great drum." Slave-owners know "he will serve us better if we bring him from Africa naked and thing-less," so drums are forbidden, but "Cuffy seized his drum and hid it in his skin, under the skull bones. . . . He laughed with cunning and said, 'I, who am borne away to become an orphan, carry my parents with me. For Rhythm is she not my mother and Drama is her man?' So he groaned aloud in the ships and hid his drum and laughed" (29–30). Hurston thus presents the drum as a triumphant agent of coded, communicative folk laughter, one specifically African, which the call-and-response mode of the black church echoes.[35]

Hurston quickly returns to the present and offers, via Bully's calls, comic mininarratives, such as:

> Ole cow died in Tennessee
> Send her jawbone back to me
> Jawbone walk, Jawbone talk
> Jawbone eat wid uh knife and fork. Ain't Ah right?
>
> Chorus: Yeah!

The narrator comments, braiding together the past and the present: "Ibo tune corrupted with Nango. Congo gods talking in Alabama" (30). Clearly, the gods have a sense of humor, one shared with the people via call and response. Thus Hurston draws a scene from the present, couples it with an impressionistic vision of the cultural past, and somehow anneals the two seamlessly in a sweeping gloss on cultural production and continuity.[36]

The sense of humor of the gods and of the community plays a more obvious and serious role in this last section of the novel. One scene brings us to yet another reading of the original title "Big Nigger," for several times the community tries to pull John down. As his friend Hambo tells him late in the book, "'You know our people is jus' lak uh passle uh crabs in uh basket. De minute dey see one climbin' up too high, de rest of 'em reach up and grab 'em and pull 'im back. Dey ain't gonna let nobody git nowhere if dy kin he'p it'" (169), a corroboration of Bakhtin's assertion of the "leveling," "uncrowning" impulse of much of folk humor. Hurston would elaborate on this theme in much of her work, particularly in *Moses*, where the stiff-necked Hebrews repeatedly buckle under Moses' rule.[37]

Some community members rail against such perceived "big nigger" behavior at the formal school closing ceremony. Lucy's starring role generates considerable envy. Parents in the audience, in a critique of the kind of cultural elitism that hurts Lucy and John throughout the book, mutter about favoritism ("dey muches her up") and swear they'll take their children out of the school: "'Dey makes cake outa some uh de chillun and cawn bread outa de rest'" (36).

Most of this comic correction follows Lucy's death and John's subsequent unhappy marriage to Hattie. At this point the narrative plays a counterpoint of duets, one between John and his sage friend Hambo, another between Hattie and the "Judas" Deacon Harris, who envies John and sees in the minister's angry wife a way to cut the proud gourd vine down. He feels like "a cat in Hell with no claws" (153), and Hattie offers what he lacks. Their scheming has a comic edge. When the Deacon urges Hattie to divorce John, she chides him, "'Chile, he wouldn't care. . . . He'd be glad, Ah speck, so he kin run loose wid dat Gertie Burden.'" Harris replies, "'Who you tellin'? Ever since she wuz knee high. Us knowed it all de time, but thought yuh didn't.' 'He don't try tuh keep it out mah sight. He washes mah face wid her night and day.' 'You jokin'!'" (154). This exchange extends the washing imagery, and indeed, the deacon's visit interrupts Hattie's washing of the family's "white things." They are examining the "dirty linen" they need to do John in, and he supplied it all.

Harris represents an entire faction of the community, and through him we often see how the community reacts to John's infidelities. Sometimes Harris's venom, and thus the community's, seems justified, as he smolders over John's appetite for power and women. John doesn't understand Harris's hostility, for "he had taken no woman who loved Harris, for none had wanted him. His incompetence was one of the behind-hand jokes of the congregation. . . . Harris hated him with all the fury of the incompetent for the full-blooded loins" (166). We have already heard Harris's side, however: "Harris knew that he must find some other weapon to move the man who had taken his best side-girl from him" (159). Later, Hambo confirms Harris's sins, saying at the divorce trial, "'G'wan talk, Harris, you and de rest dat's so anxious tuh ground-mole de pastor, but be sho and tell where *you* wuz yo'self when you seen him do all of dis y'all talkin' 'bout. Be sho and tell dat too. Humph! Youse jes' ez deep in de mud ez he is in de mire'" (172).

Hambo may be John's best friend, but he clearly functions as the community's conscience and leads a party of his fellow deacons to chastise and "correct" John. When John asks how Hambo does, he replies, "'Don't do all dey say, but Ah do mah share, and damned if you don't do yourn'" (137). John at first views this as merely a joke, but soon sees it as a joke with a purpose. "He started to laugh, then looked at the men's faces and quit" (137). Hambo continues in this vein, calling John's attention to the children's needs: "'They's 'round de streets heah jes' ez raggedy ez jay-birds in whistlin' time. Dey sho ain't gittin' uh damn bit uh 'tention.'" Elaborating and signifying further on John's lazy new wife, Hattie, Hambo charges:

> "Dat strumpet ain't never done nothin' but run up and down de road from one sawmill camp tuh de other and from de looks of her, times was hard. She ain't never had nothin'—not eben doodly-squat, and when she gits uh chance tuh git holt uh sumpin de ole buzzard is gone on uh rampage. . . . Ah ain't gonna bite mah tongue uh damn bit. . . . Ahm three times seben and uh button! . . . Ah ain't gonna wait nothin' uh de kind. Wait broke de wagon down. Ah jes' feel lak takin' uh green club and waitin' on dat wench's head until she acknowledge Ahm God and besides me there's no other. . . . Ah ain't come tuh make yuh no play-party. Stoopin' down from where you stand, fuh whut? . . . Jus 'cause you never seen no talcum powder and silk kimonos back dere in Alabama." (139)

This scene establishes Hambo as a kind of comic counsel to John; both his wisdom and his love of John are cloaked in a rough humor and folk demeanor that recalls the classic figure of Silenus, teacher of Bacchus, who had an ugly exterior but a beautiful soul. Hambo "categorizes" Hattie with well-chosen words: "strumpet," "buzzard," "wench." But his epithets are humorously dramatized as well, picturing a "poor whore corps" Hattie in constant motion "on the road," trying to drum up business, then shifting not just to the buzzard but a buzzard seen gobbling ("on uh rampage"). Hambo indicates his stance as a corrective God to John's sin by substituting Hattie; he actually directs his demand that she acknowledge "'Ahm God and besides me there's no other'" at John, as he ultimately admits, by denying he's come to make him "a play-party." He leaves John a comic alibi, however, which enables him to save face, while reducing Hattie to her props; John the rube from the Alabama backwoods has really been seduced by "talcum powder and silk kimonos," a false image of culture. While the diatribe is misogynist in the way an Old Testament prophet's would be, it interestingly and shrewdly subtracts the woman's body from the equation, implicitly mocking its power by ignoring it.

Hattie, hidden, hears everything, but gloats that she's invulnerable, for she significantly and secretly carries in her hair a piece of John-de-conquer root, the most powerful charm in hoodoo, which can only gain in significance through the ironic coincidence of her husband's name.

Hattie tries to keep John through sex, but he turns her away: "'It don't seem lak iss clean uh sumpin,'" and charges her with not being Lucy, inspiring a rush of signification from her: "'Naw, Ah ain't no Miss Lucy, 'cause Ah ain't goin' tuh cloak yo' dirt fuh yuh. An ain't goin' tuh take offa yuh whut she took so you kin set up and be uh big nigger over mah bones. . . . You fool wid me and Ah'll jerk de cover offa you and dat Berry woman. Ah'll throw uh brick in yo' coffin and don't keer how sad de funeral will be'" (145). Her pronouncements here summon up Lucy well, for while her comic spunk has the malicious spice that Lucy lacked, her willingness to put John's name in the street reverses Lucy's corrective approach. Both her remarks and John's rehearse the cleanliness theme, while her charge of "big nigger" brings up the "uppity" issue that so transfixes the community. John's final, violent showdown with Hattie obviously cannot be read with late twentieth-century values in mind. Her hoodoo and conjure are exposed, and John is advised to beat "'de blood out her. When you draw her wine dat breaks de spell'" (162), and he complies.

How does Hurston feel about this? It seems obvious that she views Hattie as totally evil. One searches in vain for any redeeming qualities in the woman. More light is shed on how John responds to her conjuration by understanding that when Hambo tells John "'She been feedin you outa her body for years'" (161), he means it literally. Hurston's *Journal of American Folklore* piece, "Hoodoo in America," lists a hoodoo formula from Palatica, Florida: "To make a man love you . . . put either urine or menstrual discharge in his food secretly" (395). Moreover, Hattie's portrayal owes much to Hurston's lifelong animus toward her stepmother, clearly Hattie's model. As she said in *Dust Tracks,* "God, how I longed to lay my hands upon my stepmother's short, pudgy hulk! No gun, no blade, no club would do. Just flesh against flesh and leave the end of the struggle to the hidden Old Women who sit and spin" (98). In fact, in one of the most terrifying scenes in the book, she has a violent fight with the woman: "Her head was travelling between my fist and the wall, and I wished my fist had weighed a ton" (102).[38] Although the language Hurston uses in these descriptions is clever, any humor involved is grim indeed. The ending of the novel leaves no doubt that Hattie's real-life version was "beyond the Pale" of sisterhood for Hurston.

When Hattie's vindictive, individual campaign for John's "correction" fails, she sues for divorce, this time literally putting his name in the white man's street. John feels shame in the white courtroom at the "smirking anticipation on the faces of the lawyers, the court attendant, and the white spectators and felt as if he had fallen down a foul latrine." The scene has a kind of surreal humor, rather like that of *Alice in Wonderland,* as "his honor took his seat as a walrus would among a bed of clams." "'Now, how was it Hattie?' They look around the room at the other whites, as if to say, 'Now listen close. You're going to hear something rich. These niggers!'" (167). The insulting line of white courtroom argument applies to both sides: "'Ha! ha! couldn't you get yo'self another man on the side? . . . You got divorce in yo' heels, ain't you? You must have the next one picked out. Ha! ha! Bet he ain't worth the sixty dollars'" (167). John in fact takes grim comfort and laughs inside to see the witnesses for Hattie squirm, but because he refuses to provide an occasion for jeering racist laughter, he agrees to all of Hattie's charges.[39]

John's dignity in the courthouse and his reply to Hambo's joking desire to expose Hattie's promiscuity to the court illustrate what Hurston meant when she indicated her desire to portray "a Negro preacher who is neither funny nor an imitation Puritan ram-rod in pants." In one of the book's great passages, John eloquently insists on the dignity of individual and racial privacy:

> "Ah didn't want de white folks tuh hear 'bout nothin' lak dat. Dey knows too much 'bout us as it is, but dey some things dey ain't tuh know. Dey's some strings on our harp fuh us tuh play on and sing all tuh ourselves. Dey thinks wese all ignorant as it is, and dey thinks wese all alike, and dat dey knows us inside and out, but you know better.

Dey wouldn't make no great 'miration if you had uh tole 'em Hattie
had all dem mens. Dey spectin' dat. Dey wouldn't zarn 'tween uh woman lak Hattie and one lak Lucy, uh yo' wife befo' she died. Dey thinks
all colored folks is de same dat way. De only difference dey makes is
'tween uh nigger dat works hard and don't sass 'em, and one dat don't.
De hard worker is uh good nigger. De loafer is bad. Otherwise wese
all de same. Das how come Ah got up and said, 'Yeah, Ah done it,'
'cause dey b'lieved it anyhow, but dey b'lieved de same thing 'bout all
de rest." (169)

As John's speech shrewdly reveals, the self-serving racist humor of the
whites seeks to level too; by finding a low common denominator, this
ugly humor establishes a ground for the charge "they're all the same."
The courtroom scene thus reveals a gap in cross-racial humor.

There is an "ugly" side to humor within John's home community
as well; we continue to learn about the hypocrisy of Sanford after the
divorce. Old friends refuse to give John carpentry work and others,
who owe him money, comically and smugly decide "it would be lacking in virtue to pay carpenter-preachers who got into trouble with
congregations" (182). Similarly, "Every bawdy in town wept over her
gin and laid her downfall at John's door. He was the father of dozens of children by women he had never seen." One man, speaking
for many, says, "'Well, since he's down, less keep 'im down'" (183),
yet another reminder of the basket of crabs. Their hypocrisy and
exaggerated sense of self-serving righteousness amuses us, but in fact
does help correct John.

John doesn't lose his sardonic sense of humor completely, however, for when the carpentry business fails, he wryly comments, "'All de
lies dese folks strowing 'round 'bout me done got some folks in de
notion Ah can't drive uh clean nail in they lumber. Look lak dey
spectin' uh house Ah build tuh git tuh fornication befo' dey could
get de paint on it'" (183), a configuration that creates a surreal bit
of hilarity.

The Cosmic Comedy of History and Time

The cosmic language Hurston so often favors proves especially useful in spanning time: "The Lord of the wheel that turns on itself slept,
but the world kept spinning, and the troubled years sped on" (141).
These ennobling but nevertheless domesticating references are extended in passages such as "The old black woman of the sky chased
the red-eyed sun across the sky every evening and smothered him in
her cloak at last" (147). This lifts the narrative into the transcendent,
but also prefigures Hattie's revenge on John.

Much of this language and its images come from the book of Revelation, like the following: "By that time the sun was washing herself in the bloody sea and splashing her bedclothes in red and purple" (94). It occurs just after one of John's most scandalous absences; while he cavorts with a woman named Delphine, Lucy gives birth to their first daughter and immediately afterward has their marriage bed (a gift from Alf Pearson) pulled from under her by her cruel brother Bud in payment for a debt. John's triple betrayal of duties as provider, father, and defender aptly fits against this seemingly simple apostrophe to the sun, which is taken from Rev. 17:5: "And the woman was arrayed in purple and scarlet colour . . . having a gold cup in her hand full of abominations and filthiness of her fornication"; Hurston has conjured up, at an appropriate moment, the whore of Babylon.[40]

John's greatest sermon at Zion Hope, his last, comes from a mimeoed sermon Hurston uses virtually verbatim, originally preached by the Reverend C. C. Lovelace of Eau Gallie, Florida, on May 2, 1929. The powerful cosmic poetry of the piece offers compelling proof of the sources of Hurston's cosmic metaphors and how she used the sacred to create a transcendence for the profane. The references to the "hammers of creation," the "anvils of time," "the rim bones of nothing," the "scepter of revolvin' world," the sun gathering up "de fiery skirts of her garments" echo in all of Hurston's novels and stories, which expand their power to move us exponentially by the deepening of the frame of reference. We are only a step away from the famous beginning of *Their Eyes,* where ships are on the horizon with every man's wish aboard and the Watcher is mocked to death by time, or from "The Gilded Six-Bits," where Joe's discovery of his wife's infidelity stuns him and "the great belt on the wheel of Time slipped and eternity stood still." This line comes directly from John's "train sermon" as he describes Christ crucified: "He died until the great belt in the wheel of time / And de geological strata fell aloose" (180). Passages such as this establish a historical as well as a biblical cosmology.

These transcendent apostrophes to time underscore Hurston's attempt to act as griot/chronicler for an age that was slipping away. The generations of *Jonah* reenact the great dramas of Reconstruction and the nadir, the great migration, and black involvement in World War I. The intersection of these events with the familial and local Eatonville culture she was also resurrecting results in dramatic and enlivened presentation of both the structures of everyday life and the effect upon them of larger events, part of the pattern of doubling that one finds everywhere in Hurston's work.

We may profit from an inspection of just how Hurston accomplishes this by returning to sections of the book already visited with these points in mind. Early on, when the ex-slave Ned proposes to hire his stepson out to the ex-overseer Mimms, John's mother criticizes "the man" in a comic and devastatingly sarcastic way while providing us with a historic context consonant with the generalized references to slavery: When "'Massa Pinckney got kilt in the war,'" Mrs. Pinckney married Mimms, her oafish overseer, to maintain effective control over her property, despite the fact that "'he wasn't nothin' but uh overseer, lived offa clay and black m'lasses. His folks is so po' right now dey can't sit in dey house. Every time you pass dere dey settin' in de yard jes' ez barefooted ez uh yard dawg. You ain't gwine put no chile uh mine under no Mimms'" (7). Despite this devastating signification, which employs leveling humor based on hierarchies of racial and economic class, John tells his brother Zeke, "'Ah jes' ez soon be under Mimms ez pappy. One 'bout ez bad as tother. . . . Dis ain't slavery time and Ah got two good footses hung onto me'" (8), a telling comment on how the patterns of patriarchal oppression have filtered down into the black community and family.

This same sort of language introduces historic events, such as migration and war. Precisely at the middle of the novel, when John escapes a sticky situation in Alabama by fleeing to Florida, necessitating his long-desired first train ride, we are seeing a moment of transition that signaled the great shift from an agricultural to an industrial nation. Hurston limns it in epic fashion, in prose simultaneously comic and evocative:

> To him nothing in the world ever quite equalled that first ride on a train. The rhythmic stroke of the engine, the shiny-buttoned porter bawling out the stations, the even more begilded conductor, who looked more imposing even than Judge Pearson, and then the red plush splendor, the gaudy ceiling hung with glinting lamps, the long mournful howl of the whistle. John forgot the misery of his parting from Lucy in the aura of it all. . . . He got off the train at every stop so that he could stand off a piece and feast his eyes on the engine. The greatest accumulation of power that he had ever seen. (104)

And at the same time we feel John, as a representative of his culture, moving forward. Instead of emphasizing the car as a Jim Crow one or having the white railroad personnel hurl insults at John, Hurston through this train ride gives John and his people a personal and symbolic sense of empowerment.

An even more compelling use of cosmic language wrapped around comedy and delivered in folk expression marks the advent of war and change: "A fresh rumor spread over the nation. It said war. It talked of blood and glory—of travel, of North, of Oceans and transports, of white men and black. And black men's feet learned roads. . . . The wind said North. Trains said North. The tides and tongues said North, and men moved like the great herds before the glaciers" (148). We can see how this section encapsulates not only military conscription but also the great migration that was generated by the war. Here the phallic symbol of the train becomes the empowering liberation of the exodus to the North.

Once again an impressionistic, biblical, and somewhat apocalyptical language paints the scene: "Conscription, uniforms, bands, strutting drum-majors, and the mudsills of the earth arose and skipped like the mountains of Jerusalem on The Day. Lowly minds who knew not their State Capitals were talking glibly of France" (148). Hurston follows this passage with a comic but bitter chorus of anonymous voices:

> "Gen'l Pushin,' Gen'l Punishin', Gen'l Perchin', Gen'l Pershin. . . . De black man ain't got no voice but soon ez war come who de first man dey shove in front? De nigger! Ain't it de truth? Bet if Ole Teddy wuz in de chear he'd straighten out eve'ything. Wilson! Stop dat ole lie. . . . Ain't never been two sho' 'nuff smart mens in dese United States— Teddy Roosevelt and Booger T. Washington. Nigger so smart he et at the White House. Built uh great big ole school wuth uh thousand dollars, maybe mo'. Teddy wuz allus sendin' fuh 'im tuh git 'im tuh he'p 'im run de Guv'ment. Yeah man, dat's de way it 'tis—niggers think up eve'ything good and de white folks steal it from us. Dass right. Nigger invented de train. White man seen it and run right off and made him one jes' lak it and told eve'ybody he thought it up. Same way wid 'lectwicity. Nigger thought dat up too. DuBois? Who is dat? 'Nother smart nigger? Man, he can't be smart ez Booger T.! Whut did dis DuBois ever do? He writes up books and papers, hunh? Shucks! dat ain't nothin', anybody kin put down words on uh piece of paper. Gimme da paper sack and lemme see dat pencil uh minute. Shucks! Writing! Man Ah thought you wuz talkin' 'bout uh man whut had done sumpin. Ah thought maybe he wuz de man dat could make sidemeat taste lak ham." (148)

This passage, written in dialect replete with folk expressions, amuses because of the combination of sophisticated political commentary and rustic voice. It follows the time-honored American tradition of backwoods wisdom that began with colonial America's Brother Jonathan[41] and continued on through Finley Peter Dunne's Mr. Dooley and Langston Hughes's Jesse B. Semple. Writing in dialect enabled these writers to say things that would otherwise be offensive to the intended audience among the privileged. Baiting the hook with humor helped drive the point home. As Dunne put it, "While I was writing editorials for the *Post,* we became engaged in a bitter fight with the crooks in the city council. . . . It occurred to me that while it might be dangerous to call an alderman a thief in English no one could sue if a comic Irishman denounced the statesman as a thief" (240). Hurston similarly uses a dialect mask (and anonymous voices) to make people understand that African Americans were playing key roles in their nation's history, even though they were being denied equal access to full citizenship; that they were aware of the discrepancy between their contributions and their rewards; and that they were fully cognizant of the significance of the sweeping events they were helping to create, such as World War I and the great migration. She was perfectly willing to wear her customary comic mask to do so.

We thus see in *Jonah* a bitter, communal amusement at the way war merely replicates everyday realities, for the silenced black man must defend free speech with his rifle and his life. General Pershing thus did indeed "push" and "punish" the black man while "perch"ing on the hypocritical standard of a war to save a democracy that did not in fact exist for many American soldiers.

Hurston's valorization of Booker T. Washington and Teddy Roosevelt cleverly elevates the former to the position of the latter, while honoring her own long-term commitment to the Republican party, which we would do well to remember was the preferred party of many blacks at this time because of its history, strongly associated with Lincoln and Emancipation.

Hurston's antipathy for Du Bois and love for Washington, a fascinating subject that deserves extended analysis, finds further expression here, with Du Bois getting the comic needle she reserved for "dicty," elitist blacks. Making "sidemeat taste lak ham" seems to indicate that Washington did more for the lives of everyday folk.

This amazing passage goes on to summarize postwar movement to the North as well:

> "Yeah man, parlez vous, man, don't come bookooin' 'round heah, yuh liable tuh git hurt. Ah could uh married one uh dem French women but shucks, gimme uh brown skin eve'y time. Blacker de berry sweeter de juice. Come tuh mah pick, gimme uh good black gal. De wine wuz sour, and Ah says parlez vous, hell! You gimme mah right change! Comme telly vous. Nar, Ah ain't goin' back tuh no farm no mo'. Ah don't mean tuh say, 'Git up' tuh nary 'nother mule lessen he's setting down in mah lap. God made de world but he never made no hog outa me tuh go 'round rootin' it up. Done done too much bookoo plowing already! Woman quick gimme mah sumpin t' eat. Toot sweet."

World gone money mad. The pinch of war gone, people must spend. Buy and forget. Spend and solace. Silks for sorrows. Jewels to bring back joy. The factories roared and cried, "Hands!" and in the haste and press white hands became scarce. Scarce and dear. Hands? Who cares about the color of hands? We need hands and muscle. The South—land of muscled hands.

"George, haven't you got some relatives and friends down South who'd like a job?"

"Yes, suh."

"Write 'em to come." (149)

Dialect serves the writer even better here as she bravely addresses the bugaboo of interracial sex in France, a specter that horrified the white South and contributed to a resurgence of lynching after the war. Hurston's comments seem calculated to allay racist fears by indicating through humor black men's preference for black women, culminating in the cherished folk expression "The blacker the berry, the sweeter the juice." The slightly mangled, but tellingly understood French creates bicultural comedy and linguistic code-switching, but also inserts a warning; although black servicemen aren't interested in white American women as a result of their experiences abroad, they certainly have learned the values of being treated justly, and like the song says, "How you gonna keep 'em down on the farm, after they've seen Paree?" Here Hurston takes the sentiment of a popular ditty and makes it an ironic gloss on the great migration.

Hurston also describes the recruiting agents who rustled up work crews and gave them train money. It drains John's congregation, causing him to complain, "'Iss rainin' in mah meal barrel right along'" (149).[42] Together, Hambo and John offer a revealing historical panorama of the syndrome, piecing together reports from agents such as John's son in Tennessee and adding shrewd descriptions of the consequences in their own community. Hambo, a philosopher of sorts, predicts long-lasting effects: "'Iss powerful hard tuh git uh countryman outa town. He's jus' ez crazy 'bout it ez uh hog is 'bout town swill. Dey won't be back soon'" (151). And in fact, Hurston links the powerful movement to the Exodus: "The cry of 'Goin' Nawth' hung over the land like the wail over Egypt at the death of the first-born. . . . Whereas in Egypt the coming of the locust made desolation, in the farming South, the departure of the Negro laid waste the agricultural industry—crops rotted, houses careened crazily in their utter desertion, and grass grew up in streets. On to the North! The land of promise" (151). This equation of the biblical exodus with the great migration would find magnificent creative and comic expression in *Moses*.

The Ironies of Time's Great Wheel

Hurston returns to the initiation/meeting theme one last time. In yet another indication that John's life resembles a great revolving wheel that dizzily circles back to its origins again and again, he characteristically meets his last wife in a folk-based way. When she invites him to rest on a chair rather than her steps she warns, "'If you set on de steps you'll git all de pains in de house. Ha, ha! Ah reckon you say niggers got all de signs an white folks got all de money'" (186). Her declaration that her dead husband said John was "'de best preacher ever borned since befo' dey built de Rocky Mountains'" causes him to laugh "a space-filling laugh" and he waits on her lead (186). Significantly, this woman who renews John's faith in himself is named Sally Lovelace, surely after the wonderful minister who provided Hurston with John's last sermon to Zion Hope Church. Sally also offers John a pitcher of water before setting him before a groaning table, echoing once again the biblical pattern of the woman at the well greeting the stranger who will become her husband.

When John hesitates to say he'll join Sally at church she responds, "'You jokin', Ah know.'" People wasting their God-given talents are a joke, indeed. His confession of what happened in Sanford follows and ends with him sobbing with his head in her lap "like a boy of four" (189), once again emphasizing the paradoxically childish aspect of this big-voiced and muscular man. Sally's protective and comically worded growl underlines her replication of the maternal: "'None of 'em bet' not come 'round here tryin' tuh destroy yo' influence. . . . Ain't doodley squat dey self and goin' 'round tromplin' on folks dat's 'way uhbove 'em'" (189). Moreover, the semiotics of their physical postures here refigure the sheltering shade of the pieta-like gourd vine.

Sally's comically unsentimental common sense finds further expression in her suggestion of marriage: "'We ain't no chillun no mo', and we don't need tuh go thru uh whole lot uh form and fashion— uh kee-kee-in' and eatin' up pocket handkerchers. . . . Ahm gointer marry you, 'cause Ah love yuh and Ah b'lieve you love me, and 'cause you needs marryin'" (190). John agrees and suggests they catch fish afterward, something she's always wanted to do that her former husband never allowed, prefiguring Tea Cake's similar activity and doctrine of equality with Janie in *Their Eyes*. Indeed, Sally, the financially secure childless widow who says, "'Tuh think Ah lived tuh git forty-eight 'fo' Ah ever knowed whut love is'" (193) directly foreshadows Janie, even to the brevity of her last marriage and the accidental death of her husband.

Still, Hurston can't resist making a bit of fun of this good woman; when Sally sends John back for a visit to Sanford, despite his vow never to spend a night away from her, she exults "in her power and sipped honey from his lips, but she made him go, seeing the pain in John's face at the separation. It was worth her own suffering ten times over to see him that way for her" (194).

When friends ask John to return to his old town, Hurston encourages us to look down at him as he lords it over the townspeople with his big car and roll of bills: "He was grinning sardonically inside, thinking of the heat of the pavements and empty belly, the cold cruelty of want, how much men hit and beat at need when it pleads its gauntness" (195), ironically reflecting, in other words, on what he is now doing himself. Another turn of Fortuna's wheel has him at the top and at a wheel of his own.

He promptly spins it, however, in the direction of a woman. Ora, whose "egg-bag ain't gonna rest easy" until she's with John, lives up to her scandalous billing. Pleading for a ride in the car, she uses sexually charged, doubled language right out of the blues: "'Let de wheels roll. Ah loves cars. Ride me 'til Ah sweat'" (197).

After seducing John, Ora asks for money, and he spurns her after tossing four dollars down, roughly throwing her from the car. One would think the Hurston of *Their Eyes* would be more sympathetic, but her loyalties are with John, who tries so mightily to resist temptation. Ora's true nature emerges after John's departure, when she talks like an animal trickster: "'He done lef' me right where Ah wants tuh be, wid pay-day at de packin' house tuhmorrer. Jes' lak de rabbit in de briar patch'" (200).

John's death in a car-train accident after he has betrayed Sally with Ora might be meant as a modern equivalent of black folklore's Chariot of Fire, or more obviously, the Judgment Train prefigured in John's great sermon; those big wheels of justice, like Fortuna's, will inevitably turn.[43] The conclusion also echoes, however, the actual death of Hurston's father. Speaking of a conversation with her brother, Hurston relates, "My father had been killed in an automobile accident during my first years at Morgan, and Bob talked to me about his last days. In reality, my father was the baby of the family. With my mother gone and nobody to guide him, life had not hurt him, but it had turned him loose to hurt himself. He had been miserable over the dispersion of his children when he came to realize that it was so. We were all so sorry for him, instead of feeling bitter as might have been expected. Old Maker had left out the steering gear when He gave Papa his talents," a rather comic way of expressing pain and loss (*Dust*, 172). John Hurston's fictional counterpart lacks a steering gear too at the climactic moment, when the train bears down on him. The gear equates to the Christian's fortitude in turning away from temptation. Despite the residual anger at the pain her father caused his wife and children, Hurston seems, indeed, to feel that in some ways her parent had remained true to his African roots by not slavishly following the white man's dictum of the division of soul and body. This finds illustration as the book ends, when a significantly unnamed preacher eulogizes John, but with the congregation transmogrified to Africans: "They beat upon the O-go-doe, the ancient drum." The preacher's last words—"'nobody knowed 'im but God'" (202).[44]

Hurston's purpose in *Jonah* was to show the world the glory of African American folklore and language and the central role it plays in sustaining the community, particularly in the rhetoric of the minister and in the metaphors of everyday games, gossip, and sheer conversation. It was meant to do what Hurston had challenged the race in general to do in her December 29, 1934, article in the *Washington Tribune:* recognize that African American folk expression had an integrity that was every bit as fine as that of Anglo-American culture. After providing parallels and examples from both sides, she issued a clarion call: "Who knows what fabulous cities of artistic concepts lie within the mind and language of some humble Negro boy or girl who has never heard of Ibsen. . . . Fawn as you will. Spend an eternity standing awe struck. Roll your eyes in ecstasy and ape his every move, but until we have placed something upon his street corner that is our own, we are right back where we were when they filed our iron collar off." With *Jonah,* that street corner had been filled.[45]

Despite the claims I have made for *Jonah's Gourd Vine,* many critics, including Robert Hemenway, have read it as a failure, charging that Hurston couldn't bridge the gap between John's poetic magnificence and his personal crisis (*Zora* 196 ff.). Such an analysis ignores the fact that this age-old problem constitutes the very subject of the story. The paradox (and thus the divine joke of God the maker and author of the Bible) is that people's God-given sexuality, surely to be equated with the fertile imagination too, drives them ever further into Bible-defined sin. Why should Hurston be expected to untangle a problem that even the Bible fails to resolve? As Toni Morrison has stated, the novel "should have something in it that enlightens; something in it that opens the door and points the way. Something in it that suggests what the conflicts are, what the problems are. But it need not solve those problems because it is not a case study, it is not a recipe" ("Rootedness" 341). Here, for instance, the conundrum partly consists of the fact that as with Arthur Dimmesdale in *The Scarlet*

Letter (which some critics apparently believe Hurston should have mimicked by providing a similar sense of canonical resolution), the rising level of John's personal agony creates a commensurate increase in his pulpit eloquence and also in his wry and bitter ability to sound out his enemies. And virtually all the characters share this ability to fashion humor-warmed philosophy out of pain. Commenting on African American comedy, Charles Nichols puts this wound-and-bow situation into perspective: "The black writer is probably more keenly aware than most that he lives at the edge of a precipice, in constant danger of some bottomless abyss of chaos and destruction. This very consciousness heightens his wild joy. His art is his only real freedom, his mastery of the ludicrous his only redemption" (105).

Finally, we have noted Hurston's sly use and subversion of the underlying mythic foundation of the Bible, which, after all, has often served as a weapon in the white world's unceasing campaign to maintain racial hegemony. Hurston would suggest in *Moses* that the Bible's original Afro-Asian roots had been distorted by later adaptations for such purposes. *Jonah,* an initial exploration of these issues and problems, receives magnificent amplification in the later book.

Jonah's Gourd Vine succeeds on many levels, especially in raising the conundrum of the flawed minister as the ideal vessel for God's messages. Perhaps the presiding minister's assertion at the funeral of John's mystery is also Hurston's. She began *Jonah* in an attempt to understand her father by fictionalizing him, and in some ways, by appropriating his voice, by actually *becoming* him, but she seems to have ended just as mystified by the wonder of his life as before, frustrated by the failure of the English language to encapsulate him. The understanding of the drums perhaps implies that John's tragedy lies not only in the separation of his body and soul but also in the sundering of his life from his African heritage. As Mary Helen Washington has noted, although *Their Eyes* indeed revolves around a woman finding a voice, it also limns the ultimate failure of language to adequately express a woman's experience or to offer a sure path to liberation. Washington agrees with Hemenway that John Pearson uses language to gain power and status rather than "the expression of feeling" and expands this to a critique of a culture "that celebrates orality to the exclusion of inner growth" (*Lives* 247). Is it possible, however, that Hurston felt that the ultimate language of the soul, bonded forever to the body, is a submerged, all-powerful, and inexpressible meta-language that supersedes all others? Moreover, although some have charged that John Pearson never changes, only his situation remains static; his perception of it, and therefore his agony, guilt, and ever-more-painful returns to sin do chart a terrible kind of progress of moral awareness, although it may not follow the traditional Christian/capitalist narrative route to transcendence or riches.

Amazingly, these sorrowful and sacral metaphysics, approached obliquely through comic presentation, prove both instructive and even exhilarating, permitting· Hurston to come far closer to saying the unsayable. By appropriating her father's voice, she too could function like the black ministers, who she once said were "the first artists, the ones intelligible to the masses. Like Adam Bede, a voice has told them to sing of the beginning of things."[46] By basing her narrative in folk humor and legend, and through her loving decision to face her father's faults with an open heart and a multivocal text, Hurston found a code for communal explication, and correlatively, a key to the human soul.

Notes

1. Hurston's title might have suggested defiance too. The great black stage duo of Williams and Walker boldly listed themselves as "Two Real Coons" in 1896, as both an advertisement and a veiled rebuke against the widespread practice of whites playing blacks with the aid of a little burnt cork (Anderson 36–37). Similarly aggressive manipulations of stereotypes may be found in Dick Gregory's title *Nigger*, or Alfred Kazin's *New York Jew*.

2. J. Mason Brewer's *The Word on the Brazos: Negro Preacher Tales from the Brazos Bottoms of Texas* offers a cornucopia of humor. For a representative selection of preacher jokes and church tales, see Hughes and Bontemps 139–62; Dorson 363–72; Brewer, *Word* 107–41; Spaulding 208–23, 505–15; Sterling 113–38. For a racier set—especially narratives that traveled north to the cities—see Abrahams, *Deep Down* 180–97. These stories contain sexually explicit elements Hurston or her editors chose not to include in her folklore collections.

3. Zora Neale Hurston to James Weldon Johnson, Apr. 16, 1934, James Weldon Johnson Memorial Collection, Yale Collection of American Literature, Beinecke Rare Book and Manuscript Library, Yale University, New Haven, Conn.

4. Herskovits is still a central figure in the debate over Africanisms, although several of his assertions have been challenged. See Herskovits and also J. Holloway for a reading of his position and the ongoing debate.

5. Young boys incorporate references to preachers in their play, including swimming, where a favorite trick is to somehow stay partly above water, waving one's arms like a preacher, marking lines such as "Git yourselfs straight,·cause yo' time ain't long" (C. Johnson 171–72).

6. Hurston may have had the general fate of Jonah in mind as well, as he is widely known in black culture as an unfortunate figure. Bert Williams, the famous black vaudevillean, had a popular song entitled "I'm a Jonah Man":

My hard luck started when I was born.
. . . .

Dat same hard luck been my bes' fren'.
. . . .

They named me after papa and the same day papa died.
For I'm a Jonah, I'm a Jonah man.

(Anderson 39)

7. Interestingly, the adolescent Richard Wright also was fascinated by trains and used to sneak into the cabs of locomotives and pretend he was an engineer. He, too, would use train imagery to describe the path of his life: "Somewhere in the dead of the southern night my life had switched onto the wrong track and, without my knowing it, the locomotive of my heart was rushing down a dangerously steep slope, heading for a collision, heedless of the warning red lights that blinked all about me, the sirens and the bells and the screams that filled the air" (*Long* 148). Wright, however, plays it straight, while Hurston mingles the metaphor with humor.

8. For a summary and brief discussion of snake imagery in Hurston's oeuvre, consult Morris and Dunn. Howard also addresses this issue in *Jonah;* see *Zora.*

9. For a variety of this popular staple, see Rosenberg 270–79.

10. This passage helps us understand Hurston's attitude, so often discussed, against writing "propaganda" fiction. She obviously felt "preaching" of her sort about black life was preferable to "lecturing" by writers such as Richard Wright.

11. We must note, both here and in *Moses,* that Hurston was recognizing in her fiction what has only recently been acknowledged in the academy, namely that black Americans created their own religious culture in this country, one that overlaps, to be sure, with white religion, but by no means merely replicates it. The "black sacred cosmos" includes religious attitudes and worldviews from Africa, as well as structures of spirituality developed in response to Christianity.

12. This phrase has inspired the title *Changing Our Own Words,* a collection of essays by scholars in the field of black feminist criticism, edited by Cheryl Wall.

13. Richard Wright uses the same saying in a very serious way indeed in *The Long Dream,* where the young boy Fish is terrified into fainting several times by guffawing policemen who pretend they're going to castrate him; they're amazed that the adage proves to be false.

14. Hurston uses all three of these "neutral zones" for moments of liminality. Nanny, in her flight from slavery, hides in a swamp before becoming free. Moses combines two realms, crossing the Red Sea and then going through a liminal phase in the desert. Although Arvay in *Seraph* never goes into the swamp, it becomes a psychic double for her unconscious; Earl, her alter ego, dies there, and his death is a liminal experience for his mother.

15. Pearson's relation to John is more obvious in a passage deleted from the manuscript, where Pearson says, "'Ye Gods! Why he's almost as big as I am now'" (17). The published version changes this to "'Dog damn! Boy

you're almost as big as I am,'" omitting the crucial "now," which establishes a prior relation. This relationship apparently is modeled from Hurston's family history; a letter to Godmother from Hurston discloses: "Do you know that in more than fifty years of this town's [Eatonville] existence that never has a white man's child been born here? My father was a mulatto but he was born in Alabama and moved here while young, following his employer and father who settled in the white community" (May 17, 1932, Moorland-Spingarn Research Center, Howard University Library, Washington, D.C.).

16. African survivalisms such as this have received great scrutiny in the past fifteen years. For an excellent example of current scholarship, consult J. Holloway.

17. This theme surfaces in many slave narratives. Frederick Douglass, for instance, speaks of cases where the plantation mistress makes the black children of her husband "suffer greater hardships, and have more to contend with." As a "constant offence" to her, she is "ever disposed to find fault with them. . . . She is never better pleased than when she sees them under the lash, especially when she suspects her husband of showing to his mulatto children favors which he withholds from his black slaves. The master is frequently compelled to sell this class of his slaves" (23).

18. There is another possible typological reference as well. In Judges 16, a chapter that begins with Samson's visit to a harlot and ends with his death after paying for his weaknesses with women with his eyesight, the fallen hero prays to God: "I pray thee, on this once, O God, that I may be at once avenged of the Philistines for my two eyes" (18). This is the only passage in the Bible that couples the words "two eyes," and it is telling that it comes in the chapter devoted to a womanizer who dies tragically. Furthermore, Hurston used materials from this book of the Bible repeatedly, especially in *Mule Bone*.

19. Although the dozens is usually a game for boys, girls are sometimes skilled players. For a discussion of female dozens playing, see Smitherman 128–34.

20. Hemenway links this allusion to folk narratives about black angels, but doesn't discuss the humorous element involved. His illustration is taken from B. A. Botkin's *A Treasury of Southern Folklore*. For a delightful turn-of-the-century sample of African American courtship conversation conventions, see Banks and Smiley.

21. Severed tree trunks are symbolic of older, defeated generations in *Their Eyes* as well, especially with Logan Killicks and Nanny.

22. For a full definition of these terms and their use, consult Abrahams ("Negro Stereotype," *Positively Black*, "Joking," and "Training") and Hannerz. In many ways, the terms "talking broad" and "talking bad" are interchangeable. The key distinction is between "talking sweet" and "talking broad," a subject Hurston develops to much greater effect in her characterizations of Moses and Aaron.

23. In "Characteristics of Negro Expression," Hurston describes this element of black discourse. She feels blacks create "action words" such as "chop-

axe," "sitting-chair," and "cook-pot," resulting in a pictoral language, which she calls hieroglyphics. Consequently, mere gesture and pose, without words, can frequently send a message. She also claims that the will to adorn is everywhere in black speech and gives many examples centered in the use of metaphor and simile, the use of the double descriptive, and the use of verbal nouns, all designed to "make over a great part of the tongue to" black people's "liking," as part of their "desire for beauty" ("Characteristics," 39). The general theory of language here is based on an analogy that presents black speech as a kind of "primitive" speech (primitive, we must remember, had not acquired its present negative connotation in 1934). Hurston in effect makes a case for the black speaker as poet: "The primitive man exchanges descriptive words. His terms are all close fitting." Compare this with Emerson's observations that "words are signs of natural facts. . . . Children and savages use only nouns or names of things, which they convert into verbs, and apply to analogous mental acts." Because "things are emblematic," words for natural things are spiritual, for "every natural fact is a symbol of some spiritual fact," so "as we go back in history, language becomes more picturesque, until its infancy, when it is all poetry; or all spiritual facts are represented by natural symbols." Emerson thus felt that latter-day Americans, isolated in the country (like Hurston's folk) were akin: "It is this which gives that piquancy to the conversation of a strong-natured farmer or back-woodsman, which all men relish" (31–34). Neither writer dwells on the comic aspect of such language, but surely the "piquancy" Emerson details and Hurston suggests throughout her essay points to the comic aspects of a language based in nature and the pictoral.

This could also be a literal description of Lucy's ability to "shape-note sing." Although waning in popularity in New England much earlier, shape-note singing thrived in the South and in rural areas well into the twentieth century. The system allowed untrained singers to read the music according to the shape of the note heads, which, in most cases, were squares, circles, triangles, and diamonds.

24. This is illustrated by a popular comparative-denominational joke. Black Baptist, Presbyterian, and Methodist preachers share a haunted room. When ghosts enter, the Baptist starts singing to no effect. The Presbyterian prays with the same lack of success. Finally, the Methodist takes up a collection and the haints leave (Dorson 372).

25. Roger Abrahams has delineated the "training of the man of words" and depicted rapping and capping as art in three key articles ("Rapping," "Joking," "Training"). For an amplification and qualification of Abrahams, consult Hannerz 119, 129, 133–35.

26. Hurston is obviously presenting John in yet another liminal way by positioning him where her father was, in a period of change and adjustment for the African American minister. In many ways John's training for the pulpit and his background make him heir of the long lineage of slave preachers, heroic figures who nonetheless sometimes became the brunt of their congregations' jokes. At the same time, as the comic "duel" with the new minis-

ter demonstrates, black pulpit performances were changing, as Hurston well knew. In both eras, however, ministers were expected to take their texts from life, employing stories—sometimes humorous ones—to illustrate problems blacks faced, and thereby suggesting possible solutions. For an analysis of the development, function, and importance of slave ministers, a subject I am unable to fully address here, the key resource is Albert J. Raboteau's *Slave Religion;* see also the work of Owens, Levine, Genovese, and Blassingame.

27. In *Their Eyes,* Jody Starks (clearly modeled on Joe Clarke) is the first mayor. In this book Hurston is more faithful to the actual facts and names of Eatonville, although she scrambles the chronology. The real Joe Clarke was mayor from 1900 to 1912, Hurston's father John from 1912 to 1916, Matthew Brazell from then to 1920, followed by Sam Mosely from 1922 to 1924. All four of them play themselves in Hurston's fiction, while her father becomes John Pearson. Brazell's mule (Bonner's mule in *Their Eyes*) becomes more famous than his owner (Otey 16–22).

28. Joseph Heller has seen the comic possibilities of King David's narrative. His *God Knows* (1984), an uneven but frequently hilarious novel, uses humor to make profoundly serious points about God, sexuality, racial leadership, and global politics. It offers fascinating parallels with Hurston's *Moses.*

29. In 1947 Hurston would expand this tale into the story/fable "The Lost Keys of Glory." The manuscript shows how far Hurston had come from the feminist formulations of *Their Eyes;* much of it reads like the "fascinating womanhood" arguments voiced by reactionary women's groups. She makes her point specific and contemporary: "In 1947, women have entered every profession and skill that men follow for a living. There is no doubt that women are taking themselves quite seriously as the equal of men in all of these pursuits. It is obvious, however, that women are not adequate to the struggle. Like the brief time when Man first got his superior strength, the women have not realized that it is so. . . . It is nevertheless true that women in any particular field have never been able to come up to a standard of excellency equal to the best men in that same profession" (9).

30. Booker T. Washington commented tellingly on this phenomenon: "A large proportion took up . . . preaching as an easy way to make a living. . . . The ministry suffered . . . on account of not only ignorant but in many cases immoral men who claimed that they were 'called to preach.' In the earlier days of freedom almost every coloured man who learned to read would receive 'a call to preach'. . . . The supply of ministers was large. . . . I knew a certain church that had a total membership of about two hundred, and eighteen of that number were ministers." Later, Washington tells a joke on this subject: "A coloured man in Alabama . . . one hot day in July, while he was at work in a cotton-field, suddenly stopped, and, looking toward the skies, said: 'O Lawd, de cotton am so grassy, de work am so hard, and the sun am so hot dat I b'lieve dis darky am called to preach!'" (72, 97).

31. Addison Gayle flatly states that Lucy, "because of her loyalty, courage, and perseverance, stands out as the dominant character in the novel." For him, she is the "black woman come to maturity in a new South and a new

age," but he principally lauds her for "her willingness to suffer for her man and her children, an important element in her makeup as a black woman," yet he also calls her "a delectable morsel" (142–44). Although we might agree that Lucy is an arresting character, these cited attributes are hardly "new" in black female portraiture, and that she scores higher than John in moral goodness doesn't mean she's therefore the center of the novel. Mary Helen Washington, by contrast, is just as definite as Gayle, but asserts (correctly, in my view): "John Pearson is unambiguously the heroic center of *Jonah's Gourd Vine*. He inhabits the entire text, his voice is heard on nearly every page, he follows his own dreams, he is selected by the community to be its leader and is recognized by the community for his powers and chastised for his shortcomings" (*Invented* 250). Her remarks here are part of a fascinating comparison of John and *Their Eyes*'s Janie.

32. The comic debates of the church committees in *Jonah* are similar in structure to the second act of *Mule Bone*. There rival churches sit on either side of the stage as a comic trial, administered by the mayor, takes place.

33. Those who feel Lucy is the gourd vine cite Hurston's letter to Carl Van Vechten: "Oh yes, the title you didn't understand. (Jonah 4:6–10). You see the prophet of God sat up under a gourd vine that had grown up in one night. But a cut worm came along and cut it down. Great and sudden growth. One act of malice and it is withered and gone" (Feb. 28, 1934, James Weldon Johnson Memorial Collection, Yale Collection of American Literature, Beinecke Rare Book and Manuscript Library, Yale University, New Haven, Conn.). The act of malice is seen as John's slapping of Lucy; but we should remember that Deacon Harris's malice is directed toward cutting down that "Jonah's gourd vine" (154), and that there are several other possible meanings for the title.

34. Hurston has played with this scene in more than one way. This is the first treatment of her mother's death and comes in a work of fiction. Yet she recycled it, virtually intact, for her autobiography many years later. We see Hurston merging fact into fiction again in this novel. Although this story only echoes the facts of Hurston's parents' romance, notice that Lucy's six brothers and one sister exactly duplicate the number and sexes of Zora's siblings, at least as she recorded it. We now know there were nine children; a son, Isaac, died before Zora was born (Bordelon 8).

35. Later, in a more somber and cosmic moment, the drum mourns John's death. This passage also suggests that the terrors of the middle passage and its sequels were made more manageable by psychic doubling and a bitter, terrible, but sustaining inner laughter.

36. Hurston was intent on emphasizing Africanisms at least partly to demonstrate the strong power of African survivals in black Florida folklife, humor, and religion. Her work in this area has recently been validated by Robert L. Hall, who comments extensively on late nineteenth-century African religious retentions in Florida; see his essay "African Religious Retentions in Florida," in J. Holloway, 98–118.

37. This charge, however, has another side to it, whether Hurston wished

to show it or not. John O. Killens in his novel *Youngblood* has one character, an Uncle Tom school principle, lecture a teacher about the inability of blacks to accept the dominance of a leader. Richard Myles, the teacher, responds, "'As far as that parable about the crabs is concerned—People are a little bit different from crabs. It's not those at the bottom that pull down the others trying to get to the top. That's not the problem at all. Some of those that get half way up turn around and when they see the millions of black hands reaching up to them for a helping hand, they take baseball bats and beat them on their knuckles. But the most important question is to concentrate on the man who put you in the bottom of the basket in the first place. He's the main one seeing to it that we don't get out'" (297). We might also note that the process of "leveling" was a prime function of African American religion; conversion implied equality with whites, with all sinners made equal before God. This works within the race as well, of course, and Hambo's remarks have equal relevance to communal judgment of sin and sinning, and these too may be expressed in a comic manner.

38. Nor was this the end of Hurston's hatred. She relates that years later, doing research for her Columbia degree, she drove twenty miles out of her way to where she learned her stepmother was living "to finish the job," but finds she's dying with a neck tumor. "I turned back, all frustrated inside. All I could do was to wish that she had a lot more neck to rot" (*Dust Tracks,* 103). Hurston may have also known that African religions judge weak figures (lacking "life force") who subvert power from strong life-force figures as profoundly evil (Mbiti 258). Hattie's model, Mattie Hurston, was in fact married (apparently happily) to John Hurston until his death. According to Winifred Hurston Clark, Zora's niece who grew up in Memphis, where Mattie and John resided for many years, John's grandchildren for a long time thought Mattie was their natural grandmother and adored her. Moreover, in 1910, five years after their marriage, Mattie and John were still caring for Zora's younger siblings, Joel, Ben, and Everett. They were *not* in foster homes (Bordelon 12–13).

39. The phrase "divorce in your heels" was used earlier in the book by a character named Exie to describe herself. There, however, it was funny, because it was self-reflexive and an inside joke. Context, in ethnic humor, is all. Here, because of the joker, his audience, and the setting, the jokes are merely racist.

40. This and so much else in Hurston's repertoire of images comes from the Bible and traditional black sermons. The sermon, with its emphasis on the Creation, strongly suggests James Weldon Johnson's poetic setting of the same theme, and his response to the original sources surely echoes what Hurston felt as she set Lovelace's gem. He relates that hearing a black evangelist preach in Kansas City "tempered me to just the right mood to go on with what I had started when I wrote 'The Creation.' I was in touch with the deepest revelation of the Negro's soul that has yet been made, and I felt myself attuned to it. . . . As I worked, my own spirit rose till it reached a degree almost of ecstasy" (*Way* 377).

41. For a full discussion of this tradition in American culture, see Constance Rourke's classic text *American Humor.*

42. The great migration has received much attention of late, especially in the work of Nicholas Lemann and Carole Marks; her bibliography is useful as well.

43. Hurston wrote but never published a comic one-act play drawn from folklore about this, "The Fiery Chariot." See also Ernest Gaines's use of this motif in the death of Albert Cluveau in *The Autobiography of Miss Jane Pittman.*

44. This curiously echoes Isabel's final cry over the dead body of her lover-brother Pierre, "'All's o'er, and you know him not!'" (362), in Melville's *Pierre.* The title character, like John, is a highly doubled and ambiguous hero who alternates between the sinful and the holy in a search for truth. Isabel's cry similarly comes on the last page of the novel. Were both Melville and Hurston mocking their readers? Or themselves, as failed artists? Or both?

45. Hurston's pronouncement appeared in her essay "Race Cannot Become Great Until It Recognizes Its Talent."

46. Zora Neale Hurston to James Weldon Johnson, May 8, 1934, James Weldon Johnson Memorial Collection, Yale Collection of American Literature, Beinecke Rare Book and Manuscript Library, Yale University, New Haven, Conn.

THREE

Laughin' Up a World:
Their Eyes Were Watching God and
the (Wo)Man of Words

[The] ability of a person to use active and copious verbal performance to achieve recognition within his group is observable throughout Afro-American communities in the New World. It has given rise to an observable social type . . . called "the man-of-words." His performances are typified by his willingness to entertain and instruct anywhere and anytime, to make his own occasions. In all he does, he attempts to dazzle as well as amuse. And in each performance he must incessantly call attention to himself as an unexcelled speaker or singer.

—*Roger D. Abrahams*

There is no such thing as a Negro tale which lacks point. Each tale brims over with humor. The Negro is determined to laugh even if he has to laugh at his own expense. By the same token, he spares nobody else. His world is dissolved in laughter. His "bossman," his woman, his preacher, his jailer, his God, and himself, all must be baptized in the stream of laughter.

—*Zora Neale Hurston*

Jonah provided Hurston a great rehearsal for the issues she would raise in her masterwork, *Their Eyes Were Watching God*. In some ways, Janie's story resurrects Lucy, now free, to go forward and preach the great sermon that her social role in the earlier novel denies her. Janie, child-free, financially secure, leaves one husband, buries two others, and finds the "pulpit" Lucy always deserved. She does so, as her predecessor attempted without success, by using that fearful weapon John alludes to in *Jonah:* "'Jes' cause women folks ain't got no big muscled arm and fistes lak jugs, folks claims they's weak vessels, but dass uh lie. Dat piece uh red flannel she got hung 'tween her jaws is equal tuh all de fistes God ever made and man ever seen. Jes' take an ruin a man wid they tongue, and den dey kin hold it still and bruise 'im up jes' ez bad'" (158).

Janie, however, will go far beyond this description, for she learns that humor can be constructive, supportive, and joyous, and that it can create personal and communal harmony as well as discord. She also seems to understand that even language has its limits, however, and that the search to express many of life's mysteries must be ultimately surrendered to the "inaudible voice of it all" (24).

Although the text signals Janie's achievement of voice to the reader in various ways, the most telling lies in her overarching transmission of her story to her friend Pheoby, who learns and grows from her sister-in-the-spirit's tale. Pheoby then tells the story to others, taking in her turn the expression so key to the novel, "mah tongue is in mah friend's mouf" (17).

This phrase appears in Swift's *Gulliver's Travels* during the voyage to Laputa. In the kingdom of Luggnagg, Gulliver has been taught, without understanding the words themselves, the local way to say to the king, "My tongue is in the mouth of my friend"; Gulliver tells us that "by this expression was meant that I desired leave to bring my interpreter" (Swift 166). Whether Hurston took the expression from Swift or directly from folk culture seems less interesting than Swift's own recognition of the need for linguistic bridges, be they between people or cultures, and the usefulness of "translators" and "friends"; above all, however, Swift, like Hurston, understood the great role humor could play in that endeavor.[1] Accordingly, the tongue Janie wields in *Their Eyes* is honed by humor and the ability to "talk that talk," for she achieves maturity, identity, and independence through the development of a voice, one that treats narrative as a repository and display piece for her hard-won, humorously expressed wisdom.

The book's justly famous opening leans more to the cosmic than the comic, but even here the two realms merge: "Ships at a distance have every man's wish on board. For some they come in with the tide. For others they sail forever on the horizon, never out of sight, never landing until the Watcher turns his eyes away in resignation, his dreams mocked to death by Time. That is the life of men" (9). Thus we see right away the possibility of God the joker, an idea everywhere in Hurston's works; for Time/God, Watcher/Man, and the promise of life itself are all subject to interpretation as a series of cosmic jokes, a race that must be run but never won. This somewhat ominous opening should be borne in mind by those who see the book as a "simple" and "joyous" tale and nothing else.[2]

Their Eyes describes a woman's quest for identity and, like most quests, ends with the heroine's returning to the community for re-integration; she thereby achieves wholeness while enriching the community with her newfound insights.³ Most critics have quite rightly concentrated on this search for a voice; as the second paragraph tells us, for women "the dream is the truth. Then they act and do things accordingly" (9). It takes Janie more than a little while (over twenty years) to find her dream, but she does indeed "act accordingly" once she finds it, concordantly with a voice. While criticism focusing on this aspect of the book has been quite persuasive and illuminating,⁴ most scholars have entirely neglected Janie's skills as a narrator who entertains, indeed, mesmerizes, and much of this comes from her considerable gifts as a humorist. Rewarding, reciprocal love with Tea Cake and self-expression come from the mastery of laughter and its language, which subsequently becomes a bond between Janie and her community.

Henry Louis Gates, Jr., in *The Signifying Monkey* provides an intriguing reading of *Their Eyes,* demonstrating Hurston's success in creating what he calls a "speakerly text," which introduces free indirect discourse into African American narration. Doing so enables her to gradually annul the distance between her own authorial voice and those of her characters, especially Janie's, a device that enables the intimacy of first person narration while avoiding its restrictions. The speakerly text privileges its own folk-centered, vernacular mode of narration over all other structural elements. Gates does especially well in linking signification with the pattern of play and gaming in the novel, although after touching on this he goes on to his real interest, Hurston's narrative play. I would add that humor constitutes a key ingredient in Hurston's craft and especially in the play aspect that so intrigues Gates. Dialect, after all, finds its shape and form from folk content, and humor functions as the heart and soul of both Hurston's idiomatic prose and presentations of play.

Hurston signals the importance of Janie's linguistic maturity by emphasizing through the frame story the verbal tools she bears within her as she marches back into Eatonville at the opening of the novel. In this respect she proves fortuitously armed, for the community has an arsenal of scorn waiting for her: "Seeing the woman as she was made them remember the envy they had stored up and swallowed with relish. They made burning statements with questions, and killing tools out of laughs" (10). This returns us with a vengeance to Freud's concept of humor as an aggressive force. Their cruel laughter has a base in presumed dichotomies, always a rich source of mirth;

the blue satin dress of her departure against the overalls of her return, the money left by Jody and the money now presumed squandered, the woman of forty with the loose hair of "some young gal," but most of all, the woman of forty alone, not the woman who left with "dat young lad of a boy." Janie, they hope, will turn out to be a comic script they know well and hope to use, for they intend their humor to "uncrown" Janie, as Bakhtin would say, to make her "fall to their level" (11). The women hoard up this image, knowing they might need it, for their men are also "reading" this text, seeing Janie's "firm buttocks like she had grape fruits in her hip pockets" and her "pugnacious breasts trying to bore holes in her shirt" (11). A comic contrast develops between the men's richly appreciative and sly appraisal of the body and the women's smugly snickering scorn, but both depersonalize her. After Janie wordlessly enters her gate and slams it behind her, "Pearl Stone opened her mouth and laughed real hard because she didn't know what else to do" (11). Like Hester Prynne in the opening pages of *The Scarlet Letter,* Janie will be the victim of cruel, unthinking humor until she silences it, and unlike Hester, she must cap the discussion by having the last laugh herself.

The figuration of Janie's buttocks and breasts as grapefruits and weapons would seem to be mere significations upon the object of desire, but in fact meld and reverse traditional associations. The breasts would ordinarily be associated with food, but here become weapons; the buttocks, traditionally associated with ridicule (the "butt" of jokes) become not only food, but local food (grapefruit), and thus a sign of bounty, as they literally "grow on trees" all around. Thus Janie, potentially nutritive and destructive, represents both promise and threat. She embodies, in short, mystery. A concentration on her buttocks and breasts in this particular way suggests both possibilities of her return. She will either become a recurring victim of men's lust, the way the pathetic Mrs. Tyler has been with her succession of young male lovers, or she will be revealed as someone who actually learned from her absence, thereby presumably strengthening her preexisting separation from the community. If she is set apart because of her class, her breasts cannot be sexually enjoyed, and thus nutritive to the male ego, but taunting, inaccessible weapons. Janie's overalls would seem to signal the "fall" the women wish, but they actually make even her sexual identity puzzling, feeding into a general air of mystery that the town feels as she reenters their world. By treating her humorously, they attempt to reduce her mystery to a mere riddle that may be solved.

Janie wants to refamiliarize herself with the town, to use her narrative to annul the differences separation and absence create. In her case, however, her mystery goes further, as her name suggests, for "Jan(ie)" stems from Hurston's birth month, January. Janus was a god unique to the Romans; he has no Greek equivalent. Even the Romans were unable or unwilling to assign him a specific meaning; like Janie's all-purpose tabula rasa status among the white Washburn children, who appropriately name her Alphabet, Janus was a god whose sign could be created by his worshippers, yet he was seen and worshipped as one of the "oldest, holiest, and most exalted of gods" (Seyffert, Nettleship, and Sandys 328). At sacrifices, he was invoked first; prayers to him preceded even those to Jupiter. Originally, he was the god of sun and light who opened up the gates of paradise when he went out in the morning and closed them when he returned at night. Eventually, he was termed the god of going out and coming in and identified with all doors and gates, which were holy to him and often dedicated to him. Indeed, his image, remembered by us as merely his doubled head, was also a gatekeeper with a staff and a key in his hands. His face was not just looking forward and backward, but also in and out, signifying his governance over time. Therefore, the beginnings and ends of things were sacred to him. His chief festival date was January 1, when he was honored with cakes of meal. Gifts of sweets were exchanged between celebrants. Furthermore, the origin of all life was associated with him and he was also known as the "sower." More generally, however, he was known as the "Custodian of the Universe."[5]

Hurston's strong identification with and interest in folklore and myth influenced her work continuously. Hurston's particular attraction to the Janus myth, however, may have affected decisions about her personal life. According to the family Bible, Hurston was born on January 15, 1891, although census records indicate she was born on January 7 of that year. All during her life, however, she often listed her birthday as January 1, 3, or 7 and the year of her birth as 1901 or 1903, even on official identification such as her driver's license. Furthermore, her religious sensibility, particularly after her hoodoo research, was always multicultural, syncretic, and personal. *Moses* demonstrates her brilliant conflation of the title figure and Damballah, the West African God. Janus, with his two heads, his mystery, his depiction as both laughing and serious, and the obvious parallel this forms with the masks of attic tragedy and comedy would make him a double of the two-headed man, the conjurer, and an associate of the trickster in folk comedy as well. An African parallel exists; Henry Louis Gates, Jr., has pointed out that the Fon people's primal god has two sides; these represent male and female divinities, Lisa and Mawu, whose eyes respectively form the sun and the moon. This mode of characterization also appears in certain depictions of Esu, reconciling the opposite poles of discourse (*Signifying* 23, 29, 34).

In *Jonah* Hurston had already played on the Janus imagery. The entire book rings with the comedy of initiation and of the greenhorn, which shows Janus's obvious link with liminality. Hurston made the central couple, Lucy and John, radically different people who nevertheless live together—an obvious manifestation of Janus's opposed identities. As we saw, Lucy's birthday, December 31, contrasts dramatically with John's, January 1. She represents the traditional, the tried, the true, home and hearth, while he stands for the new, the forbidden, the uncharted.

Hurston provides obvious references to Janus throughout *Their Eyes*. Janie repeatedly gets associated with doors, thresholds, gates, and gateposts, and we know from *Dust Tracks* that Hurston's favorite picture of herself was that of a young girl leaning over the gatepost looking down the glistening shell road and dreaming of horizon (36, 45). It was also an image she associated with freedom, for in a 1932 letter to Godmother anticipating the day in which she would be financially independent, she says only then will Godmother be able to see her again as "the Zora of the Eatonville Gatepost."[6] And Janie begins her story by deciding "her conscious life had commenced at Nanny's gate" (13). She must have seen the intersection of the actual road and the cosmic horizon and related it to her internal dreams. Tea Cake several times tells Janie she has "the keys to the kingdom," reminding us of the black woman's role as gatekeeper and Hurston's constant reference to the folktale concerning woman's domestic "keys."

Food continues the overt Janus references throughout the novel. Janie's decision to leave Jody comes as she flips a hoe-cake onto its other side. The two faces of the cake sacred to Janus of course augur a new beginning, and Janie soon darts out the door, tossing her apron on a bush. Similarly, in the frame tale, Pheoby comes bearing a gift of mulatto rice (red and white rice, or beans and rice), a "sweetmeat" appropriate for exchange among celebrants of Janus, and indeed, in the South, January 1 can begin a string of bad luck unless one eats a goodly quantity of black-eyed beans and rice seasoned with hog's jowl (significantly, meat from the mouth). Pheoby's gift, also referred to as a "covered bowl" (13), could have another, darker, classical allusion as well, the gifts for the dead mentioned in the title of Aeschylus's *The Libation Bearers*.

More often, however, Janus plays a less direct but more significant role. The narrative itself, for instance, begins Janus-like, looking forward and backward, as the townspeople and readers try to piece together Janie's past in an effort to predict her future. Appropriately, for a book that will repeatedly focus on humorous modes of address and description, Pheoby presents Janie's case to the other women with a scornful humor: "'De way you talkin' you'd think de folks in dis town didn't do nothin' in de bed 'cept praise de Lawd'" (13). She greets Janie's arrival more positively: "'Gal, you sho looks *good*. You looks like youse yo' own daughter.' They both laughed" (14). The irony and therefore the doubling of the joke lies in the fact that Janie, in a metaphorical sense, *is* her own daughter, in that she has created a new persona out of the woman who left town with Tea Cake. Pheoby's joke fits with her entrance to Janie's yard through the "intimate" gate, for her humor, always useful in establishing intimacy, brings the two old friends together quickly.

Janie exuberantly expresses her appreciation for the dish Pheoby has brought her: "'Gal, it's *too* good! you switches a mean fanny round in a kitchen'" (15). This inaugurates her in the reader's mind as a woman versed in folk wisdom and humor and signals that, like Pheoby, she knows how to use a joke to initiate warmth and welcome.[7] The dish itself, mulatto rice, constitutes a joke too, since Janie's white blood relates her to the food and causes jealousy within the community. Hurston extends the food/eating metaphor further; as Janie eats, she comments that "'people like dem wastes up too much time puttin' they mouf on things they don't know nothin' about. Now they got to look in to me loving Tea Cake and see whether it was done right or not! They don't know if life is a mess of corn-meal dumplings, and if love is a bed-quilt! . . . If they wants to see and know, why they don't come kiss and be kissed? Ah could then sits down and tell 'em things. Ah been a delegate to de big 'ssociation of life. Yessuh! De Grand Lodge, de big convention of livin' is just where Ah been dis year and a half y'all ain't seen me'" (17–18). People "like dem" can be heard laughing up the road, and Janie immediately comments, "'Well, Ah see Mouth-Almighty is still sittin in de same place. And Ah reckon they got *Me* up in they mouth now,'" a cogent comment on the judgemental, rigidly righteous neighbors (16).

Although Janie jokes that "'if God don't think no mo' 'bout 'em then Ah do, they's a lost ball in de high grass,'" she knows she has an interest in the social game, and the ensuing story of her wanderings told to Pheoby appears meant to bring the players together again (16). As John Callahan has demonstrated, Janie tells her story to Pheoby because, unlike the community as a whole at this point, Pheoby eagerly listens, responds, and urges on the narrative. As Hurston states, "Pheoby's hungry listening helped Janie to tell her story" (23). Callahan usefully points to the way this structural device, taken from the modes of black discourse in general and the black church in particular, supports the achievement of what he calls a rhetoric of "intimacy and immensity" throughout the entire book (115–49). Although Callahan does not discuss the role of humor, his terms here are similar to those I have identified as key to Hurston's comedic world: the systolic system she creates by recognizing the "co(s)mic," humor's paradoxically central role in the cosmos, but also its ability to cancel voids by the achievement of intimacy. As I see it, the intimacy Callahan traces so diligently comes from the humor of the characters and the culture in addition to the structural device of call and response.

The retrospective narrative of Janie's life significantly begins with a joke she remembers was played on her as a child. Raised with the white Washburn children, she doesn't identify herself as black until all the children view a group photograph. When she exclaims, "'Where is me?'" Janie's distinguishing question throughout the book, the assembled group laughs at her. "'Miss Nellie . . . said, "Dat's you, Alphabet, don't you know yo' ownself?" . . . Ah said: "Aw, aw! Ah'm colored!" Den dey all laughed real hard. But before Ah seen de picture Ah thought Ah wuz just like de rest'" (29). Here laughter, although loving, also becomes isolating. Conversely, the black children at school tease Janie about "livin' in de white folks backyard." Although Hurston doesn't see fit to stress the fact, Janie's octoroon status causes her to catch comic venom from both sides throughout the book. A "knotty head gal name Mayrella" teases her relentlessly because the white Mis' Washburn favors Janie and dresses her beautifully. Mayrella incites others, so their play forestalls Janie's, significantly pushing her out of "de ring plays," the African-derived circle games that here obviously signify membership in African American society.

The frame story of the novel repeats this situation, for once again Janie's identity becomes a burning issue for a circle of questioning faces, but this time Janie herself provides the answers, fighting the firestorm of cruel, aggressive laughter with narrative, uniting, communal laughter, refusing to let the circle of fellowship become broken. Her voice, multiplied by those of the characters who have shaped and been shaped by her life, does indeed become an alphabet at last, one that spells out the human comedy and condition.

Hurston's narratives are replete with tragedy as well, but virtually everyone in the book has some comic lines. Nanny offers no exception to this, but she can only joke after Janie has been safely married off. In some ways, we may posit Nanny's mode of narration as generated by her harsh experiences and thus representative of both slave narratives and what would become known as "protest literature" after Richard Wright exploded on the literary scene.[8] Hurston ingeniously presents us with this representative history and then has the text ask, through Janie, will a tragic history (as expressed through Nanny and Leafy) take the pleasure out of present black life (Janie's)? For a time, the answer seems to be yes.

In her desire to provide Janie "security" before her own death, Nanny marries her to Logan Killicks, a work-deadened but decent older man who appears to be almost as imprisoned by sharecropping as his ancestors were by slavery. His stunted manhood finds its symbol in the metaphor Janie chooses to describe his farm, "a lonesome place like a stump in the middle of the woods where nobody had ever been" (39). The stump imagery links Logan with Nanny's despair; she wears dead palma christi leaves (thought to be poisonous by rural communities) around her head for coolness and refers to black people as "branches without roots" (31). The amputated stump suggests Logan's notably unadorned speech as well. Hurston said "Negro expression" is always characterized by the "will to adorn," which "satisfies the soul of the creator" ("Characteristics" 39). Nanny's and Logan's barren signifiers stand in stark contrast to Janie's glorious flowering pear tree, where she dreams of love and eternity.

When Janie's expectation of falling in love with Logan is not met, she seeks advice from Nanny, who erupts in revealing, dialect-driven, comic invective. She employs "black on black" signification and a telling malapropism: "'Ah know dat grass-gut, liver-lipted nigger ain't done took and beat mah baby already! Ah'll take a stick and salivate 'im!'" (40). This does not indicate surprise at Janie's being beaten, but that she has been beaten so soon. The "liver-lipted" reference is part of black-on-black humorous tradition, and the reference to his "grass-gut" transforms him into a cow and thus feminizes him. Her previously unstated reservations about Logan find further expression when Janie adds, to be fair, that Logan draws water and chops wood for her. "'Humph! don't 'spect all dat tuh keep up. He ain't kissin' yo' mouf when he carry on over yuh lak dat. He's kissin' yo' foot and 'tain't in uh man tuh kiss foot long. Mouf kissin' is on uh equal and dat's natural but when dey got to bow down tuh love, dey soon straightens up.'" Nanny offsets her comic skepticism, however, with her respect for material things: "'If you don't want him, you sho oughta. Heah you is wid de onliest organ in town, amongst colored folks, in yo' parlor. Got a house bought and paid for and sixty acres uh land right on de big road and . . . Lawd have mussy! Dat's de very prong all us black women gits hung on. Dis love!'" (41–42). Nanny's discourse has two embedded sexual jokes in it. Janie has an "organ" in her parlor now, but neither she nor Logan can make "music" with it. And clearly the "prong" women get "hung on" is more than just "dis love."

Nanny thus correctly reads Janie's sexual frustration, seen most prominently in the young bride's cry, "'Ah hates de way his head is so long one way and so flat on de sides and dat pone uh fat back uh his neck. . . . His belly is too big too, now, and his toe-nails look lak mule foots. And 'tain't nothin' in de way of him washin' his feet every evenin' before he comes tuh bed'" (42). This signifying address affords a fine example of a technique we have seen before, where a character may speak in deadly earnest, even in pain, but Hurston sees to it that the dialogue is comically adorned for the reader's benefit. This suggests (as we saw in the conversations between Amy and Ned in *Jonah*) that comic expression of the most painful things somehow eases heavy psychic burdens, even if the characters speaking and listening do not necessarily seem amused at the utterance.

The drama of Jody's explosion onto the scene profits from his contrast with Logan, a figure notably lacking in many traits, but especially humor. After Nanny's death, Logan decides to quit hauling wood and drawing water for Janie, as Nanny predicted; he even wants his wife to start plowing. This draws a comic tirade from Janie, a play on words that nevertheless sends a message: "'Scuse mah freezolity, Mist' Killicks, but Ah don't mean to chop de first chip'" (44). Her "freezolity" combines a sense of iciness and frivolity, expressing both the way she feels and how she knows he will interpret her emotion.

Logan's response to her supposition that she might leave him represents his only comic moment, and he uses humor aggressively, to hurt. "'You won't git far and you won't be long, when dat big gut reach over and grab dat little one. . . . Ah'm sleepy. Ah don't aim to worry mah gut into a fiddle-string wid no s'posin'" (52). When he demands that Janie come out and help him shovel manure the next day, that is the final straw. Logan doesn't know that Janie thinks he looks at this moment "like a black bear doing some clumsy dance on his hind legs" (52); the reader goes further, and sees that Logan is figuratively as well as literally "shoveling shit."

It thus comes as no surprise when Janie falls for the flashy, ambitious, and apparently fun-loving Jody Starks, even though he "did not represent sun-up and pollen and blooming trees, but he spoke for horizon. He spoke for change and chance" (50). He comes into the novel audibly first, through his cheerful whistle. Because he does not look her way, Janie labors furiously at the pump to get his attention, which (accidentally?) causes her hair, always mentioned as her sexual glory, to fall down. Jody's immediate interest and his request for a drink of water provides us with yet another biblical woman-at-the-well scenario. Moreover, "It had always been his wish and desire to be a big voice," and he intends to develop it in Eatonville, an all-black town where a man can have a chance. His abundant humor adds an ingredient; he makes Janie laugh: "'You behind a plow! You ain't got no mo' business wid uh plow than uh hog is got wid uh holiday! . . . A pretty doll-baby lak you is made to sit on de front porch and rock and fan yo'self'" (49). Over the next twenty years, however, this joke pales, for it proves grimly prophetic. His appellation of "doll-baby" falls alarmingly close to Logan's pet name for her, "L'il Bit."

Jody's entry into Eatonville with Janie on his arm leads to his first comic deflation, following a discussion with two men "sitting on their shoulderblades" who "almost" sit upright at "the tone of his voice," which he characteristically raises in demand: "'I god, where's de Mayor.'" This question doubles as an assertion—he's God, so the mayor, if there is one, must be lesser, and if no one has been elected, he's an obvious candidate. His posture, however, as so often happens later in the book, instantly collapses, as one of the men slyly asks, "'You and yo' daughter goin' tuh join wid us in fellowship?'" (57).

Up until now we have largely drawn our opinions of Jody from Janie, and they have been positive. The two men, however, watch Janie and Jody depart, and in a comic variant of stichomythia, provide a "reading" of the pair:

> "Dat man talks like a section foreman. . . . He's might compellment."
> "Shucks! . . . Mah britches is just as long as his. But dat wife uh hisn! Ah'm uh son of uh Combunction if Ah don't go tuh Georgy and git me one just like her."
> "Whut wid?"
> "Wid mah talk, man."
> "It takes money tuh feed pretty women. Dey gits uh lavish uh talk."
> "Not lak mine. Dey loves to hear me talk because dey can't understand it. Mah co-talkin' is too deep. Too much co to it." (58–59)

This exchange deepens the narrative considerably, for it provides the first manifestation in the story proper of the "choral" function the townspeople play, a role virtually always adorned, as here, with hu-

mor. It provides a kind of frame within the frame as well, both verbally and visually, for we "see" as well as hear: "Already the town had
found the strangers. Joe was on the porch talking to a small group
of men. Janie could be seen through the bedroom window getting
settled," icons for the gendered roles associated with jocular speech
and silent domesticity (59).

Finally, the humorous speculations of these two townsmen "flip"
our understanding of Jody, a process Janie will painfully and gradually experience over the years. This narrative process of shaking things
up, over, or inside out becomes a repeated motif in the book, one
frequently associated with humor, as disjunction often is. In her final
exchanges with Logan, Janie feels she's "turned wrongside out just
standing there and feeling" (53). Her final decision to leave comes
with a laugh, when she flips over a hoe-cake. Years later, this scene
finds its darker double when disenchantment with Jody causes Janie
to discover she has an "inside" and an "outside."

The visual images of Janie and Jody soon find verbal comic expression. Indeed, as Houston Baker has astutely noted, Joe Starks, rather than being the "careless," pollinating "love bee" Janie desires, actually represents a worker bee, busily engaged in a parody (as Logan
was on a lower level) of white entrepreneurial economics (*Blues* 58).
But Jody can use humor too, especially to transact business. He does
so in making his first public point—that the town needs to buy more
land from "Cap'n Eaton": "'Y'all ain't got enough here to cuss a cat
on without gittin' yo' mouf full of hair,'" but the men's disbelieving
laughter comes from the idea of buying more land, period, rather
than the expression: "The idea was funny to them and they wanted
to laugh. They tried hard to hold it in, but enough incredulous laughter burst out of their eyes and leaked from the corners of their
mouths." Joe notices and senses a test, and indeed, several go with
him to show him the way to Maitland and "to be there when his bluff
was called" (61). This male testing of Joe has a parallel with Janie,
for Hicks significantly "mounts" the porch to try to make time with
her. Janie doesn't respond to his loaded offer: "'Anything *Ah* kin do
tuh help out, why you kin call on me,'" prompting his "'Folks must
be mighty close-mouthed where you come from,'" enabling her to
"cap" him with "'Dat's right. But it must be different at yo' home'"
(61).

In a key passage, Hicks learns Jody actually bought twenty acres and
plans to set up a store and post office. "He wasn't ready to think of
colored people in post offices yet. He laughed boisterously. 'Y'all let
dat stray darky tell y'all any ole lie! Uh colored man sittin' up in uh

post office!' He made an obscene sound" (63). Hurston clearly wants to show how white culture has made the idea of black men in authority ridiculous for so long that the victims themselves have come to believe in the ludicrous images that were popular in the press, such as the exaggerated cartoons of black ape-like congressmen lolling in legislative halls during Reconstruction. Coker, however, has learned the lie of this from Jody's actions and reproves Hicks's self-defeating laughter: "'Us colored folks is too envious of one 'nother. Dat's how come us don't git no further than us do. Us talks about de white man keepin' us down!'" (63). This scene clearly echoes Hambo's basket of crabs in *Jonah.*

In a brilliantly managed scene, Joe emerges as town leader at the purposely ceremonial dedication of his store, which he intends to be the heart of the town. Cleverly, he has Tony Taylor act as chairman, for the latter's lack of verbal ability underlines Jody's mastery. Tony's bumbling speech gets interrupted repeatedly by raucous, mocking laughter. When he wants to know why, he's told, "'Cause you jump up tuh make speeches and don't know how. . . . You can't welcome uh man and his wife 'thout you make comparison about Issac and Rebecca at de well,'" and others "titter" at "his ignorance" (68). Hurston thus signals the importance of verbal ability to the reader as well, significantly through the community's cruel but nevertheless corrective laughter. We also notice the people's expectation of biblical knowledge, which sets the "text" of even secular "sermons."[9] Jody recognizes and carefully orchestrates a ritualistic occasion, dressing Janie totemically in wine-colored silk. He seizes the opportunity to preach his secular gospel, ending with "Amen." His anointment as mayor unsurprisingly follows immediately, but in his first act he silences Janie; she's called on to make a speech, but Jody intervenes: "'Thank yuh fuh yo' compliments, but mah wife don't know nothin' 'bout no speech makin'. Ah never married her for nothin' lak dat. She's uh woman and her place is in de home'" (69). A disturbed Janie forces herself to laugh in response—apparently this is what a decorative woman does, giggle and be still—and thus dons a mask she will wear for years.

Joe's identification of Janie with his "high class" position dictates this pose. But later in the narrative Hurston demonstrates that the other women of Eatonville have considerably more verbal freedom. Joe forbids Janie to attend the mock-funeral of Bonner's mule, but other women go. They get "mock-happy," shout, and require the men to hold them up, mimicking their weekly behavior in church, a demonstration of healthy self-parody and creativity on their part and yet a welcome reminder to readers (especially those who haven't read *Mules and Men*) that Janie's exclusion from the realm of comic creativity should not be read as representative of all black women.[10] Thus there are women in the community with the creative and emotional energy to compete with the men verbally, but Janie's orders are to "class off" from such behavior.

Laughter aplenty, however, gushes out in the years that follow from the salty, humor-drenched "lyin'" sessions on the porch of his store. Hurston obviously relishes the opportunity to reprise material first used in *Mules* and "The Eatonville Anthology." Although Joe forbids Janie to take part, she obviously listens well: "When the people sat around on the porch and passed around the pictures of her thoughts for the others to look at and see, it was nice. The fact that the thought pictures were always crayon enlargements of life made it even nicer to listen to" (81). As this passage shows, Janie's silences are pregnant with creativity and explode later in her great tirade against Jody. Furthermore, since crayons are associated with a rainbowlike array of vibrant colors and crayon-colored photographs would be "adorned" representations, we may view the store-porch tales and signifying Janie describes as "crayon enlargements of life" as equivalent to the colorful "verbal hieroglyphics" Hurston discusses in "Characteristics"; obviously, much of the "coloring" involves the bright hues of humor.

Meanwhile, the introduction of Matt Bonner's skinny yellow mule into the narrative provides great fun, initially through a whole series of jokes played on Bonner. The town has a genuine animus toward Bonner because of his stinginess. Victor Raskin has demonstrated that ethnic jokes usually take one of two routes; jokers view their victims as stupid, lazy, and dirty or cunning and stingy (Raskin 194). The jokes against Bonner thus have an edge of malice in them, for he is certainly cunning and stingy, which makes him all too like slaveowners and contemporary white bosses. In a sense, then, the comic assaults directed at him are really aggressive ethnic jokes against negative "white" qualities. The humor, however, masks a veritable palimpsest of serious meditations on the mule's symbolism in black culture. Earlier, of course, Nanny bemoans the black woman's fate as the "mule of the world" (29), and here the beast becomes a general symbol for all black people under white oppression, but also for silenced black women like Janie, also "yaller," like the mule. Bonner has obviously mistreated the animal, but in a comic exchange with the townsmen, assigns the blame to the victim, just as slaveowners did: "'Ah does feed 'im. He's jus' too mean tuh git fat. He stay poor and rawbony jus' fuh spite. Skeered he'll hafta work some.' 'Yeah, you feeds 'im. Feeds 'im offa 'come up' and seasons it wid raw-hide'" (83). As with Tony Taylor earlier, Bonner suffers doubly as a butt because of his inability to answer in kind, a verbal failure exacerbated by Hurston's exploitation of his stutter, a rather cruel but effective comic technique used by many writers as a mode of caricature.

Other barbs, however, are more playful: "'De womenfolks got yo' mule. When Ah come round de lake 'bout noontime mah wife and some others had 'im flat on de ground usin' his sides fuh uh wash board.' . . . Janie loved the conversation and sometimes she thought up good stories on the mule, but Joe had forbidden her to indulge. He didn't want her talking after such trashy people. 'You'se Mrs. Mayor Starks Janie'" (85). This dictum against joking adds to Janie's estrangement from the people: "She slept with authority and so she was part of it in the town mind. She couldn't get but so close to most of them in spirit" (74); much of this distance comes from her forced sobriety, for humor often offers the quickest bridge to intimacy.

Jody's orchestration of Janie's role may make her the "bell-cow," but the details of his other actions make it plain that he unconsciously has parodied the white culture he saw when working in a bank in Atlanta. His props—white man's desk, spittoons, the "gloaty white" paint on what the townspeople call his "big house," surrounded by the "quarters" of the rest of the town—are all drawn from the white world. Janie, his centerpiece, seems intended as a replica of "Big Missy." The most significant material prop may consequently be her stand-in, the dainty, floral-painted "lady-size spittin pot" he buys for her, and it truly alienates the town. "It was like seeing your sister turn into a 'gator. A familiar strangeness. You keep seeing your sister in the 'gator and the 'gator in your sister, and you'd rather not" (76). The humor here proves revealing, for it indicates the folk feel Janie has been "conjured" into a spittoon by white materialism. This comic but deeply disturbing fetishization of Janie has another ironic dimension, for Nanny states earlier that she wants to prevent Janie being turned into a "spit-cup" for black or white men. Nanny, as she so often does, employs a sexual metaphor; ironically, Janie is turned into a spit-cup, but an asexual one, a commodity that functions as a somber and alienating sign of Joe's "white" success. His increasing verbal abuse of her fits here too, for she silently accepts and accumulates them, the way the pot does spit.[11]

Joe does, however, notice Janie's outrage over the cruel physical torture of the old mule, one of the clearest demonstrations in the book that human humor can sometimes be despicable. He buys the animal and pastures him just outside his store, as a gesture of largesse, but we realize this ironically creates more of a display of power rather than of charity.

This gesture moves Janie, however, and in her "maiden speech" acclaims Jody in front of the town as "'uh mighty big man . . . something like George Washington and Lincoln. Abraham Lincoln, he had de whole United States tuh rule so he freed de Negroes. You got uh town so you freed uh mule. You have tuh have power tuh free things and dat makes you lak uh king uh something.'" Hambo in turn praises Janie as "'uh born orator. . . . Us never knowed dat befo'. She put ju's de right words tuh our thoughts'" (92). Readers, though, see the irony; unlike the mule, Janie remains indentured. People never "knowed befo'" because Jody, like Bonner, continues to be stingy with her liberties. Moreover, an underlying comic disjunction underlies her analysis of Jody, certainly no Washington or Lincoln. True, he "frees," but only because he's a tyrant, "uh king," who's trying to be seen as benevolent. And indeed, his generosity seems always before the public as "new lies sprung up about his free-mule doings," making the mule rambunctious, intrusive, and a metaphor for all freed slaves, virtually transforming the traditional signifying monkey into the signifying mule. The animal's liberating humor, really that of the folk, undercuts all modes of authority in the town, including Jody's. In one story, the mule sticks his head in the Pearsons' window while the family is eating; Mrs. Pearson mistakes him for Rev. Pearson and hands him a plate. Obviously, this vignette constitutes Hurston's personal contribution to the comic preacher tale tradition.

When the mule dies, the big voice and sense of humor that Joe used to win Janie are effective with the town as well; at a sham funeral that mocks "everything human in death," he leads off with a great comic eulogy on "our departed citizen, our most distinguished citizen" (95). He makes sure to attend, for as he tells Janie before the event, "'They's liable tuh need me tuh say uh few words over de carcass, dis bein' uh special case'" (94). Significantly, when he rises from the table after saying this, he wipes ham gravy off his lips. Joe, a linguistic performer, a "ham," who never misses a chance for a dramatic performance, especially favors secular occasions that call for a parody of religious ritual, such as his pseudo-religious ritual of lighting the town's first streetlamp.[12]

The mule's funeral offers a perfect example of what Bakhtin calls a carnival pageant, and indeed, in medieval Europe there was a mock "feast of the ass." The animal-inspired mock masses featured braying priests; laughter was the leading motivation, for, as Bakhtin notes,

"The ass is one of the most ancient and lasting symbols of the material bodily lower stratum, which at the same time degrades and regenerates" (*Rabelais* 78). Obviously, since the mule has frequently been used as a metaphor for black people, this one's comic funeral represents the people's triumph over their fear of death. As Hurston says, "They mocked everything human in death" (95). Bakhtin would add, "The people play with terror and laugh at it; the awesome becomes a 'comic monster'" (*Rabelais* 91). Moreover, here, as in the festivals he describes, "the basis of laughter which gives form to carnival rituals frees them completely from all religious and ecclesiastic dogmatism" and they are free to parody the church's forms. Another benefit: no distinction exists between actors and spectators in carnival; everyone participates. "Carnival is not a spectacle seen by the people; they live in it, and everyone participates because its very idea embraces all the people" (5–7). Jody understands this, and another reason for his attendance may be that he fears the townspeople will seize the occasion to signify on him if he isn't there. Although his very participation in this "'mess uh commonness,'" as he describes it to Janie, has the potential to "uncrown him," staying away might be worse.

Sam Watson's speculations about "mule heaven" parody the folktales about blacks flying around Heaven, utilizing the absurd image of mule-angels: "'Miles of green corn and cool water, a pasture of pure bran with a river of molasses . . . and . . . *No* Matt Bonner. . . . Mule-angels would have people to ride on'" (95). This particular image recalls folktales about the trickster rabbit conniving the fox to ride him on his back. These comic reversals are ubiquitous in black folktales that offer basic images of social inversion. Once again, we have a parody of a parody, and yet more, for the signification on "mule heaven" may be Hurston's sly dig at the white folks' love of the play *Green Pastures,* which she hated.

We have talked of silences being eloquent. Jody knows that his mule speech will be received more attentively precisely because he has marshaled his "big voice" carefully: "He bought a desk like Mr. Hill or Mr. Galloway over in Maitland with one of those wing-around chairs to it. What with him biting down on cigars and saving his breath on talk and swinging round in that chair, it weakened people" (75–76). As Klaus Benesch has observed, this "smug reticence" adds to the image we have of Jody's "acting white" and adds substantially to what Benesch sees as "an extremely effective caricature" of this "big man" (632). Although we do not know what Jody says on this occasion, we understand his words must have been funny. We acknowledge here, as Hurston seems to, that humor can deceive as well, for she tells us that Jody's comic speech makes him "more solid than building the school-house had done" (95), a tribute to the role humor plays in creating a long-desired sense of intimacy (on their part) between the people and their mayor. His coming down to their level pleases them, but their elevation of empty rhetoric above a truly useful deed points to the dangerous role humorous discourse can play in the machinations of a demagogue.

Janie also learns how powerful the omission of events, speeches, and commentary can be. Surely the fact that she as narrator omits any detail of Joe's greatest oration, the mule's eulogy, means something (especially since she excerpts Sam's), and indeed it does, for it sets up what follows. In a daring move, Hurston extends the scene into the realm of the surreal by adding a parody of the parody: after the humans leave, a group of vultures headed by their "Parson" descends on the carcass. "'What killed this man?'" cries the "minister" in his first "call." The response: "'Bare, bare fat.' 'Who'll stand his funeral?' 'We!!!!' 'Well, all right.' So he picked out the eyes in the ceremonial way and the feast went on" (97). Since Janie is telling the tale to Pheoby, this becomes *her* added touch, *her* "mule story," voiced at last, and also revenge against Jody, who forbade her to attend the ceremony, much less speak of it.

Moreover, her comic signification contains a moral lesson, one connected with the title. The leader of the buzzards has a white head. He and his kin can do as they will with a "dead" animal. In picking out the eyes, he selects the choicest bits, for as the book repeatedly emphasizes, truly "seeing" provides the key to truly living. White culture first deadens minorities through economic and social oppression and then steals their positive images of themselves. Jody, a prosperous man, nevertheless seems spiritually dead, and the white world has indeed plucked out his eyes for his values are entirely supplied by the white world. The "fat" that killed him? The deadening substitution of material value for the spiritual in his daily diet. Thus Janie not only has revenge for being silenced at the time but also the last word on Joe's entire life.[13]

Jody, who seemed to relish the mock funeral, takes on a smug, "dicty" attitude of disapproval after the fact in a revealing passage: "'Ah had tuh laugh at de people out dere in de woods dis mornin', Janie. You can't help but laugh at de capers they cuts. But all the same, Ah wish mah people would git mo' business in 'em and not spend so much time on foolishness'" (98). Janie's response suggests Hurston has in mind here those Harlem Renaissance critics who accused her of cuttin' the monkey for the white folks. "'Everybody can't be lak you, Jody. Somebody is bound tuh want tuh laugh and play'"—a reflection of Janie's inner yearnings. (99).

Jody "has to laugh," too, at the verbal duels of Sam Watson and Lige Moss, regulars on the store porch. Hurston gives them some choice lines from her Eatonville folklore collections, in tales of sheer hyperbole. Some are saucy comments to the young women passing, but "the girls and everybody else help laugh. . . . They know it's not courtship. It's acting-out courtship and everybody is in the play" (108), an indication of the importance of communal parody in this culture.[14]

Hurston significantly inserts an ugly scene in the midst of these comic ones. Janie, normally a good cook, one day prepares what Hurston comically describes as "a scrochy, soggy, tasteless mess" that some "fiend" has slipped into her pots and pans (112). Joe, enraged, slaps Janie for the first time, but chooses to tell her "about her brains" instead of her cooking. Janie's reaction sets up a paradigm for understanding the rest of the book:

> She stood there until something fell off the shelf inside her. Then she went inside there to see what it was. It was her image of Jody tumbled down and shattered. But looking at it she saw that it never was the flesh and blood figure of her dreams. Just something she had grabbed up to drape her dreams over. . . . She found that she had a host of thoughts she had never expressed to him, and numerous emotions she had never let Jody know about. Things packed up and put away in parts of her heart where he could never find them. She was saving up feelings for some man she had never seen. She had an inside and an outside now and suddenly she knew how not to mix them. (112–13)

In an earlier version of this scene struck from the original manuscript, Hurston sets the episode in the second rather than seventh year of Janie's marriage, and before the slap scene, Janie lives "with her insides turned outward towards Joe, her Jody." After the slap, however, the manuscript states, "she began to fold in on herself and to take without giving. Saving up feelings for a man she had never seen" (30). In the published version the statement "No matter what Jody did, she said nothing" follows the slap. Although Janie's voice has been said to begin after the slap, with the awareness of an inside and an outside, and thus the separate parts of her identity (B. Johnson 212), one can see the opposite process described here, one of silence, one of flowers closing inward.

At least ten years pass before she finally explodes into "killing" signification. The "unpacking" of the drawers of her heart takes place later, when Tea Cake tells her she has the keys to the kingdom, which are also the keys to those compartments in her heart. The original manuscript makes this clear too: "Everywhere there were little compartments with doors. Doors shut tight and locked. She had key symbols of life but she wasn't living. And she had so meant to live. Here she was inching along with keys" (30).[15]

A fascinating parallelism emerges here in the paired images of the sacred compartments of her heart and the foul repository of the spittoon, her other sign. Jody's ugly, slighting humor builds up, like spit, while her love thoughts and, I would suggest, her comic thoughts build up and are stored away for future use, for in lines such as "Janie loved the conversation and sometimes she thought up good stories on the mule" (85) indicate an active, but silent, comic creativity.

Janie's acquisition of how to handle Jody with silence and "taking without giving" suggest Janie's mastery of "fronting." Thomas Kochman defines this as a mechanism whereby African Americans are "consciously suppressing what they truly feel or believe." As he notes, blacks often have good reason to distrust the seemingly detached mode whites use in all manner of debates. Fronting becomes a daily reality for African Americans from childhood on. As W. E. B. Du Bois claimed, all members of the race are born with a "double-consciousness" (364), which he surely would agree generates fronting ability. Fronting thus represents the prudence of silence when speech would likely involve risk (*Black* 22).

Her acknowledgment of this conscious strategy of silence could be considered one of Janie's acquisitions of "voice"; silence, after all, may paradoxically constitute a voice as well as a lack of one. After the slap she can wield this new weapon more effectively, for she had been using it in her dealings with the white community all along.. She surely had an awareness of an inside and an outside long before this scene, but she had just never applied it to her marriage. This implies that henceforth she must relate to Jody as if he were white.

Hurston quickly returns to comic matters, however, enclosing this very serious scene within an envelope of mirth. One of the funniest episodes in the book reprises "Mrs. Tony," the begging woman from "The Eatonville Anthology." Once again, she begs Joe for some meat—for "'Tony don't fee-eed me!'" Hurston adds some delicious details: "The salt pork box was in the back of the store and during the walk Mrs. Tony was so eager she sometimes stepped on Joe's heels, sometimes she was a little before him. Something like a hungry cat when somebody approaches her pan with meat. Running a little, caressing a little and all the time making little urging-on cries." But when Jody cuts off a smaller piece than she wants "Mrs. Tony leaped away from the proffered cut of meat as if it were a rattlesnake. 'Ah wouldn't tetch it! Dat lil eyeful uh bacon for me an all mah chillun!' . . . Starks made as if to throw the meat back in the box. . . . Mrs. Tony swooped like lightning and seized it, and started towards the door. 'Some folks ain't got no heart in dey bosom'. . . . She stepped from the store porch and marched off in high dudgeon!" (113–15).

Some of the men laugh, but another says that if she were his wife, he'd kill her "cemetery dead," and Coker adds, "'Ah could break her if she wuz mine. Ah'd break her or kill her. Makin' uh fool outa me in front of everybody'" (116).

Although Mrs. Tony's caricature amuses, it also has much to do with several levels of the plot, and offers a fine example of the way Hurston uses humor to convey a serious meaning. Mrs. Tony, urging Jody on, calling him a "king," exposes Stark's enjoyment in playing the "great man," the man who can afford to be generous in public, as he was earlier when he paid for the mule's "retirement" fund. Furthermore, the scene brings out Jody's falsity since he charges Tony's account anyway and comically underlines his marital stinginess toward Janie—he doesn't "fee-eed" her spiritually or emotionally. Finally, the men's communal insistence on the propriety of using violence to "break a woman" and the shared assumption that Mr. Tony rather than his wife is the ultimate butt of their humor lends male communal sanction to Jody's slap and prepares the reader for Janie's final public showdown with Jody.

When Jody's youth and good health begin to wane, he tries to draw attention away from himself by publicly ridiculing Janie. "'I god amighty! A woman stay round uh store till she get old as Methusalem and still can't cut a little thing like a plug of tobacco! Don't stand dere rollin' yo' pop eyes at me wid yo' rump hangin' nearly to yo' knees'" (121). Such a ritual insult, "talkin' under clothes," if directed at a man would possibly initiate a game of the dozens or physical violence, but Jody, assuming Janie will know her place and not engage in a forbidden joking relationship, expects her silence. Instead, she accepts his challenge and powerfully concludes a spirited exchange of charges with him: "'You big-bellies round here and put out a lot of brag, but 'taint nothin' to it but yo big voice. Humph! Talkin' 'bout *me* lookin' old! When you pull down yo' britches, you look lak de change uh life.' 'Great God from Zion!' Sam Watson gasped. 'Y'all really playin' de dozens tuhnight'" (123).[16]

Not only has Janie dared to play a male game, she has "capped"

Joe forever with this ultimate insult, and in fact, in the eyes of the community, has effectively emasculated him. "They'd look with envy at the things and pity the man that owned them . . . and the cruel deceit of Janie! Making all that show of humbleness and scorning him all the time! *Laughing at him!* and now putting the town up to do the same" (124; my emphasis). In fact, Janie's charge immediately inspires rebellion from the male ranks of his followers as well, for Walter taunts, "'You heard her, you ain't blind,'" a joke within a joke, clearly "sounding."

What Jody expresses here is more than a sense of betrayal; he actually casts Janie in the diabolical role of trickster, that omnipresent menace of folktales, who like the Signifying Monkey or Brer Rabbit, two of his avatars, strikes down his physical superiors, as David slew Goliath. Significantly, however, Joe refuses to consciously give her this much credit, and so compares Janie to Saul's scheming daughter, a figure who publicly mocks her husband for drunkenly dancing in the streets and accidentally exposing his genitals. Michal's outcry, however, has the effect of publicizing something few actually saw and thus functions on the level of Janie's public "exposure" or "talkin' under clothes." As a result David spurns Michal's bed and she dies childless, a condition shared by Janie (2 Sam. 6:15–23).

Moreover, in this ultimate explosion of signification against Jody, we see the symbolic "overturning" or inversion of the years of epithets he hurled at her. No longer an "object," mute and decorative like the spittoon, but a speaking, acting, fighting human being, Janie utilizes the linguistic resources of her culture. This surely represents an extreme example of what Hurston refers to as the "baptism of laughter."[17]

We identify spit, as a bodily fluid, with excrement, and the contents of a spittoon would be brown from tobacco. Hurston thus creates one of those cherished confrontations of the intellect and the buttocks that Bakhtin delineates, always a comic occasion. This also fits with another line that describes Janie's eleven years of relative silence: "She received all things with the stolidness of the earth which soaks up urine and perfume with the same indifference" (119). The earth, however, sometimes has volcanic eruptions.

When Janie later tells this story to Pheoby in the framing device and, by extension, the community, she does so from a somewhat privileged position. She is free from many of the restrictions against expressing herself humorously in public in this private situation, but remember, the story is meant to be "passed on." In many cultures older women, especially after menopause, are permitted much more verbal freedom and eventually are allowed to compete with men, if they so choose (Apte 79). In this sense, Janie's story and her earlier challenge of Jody in the male territory of tall tales, verbal dueling, escalating insults, and capping doesn't outrage the community as it might have years earlier, for she is mature, experienced, and widely recognized as a relatively wealthy, independent woman and presumably not vulnerable to sexual manipulation and appropriation.

After Jody's death, part of Janie's gradually revealed exuberance comes from shedding the duty of clerking in the store, something she entrusts to Hezekiah. This seventeen-year-old imitation of Joe practices smoking cigars and rearing back in his swivel chair. His attempt to make a prosperous paunch out of his trim abdomen reminds us of Joe Banks's similar imitation of Slemmons in "The Gilded Six-Bits." Janie openly laughs at Hezekiah's comic parroting of Jody's expressions, as when he tells a customer asking for more credit, "'I god, dis ain't Gimme, Florida'" (142). Janie laughs, partly in joyous acknowledgment that a copy stands before her, not the real thing. We are hearing the laughter of liberation.[18] Some men in the community, however, don't understand this. Another reason Janie learns to laugh again stems from the hypocrisy of her abundant suitors: "Janie found out very soon that her widowhood and property was a great challenge in South Florida. . . . 'Uh woman by herself is uh pitiful thing,' she was told over and again" (139). But Janie has different plans. Like the woman who thinks she's become a widow in Kate Chopin's "The Story of an Hour," Janie exults because "she would have the rest of her life to do as she pleased" (137).

Her relationship with her next husband, Tea Cake, central to the book's meaning, begins on a note of humor. He walks into the store on a slow day; most of the community is off at a ball game in Winter Park. "'Good evenin', Mis' Starks,' he said with a sly grin, as if they had a good joke together. She was in favor of the story that was making him laugh before she even heard it" (144). Their entire first interchange consists of a series of little jokes, and Janie's thrilled reaction to his invitation to play checkers could just as well apply to his subsequent willingness to privilege her as his comic equal: "She found herself flowing inside. Somebody wanted her to play. Somebody thought it natural for her to play. That was even nice" (146). Tea Cake wants her to play in every sense of the word, ending the long line of nay-sayers that stretches back to Nanny.

It interests us that Janie does not learn his name, Vergible Woods, until the entire afternoon has been spent together in play; but folks call him Tea Cake. Janie laughs and makes a joke: "'Tea Cake! So you sweet as all dat?' She laughed and he gave her a little cut-eyelook to get her meaning. 'Ah may be guilty. You better try me and see. . . . B'lieve Ah done cut uh hawg, so Ah guess Ah better ketch air.' He made an elaborate act of tripping to the door stealthily. Then looked back at her with an irresistible grin on his face. Janie burst out laughing in spite of herself. 'You crazy thing!'" (149). But Tea Cake remains. "They joked and went on till the people began to come in. Then he took a seat and made talk and laughter with the rest until closing time" (150).

It seems important to note here that Tea Cake courts Janie both in private and in public. His second visit again involves a game of checkers, but this time they play in front of an audience. "Everybody was surprised at Janie playing checkers but they liked it. Three or four stood behind her and coached her moves and generally made merry with her in a restrained way" (154).

Janie and the rest of the community come to love Tea Cake for his spontaneity, creativity, and positive attitude toward life. He and Janie are always making "a lot of laughter out of nothing" (154), an obvious parallel to the ubiquitous expression in African America, "making a way out of no way." In a moving scene, Hurston pinpoints his tenderness and his teaching quality. Tea Cake combs Janie's hair for her and says, "'Ah betcha you don't never go tuh de lookin' glass and enjoy yo' eyes yo' self. You'se got de world in uh jug and make out you don't know it. But Ah'm glad tuh be de one tuh tell yuh.'" [19] When Janie objects that he must tell this to all the girls, he replies, "'Ah'm de Apostle Paul tuh de Gentiles. Ah tells 'em and then agin Ah shows 'em'" (157–58). Tea Cake's gospel of laughter here becomes the New Testament revision of the black aesthetic, replacing the tragic "Old Testament" litany of Nanny and others like her who still labor under the stubborn heritage of slavery. Nanny, we remember, believes that "'folks is meant to cry 'bout somethin' or other'" (43), and Tea Cake's creed reverses this. His forward-looking stance thus provides the encouragement Janus/Janie has always needed for that part of her personality. His doctrine rings out as profoundly American and hopeful, even though he too has been and will be the victim of white racism; indeed, one could argue he dies from it, in his crazed belief that Janie wants to leave him for a lighter-skinned man.

Like Hurston, Tea Cake refuses to let racial oppression blind him to the glories of the world or to define the possibilities of the self. As Emerson and Whitman urged, he believes in living in the now, but his self-love and sheer joy in living come out of a black heritage, and his admonition to Janie echoes a traditional blues lyric: "Baby, Baby, what is the matter with you? / You've got the world in a jug / Ain't a thing that you can't do." His identification with present tense throws him into contrast with Nanny, who operates entirely out of an obsession with the past, and Killicks and Starks, who mimic white culture by constantly building up financial capital for the future at the expense of emotional and spiritual health.

This sense of the present moment and its possibilities functions importantly in the world of play. Huizinga has proven play to be a basic human need, which strongly relates to laughter; play, he flatly states, is an instinctual impulse that must be satisfied. Janie, who said as much to Jody, wants no exception to this rule and relishes her third husband's sense of play and laughter. She learns as much as she can from him on this subject during their brief two years together. The verb "to laugh" crops up again and again in the chapters devoted to their marriage.

Play frequently occurs within social parameters (as with the communal game of checkers, card games, the evenings with the people in the Everglades), but it often takes place on the periphery of convention or even outside it. At one point Janie and Tea Cake go fishing in the middle of the night: "It was so crazy digging worms by lamp light and setting out for Lake Sabelia after midnight that she felt like a child breaking rules. That's what made Janie like it" (155). Tea Cake seems to be a master of breaking rules and conventions, even inverting night into day, but in an "even nice" way. One feels Janie also delights in breaking the "rule" of age in taking up with a man at least twelve years her junior, one of Hurston's lifelong habits. Janie herself refuses to abide by the rules during their first checker game, objecting when Tea Cake legitimately takes her hard-won king (a figuration on "uncrowning"), and eventually she upsets the board. But this may be a momentary urge from a woman still laboring under the legacy of twenty-odd years of silencing by a real-life "king."

The games Janie loves most are those that involve Tea Cake's imagination and creativity. Early in their relationship he pretends to play on an imaginary guitar. Later, arriving in a battered car, he jumps out and makes the gesture of tying it to a post. But he brings the car because he wants to teach Janie how to drive, how to have and relish the power of mobility. As she tells Pheoby, "'Ah always did want tuh git round uh whole heap, but Jody wouldn't 'low me tuh'" (169). He also instructs her on how to plant seeds in her garden and chops down an ugly tree by the window she has always hated that Jody probably liked. All this obviously translates into metaphors for freedom, growth, the cutting down of rigid patriarchal traditions, and the general power of self-assertion. Tea Cake tells her to "'have de nerve tuh

say whut you mean'" and shows her how to have the nerve to be creative, prune away dead limbs on her spiritual tree, and make joyful
plans for a mobile future, one not tied down to her possessions.

Paradoxically, the town sees all this as "signs of possession" and
thinks that "Poor Joe Starks" must be turning over in his grave. They
fail to realize that they're still looking at Janie as an extension of Joe,
as his spoils, waiting to see if an appropriate claimant will come along,
someone like the oft-mentioned undertaker from Sanford. They fail
to "see" because their eyes are watching the wrong god: Mammon. The
humorless nature of their communal discourse here testifies to a blind
adherence to a joyless Puritan ethic. Even the usually astute Sam fails
this test; he rightly and wryly detects Janie's growing love for Tea Cake:
"'New dresses and her hair combed a different way nearly every day.
You got to have something to comb hair over. When you see uh woman doin' so much rakin' in her head, she's combin' at some man or
'nother. . . . Tea Cake can't do nothin' but help her spend whut she got.
Ah reckon dat's whut he's after. Throwin' away whut Joe Starks worked
hard tuh git tuhgether'" (167). Pheoby agrees and favors the undertaker because "'de man's wife died and he got uh lovely place tuh take
her to—already furnished. Better'n her house Joe left her'" (167). Both
speakers discount the idea of choice and creativity, preferring a life
"already furnished," one defined by possessions. Neither see the creativity Tea Cake awakens in Janie, which the varying attire and hair
styles suggest. Their sense of Janie "throwin' away Joe" shows that even
her best friend and the relatively sensitive Sam still define her through
a dead man. The fact that they favor a new suitor known only by his
extremely unplayful trade fits in well.

Eventually Pheoby "picks" her way to Janie's, comically "like a hen
to a neighbor's garden," talking with people on the way, "going
straight by walking crooked" (169) so as to appear to be dropping
advice on Janie by accident, a charming bit of folk custom that relates to the indirection of humor.[20] The case she makes to Janie on
behalf of the community's outrage over Tea Cake's dragging her
down from her class begins censoriously, with "everybody's talkin',"
but humor punctuates their conversation, especially when it drifts to
intimate matters. Letting Pheoby know she's been sleeping with Tea
Cake ("'We'se just as good as married already'") Janie adds, "'Ah ain't
puttin' it in de street. Ah'm tellin' *you*,'" to which Pheoby replies, "'Ah
jus lak uh chicken,'" fitting with her "picking" her way to Janie's "like
a hen"; "'Chicken drink water, but he don't pee-pee,'" and Janie concludes, "'We ain't shame faced. We jus' ain't ready tuh make no big
kerflommuck as yet'" (173).

In still another comic inversion, Janie has flipped the town's expectations; instead of mourning atop the pedestal Jody created for her, she has lost her "class" by gambling on Tea Cake and love. They want her back as an icon of respectability, but that isn't what they say. Pheoby, their emissary, warns Janie, "'You'se takin' uh awful chance,'" to which Janie, twice-married already, replies, "'No mo' than Ah took befo' and no mo' than anybody else takes when dey gits married. . . . Dis ain't no business proposition, and no race after property and titles. Dis is uh love game'" (171), thereby setting the play element of their relationship out for the community.

This statement needs to be taken more seriously than it has been. Tea Cake is a teacher, as the first part of his name and all of his relations to Janie suggest, and teachers give tests. Janie's faith, and ours as readers, gets sorely tested in Jacksonville, for during their honeymoon there, Tea Cake vanishes with her hidden two hundred dollars. Many students and some critics have been upset by this, and the scene has increasingly been brought into service for the growing attack on Tea Cake in Hurston criticism. Michael Awkward has said that Tea Cake "steals" from Janie (17). Writing Tea Cake off as a bum, a thief, and a "wife-beater," which some presentist readers seem to be doing, makes seeing his real role in the novel impossible. We need to remember that he has insisted, prior to this, that he finance their expeditions, that he buy groceries for their church picnic even though Janie owns a store, and that he is often absent because he is working for this courtship money. Hurston never suggests a scheme to appropriate Janie's real hoard, which still awaits her in the bank when she returns to town after burying Tea Cake. He terrifies Janie when he comes back from his gaming wounded, but as she tends to him he gives her the $322 he has won, Hurston's metaphorical comment on the exponential rewards of trusting the "love game" and her folk illustration of the biblical injunction to cast your bread upon the waters.

Tea Cake tells her to put the original $200 back in the bank, but that is beside the point. He simply does not value money the way most of us do. He sees more in life than the building up of capital. Although we may prefer to believe we are offended here by a violation of Janie's trust, we must face the fact that we may be led to that position because Tea Cake has actually offended our capitalist values. If so, we have failed a test Hurston has provided for readers by identifying Janie through her possessions. As Janie said, "'Dis ain't no business proposition. . . . Dis is uh love game,'" and love games put your faith and trust on the line. Hurston as narrator thus uses a practical joke to teach. Janie learns here to trust herself as well as others, but also to take chances. She bears up under the strain and is still there, waiting, when Tea Cake comes home.

His humorous assurance nevertheless glistens with sincerity: "'You doubted me 'bout de money. . . . De girl baby ain't born and her mama is dead, dat can git me tuh spend *our money* on her. Ah told yo' before dat you got de keys tuh de kingdom'" (181; my emphasis). His roistering narrative of the party he has given for his friends constitutes a comic masterpiece, replete with revelry, feasting, fighting, and jokes. When Janie asks him why he didn't invite *her* (our question as well), we find she isn't the only one who has had doubts. If she has questioned whether he could really love an older woman, he has doubted she could accept his friends: "'Dem wuzn't no high muckty mucks. . . . Ah wuz skeered you might git all mad and quit me fo takin' you 'mongst 'em. . . . 'Tain't mah notion tuh drag *you* down wid me,'" a telling illustration of the way white class patterns can disrupt even the most loving relationships. Janie's instructive response proves she can teach with jokes too and will be heeded during the rest of the book: "'If you ever go off from me and have a good time lak dat and then come back heah tellin' me how nice Ah is, Ah specks tuh kill yuh dead. You heah me?'" (186). Ironically, this has much to do with why she has to kill him, for in his rabid state he thinks she's too nice to really love a black black man.

Tea Cake subsequently isn't afraid to suggest their removal to the Everglades "muck" community. The learning experience among the common folk there seems just as important to Janie as Tea Cake's love in making her complete and whole, which is instigated by him as teacher. In this folk "classroom," folks "'don't do nothin' . . . but make money and fun and foolishness,'" and Janie grows there, like everything else: "'Ground so rich that everything went wild. . . . People wild too'" (193).

Janie's "education" proceeds a bit before the bean harvest begins, when Tea Cake insists, via a joke, on teaching her how to fire a weapon and hunt: "'Even if you didn't never find no game, it's always some trashy rascal dat needs uh good killin''" (195). In a terrible irony, rabies later turns him into a murderous "rascal," forcing Janie to shoot him when he attacks her. The joke doubles yet again, and terribly, by the idea that in killing him she kills the "love game" he represents.

Here on the muck, Tea Cake, with his guitar, his songs, his infectious laughter, plays Orpheus for the folk. This extends a pattern established earlier, for back in Eatonville we saw him simultaneously joking and playing a mean blues piano, twining together the folk traditions of humor and music.

Janie's growing ability to joke and laugh soon makes her a favorite with the people too, especially after she starts working alongside Tea Cake in the fields. We note here that she does so because he misses her so much during the day, quite opposite to Logan Killicks's desire to have her plowing. When she and Tea Cake carry on behind the boss's back, "It got the whole field to playing off and on," recalling the role humor played in relieving the drudgery of field work during slave times (199). Soon, Janie joins Tea Cake in storytelling for the appreciative audience that gathers each night at their shack: "The house was full of people every night. . . . Some were there to hear Tea Cake pick the box; some came to talk and tell stories, but most of them came to get into whatever game was going on or might go on. . . . Outside of the two jooks, everything on that job went on around those two" (200–201). Janie learns to "woof," to "boogerboo," to play all the games, and through it all, "no matter how rough it was, people seldom got mad, because everything was done for a laugh" (200). In this school and laboratory, Janie "marks" (imitates) the other storytellers and becomes an accomplished comedian/"liar" herself.[21]

In particular, life on the muck acquaints us with all sorts of card games and their comic lingo, as expertly played and "sayed" by folk comedians whose very names, such as Sop-de-Bottom, Bootyny, Stew Beef, and Motor Boat, cause a smile. Their lingo, emerging directly from black folk culture, is equally tinged with violent menace and outrageous, creative play, as when they raise stakes: "'Ah'm gointuh shoot in de hearse, don't keer how sad de funeral be'"; "'You gointuh git caught in uh bullet storm if you don't watch out.'" Black-on-black jokes play a role as well: "'Move from over me, Gabe! You too black. You draw heat'" (201).

The happy times don't last, however, and after the hurricane, when they are safe in Palm Beach, Tea Cake asks Janie if she had expected all this when she took up with him. Her answer says much: "'Once upon uh time, Ah never 'spected nothin' Tea Cake but bein' dead from the standin' still and tryin' tuh laugh. But you come 'long and made somethin' outa me'" (247). Life and laughter are the equation for fulfillment.

More so here than in any other place in Hurston's oeuvre, Janie and Tea Cake in their scenes on the muck, surrounded by their people and enjoying and creating black folk culture, best express what Alice Walker has called "racial health; a sense of black people as complete, complex *undiminished* human beings" (*In Search* 85).

An extremely important passage regarding Hurston's feeling about black laughter comes in this section, when Janie meets the near-white

Mrs. Turner. This color-struck troublemaker hates her own race and tells jokes a klansman could love, as when she repeats her son's crack that some people are so black they draw lightning. As always, context is all. Black Gabe's friend earlier made the same kind of joke, but affectionately, and within the group. Here, Mrs. Turner, making the same remark, but to an equally light-skinned (and presumably "dicty") audience really intends to project contempt. Her ordinary conversation is no better. Damning color again, she asks, "'Who want any lil ole black baby layin' up in de baby buggy lookin' lak uh fly in buttermilk? Who wants to be mixed up wid uh rusty black man, and uh black woman goin' down de street in all dem loud colors, and whoopin' and hollerin' and laughin' over nothin'?'" (210–11).[22] Mrs. Turner, who has her own brother in mind, urges Janie to marry a whiter man than Tea Cake. When Janie asks her, point-blank, "'How come you so aginst black?'" she immediately replies, sounding much like Jody: "'Dey makes me tired. Always laughin'! Dey laughs too much and dey laughs too loud. Always singin' ol' nigger songs! Always cuttin' de monkey for white folks. If it wuzn't for so many black folks it wouldn't be no race problem. De white folks would take us in wid dem. De black ones is holdin' us back'" (210). She brags about her almost white brother, who tore Booker T. Washington to pieces in a speech. "'All he ever done was cut de monkey for white folks. So dey pomped him up. But you know whut de ole folks say, 'de higher de monkey climbs de mo' he show his behind' so dat's de way it wuz wid Booker T.'" (212). Mrs. Turner thus becomes Hurston's surrogate for all those critics who accused *her* of cuttin' the monkey for white folks, and it reminds us that though Janie functions as Hurston's alter ego in the novel, so does Tea Cake, for here he becomes the polar and positive opposite of Mrs. Turner, as an agent of the laughter she hates, and he plots her banishment after overhearing her diatribe against blacks in general and him in particular from the adjoining room. Mrs. Turner's speech provides reader-author irony at her expense as well, for she rails against black culture by using its resources in her pungent citation of the "ole folks."

Hurston does not stop with Mrs. Turner, either; she exposes the similarly color-struck and sexist views among black men, whose repository of "black black women" jokes she despised. When Tea Cake slaps Janie for supposedly flirting with Mrs. Turner's brother, Sop-de-Bottom compliments him for having a light-colored woman:

> "Uh person can see every place you hit her. Ah bet she never raised her hand tuh hit yuh back, neither. Take some uh dese ol' rusty black women and dey would fight yuh all night long and next day nobody

couldn't tell you ever hit 'em. Dat's de reason Ah done quit beatin'
mah woman. You can't make no mark on 'em at all. . . .

"... Mah woman would spread her lungs all over Palm Beach County, let alone knock out mah jaw teeth. . . . She got ninety-nine rows uh
jaw teeth and git her good and mad, she'll wade through solid rock
up to her hip pockets." (218–19)

Yet after this Sop-de-Bottom agrees that Mrs. Turner is "color-struck"
and helps to run her off the muck. Hurston's clever juxtaposition of
these sentiments could hardly be more ironic or more damning.

Still, here as elsewhere, Hurston refuses to stop the action for a
righteous lecture on the errors of Sop's ways. She obviously appreciated humor, even when it expressed views she didn't share, a quality
that any anthropologist would have to cultivate. As Mary Douglas has
demonstrated, a joke is primarily a play upon form; but to appreciate it properly, you must have the context of the joke. If the play on
form is missing, what you have, in most cases, is ordinary insult ("Social" 365). Black-on-black jokes, while unfortunate, are almost always
examples of the former. Should anyone doubt Hurston's abhorrence
of these attitudes toward her darker sisters, they should consult *Dust
Tracks* (225–26), where she expresses devastating contempt for the
tradition. She also discussed this syndrome's other aspect, its grudg-
ing admiration for the strength of very dark women, in "Characteristics" (45).

Although Hurston would probably be surprised, the scene where
Tea Cake slaps Janie inevitably causes a great deal of discussion in the
classroom. Some students regard it as a sign that Tea Cake is an abusive husband. While this violence against Janie should disturb us, and
it is gratifying to see students object to such behavior, we need to
avoid reading the scene out of context, with contemporary values. We
must recognize that Hurston's narrative takes place in a relatively
violent southern society of the 1930s, where many people, men, wom-
en, and children of both races, frequently experienced physical abuse
from their loved ones, beginning with whippings as children, and
offered the same in return. A biblically inspired people takes seriously
the various biblical dictums sanctioning punishment, and in fact,
frequently equates corrective violence with love.

Moreover, Janie and Zora do the same. We should remember that
Janie reacts to Nunkie's attempts to seduce Tea Cake by physically
striking him, and that in her role as author she specifically tells us
Tea Cake's slapping of her was just that: "No brutal beating at all . . .
two or three face slaps" (218). I would also point to Hurston's own
physical fights with her stepmother, which she apparently remem-

bered with relish and the portions of *Dust Tracks* that detail her violence against men in her life.

Most importantly, Tea Cake only does this to signal to Mrs. Turner and the community that he refuses to give up his woman to a light-skinned man without a struggle. Critics who complain about his sense of male possessiveness miss Hurston's frequent demonstration that love, if genuine, is possessive by definition, no matter which sex is involved. Here he seems to be in danger of losing what matters most to him because of the color of his skin: "'Ah didn't whup Janie 'cause *she* done nothin'. Ah beat her tuh show dem Turners who is boss. Ah set in de kitchen one day and hear dat woman tell mah wife Ah'm too black fuh her. She don't see how Janie can stand me'" (220). Critics who cite this section as one of Janie's "silences" because she doesn't tell us how she felt usually ignore this comment and also the possibility that Janie in retrospect sees nothing wrong with what Tea Cake did, after realizing, as the text clearly indicates she did, what motivated such behavior.

This is not to condone Tea Cake's actions; violence against women (and men, for that matter) is always deplorable. But readings that insist on applying contemporary standards to texts written in and about a different culture almost sixty years in the past are simply ahistorical presentist interpretations of both literature and culture. It is worth noting that until this line of argument was raised, many critics quite rightly praised this novel as one of the great love stories in our literature; unfortunately, that reading seems to be receding as an important but not definitive detail of the narrative has been interpreted out of context.

In any case, Tea Cake soon finds a better way to deal with the troublemaker Mrs. Turner, significantly involving humor. The wild melee he and the other men stage in Turner's restaurant provides an excuse to wreck the place; while the destruction goes on, they pay elaborate compliments to their distressed hostess. Tea Cake yells out, "'If you don't want tuh respect nice people lak Mrs. Turner, God knows you gointuh respect me!'" (224). The scene releases the chaotic energy of the Marx brothers films, but we see the serious purpose; clearly the real message is for Mrs. Turner and gets summed up in the last two words of Tea Cake's dictum. Mrs. Turner scurries away to Miami, "'where folks is civilized'" (226) and, presumably, less humorously inclined.

When the folk on the muck fear the coming hurricane, they turn to the cheering resources of their culture; they first sit in Janie and Tea Cake's house and tell stories about Big John de Conquer and his feats and tricks.[23] They also listen to Tea Cake's guitar and then sing a song that comes from the dozens:

> Yo' mama don't wear no *Draws*
> Ah seen her when she took 'em *Off*
> She soaked 'em in alco*Hol*
> She sold 'em tuh de Santa *Claus*
> He told her 'twas aginst de *Law*
> To wear dem dirty *Draws*.
>
> (232-33)

The combination of the hilarious John de Conquer stories and snippets of bawdy dozens lines helps the figures gird up their loins against cosmic forces. John, a traditional and daring figure, frequently gambles with both God and the Devil; similarly, the defiance of the dozens humor seems directed against a malevolently approaching storm. A beneficent Culture attempts to ward off a threatening Nature. Eventually they have to leave the shack and face the storm in a struggle to reach higher ground, an effort that ironically fulfills yet another of Nanny's dreams/prophecies of taking "a stand on high ground" (32).[24]

Tea Cake and Janie are amused when they find that Motor Boat, whom they left dozing in a house at the height of the storm, slept through it all and survived, even though the raging waters moved the house. They joke about it: "'Heah we nelly kill our fool selves runnin' way from danger and him lay up dere and sleep and float on off!'" (256–57). Weeks later, their amusement pales, for if they had stayed with Motor Boat, Tea Cake would never have been bitten by what they now know was a rabid dog.[25]

In the aftermath of the hurricane, whites impress Tea Cake for a burial squad and several other examples of racial oppression are raised. The situation becomes less oppressive through a terrible kind of levity, also a quality of the hurricane scenes. The grim sequence of events that lead to Tea Cake's infection with rabies is chilling, but looked at with a surrealist's detachment, getting bitten by a mad dog that is riding the back of a cow in a hurricane is wildly funny, a scene only a cosmic joker could write. And in fact, when Janie ponders, "Did He *mean* to do this thing to Tea Cake and her? . . . Maybe it was some big tease and when He saw it had gone far enough He'd give her a sign" (264), it seems the biggest joker in the book, on whom all eyes are turned, has to be God.[26]

Humanity has its own absurdities, however; making the impressed men determine whether the bodies are white or black so as to bury them in segregated graves creates gallows humor with a vengeance. Only the whites get cheap pine coffins, causing Tea Cake to say, "'They's mighty particular how dese dead folks goes tuh judgement. Look lak dey think God don't know nothin' 'bout de Jim Crow law'" (254).

Interracial humor permeates the penultimate scenes. Tea Cake bitterly remarks, "'Every white man think he know all de GOOD darkies already. . . . All dem he don't know oughta be tried and sentenced tuh six months behind de United States privy house at hard smellin'. . . . Old Uncle Sam always do have de biggest and de best uh everything. So de white man figger dat anything less than de Uncle Sam's consolidated water closet would be too easy'" (255). The bitter pun implicit in United States privy/United States privileges appropriately bristles. When Tea Cake comments further on the dangers of being "'strange niggers wid white folks'" Janie adds, "'Dat sho is de truth. De ones de white man know is nice colored folks. De ones he don't know is bad niggers,'" which causes Tea Cake to laugh too, helping both of them to bear an unbearable situation (255). Those who think Hurston glibly accepts American racism should reread these scenes, alongside her bitterly comic diatribe, "Crazy for this Democracy," where the "Arsenal of Democracy" receives refiguration/conjuration as the "Ass-and-all of Democracy" ("Crazy" 45).

More of this ugly humor occurs when Tea Cake lies dying of rabies, and Janie summons a white doctor to make a diagnosis. We remember Mrs. Turner's earlier statement: "'Don't bring me no nigger doctor tuh hang over mah sick-bed'" (211), and here we see her preference tested. This physician initially greets his patient with some racist jocularity: "'Tain't a thing wrong that a quart of coon-dick wouldn't cure. You haven't been gettin' yo' right likker lately, eh?' He slapped Tea Cake lustily across his back and Tea Cake tried to smile as he was expected to do but it was hard" (261). To be fair, however, we should remember that this same man testifies on Janie's behalf during her murder trial.

The grim absurdity of the courtroom scene seems oddly "funny too. Twelve strange [white] men who didn't know a thing about people like Tea Cake and her were going to sit on the thing" (274), a not-so-subtle comment on the gross injustices of southern juror selection in the 1930s.

As narrator of the book, Janie chooses to be silent about her exact testimony in court, which has troubled several critics, notably Michael Awkward and Mary Helen Washington. Perhaps one of the reasons Janie omits her speech to the jury may be found in a short story Hurston published in the *Saturday Evening Post* in 1950, "The Conscience of the Court." The tale describes the trial of a domestic servant, Laura Lee, for beating up a black loan shark, Beasley. The villain takes advantage of the absence of Mrs. Celestine Clairborne, Laura Lee's lifelong employer, to demand her valuable antiques as payment for a note he holds. The impoverished white woman took out the loan to bury Laura Lee's husband "like a big mogul of a king" (21). Beasley attacks Laura Lee after she defends the property; she subsequently beats him to a pulp, prompting the lawsuit. Miss Clairborne, away on vacation, can't be reached. After hearing damning but false evidence against her, Laura Lee cleverly makes capital out of her status: "'I am a unlearnt woman and common-clad. . . . I ain't never rubbed the hair of my head against no college walls'" (20); she tells the moving but maudlin story of her childhood with Miss Celestine, the death of the latter's young husband, and the mutual devotion of maid and mistress. As Laura Lee speaks, Hurston notes the shift in sentiment in the crowded white courtroom. Hurston establishes interracial communitas through a narrative that creates intimacy and understanding, partly by humor, but mostly through pathos. A touch of the "noble savage" crops up: "With the proud, erect way she held herself, she might be some savage queen. The shabby housedress she had on detracted nothing from this impression" (17). The judge dramatically produces the loan note and reveals the months-away due date, adding that the plaintiff intercepted Laura Lee's letter to Mrs. Clairborne. Laura Lee, acquitted, goes home realizing she wrongfully thought her mistress had deserted her.

I present this story at length to show what we miss through Janie's silence. Like Laura Lee, if she *truly* has the personal and verbal resources we think she has at this point in the book, Janie would have to employ them in a demeaning way before a white jury, something John Pearson refuses to do in the courtroom scene in *Jonah*. This late short story reprises Janie's courtroom, treats a recent widow whose husband received a regal burial, dresses her shabbily, reduces the supportive white women to one, recreates the "hushed" response to a pathetic story, and demonstrates the special need for eloquence and silence the black community has when placed in the jaws of an unjust legal system. Perhaps because she had recently been a victim of the legal system herself, the Hurston of the 1950s wanted to ironically remind white America of this. She has her "good" judge intone that "'the protection of women and children . . . was inherent, implicit in Anglo-Saxon civilization, and here in these United States it had become a sacred trust.'" We note that he doesn't allocate this trust only for Anglo-Saxons.[27]

Most importantly, however, the defendant's real enemies (indeed, in Laura Lee's case, the plaintiff) are from the black community. In *Their Eyes,* the courtroom "tongue storm" of black voices, tongues "cocked and loaded," provides a threatening communal symbolic replication of the natural disaster of the hurricane and the individual threat, which gets met in kind, of Tea Cake's gun. This "killing" humor seems to be less directed at Janie per se than at the black spectators' bitter perception of the injustices of white law and their knowledge that their "tongues cocked and loaded" are "the only real weapon left to weak folk. The only killing tool they are allowed to use in the presence of white folks" (275). Thus the bitter acknowledgment "'you know whut dey say "uh white man and uh nigger woman is de freest thing on earth." Dey do as dey please'" (280). So Janie must talk, not walk, her way through a gauntlet of hostile auditors. The potentially killing tongues also look forward in the chronological narrative to the gauntlet of killing laughs and tongues Janie will face in Eatonville.

Janie buries what she actually said in the courtroom in two brief paragraphs of vague prose. This suggests she wants to hide something, namely that her performance in court was in some ways a pose, a careful manipulation of her now-developed vocal power to literally save her life by creating the image the jury wants of a "broken woman." Her equally manipulative but honestly felt and expressed version of the same story in the black community signals not only the truth of what happened, minus her exact testimony, but offers eloquent proof of her confident identity as a black woman, signaled by her mastery of humorous, inventive, and captivating narrative, something that would not have worked in the white courtroom.[28] Thus her manipulation of narrative, in white society, in the larger version told to Pheoby, the community, and us, demonstrates the accuracy of Glynis Carr's perception that Hurston "offers storytelling as the sine qua non of black life. In fact, storytelling for Hurston is synonymous with the mastery of life" (190).

Simultaneously, Janie's performance in court offers another example of that skill she acquired during her marriage with Jody, fronting. This extends to narration of the book as well; Janie has already learned how to edit things from her story, for earlier she had decided to omit Jody's oration over the mule. During her narration of the trial, Janie's silence keeps us from reading her story the way the white jury apparently does, for they are charged to choose whether she is a "wanton killer" or "a poor broken creature" (279), melodramatic or pathetic terms. Surely one of the most vital uses of the syndrome of fronting for African Americans has been in life-or-death situations like these, legal minefields, where the letter of the law can mean anything if you're black. The detached modes of discourse we examined in connection with this concept earlier surely find their most salient example here. Silence, or stories that mask hidden facts, become life-saving devices. Another reason for fronting would be the loss of dignity, a scenario John faces in the similar courtroom scene in *Jonah,* where he refuses to reveal Hattie's evil ways, particularly her negative use of hoodoo, before the mocking white judge and jurors.

One further aspect of Janie's various narrative voices seems pertinent. The power of *Their Eyes,* as John Callahan has demonstrated, comes from the scaffolding of call-and-response patterns that supports virtually every scene, but particularly in the frame, where Pheoby and Janie personify this format. The white courtroom, with its de jure mode of oral argument, erases any possibility of this call-and-response narrative. Further, it obviously functions within the narrative as a representative of white/black discourse in general, which similarly breaks down when racial scenarios produce monologism rather than dialogism.

As readers, we also object to this scene because the rest of the novel succeeds so well in indoctrinating us in the modalities of black linguistic activity, which always proceeds with the assumption that ideas must be tested and validated verbally, with all involved parties participating in the process. Janie's performance here no doubt works in tandem with the white doctor's testimony; he acquaints the court with the seriousness of Tea Cake's illness, Janie's tender care, and the threat rabies presents to the whole town. The perceptive reader will see that the latter fact probably sways the white jury more than anything else he says and that whatever Janie offers the court must be subservient to the doctor's testimony as a white man, one respected as a "diagnostician"/reader of humanity.

Hurston would later exploit this technique of omission extensively in *Dust Tracks,* which has repeatedly been attacked (unjustly, in my view) for its many silences on issues such as Hurston's love life, particulars of her religious beliefs, details of controversial relationships, and the like. We would do well to remember that such expectations come from a tradition of white autobiography, and although unconscious, a lack of understanding of black discursive practice. Hurston was astute enough to realize that by writing an autobiography, she was placing herself in the dock (as all autobiographers do) before a largely white audience, and her mode of narration followed accordingly. She skillfully masks many of these silences through humorous diversions, a sign that she was well aware of the judgmental expectations of her readers.

These expectations apply to Hurston's fiction too. Rachel Blau DuPlessis has demonstrated that the whole of *Their Eyes* centers on the notion of trials, "one by white people's rules, another by black men's rules, a third by the rules of 'Mouth-Almighty'—her black working-class rural community." Pheoby, as auditor, represents a "proper jury" (a peer) *and* judge (106). I would add that the book tests the reader's preconceptions about a number of issues and attitudes as well. Obviously, Janie's exuberant story of liberation, as told to Pheoby, forces us to radically different conclusions from the white jury's; to us, she seems neither a "wanton killer" nor a poor "broken creature," and we arrive at our decision largely on the evidence of her convincing comic creativity.

The anger of Tea Cake's male friends, led by Sop-de-Bottom, over Janie's acquittal becomes more understandable if one figures in the mocking "justice-for-blacks-is-a-game" attitude of the white courtroom, led by the judge himself. If Janie had killed a white man, the tone and outcome would have been very different, and everyone knows it. Hurston knew a woman, Babe, from Polk County, who had shot her husband to death, fled to Tampa, bobbed her hair, and eluded capture, but was finally arrested. Eventually the authorities released Babe, and the case was forgotten. "Negro women *are* punished in these parts for killing men, but only if they exceed the quota. I don't remember what the quota is. Perhaps I did hear but I forgot. One woman had killed five when I left that turpentine still where she lived. The sheriff was thinking of calling on her and scolding her severely" (*Mules and Men* 65). Hurston inserts a very serious issue here under the garb of a comic presentation, but in *Their Eyes* the perspective becomes quite different. Reading racist humor correctly reveals multiple modes of judgment at work during Janie's trial.

Janie obviously understands and sympathizes with the men and thus finds her way to reconciliation with them. Presumably, she has seen to it that the actual facts have filtered out, at least to the people who were with them on the muck, for Sop-de-Bottom testifies to a new understanding of what happened. In a prefiguration of Pheoby's role in Eatonville, he explains and reverses his earlier reading of Tea Cake's death and simultaneously "testifies" for Janie: "'Naw, Ah ain't mad wid Janie,' Sop went around explaining. 'Tea Cake had done gone crazy. You can't blame her for puhtectin' herself. She wuz crazy 'bout 'im. Look at de way she put him away. Ah ain't got anything in mah heart aginst her. And Ah never woulda thought uh thing, but de very first day dat lap-legged nigger [Mrs. Turner's brother] come back heah makin' out he was lookin' fuh work, he come astin' me 'bout how wuz Mr. and Mrs. Woods makin' out'" (282). The men run the brother, now their comic scapegoat, off the muck yet again, thereby purging any animus left toward Janie, demonstrating that even the "killing" humor can be productive.

But just how do readers assess the circumstances of Tea Cake's death? An ominous prefiguration occurs in a seemingly innocuous scene early in the novel, when Jody asks Janie her name. She tells him it used to be Janie Mae Crawford, but now it's Janie Mae Killicks. We notice the way marriage repeatedly stifles Janie, sometimes even with Tea Cake, the "bee" for her "blossom," as the scenes on the muck so abundantly prove. It does change her from a Janie Mae Crawford who "may" "crawl forth" from her tragic origins into selfhood into a frustrated woman, Janie-may-kill, as the wife of both Logan and Jody. Of course, Janie has innocently but ironically stated, much earlier in the narrative, that she loved Tea Cake "fit tuh kill" (168).

Paradoxically, both these identities come into play simultaneously, as the various sides of Janie merge after Tea Cake's death. Janie Woods comes back to the community bearing seeds, completed and generative with her story, yet she has killed the one husband who belied the prophecy of her first change of name. On the other hand, setting Tea Cake's actual identity and undeniable worth aside, only after she "kills" oppressed versions of herself (married/man-defined woman) can her individual self clearly "crawl forth" as a separate entity. This final crawling forth and, presumably, standing represents a further development of being drawn out of the ordinary by love. Just before going on the muck with Tea Cake she looks down on him as he sleeps and feels "a self-crushing love. So her soul crawled out from its hiding place" (192).

Her use of the term "Mouth Almighty" in the first chapter to describe the communal critics judging her return to Eatonville constitutes more than an epithet: it has a double meaning, like many other terms in the novel. While it labels the smug appropriation of Godlike powers of judgment, it simultaneously offers tribute to the justice of communal debate and deliberation, which her tale-telling tacitly acknowledges by being given to them through their agent, Pheoby. For Janie had known what to expect from the town; "'sitters-and-talkers gointuh worry they guts into fiddle strings till dey find out'" (284), and Janie intends her tale, told to Pheoby, to function like Tea Cake's bundle of seeds, which Janie has brought with her. Their story is meant for planting in the community, which needs the laughing, loving example this pair of lovers offers. This intention finds results in Pheoby's reaction: "'Lawd! . . . Ah done growed ten feet higher from jus' listenin' tuh you, Janie. Ah ain't satisfied wid mahself no mo'. Ah mean tuh make Sam take me fishin' wid him after this. Nobody better not criticize yuh in my hearin''" (284).

There are three interesting aspects to this seemingly simple utterance. First, it precludes closure to the narrative. Second, it earmarks Sam as the next candidate to be reformed by Janie's story. Finally, it introduces the completion of a pattern of imagery that has been somewhat submerged, the linkage of Janie and Tea Cake to a mythic mode of representation that centers on the figures of Isis, Osiris, and St. Peter.

Pheoby's announcement precludes closure to the story, for its continual telling means that the "seeds" (words) planted here will sprout. Sam Watson will be the next to benefit from Janie's story. He and Pheoby thus become Janie's ambassadors to the worlds of male and female discourse within the community. Sam would appear to be the perfect figure to intercede for Janie in another sense too, for Janie herself says of this comic King of the Porch early in the novel, "'Sam is *too* crazy! You can't stop laughin' when youse round him'" (16). His comic approach to life makes Pheoby's affinity to Janie stronger in this ongoing marriage's parallelism with Janie and Tea Cake's and makes the sense of continuity and regeneration at the end of the book even stronger too.

Tea Cake's seeds and their link with the sprouting of the story itself are part of the network of Egyptian symbolism that pervades the novel. Tea Cake is buried "like a Pharaoh" with a guitar in his hands; he is repeatedly described as the sun of the Evening Sun; and the circumstances of his death associate him with flood, thus figuring him as an avatar of Osiris. Further, he resembles the Egyptian black god of fertility, ruler of the lower world, whose symbol was an eye opened wide as a sign of his restoration to light by Isis (Seyffert, Nettleship, and Sandys 439). The novel begins with Janie described as "a woman . . . come back from burying the dead . . . eyes flung wide open in judgment" (9). In the novel's final scene, Janie climbs the stairs with a lamp; soon after, Tea Cake appears to her, "prancing around her," reborn like Osiris, who was also king of the upper air and of light.[29]

Osiris was brother, lover, and equal to Isis. Hurston, we remember, chose to name her fictional equivalent Isis in "Drenched in Light" and *Jonah*. The goddess, like Osiris, was associated with the flood, and her symbol was the cow, which may well account for the awkwardness of the mad dog scene in *Their Eyes*. She was also the goddess of ships and navigation (Seyffert, Nettleship, and Sandys 324–25) with obvious ties to the sea.[30]

Sam and Pheoby will really go fishing; Janie with her "net" symbolically does so at the end of the novel, and this brings us to Hurston's daring overlay of the Osiris/Isis imagery with that associated with St. Peter. Tea Cake asserts repeatedly that Janie has "the keys to the kingdom." We have seen that the woman with keys comes from a black folktale about woman's power, but keys play an important role in the Bible as well. Peter, formerly a fisherman, and then a "fisher of men," is awarded the keys to the kingdom by Christ, who says he will build his church on this rock (Matt. 16:18–19). In the gospel of John, the risen Jesus (like Tea Cake here) appears again to his disciples and bids them cast their nets on the right side of the boat: "Simon Peter went up, and drew the net to land full of great fishes, an hundred and fifty and three, and for all there were so many, yet was not the net broken" (John 21:11). Janie, taking her light up the stairs (echoing the spiritual, "this little light of mine / I'm gonna let it shine") has already demonstrated her fitness to carry forth Tea Cake's "religion" of fully lived life and in fact has made her first convert in Pheoby.

Recognizing this pattern suggests a future for Janie beyond sitting in her room and living off memories. Peter, after all, was a great preacher, so perhaps Janie will become one too. We should remember that all of Nanny's fears/prophecies for Janie have come true. Janie is transformed into a mule, first of work, by Logan, then of decorative leisure, like Bonner's mule, by Jody. She does become a spit cup, as we have seen. Janie has already preached one sermon "from on high," as Nanny wished, and it may be that the novel's conclusion predicts many more.

On the other hand, a curious scene in the novel might be read as a caution against making too much of this Christian mythic patterning. One of the men on Jody's porch tells a comic Big John de Conquer story, claiming ole John was gone for centuries because he was in Egypt, hanging around, eating up "'dem Pharaoh's tombstones. Dey got de picture of him doin' it. Nature is high in uh varmint lak dat'" (104). African American mythology ultimately and joyously gobbles up all others in this narrative.

We know this story has to be told for another reason. Earlier, Mrs. Annie Tyler brought out the cruel side of the community's humor. Seduced, abandoned, and robbed by a series of young men, this older woman goes off laughing on her final fling with yet another younger man named, appropriately, Who Flung. Two weeks later a pitying Eatonville man finds her abandoned and penniless in Tampa; she becomes the laughingstock of the community upon her return. Similarly, at the beginning of the frame story, when Janie returns alone, the neighbors' "burning statements" and killing laughter once again create mass cruelty. (10). Janie's transformation, however, gives her words to soothe these sentiments and to turn them to her favor since her story, which cheers and illuminates, points the way toward personhood. The opposition here is not just between Janie and the community, but between modes of comic creativity. Like the Hindu godhead, humor has both a healing, preserving, uniting aspect (Vishnu) and a destructive, revenge-seeking, purging one (Shiva), once again pointing to the Janus imagery. Janie magically transforms this communal energy into something constructive and uniting—her story.

This has importance beyond the pertinent details of the scene. Black literature, especially that written in dialect, has often been accused of locating itself in a narrow orbit between "humor and pathos," as James Weldon Johnson once put it (*Poetry*), which could translate as "between minstrelsy and melodrama." Janie wants to avoid both extremes—being cast as the butt in a comic script like Mrs. Taylor or being seen as a pathetic "broken woman," the way the white judge and jury choose to read her.

Back in Eatonville, Janie has to "make her case" among her people, with their involvement. Individual achievement finds its ultimate fulfillment in conjunction with others, and as Mary Helen Washington wisely observes, "the deepest and most lasting relationships occur among those black people who are most closely allied with and influenced by their own community" (*Black-Eyed* xxx). Janie instinctively knows that she can find peace only when the story untold at the trial becomes lodged in the figurative bosom and collective memory of her home community. The telling of her story, in the people's own loving, laughing voice, confirms its communal, cultural relevance, assures its immortality, and embalms her love for Tea Cake.

Throughout *Their Eyes Were Watching God* Hurston indicates that in refusing one's heritage, a person commits cultural suicide, and the loss of laughter represents an early symptom of that internal death. In a unique way, both Janie Crawford Killicks Starks Woods and Zora Neale Hurston recognized and harnessed humor's powerful resources; using its magical ability to bring people together, they established the intimacy of democratic communion.

On the other hand, Washington has also warned us against reading this novel too positively, for Janie indeed is silenced at any number of places, and we have no assurance that her voice will reverberate in the community again beyond the telling of her story through Pheoby. Janie herself issues a qualification as she summarizes the buzzing curiosity and gossiping of the townspeople to Pheoby: "'Dem meatskins is *got* tuh rattle tuh make out they's alive. Let 'em consolate theyselves wid talk. 'Course, talkin' don't amount tuh uh hill uh beans when yuh can't do nothin' else. And listenin' tuh dat kind uh talk is jus' lak openin' yo' mouth and lettin' de moon shine down yo' throat. It's uh known fact, Pheoby, you got tuh *go* there tuh *know* there. . . . Two things everybody's got tuh do fuh theyselves. They got tuh go tuh God, and they got tuh find out about livin' fuh theyselves'" (285). Ultimately, as this passage suggests, language itself becomes limited, unable to reach what Hurston calls that "gulf of formless feelings untouched by thought" (43). People thus need the other arts and any other feeble tool they can create to assault the voids of silence that divide us.[31]

Humor, I would suggest, springs from the failures of ordinary, standard language to adequately communicate human needs, emotions, and expressions. It offers an expansion of language that goes even beyond metaphor. Indeed, as Hurston indicates in "Characteristics of Negro Expression," humorous gestures can function as communication, displacing and frequently transcending the limitations of spoken or written discourse. Comic creation of all types, however, paints, as Hurston might say, a "hieroglyphics" of mirth, speaking to us in a way that unadorned speech never can, moving us as close as language can ever get to what Janie instinctively understands as "the inaudible voice of it all." (24).

Notes

1. Hurston knew Swift's work as a child; some white women sent her a set of books that included *Gulliver's Travels* (*Dust Tracks,* 53). I thank my friend Asun Elizagierre for drawing my attention to this line in Swift.

2. Several early and appreciative critics nevertheless read the novel reductively. See, for example, George Stevens, who finds the book "simple and nonpretentious" (3). More damningly, Hurston's friend/enemy/sibling rival Alain Locke declared the novel "folklore fiction at its best," but added "when will the Negro novelist of maturity who knows how to tell a story convincingly—which is Miss Hurston's cradle-gift, come to grips with motive fiction and social document fiction? Progressive southern fiction has already banished the legend of these entertaining pseudo-primitives whom the reading public still loves to laugh with, weep over, and envy. Having gotten rid of condescension, let us now get over over-simplification!" ("Jingo" 10).

3. Joseph Campbell's formulation of narrative pattern in heroic quest is enumerated in his *The Hero with a Thousand Faces.*

4. See especially Missy Dehn Kubitschek's reading. Other articles on this topic are listed in Awkward.

5. *Columbia Encyclopedia,* 3d ed. Cyrena Pondrom has made a strong case

for Frazer's multivolume *Golden Bough* as the source for much of Hurston's detailed knowledge of classical myth. There Janus/Jana (the male/female pair) is interchangeable with Diana. I would add that Jana/Diana was embraced in the sacred grove of Nemi by the King of the Woods, Virbius, whom Frazer claims was merely a local form of Jupiter in his aspect as god of the Greenwood. Virbius's union with Jana/Diana constituted a regal couple, the King and Queen of the Woods, and he was charged with the protection, "*at the peril of his life,*" of the sacred oak (376–87; my emphasis). The royal union was deemed essential for the fertility of the earth. Clearly, Virbius would be an obvious source for Vergible Woods, whose last name suggests the sacred grove. Tea Cake does indeed die as a result of trying to protect Janie, who identifies with the pear tree. Hurston intrigues us by her decision to identify Janie with a male god rather than with his female counterpart, saving that maternal, moon-associated aspect for Pheoby.

6. Zora Neale Hurston to Charlotte Mason, Sept. 28, 1932, Moorland-Spingarn Research Center, Howard University Library, Washington, D.C.

7. As Lawrence Levine reminds us, Hurston's great contemporary, the stand-up comedienne Moms Mabley, frequently used down-home food and humor together to create intimacy between herself and her audience. Appearing in Washington, D.C., she told an audience, "I'm telling you I'm glad to be at *home.* And I had my first real meal in months. My niece cooked me some hog *mawwws,* and some cracklin' corn *b-r-e-a-d,* and a few greens on the side. *Thank* the Lord I'm talking to people that know what I'm talking *about*" (363).

8. Wright wrote a scathing review of *Their Eyes* ("Between Laughter and Tears"), dismissing it as a form of minstrelsy; he found its humor inappropriate for a novel about black life, a collective history he could only read as overwhelmingly tragic. A passage that Wright must have found more to his liking, Nanny's moving and eloquent personal history, which comprises most of chapter 2, is appropriately sober and heartbreaking.

9. This scene is further proof that Hurston's entire career may be understood as a kind of preaching. Her novels have biblically inspired titles, which "set the texts"; within them, one finds symbolic references to biblical themes, which are then illustrated by ensuing narrative events, all of which have both surface and deep messages. Furthermore, in virtually every case, the biblically inspired scene has a comic and a serious interpretation. For example, the motif of a stranger receiving water at a well from a woman is employed in all her novels and sets the text for ensuing narrative events that are both comic and serious, as when John first meets Lucy in *Jonah.*

10. More evidence is provided by "The Bone of Contention," which served as the basis for *Mule Bone.* As in the play, Joe (named Clarke rather than Starks) presides over a trial that pits a Baptist against a Methodist, and therefore their congregations exchange verbal blows as well. A hilarious exchange between Sister Lewis, a Baptist, and Sister Taylor, a Methodist, offers a good example of what Jody refuses to let Janie do, signify in public: "'Some folks,' she said with a meaning look, 'is a whole lot mo' puhtic'lar

bout a louse in they church than they is in they house.' A very personal look at Sister Lewis. 'Well' said that lady, 'mah house mought not be exactly clean, but nobody caint say *dat'*—indicating an infinitesimal amount on the end of her finger—'about my chaRACter! They didnt hafta git de sheriff to make Ike marry ME!' Mrs. Taylor leaped to her feet and struggled to cross the aisle to her traducer but was restrained by three or four *men* [my emphasis]. 'Yas, they did git de sheriff tuh make Sam marry me!' She shouted as she panted and struggled, 'And Gawd knows you sho oughter git him agin and make *some* of these men marry yo' Ada'" (8–9). Joe Clarke/Starks orders these "moufy wimmen" to "'Shet up,'" but both he and Lum Boger, the marshal, are cowed by the women's fiery frowns.

11. Rachel Blau DuPlessis has also written about the spittoon as the fulfillment of Nanny's feared projection and as one of the signs (the other, of course, is the mule) "under which Janie's marriage to Joe Starks unfolds" (112). Although DuPlessis sees the humor associated with the mule, she doesn't extend this argument to the spittoon.

12. In these scenes, Hurston once again makes use of "The Bone of Contention." In that sketch Lindsay agrees with Rev. Simms's demand that Mayor Joe Clarke build a jail and tells the latter, "'Jus' cause you stahted the town, dat dont make yo' mouf no prayer book nor neither yo' lips no Bible. They dont flap lak none tuh *me*'" (4).

13. The scene also bears a remarkable resemblance to one of Thomas Nast's most famous cartoons, which depicted Boss Tweed and his gang around a public's carcass. The leader asks, "Shall we pray?" The cartoon was recycled by Herblock during the Watergate crisis, substituting Nixon and his henchmen for the Tweed gang.

14. Several passages devoted to the humor directed at and fielded by Daisy Taylor are taken from *Mule Bone*. There and here, Jim and Dave are rivals for Daisy's attention and engage in yet another comic verbal duel, reprising and foreshadowing much of the humor of courtship so central in both *Jonah* and *Seraph,* with comically exaggerated declarations of love, such as "'A'll take uh job cleanin' out de Atlantic Ocean fuh you any time you say you so desire'" (108). Hurston the anthropologist thereby signals to us the ritualized nature of Eatonville humor and the value it has in courtship and for the community, but once again underlines Joe's exclusion of his wife, as he orders her into the store.

15. This conceit reminds us of Emily Dickinson's poem:

> The Bustle in a House
> The Morning after Death
> Is solemnest of industries
> Enacted upon Earth—
>
> The Sweeping up the Heart
> And putting Love away
> We shall not want to use again
> Until Eternity.
>
> (242)

16. As Michael G. Cooke notes, however, Janie and Jody are not technically playing the dozens. She *categorizes* him ("big-bellies"); as Cooke states, she "seems to crash through signifying and into denunciation" (77).

17. The scene also has important comic and structural parallels with Ralph Ellison's hilarious episode in *Invisible Man* where the narrator, significantly dressed in overalls, passes through the Men's House in New York. He thinks he sees President Bledsoe, who betrayed him with false letters to northern entrepreneurs. Outraged, he empties a nearby spittoon on his head, but flees when it turns out the man is a Baptist preacher; the parallels between secular and sacral language and duplicity are obvious. The narrator is later told by an amused porter that he's been banned from the Men's House, and "'after what you did, I swear, they never will stop talking about you. You really baptized ole Rev!'" (258). The porter delights in one of his fellows on the lower end of the social totem pole inverting the social order, just as we do with Janie's signifying on Joe. Paradoxically, although both Ellison's narrator and Janie have violated the sanctum sanctorum of the "Men's House" of male discourse, they have both proved they are more than eligible for inclusion.

18. Hezekiah's portrait may operate on yet another satirical level. Hurston's oldest brother was named Hezekiah Robert. This satirical portrait is akin to the one Hurston painted of her sister Sarah in the character of Larraine in *Seraph*. There has been some confusion as to the names and ages of Hurston's siblings. Hemenway doesn't provide a list and mentions only a few of them in his biography. Hurston listed them, however, presumably in chronological order, in a letter to Godmother: "H. [Hezekiah] R. [Robert] Hurston, Physician and surgeon, Memphis, Tenn.; John Cornelius Hurston, Meat market and Florist shop, Jacksonville, Fla.; Richard William Hurston, mechanic, Newark, N.J.; Sarah Emmeline Hurston Mack, housewife, Asbury Park, N.J.; Joel Clifford Hurston, rural education, Montgomery, Ala.; Ben Franklin Hurston, PhC., Drugstore proprietor, Memphis, Tenn.; Zora Neale Hurston, bum and Godmother's pickaninny, New York City; Edward Everett Hale Hurston, P. O. clerk, Brooklyn N.Y." (Dec. 20, 1930, Moorland-Spingarn Research Center, Howard University Library, Washington, D.C.). However, the family Bible lists nine children, in this order: Hezekiah Robert, Isaac, John Cornelius, Richard William, Sarah, Zora Neal Lee (note the spelling), Clifford Joel, Benjamin Franklin, and Everett Edward. All but the last three are listed as being born in Notasulga (for details see Bordelon). In the letter the characteristic self-effacement before Godmother surfaces in the "bum/pickaninny" soubriquet, but also serves to contrast with and underline Hurston's justifiable pride in her siblings' accomplishments.

19. See 1 Cor. 13:12. Paradoxically, Tea Cake's mode as a teacher may doom him as a character, for as Claire Crabtree claims, Hurston seems to be determined to privilege folktale over novel in her narrative structure. In the folktale, Crabtree reminds us, "the magical teacher is dispensed with as the hero triumphs, and so is Tea Cake left behind on Janie's journey" (65). Additionally, this scene is likely the basis for Alice Walker's similar one in *The Color Purple*, where Shug gives Celie a mirror and urges her to examine

and get to love every part of her body. Mary Helen Washington, however, has told me that consciousness-raising groups began urging women to do this in the early days of the contemporary women's movement, so this could be Walker's source as well. This latter phenomenon was satirized with a vengeance in the novel and film *Fried Green Tomatoes*.

20. Pheoby's mode of navigation is also a reflection of one of Hurston's favorite expressions, "hitting a straight lick with a crooked stick," and an illustration of a concept she discusses in "Characteristics" under the topics of angularity and asymmetry. She finds this in black dancing, furniture arrangement, and other aspects of black life and attributes it to African aesthetics, seen in African sculpture and doctrine. African Americans are pictured as intent on avoiding "the simple straight line." Paradoxically, however, as Hurston remarks, the asymmetry of the dancing is simultaneous with the regularity of musical rhythm. Although she doesn't say so, the angular placement of furniture depends on the geometric regularity of the interior space (41). We may go further and suggest that the dialectical and grammatical rupturing of standard English, which is very important in the role speech plays in black humor, operates similarly, causing the "liberation" Freud speaks of in *Jokes*. The "angularity" of approach also stems from the need for linguistic caution (and thus indirection and coded allusion) in a dangerous racist society. Curiously, although Hurston has a "dialect" section in "Characteristics," she doesn't make this connection.

21. Mary Helen Washington has argued that Janie's quest for identity is also a quest for blackness, a frame of reference that is achieved through authentic mastery of folk language, black culture ("Zora" 68ff.). Surely the acquisition of comedic styles, repertoires, and attitudes plays a key role in both activities and educates the reader simultaneously. Melvin Dixon, in a fine essay on Hurston's use of geography and geographical imagery in *Their Eyes*, notes that Janie walks back into town with black mud on her overalls, "proof of her new baptism" (94). Although he doesn't say so, he (and Hurston) surely suggest an immersion/baptism in blackness, the kind Washington has in mind, and this returns us to this chapter's epigraph, for Janie indeed is baptized with humor, one of the things the "black mud" symbolizes. Baptism also fits with Robert Stepto's claim that *Their Eyes* is "quite likely the only truly coherent narrative of both ascent and immersion" in black literature (164), an assertion he subsequently undercuts by discounting the novel's mode of narration. Nevertheless, his initial observation stands.

22. These passages remind us of the dicty blacks' color prejudices satirized by Nella Larsen in *Quicksand* (1928), especially in the scenes set at Naxos College, and of the treatment the very dark heroine receives from her family and college classmates in Wallace Thurman's *The Blacker the Berry* (1928), books Hurston surely had read.

23. Hurston's juxtaposition of humor with an encroaching natural disaster, the hurricane, is stunning, and was based on actual events. The legendary Florida hurricane of September 1928 devastated the state, killing thousands and causing tremendous damage to property. Another storm killed 425 in 1935, just before Hurston wrote *Their Eyes* (Federal Writers' Project 61–

62). Furthermore, Hurston was in the Bahamas in October 1929, where she survived a terrible hurricane (Hemenway 127). Several novels featuring hurricanes had been written, including one Hurston may have known. Theodore Pratt's *Big Blow* (1936) is set in the very same area near Lake Okeechobee and came out just a year before *Their Eyes*. Interestingly, Pratt, who had come to Florida from New York in 1934 and would write about the state in many novels and nonfiction works during the rest of his career, would get to know Zora quite well, attend her funeral, and write a number of essays about her. Most of the hurricane-genre books routinely use the storm as Hurston does, placing it at the end of the book to bring the narrative to an exciting conclusion. Pratt's, however, combines the threat of a double lynching (of a white and a black man, both in trouble with local "trash") with the storm tradition. Nature, there, however, is a somewhat melodramatic agent of justice, for the "trash" are killed violently by the storm before accomplishing their goals, and long-yearning lovers finally embrace as the storm's last winds roar past. Pratt's description of the storm and its effects is powerful and detailed. Hurston possibly borrowed the idea of using a piece of roofing from him.

24. The theme of higher ground has set many a text for the black pulpit and is also the subject of the popular Baptist hymn "Higher Ground":

> I'm pressing on the upward way,
> New heights I'm gaining ev'ry day;
> Still praying as I onward bound,
> Lord, plant my feet on higher ground.
> Lord, lift me up and let me stand,
> By faith, on heaven's tableland,
> A higher plane than I have found;
> Lord, plant my feet on higher ground.
>   (Sims 319)

25. Hurston here uses graveyard irony and thus echoes a classic story of a Baghdad merchant, the epigraph of John O'Hara's brilliant novel *Appointment in Samarra* (1934), a book she could have read. The merchant's servant runs into Death in the marketplace, who makes a threatening gesture. The servant tells his master he's fleeing to Samarra. Momentarily, the master sees Death in the marketplace and asks him why he threatened the servant. Death's reply is: "That was not a threatening gesture . . . it was only a start of surprise. I was astonished to see him in Baghdad, for I had an appointment with him tonight in Samarra."

26. In these indirect speculations about God, also found in *Moses*, Hurston sounds similar to Jung, who specifically stated: "If we consider, for example, the daemonic features exhibited by Yahweh in the Old Testament, we shall find in them not a few reminders of the unpredictable behaviour of the trickster, of his pointless orgies of destruction and his self-appointed sufferings, together with the same gradual development into a saviour and his simultaneous humanization" (196).

27. Hurston was clearly working out some of the bitterness she still felt

in 1950 about the most devastating event of her life, her unjust accusation in 1948 by a black woman of sexually molesting a young black boy. Although the charges were dismissed, the black press across the nation had picked up the story; Hurston felt her race had betrayed her, as an October 30, 1948, letter to Carl Van Vechten reveals (James Weldon Johnson Memorial Collection, Yale Collection of American Literature, Beinecke Rare Book and Manuscript Library, Yale University, New Haven, Conn.).

28. Richard Wright, in the title of his *New Masses* review of the book, might have seemed to be signaling Hurston/Janie's success at navigating between these two modes of presentation. However, a humorless Wright finds her guilty of a new kind of minstrelsy.

29. As Cyrena N. Pondrom has shown us, both Tea Cake and Osiris are twenty-eight. She has also noted a few of the other similarities I have pointed out here. She leans much more heavily toward Tea Cake as Tammuz, however, and brings in other gods as well. She takes the same approach with Janie. Hurston was much more attracted to Egyptian myth than to those of other cultures, such as the Babylonian and Greek myths Pondrom highlights, because she believed that as Africans the Egyptians were black.

30. Hurston, ever the mythic synthesist, had no doubt considered the obvious parallels with Christ. Tea (red, like blood) Cake (the body), like Christ, is sacrificed so that others (first Janie, then the community who hears his story), might "live."

31. Pheoby's name may be important here as well, since the appellation "Phoebe" was associated with the goddess Artemis in terms of her role as moon goddess (Seyffert, Nettleship, and Sandys 486, 573). Hurston's reference to gossiping talk as moonshine underlines Pheoby's doubled role, both as someone who has heard gossip and then sped to solace its object only to find that she will be able to silence the original tales by narrating Janie's canceling narrative. The moon, of course, relays light to earth it reflects from the sun, the orb constantly associated with Janie. Lucy Hurston's advice to her children to jump at the sun, and maybe you'll at least get the moon (which becomes Lucy's advice to John in *Jonah*), has ironic relevance here, since Janie-the-Sun's neighbors do indeed "jump" her in the novel's opening, but they have to be content with getting her story/reflection second-hand from Pheoby-the-moon. Rachel Blau DuPlessis has similarly noticed the classical derivation of Pheoby's name and linked her with the moon as a reflector of the sun.

FOUR

Signifying on God:
Moses, Man of the Mountain

He had given Israel back the notes to songs. The words would be according to their own dreams, but they could sing. They had songs and singers.

—*Zora Neale Hurston*

And when the next missionary comes on to you about nonviolence use his own bible as your lever, pointing out that the God of the Jews was not particularly interested in turning cheeks, *viz.*, all those drowned Egyptians.

—*Amiri Baraka*

Zora Neale Hurston startled many of her aficionados when she set down her version of the Moses story in novel form in 1939. Written in contemporary black dialect, the tale took liberties with the biblical narrative; for example, Moses is not Hebrew, but Egyptian and therefore black. On the other hand, from the evidence of their language and customs, the children of Israel seem to be stand-ins for African Americans, and the backsliding of these "chosen people" appears to echo traits Hurston sometimes bemoaned in the phrase she used to title a chapter in her autobiography: "My People! My People!" The book comments eloquently on the history of slavery that the Israelites and African Americans had in common, but also encompasses group dynamics, the problem of racial leadership, sibling rivalry, father-son relations, people's connection to God, and the sacral quality of life.

The biblical tale recounts the story of a Hebrew baby whose parents, Jochebed and Amram, seek to circumvent Pharaoh's death decree for

newborn Hebrew sons by hiding him in an ark among Nile bullrushes, stationing his sister Miriam nearby as a sentry. She watches as the
bathing princess discovers the baby and takes him to the palace;
Jochebed then secures a position as his wet nurse. Raised as a prince
of Egypt, he grows to sympathize with the Hebrew slaves and finally kills
an Egyptian overseer who abuses them. This forces him to flee to Midian, where he settles down with Jethro's tribe, marrying his host's
daughter, Zipporah. Years later, God calls him to go back to Egypt and
demand the freedom of his people, which he secures by the aid of his
brother Aaron and plagues sent by God. Forty years of wandering in
the desert follow, as the Israelites' disobedience angers God. Moses,
too, disobeys and is guilty of striking a rock with his magic rod to get
water without God's permission. Consequently, although God allows
him to see Canaan, he takes his servant to Heaven just before Joshua
leads the people into the homeland.

The central drama in Hurston's retelling, however, involves Moses'
ethnic dilemma. Raised a prince, he has successfully conquered new
lands as head of Pharaoh's army and suffered a political marriage with
an Ethiopian princess. His growing interest in the plight of the oppressed Hebrews pushes him closer to choosing between a privileged
life as Egyptian royalty and a sacrificing life of exile and deprivation.
By killing the Egyptian overseer Moses puts an end to his own life of
royalty as he is forced to flee to Midian toward a fulfilling pastoral life
with Jethro's family. Jethro's pressure on Moses to employ his gift for
leadership and hoodoo heroically forces him to choose again, this time
between the pleasures of a quiet personal life and troubled racial leadership. Finally, when the Israelites reach the border of the promised
land, Moses must decide between wearing a crown or withdrawing into
an anonymous life; he opts for anonymity after faking his death on
Mount Nebo. Although the narrative sets up a dialectical tension between Moses and the people, in many ways his story represents their
story, a collective spiritual journey epitomized through the transformation of their leader. The Israelites are constantly faced with a choice
as well; obedience to God's laws and commandments, as expressed by
Moses, his agent and their leader, or personal, independent action that
could be described as creative rather than merely rebellious.

These ponderous themes are freshened by being presented in an
ethnic manner, with large doses of folk-inspired humor. Cross-ethnic
touches are abundant, as Hurston comically signifies upon black, Jewish, and American stereotypes, folktales, and idioms. The novel as a
whole has metaphoric significance for all American ethnic minorities
and the double binds they face as hyphenated Americans, but it also

speaks to one of the most basic paradoxes of human existence, the opposed struggles for individual freedom and group solidity and security. Despite their seriousness, all these subjects are treated comically, as Hurston employs a complex, multivocal parodic narrative to establish a sense of group identity; reveal the hidden humor of the biblical text; and to ironically signify, not just on Judeo-Christian God himself, but on all forms of authority.

I agree with Darwin Turner's early assessment that the "chief art of the book is the abundant comedy," but I disagree with his immediate qualification: "But a good joke, at best, is merely a joke. Miss Hurston's joke entertains readers but does not comment significantly on life or people" (111). Similarly, Hemenway errs in his assertion that "one must be careful not to overemphasize the comic qualities of the novel; for, contrary to Turner's assertion, the final direction of the book is serious" (*Zora* 268). Critical positions such as these suggest a rather limited view of humor's role in discourse, literature, and life, and thus keep us from arriving at a proper appreciation of brilliant comic achievements such as *Moses*. Here, perhaps more so than in any of her other works, Hurston proves that humor can be a magnificent vehicle for serious issues.

Sources, Analogues, and Motives

Those unacquainted with either American or African American literary traditions might think Hurston's decision to mount this kind of experimental narrative looks radical, even blasphemous; who is she to rewrite the word of God? In fact, resetting biblical stories into more up-to-date narrative forms and language has enjoyed great popularity in the United States from the earliest days of colonial settlement, and the black community has done so with a relish, most obviously in the spirituals but in virtually every other form of creative expression as well.

We may explore this issue a bit further by examining the typological mode of representation in American letters. Many studies have mapped this tradition's contours, most prominently those that deal with the Puritans in New England.[1] As Werner Sollors has noted, such tropes permitted a spiritualization of collective experiences, something yearned for by many American ethnic groups. Such an enterprise provided justification for various group projects, but more importantly, solidified and sacralized group identity. Moreover, in utilizing a rhetoric of a "New Exodus," writers and leaders were able to set up a continual process.

This paradigm has extended to all levels of society; popular culture has always found ways to set biblical narrative, and many such treatments have been comic. The favorite subjects have come from the Old Testament, which have been refigured in children's tales, comic books, and more recently, in a headlined event, "Bible Tales Zapped into Nintendo Land." We read of video games such as "Baby Moses," where "the joy-stick controller plays Moses' mother, helping him escape after Pharaoh ordered all male Hebrew children drowned." Only expert players succeed; all too often Egyptian soldiers capture the baby Moses (A. Banks 4F). Signification on biblical themes has similarly worked in exalted and humble, serious and comic ways in the black community. For example, the promised land becomes not only the northern bank of the Ohio River, Canada, Africa, or successful conclusions to individual civil rights movements but a broader "transcendental realm" of "true liberty" (Sollors, "Literature" 650).

These types of discursive transformations proceed from the precedent established by the "classic"—be it the Bible, a Shakespeare play, or *Uncle Tom's Cabin*. Bakhtin has remarked that "classic works" have found re-accentuation in every era; new images are frequently created from the re-accentuation of old ones, when authors translate them from one register to another, from the tragic setting to the comic, and so on (Bakhtin, *Dialogics* 421). Black Americans, from the seventeenth century until today, have constantly translated the Scriptures into their own versions of truth, frequently melding them with Afrocentric traditions; the spirituals and folktales dealing with God, angels, and the Devil are only two obvious results.

Other ready models of how to transform biblical myth into useful stories were of course handy in the inventive sermons of black preachers, among them Hurston's father, and Hurston was not the first black writer to echo their figurations in printed versions. Nor was she the first black writer, or even the first black and female American writer, to develop her own version of the Moses myth. Frances Ellen Watkins Harper, more famous as the author of the novel *Iola Leroy* (1892), wrote a long poem, *Moses, A Story of the Nile* (1869), which Hurston may have known.

Wherever she found Moses, Hurston would hardly have had to look far in the African American cultural tradition; indeed, it would have been hard to avoid him. A white minister preaching to a large black congregation in 1862 in Charleston was astonished at their reaction to his text from Exodus. He later realized that they had interpreted his figurative language literally. Albert Raboteau uses this example to illustrate how, through a long process, slaves made the Bible their own: "They creatively fashioned a Christian tradition to fit their own peculiar experience of enslavement in America" (209). Colonel Thomas Wentworth Higginson said that the songs of his Black Civil War troops would lead one to believe that their knowledge of the Bible came mostly from the books of Moses and Revelation: "All that lay between, even the life of Jesus, they hardly cared to read or to hear" (27). Moses' heroic stance appealed to African born slaves, for the African epic hero often has an unusual birth, becomes endangered or exiled during childhood, and undergoes rigorous testing before gaining power. His battles, unlike those of Western heroes, are frequently with rival politician/sorcerers rather than with warriors (Roberts 125). The debate over slavery, the appalling disappointments of Reconstruction, and the nadir made these qualities even more salient and admirable.

When Hurston was writing *Moses* in the thirties, there were still ex-slaves alive who testified to both Moses' status as a conjure man and the continuing tradition of his abilities in the folk community. A Georgia octogenarian interviewed in that decade by Works Progress Administration writers said people could still turn rods into snakes the way Moses did before Pharaoh. Moreover, "'Dat happen in Africa duh bible say. Ain dat show dat Africa wuz a lan uh magic powuh since duh beginnin uh histry? Well den, duh descendants ub Africans hab duh same gif tuh do unnatchul ting'" (28).

Mirroring the oral tradition, virtually all black writers and leaders have found the Moses story important, and most have been shaped by the Bible's importance to black culture.[2] The repeated use of Moses/Exodus/Egypt/Promised Land typology in both slave narratives and black fictionalizations of slavery hardly needs annotation here; Martin Luther King, Jr., made the most unforgettable use of this typology in his "I have been to the mountaintop" speech. Alice Walker has recalled growing up "in the Methodist Church, which taught me that Paul *will* sometimes change on the way to Damascus, and that Moses—that beloved old man—went through so many changes he made God mad" (O'Brien 194). She indicates as well that this pattern of *expected* change in the Bible shaped her method of dealing with key fictional characters. Even more recently, Bryant Gumbel used the metaphor in a looser, more universal way, speaking of his controversial leadership of the "Today" show: "And what if you're not the prophet? What if you don't lead them to the Promised Land? That's O.K. too" (Carter 66).

Moreover, the Exodus story occupies a central position in black folklore's spiritual dialogics. Even a cursory glance at Langston Hughes and Arna Bontemp's *The Book of Negro Folklore* (1958) reveals over twenty percent of the material grouped in sections labeled "God, Man and the Devil," "Do You Call That a Preacher?" "Amen Corner," and "Spirituals," and many of the other categories harbor pieces that are religious or humorous.

Hurston had been increasingly intrigued by the prospect of reinscribing the white Bible into black terms. She had already written *The First One: A Play* (1927), featuring Ham, Noah's son. A field trip to the Bahamas furnished her with several tales that signified on biblical narrative. She published them in 1930, including one that explains that Cain kills his brother and gets sent into exile because he's really Eve's illegitimate son by the Devil. Cain's subsequent marriage to a gorilla produces the entire world's progeny, thus explaining the animal in us and suggesting, beyond the text proper, what anthropologists have since discovered as fact—that human life originated in Africa ("Dance Songs" 301).[3] She briefly set Moses as a character in the sketch "The Fire and the Cloud" (1934); there he has a conversation with a wise old lizard, fakes his death (so as to keep the Israelites in the wilderness for thirty days of mourning, thereby precluding a disastrous and premature descent into the promised land), and walks away alone into the wilderness. The text focuses on Moses' rueful assessment of the costs of leadership and his laying down of the magic rod. The major elements of the novel's last chapter were created here.

Hurston's unpublished short story "Book of Harlem" comically sets a contemporary description of that city in biblical language, thereby inverting the linguistic method of *Moses*. Much later, she concluded her career by attempting to write a novelistic history of Herod the Great. A late letter to her agent indicates she was planning even further biblical transpositions, including short stories about Abraham, Sarah, and Hagar; Saul and Samuel; and another entitled "He Laughed Too Much," the story of the expulsion of Ham by his father, Noah.[4] The idea of Moses as hoodoo man was prefigured in *Mules and Men* (1935); there Moses receives his rod from God, but learns hoodoo from Jethro and acquires the ten magic making words of creation, not from God, but from a snake that lives "in a hole right under God's foot-rest" (194). *Mules* concludes by listing thirty-eight items Hurston called the "Paraphernalia of Conjure," ending with the Bible. "All hold that the Bible is the greatest conjure book in the world," she tells us, and Moses is honored as the greatest conjurer. "The names he knowed to call God by was what gave him the power to conquer Pharaoh and divide the Red Sea" (287).[5]

So there were many possible origins for Hurston's projects. Henry Louis Gates, Jr., however, believes Hurston's ultimate source for the novel was Harper's 1869 poem ("Negro" 45). While both works allegorically feature conjurers and the innovation of multiple voices, none of Hurston's papers or letters suggest that she had extensive acquaintance with the writings of nineteenth-century black writers; by the 1930s, most of their work had long been out of print. She certainly could have heard about Harper's *Moses,* however, from her literature professor at Howard, Lorenzo Dow Turner,[6] or from other scholarly contacts, and the poem receives prominently notice in her friend James Weldon Johnson's preface to his 1922 edition of *The Book of American Negro Poetry.*[7]

Harper's mini-epic interestingly begins with Moses taking leave of his presumed mother, Pharaoh's daughter; his decision to join the "fortunes of my race" appalls her. She addresses him as "my son," while he calls her "gracious princess," linguistically severing a presumed maternal tie. She doesn't object to his new affiliation on racial terms but because he has selected the "paths of labor" and the "badge of servitude and toil" (34). Harper thus problematizes the original biblical story in an interesting way by focusing on the material/class aspect as well as the racial. Furthermore, by having the princess term Moses' decision a "strange election," Harper pinpoints the crucial distinction Hurston would make: Moses *consents* to his ethnicity. Even though both his mother and father are Hebrew in Harper's version, this descent does not dictate his ethnicity. Hurston, by firmly identifying his mother as an Egyptian princess and his father as an Assyrian prince, takes it as far as possible, making the Hebrew identification entirely one of consent. Of course, we see that her obvious assumption that Egyptians are Africans—and therefore black—somewhat obviates the need for the distinction, and indeed, pushes us closer to the class component.

We would do well to consider at least one other parallel between Harper and Hurston's texts. In the poem's long flashback to Moses' birth, evoked jointly by him and the princess, we see his early bonding with his real mother, Jochebed, who in Harper's version comes to the palace to nurse the infant found in the Nile. Moses' assertion that "from her lips I learned the grand traditions of our race that float / With all their weird and solemn beauty, around / Our wrecked and blighted fortunes" (39) emphasizes the oral tradition, while the verb "float" links Moses and the endangered Hebraic culture, afloat in the corrupting influences of Egypt. By further picturing Moses sleeping in an "ark," Harper thus conflates his destiny with the very emblem of Hebraic sanctity, the ark of the covenant, which the Hebrews will carry with them through the wilderness.

Even more important than these symbolic/iconographic ties, however, is the web of linguistically received culture. Moses absorbs Hebrew culture orally early in the narrative, as in Hurston's version, which suggests the link of cultural transmission from Hebrews to African Americans. Moreover, Moses chooses to match the princess's rendition of his origins with one that explains that of his people, retelling, as his mother told it to him (and as a African griot would) the origin myth of Abraham's sacrifice of Isaac. Harper's references to Jochebed lifting her eyes to the horizon in the direction of Israel as she tells of patriarchs sleeping in distant graves clearly refers to ancestors in Africa.

Despite these interesting parallels, Hurston's text differs radically from Harper's in many ways, but most importantly in tone and style. Although both writers make the Israelites equivalents to black Americans, Harper employs stately poetic stanzas of elevated English, devoid of any folk touches and any humor. Hurston exploded the Eurocentric rewriting of what was originally an Afro-Asian composite by reinscribing its meaning through folk utterance, metaphor, idiom, and anachronisms, each element of her formula involving a rich comedic tradition as well. Doing this revitalized a desiccated text and placed the narrative back into oral tradition. To put it another way, Hurston translates the Bible back into a story of the folk out of the ornate court language of the King James Bible. Whenever oral myth becomes set in print, it in effect has ossified, particularly when the parties of codification are from social elites.

Her activity reminds us of Gavin Stevens's less productive attempt to translate the Bible back to the original Greek in Faulkner's *Go Down, Moses;*[8] but she more radically takes the text back beyond even "classical" renditions. As George Steiner has suggested, "Any thorough reading of a text out of the past of one's own language and literature is a manifold act of interpretation." Moreover, interpretation may be defined as an attempt to give language "life beyond the moment and place of immediate utterance or transcription" (Steiner 17, 27).

By going even further, Hurston was obviously signifying on God himself, but also giving the sacral narrative a specifically black voice, correcting the imposition of a white Ole Massa–like God on her people, the dire historical consequences of which were all too manifest. Correlatively, by reauthoring the Pentateuch, Hurston slyly set *herself* up as a Moses figure. She was in this respect following the lead of W. E. B. Du Bois, who in *The Souls of Black Folk* cleverly kept the Moses role for himself without directly saying so, in politely applauding Booker T. Washington's successes after devastating his failings. In a masterful signification, he stated, "So far as Mr. Washington preaches Thrift, Patience, and Industrial Training for the masses, we must hold up his hands and strive with him, rejoicing in his honors and glorying in the strength of this Joshua called of God and of man to lead the headless host" (253). In her own appropriation of Moses' mantle, Hurston achieved what Toni Morrison has claimed as one of her objectives as a novelist: "The ability to be both print and oral literature: to combine those two aspects so that the stories can be read in silence, of course, but one should be able to hear them as well" ("Rootedness" 341).

If I am correct that Hurston attempted to revise or revitalize the Scriptures in an act of cultural "translation," her attempt to read between the lines is not blasphemous at all, but restorative. As Benjamin has stated, "For in some degree, all great writings, but the Scriptures in the highest degree, contain between the lines their virtual translation. The interlinear version of the Scriptures is the archetype or ideal of all translations" (96). Hurston constantly returns to the concept of translation as a linguistic and social extension of the basic problem of a divided soul, echoed in Moses himself: "Long ago, before he was twenty, he had found out that he was two beings. In short, he was everybody boiled down to a drop. Everybody is two beings: one lives and flourishes in the daylight and stands guard. The other being walks and howls at night" (82), and each side of the psyche must be translated to the other. This idea of duality continues later when Moses sees his first mountain after fleeing Egypt. It proves to be the mountain of his destiny, and as a man tells him, it has two names: "'It's according to where you live. The people on one side of it call it Horeb. On the other side they call it Sinai'" (111). Likewise, Moses' father-in-law and second mentor is named Jethro as chief, Ruel otherwise. Significantly, Jethro speaks both the language of his tribe and Egyptian, but more importantly, "He looked as if he could understand and talk with shepherds as well as kings. So Moses was not surprised when he spoke to hear him dropping into idiom of the simple people. It took nothing from his majestic bearing, and somehow it fitted him" (117). Clearly, these concepts fit the pattern of the comic and the cosmic we have seen in Hurston's other work.

Now we have an idea of the Moses tradition in black culture and Hurston's basic conception of her narrative. Where did the idea of a comic novel based on the Bible come from? It might have stemmed from a reading of Louis Untermeyer's 1928 novel *Moses,* which offered a stylization, if not a parody, of the sacred tale. In his hands, the comedy of colliding cultures and times employs anachronistic modernist wit, costumed drama, and a forced juxtaposition of two dramatic cultural narratives, those of the sun-worshipping, monotheistic Pharaoh Aknaton and those of the multicultural, multivocal Moses. Untermeyer also highlights the complaining nature of the Hebrews and uses humor to do so: as Aaron says, "'They wouldn't be Hebrews if they didn't complain. I'm sure that Adam grumbled about the accommodations in Eden'" (177). Untermeyer, too, changes Moses' biblical identity; he presents him as the illegitimate son of Pharaoh's sister, Thermutis, who conceives him during a brief but passionate affair. However, unlike Hurston's narrative, the father is a dark and handsome Hebrew, one Amram, who in the Bible sires Moses on his Hebrew wife, Jochebed. Pharaoh's witty wife airily dismisses the problem; Thermutis can simply declare she was visited by a god and thus conceived immaculately, a ruse her royal highness employed herself when the Pharaoh was inconveniently absent fighting a war.

Similarly, rather like the "explained" version of mysteries in the gothic novel tradition, the miracles of Moses are for the most part revealed by Untermeyer to be the result of naturally occurring phenomena. Perhaps this is because Aknaton's new religion "rigorously excluded all myth, magic and sorcery" (Freud, *Moses* 26). Hurston, who had studied Egyptian religious history, clearly would shun melding this part of the story into hers since it would run counter to her plan of making Moses a practitioner of African priestly rites and rituals. This is probably why Aknaton has no role in her narrative.

Untermeyer also focuses on Moses' dilemma of deciding which heritage he will accept. As such, each story becomes a metaphor for all racial minorities and hyphenated Americans. Untermeyer's creation of Moses as a "mulatto" union of Egyptian and Hebraic blood, however, provides us with a question: since Hurston wound up transforming Moses from Hebrew to Egyptian, why didn't she do as Untermeyer did and make him heir to both cultures? Clearly she wanted to establish his identity as African, thus setting up a direct "descent" from the hoodoo tradition. On the other hand, Moses' eventual election of the Hebrew tradition makes his ethnic identity entirely one of consent rather than descent, and in many ways offers an endorsement of Hebrew culture itself, functioning here as a stand-in for African American culture.[9] Finally, the fact that she did choose to make him half Egyptian and half Assyrian makes him a "mulatto" in any case, albeit a royal one.

We have no way of ascertaining whether or not Hurston read Untermeyer's book, but we know she researched her novels thoroughly—especially "Herod the Great," her other, unfinished, biblical adaptation—and she seems to have been well aware of what was "selling" in the literary and cinematic marketplaces of the 1920s. And in fact, circumstances suggest it likelier that Hurston knew Untermeyer's work rather than Harper's. Although Untermeyer has largely been forgotten, he was a towering literary figure in the thirties and was often a guest at Carl Van Vechten's parties, where he may have met Hurston.

Even if Hurston hadn't met Untermeyer, Van Vechten was in frequent contact with her up until about 1945, and it would have been strange if he hadn't told her about Untermeyer's novel when he heard she was writing one on the same subject.[10]

When Hurston's book came out, the editors of *Saturday Review* asked Untermeyer to review it. His analysis seems rather self-serving, for in the first paragraph he notes that Freud's *Moses and Monotheism,* which also came out in 1939, uses ideas (Moses as part Egyptian and as inheritor of Aknaton's monotheistic God) Untermeyer had employed eleven years previously in his novel. Although he doesn't say so, he must have felt Hurston had borrowed from him, and he notes she used Josephus as a source. He's clearly right, for her portrayal of Moses as an Egyptian general appears only there, and she made extensive use of Josephus, while angrily correcting what she felt were his errors, when she wrote "Herod the Great." Although Untermeyer admires her "fresh" approach in making Moses the great "voodoo man of the Bible," he finds the central characterization weak, static, and superficial. But one of the chief disappointments, he feels, lies in the supposed inconsistency between the descriptive authorial commentary—which he labels "correct . . . poetic in the traditional 'white' manner"—and the dialect conversations. The racism of these remarks seems clear and reappears in his insistence that it is unfair to link Hurston's book (as other reviewers did) with *The Green Pastures,* for, according to Untermeyer, the play has a combination of "humor and poignancy" that *Moses* lacks. Obviously, Untermeyer failed to see Hurston's novel as either funny or moving because he preferred either the stereotypical minstrel-related patterns of white writers' work or the upper-class, witty type of parody he loved to write himself ("Old" 11).

Hurston knew popular comic settings by white writers of Afro-American biblical myth that had appeared earlier, especially Roark Bradford's *Ol' Man Adam an' His Chillun* (1928), a setting of sacred stories in the rural South that made biblical figures—including God ("De Lawd")—into dialect-speaking blacks. The play based upon it, Marc Connelly's *The Green Pastures* (1930), was much better known. We know Hurston had read the play and had probably seen the equally popular film released in 1936, which was quite faithful to the spirit of the play. She fumed at how far Bradford and Connelly were from actual knowledge of jokes and stories in black culture that featured biblical tales, settings, and characters; she knew and had gathered oral examples of the real thing and had studied them in unusual depth in her capacity as anthropologist and folklorist.[11] These white writers drastically transformed, simplified, and stereotyped many folkloric patterns in these traditional genres. Despite some undeniably powerful moments, both their texts are ultimately offensive, as they use minstrel-show techniques in dramatized form to retell key biblical stories. Heaven consists of one continual fish fry; Pharaoh's court is depicted as a Negro lodge. The critical reviews of the play were reverent and resounding, and virtually all applauded the "utter simplicity" and "humility of the performance." Connelly's program note stated that *The Green Pastures* represented "an attempt to present certain aspects of a living religion in the terms of its believers. The religion is that of thousands of Negroes in the deep South. With terrific spiritual hunger and the greatest humility these untutored black Christians—many of whom can not even read the book which is the treasure house of their faith—have adapted the contents of the Bible to the consistencies of their everyday lives" (Toohey 83).

Hurston was no doubt attempting to correct what she felt were flaws in these constructs, but she may have been simultaneously and paradoxically inspired by the success of the play. *The Green Pastures* ran for 640 performances in New York and won the Pulitzer Prize for 1929–30. The public's fascination with this kind of narrative must have been exciting to a writer who knew she could do a better version with more authentic materials. How pleasant it would be to correct its racist mistakes and to make money from it, especially if it led to film royalties.

In this connection she may also have had in mind erasing the memory of more overtly racist films such as *Wonder Bar* (1934), which featured Al Jolson in blackface as an old man who rides a mule to Heaven, where singing, dancing, crapshooting, watermelons, and hams play prominent roles (Campbell and Pitts 25). Hurston began discussing the possibility of her books becoming films as early as 1934, when she wrote Van Vechten that Lippincott had been talking of getting *Jonah* made into a film.[12] And in fact, on a cruder level, biblical films of the period utilized many of Untermeyer's methods, as they brought Hollywood "updatings" of biblical stories to contemporary audiences, and they must have suggested parodic possibilities to Hurston that complemented her knowledge of her own culture's parodic traditions.

Our cinema has always favored cross and javelin epics; Hurston was thus merely following tradition. Movies of biblical stories were coming out in the United States as early as L. J. Vincent's *The Passion Play* (1908) and have continued to be produced on up to the Richard Gere debacle *King David* and Martin Scorsese's notorious but successful *The Last Temptation of Christ*. Usually these treatments are rendered rather seriously, although nudity and sex have played large roles in most of them. Sometimes, a daring artist will take a contrasting comic approach, as in Monty Python's outrageous *Life of Brian* (admittedly a British import, but vastly popular in the United States as a cult film), and in print, Joseph Heller's uneven but intermittently hilarious and ultimately serious treatment of the David story, *God Knows* (1984), which has so far been ignored by Hollywood. The Moses story was twice filmed by the master of epics, Cecil B. DeMille, and Hurston probably saw the first version. Vitagraph released a five-reel *Life of Moses* in installments, from December 1909 to February 19, 1910, but Hurston may not have known this version.

Between 1908 and 1939, the year Hurston published *Moses*, over forty films based all or in part on biblical stories had been made in the United States alone, most prominently D. W. Griffith's blockbuster *Intolerance* (1916) and DeMille's *The Ten Commandments* (1923) and *The King of Kings* (1927). Interestingly, *The Ten Commandments*, like a number of silent biblical movies, pairs a biblical text with a modern story. *Noah's Ark* (1928) similarly coupled the Old Testament deluge with a modern story of a train wreck that occurs at the outbreak of World War I. Hurston might have seen in these films examples of how the ancient and the modern could be braided together, but she also would have noted the liberties many filmmakers took with biblical narrative and dialogue (Campbell and Pitts 14–21). In any case, she clearly wanted to see her works filmed by Hollywood, a desire that continued to the very end of her career, as she followed the transformation of the work of popular "religious" writers into film, such as Thomas Costain's *The Silver Chalice*, Lloyd C. Douglas's *The Robe*, and, just before her death, the second version of Lew Wallace's *Ben-Hur*.[13]

Humor, Religion, and Ethnic Identity

Hurston clearly saw that religion resembles humor and language in that it may be found in every level of human life and thought, and all three are central in a quest for identity. *Moses* blends these elements in a complex presentation of the supernatural, the historic, and the legendary, in the service of a narrative of identity that utilizes Moses' and the Hebrew people's quests as metaphors for human identity. This method brilliantly revealed humor's use as a tool for unearthing submerged serious matters that paradoxically may have been buried by "serious" but different Eurocentric narrative traditions, as in the King James Bible. Hurston employs her humor-driven, folkloric mode to comment tellingly on the hierarchies of race, class, and gender, issues already present in the biblical narrative but obscured by their mode of presentation. By dramatizing Moses' successful apprenticeship in folklore and folk linguistics, she offers testimony of the effectiveness of laughter's community-building properties, as Moses creates the kind of "secret freemasonry" among his chosen people that Bergson describes; sharing a joke creates intimacy and a sense of identification. For Bergson, laughter is "always the laughter of a group" (64). I find the "always" in this latter observation problematic, but Hurston certainly shares Bergson's idea of the utility of humor in community and nation building.

Religion and humor both allow humans to explain much that seems unpredictable, mysterious, and irregular. Biblical and racial mythologies span the gap between the psychological and cognitive poles of religion by creative use of humor. Furthermore, subtracting humor's traditional role in religion (as Eurocentric culture had done by this time) deprives spiritual folk culture of an important mechanism for combat with humanity's troubles.

We may see Hurston operating on these principles from the outset. In her "Author's Introduction" she begins with an ironic understatement, "Moses was an old man with a beard" (xxi). In doing so, she challenges us to admit our mythic stereotype of the patriarch and to move beyond it, for in the passage that follows she does little more to describe his place in the Christian pantheon; indeed, the only sacral thing about this depiction lies in the statement that "angels buried him" (xxi). She then proceeds to note that Moses plays a prominent role in other cultures, in Asia, the Near East, but more importantly,

> Africa has her mouth on Moses. All across the continent there are the legends of the greatness of Moses, but not because of his beard nor because he brought the laws down from Sinai. No, he is revered because he had the power to go up the mountain and to bring them down. Many men could climb mountains. Anyone could bring down laws that had been handed to them. But who can talk with God face to face? Who has the power to command God to go to a peak of a mountain and there demand of Him laws with which to govern a nation? What other man has ever seen with his eyes even the back part of God's glory? . . . That calls for power, and that is what Africa sees in Moses to worship. For he is worshipped as a god. (xxi)

The operative words here are "Africa" and "sees." Already the author of *Their Eyes,* which placed black eyes in white readers, Hurston decided that Africa would *tell,* as well, using the indirect mode of humorous, folk-charged narration. The book was written following the linguistic traditions of black folk culture, employing copious amounts of dialect-driven dialogue, idioms, and expressions drawn from rural southern experience (especially animist iconology), and the black variant of

America's backwoods leveling humor. Key to this comic genre is Hurston's perception, taken from the culture's term for folk-telling sessions, that oral tale-telling is a "lying" session, one with cosmic dimensions, or as she added, "that is, straining against each other in telling folks tales. God, Devil, Brer Rabbit" (*Dust Tracks* 64). Moreover, the necessity of a hermeneutical method in dealing with these "by-words" of the oral folk tradition echoed the centuries of biblical hermeneutics practiced in the same culture. As a character in *Mules and Men* remarks, "'There's a whole heap of them kinda by-words. . . . They all got a hidden meanin', jus' like de Bible. Everybody can't understand what they mean. Most people is thin-brained. They's born wid they feet under de moon. Some folks is born wid they feet on de sun and they kin seek out de inside meanin' of words'" (135–36). Zora Neale Hurston, encouraged by her mother to "jump at the sun," clearly felt she'd landed there through her study of the culture and felt ideally situated to translate both folk culture and the Bible itself, simultaneously.

Her theory of how myths and legends, both biblical and folkloric, finds fictional demonstration in the beginning of *Moses.* Hurston's narrative echoes the Bible in describing a woman named Jochebed giving birth during the time when Pharaoh has decreed death for Hebrew children. The newborn boy's sister Miriam places the cradle in the bullrushes all right, but falls asleep, then awakens to find the cradle gone. She has seen the princess bathing nearby, however, so concocts the story that the Egyptian princess found and adopted her brother. Her lie, fitting a very real need, becomes a folk myth and eventually takes on the aura of truth—perhaps Hurston's commentary on the genesis of myth and folklore, and certainly in keeping with her presentation of the "lyin'" sessions held on store porches across the South.[14] Thus Moses in this book really *is* a prince of Egypt, even though Miriam's parents start the rumor that a Hebrew is passing for the prince royal, who becomes Egypt's general. The rumors reach Moses himself and perhaps account for his sympathy for the Hebrew workers, which culminates when he inadvertently kills a foreman in an attempt to help the slaves. Taking refuge for decades with wise old Jethro in the country, he marries and studies hoodoo. Eventually, Jehovah appears to him in the burning bush and instructs him to go down into Egypt to set the Hebrews free. The rest of the story has a familiar ring, with the important exceptions that Moses, on God's order, kills Aaron, and at the end of the book, rather than dying, Moses sets out to seek an old lizard who has the memory of the world in his possession. Moses then seems ready to rejoin his wife and sons in Midian, although it appears possible that he will go on to meet still another, more important lizard (possibly a reincarnation of his Egyptian mentor, Mentu) who knows the mysteries of the universe. Then too, Moses himself might become one of these African lizard gods.

Throughout Hurston's reshaping of this narrative, she frequently uses humor to suggest and support submerged serious subjects. Sometimes, though, the subject becomes more overt, and humor sharpens our response to a truly horrific situation. Thus even Pharaoh's harsh decrees have a comic edge: "Israel, you are slaves from now on. Pharaoh assumes no responsibility for the fact that some of you got old before he came to power." Incredibly, folk language makes even whippings and infanticide resonate in a comic way: "One hundred lashes for sassing the bossman," or "Babies take notice: Positively no more boy babies allowed among Hebrews. Infants defying this law shall be drowned in the Nile" (12). Similarly, woes and complaints are made more believable by being expressed in comic vernacular; Amram, toiling for the Egyptians, hears them praise Horus and remarks, "'Horus may be all those good things to the Egyptians, brother, but that sungod is just something to fry our backs.'" His co-worker replies, "'If Horus is the weaver of the beginning of things, he's done put some mighty strange threads in his loom'" (13). Here and at many other points in the novel humor offers access to group identity and cohesiveness. As Bergson states, "Laughter always implies a kind of secret freemasonry, or even complicity, with other laughers, real or imaginary" (6) and this would seem to have increasing truth as the community of interest emerges.

We may profitably examine the more important uses of humor as a vehicle for submerged serious matters in the book by focusing on presentations of class, race, and gender. Class becomes an issue early in the book. Miriam's lie about Moses' adoption sets the scene for mother Jochebed's comic pride: "'I ain't a bit surprised to hear the Princess loved him. He is a mighty pretty child and smart as a whip for his age.'" She then gets out her red shawl, imitating the red sandals and toenails of the princess, and sets out to tell her neighbors. When Amram doubts the tale, Jochebed gets Miriam to "testify" again, then says, "'See, Mr. Smarty! Always hunting for something mean and low. You don't even believe butter is greasy. . . . Always looking for a bug under every chip'" (48). This pride in position gets extended to the entire Hebrew people in a punning parody of passing, as they gloat over the news: "'Ho, ho! Pharaoh . . . passes a law to destroy all our sons and he gets a Hebrew child for a grandson. Ain't that rich!'" prompting another to say, "'And why not? . . . There is plenty of Hebrew blood in that family already. That is why that Pharaoh wants to kill us all off. He is scared somebody will come along and tell who his real folks are.'" This sets up an extended and comic discussion of Egyptian genealogical illusion and reality but also slyly plays on racial passing in the American South. We find an echo of Hurston's own views here as well; she once asserted: "I am all for the idea of free vertical movement, nothing horizontal. . . . The able at the bottom always snatch the ladder from under the weak on the top rung. That is the way it should be. A dead grandfather's back has proven to be a poor prop time and time again" (*Dust Tracks* 345).

The comic remarks about passing have an overtly serious counterpart later in the key passage of the novel, which describes Moses' solo crossing of the Red Sea after killing the Egyptian.

> Moses had crossed over. He was not in Egypt. He had crossed over and now he was not an Egyptian. He had crossed over. The short sword was no longer the sign of high birth and power. He had crossed over so he was not of the house of Pharaoh. He did not own a palace because he had crossed over. He did not have an Ethiopian Princess for a wife. He had crossed over. He did not have enemies to strain against his strength and power. He had crossed over. . . . He felt as empty as a post hole for he was none of the things he once had been. He was a man sitting on a rock. He had crossed over. (103–4)

The high degree of repetition, the ritualistic parallelism, the incantatory tone inevitably summon up rhetorical patterns of the black pulpit and countless Sunday school lessons but also images of other destined crossings, including Caesar's over the Rubicon. More importantly we see historical moments in black American history, such as the passage over the Ohio River taken by runaway slaves, flights to Canada, or the tragic middle passage itself. This also echoes Hurston's treatment of John's passage over the creek in *Jonah*. Here, though, Hurston goes further, for she mimics and offers the reverse of passing; after the transitional years in Midian, spent studying both folk culture and hoodoo, Moses will "cross over" yet again into Hebrew culture, "passing" for Hebrew as the requirements of a people's mythic yearning for leadership swallow up his personal, familial goals. It all ends on the comic analogy with a post hole, but Moses, to use one of Faulkner's phrases, now becomes a divinely sanctioned shape to fill a lack, an empty vessel soon to be filled with the heritage of the Hebrew people and the immanence of their God.[15]

This image of Moses, Man of the Mountain, simply a man sitting on a rock, evokes typological moments of origin. We see the ark resting on Mount Ararat, ready to refigure the now blank-again page of the earth; the contrasting New Testament antitype of Peter building the church in his person on the rock; and, of course, Moses himself, as revealed "Man of the Mountain," whose position on Sinai motivates the reconfiguration of humanity's relationship to God, as the finger of God descends to inscribe the law on the tablets.

This passage also strongly echoes classic statements in black fiction uttered by those (particularly mulattoes) who suddenly became conscious of their racial identity. The narrator of James Weldon Johnson's *Autobiography of an Ex-Colored Man* remembers how he felt upon learning he was black:

> And so I have often lived through that hour . . . in which was wrought the miracle of my transition from one world into another; for I did indeed pass into another world. From that time I looked out through other eyes. . . . This gives to every coloured man, in proportion to his intellectuality, a sort of dual personality; there is one phase of him which is disclosed only in the freemasonry of his own race. I have often watched with interest and sometimes with amazement even ignorant coloured men under cover of broad grins and minstrel antics maintain this dualism in the presence of white men. (403)

This narrator, however, has hardly forgotten his "white" identity. Similarly, Moses brings with him into Midian his years of study with the Egyptian priests, the pattern of command established as an officer and prince, and the folktales and proverbs taught him by his African stableman and mentor, Mentu, a wily servant who also can wear the "minstrel" mask if necessary.

The young prince also learned about creation through Mentu's rendition of African folk legends. Clearly a surrogate for the old black narrator of conjure/animal tales, such as Joel Chandler Harris's Uncle Remus or Charles Chesnutt's Uncle Julius, Mentu's tales are closer to Nigeria than to the southern plantations. The key animal in his tellings becomes the monkey rather than the rabbit, giving the tales a more overtly African quality. Still, Mentu's creation story knits together folktales and the rudiments of Genesis: "Let there be light."

Moses in these early scenes becomes the epitome of the Jewish/black people, as folk culture shapes his imagination: "The images arose in the brain chamber of Mentu, the stableman, and stumbled off his lips and became real creatures to Moses—to live in his memory forever" (55). The animal tales dazzle and amuse him, while he notes the way the creatures comment on the ways of humans. Later, Moses the man, endeavoring to speak the language of the people, will use animal imagery in ordinary conversation; when he acquaints Jethro with a plan to capture some vandals, he says "the whole idea is to bottle those skunks up in that cave" (125). Thus Moses, before crossing over, has been providentially prepared for immersion in folk culture by the wonderful and funny stories he heard, like Uncle Remus's "white boy," from a position of privilege. His growing love for Mentu, moreover, makes him see the injustice of slavery.[16]

The idea of a double heritage resurfaces again after Moses has studied hoodoo with Jethro and read the sacred book and fought the sacred snake at Koptos, melding Hebraic and African identities, so that when he goes up Sinai to face God, the people say, using the referents of hoodoo/conjuration, "He got the black cat bone and snake wisdom. He's a two-headed man. He ain't like nobody else on earth" (280).[17] Hurston had earlier played on Moses' powers of conjuration in *Jonah*, where Deacon Harris tells Hattie why he believes in hoodoo, practicing what Herskovits and other students of Africanisms in the New World calls "syncretisms":

> "Look at Moses. He's de greatest hoodoo man dat God ever made. He went 'way from Pharaoh's palace and stayed in de desert nigh on to forty years and learnt how tuh call God by all his secret names and dat's how he got all dat power. He knowed he couldn't bring off all dem people lessen he had power unekal tuh man! How you reckon he brought on all dem plagues if he didn't had nothin' but human power? And then agin his wife wuz Ethiopian. Ah bet she learnt 'im whut he knowed. Ya, indeed, Sister Pearson. De Bible is de best conjure book in de world." (147)

Despite Harris's mention of the instruction Moses surely received from his Ethiopian wife, she plays no role here, and even Zipporah, his Midian wife, offers no instruction. Only Jethro, Moses' adoptive father, provides the knowledge Moses needs to talk to God. By linking Moses with both hoodoo and Jehovah, Jethro offers him the path to God, giving truth to the folk expression "white man got de money an' education, / De Nigguh got Gawd an' conjuration" (Brewer, *Dog* 45–46).

Perhaps Jethro's most important role is as language coach. In the biblical story, Moses depends on his "brother" Aaron to function as his spokesman to the people instead of communicating with them directly. Biblical scholars have attributed this to a speech defect; Hurston brilliantly refigures this section of the story, indicating that Moses lacks proficiency in the Hebrew dialect. As Moses tells Jethro, "'I want to talk the dialect of your people. It's no use of talking unless people understand what you say'" (121). Jethro agrees: "'And then it's always a great advantage when you're managing people to be able to speak their kind of language. Stiff words frighten poor folks'" (122). Moses, in short, sets out to learn from Jethro how to become a "man of words."

Jethro, Moses' model for tribal leadership, excels at operating as the country sage and speaks almost entirely in folk language. Leaving Moses in the desert after freedom, he says, "'Sun-up tomorrow I reckon I'll hit the grit for home. Mighty lonesome there now without you and the children. Everybody married off and out of the house'" (276). Such utterances suggest the kinetic power of slang, repetition, hyperbole, and humor in vocal performance and communication among the folk.

With Jethro's help, Moses drenches himself in the Midian culture, giving him what Robert Stepto, in his study of black literature and culture, calls an "immersion" experience.[18] Moses becomes socially renewed by immersing himself in folk culture and especially folk language. After mastering the vernacular language of the tribes, he says, "'It's no use for me to try to talk any high court language to these people. I might as well get right down with them, and you don't need to talk for me anymore, Aaron.'" The people notice: "'The more Moses gets natural with us, the stiffer Aaron gets. He tries to sound like some high-toned Egyptian talking proper—when he don't forget to do it . . . and that's what makes it funny—he forgets'" (251). The fact that they find Aaron funny doesn't mean that Moses isn't—for part of his mastery of crowd control comes with his deft insertion of humor. The difference lies in his control of the jokes; Aaron, by contrast, increasingly becomes their butt.

Obviously Hurston makes fun here of the socially ambitious "dicty" blacks, who were so often her target, and their comic tendency to reveal their folk origins in a moment of forgetfulness. We also see in Aaron and Moses both descent and ascent, with Moses starting as a prince and giving it all up to gain wisdom and humility, and Aaron, increasingly pompous, windy, elitist, and ornately dressed, becoming so puffed up with blasphemous pride as the nation's head priest that God himself takes offense and orders Moses to kill him.

It thus makes perfect sense that Moses' full acceptance by the community comes through a mastery of their speech, the repository of their culture. He makes his God-given authority palatable for the people by his translation of his rule into human terms and language. His ability to specify makes him able to communicate through verbal dueling, comic invective, and folk anecdote. His language becomes, ironically, more hieroglyphic, more "black," as he becomes less Egyptian.[19] His attempt to match the speech of his people equates well with both the playful and vernacular traditions of the African griot. Gnankouman

Doua, a griot in the Malinese *Sunjata,* tells a hunter, "'Your words are obscure. Make your speech comprehensible to us, speak in the language of your savanna'" (Okpewho 19). Doua's words are those of a teacher who knows that instruction must relate to the student's everyday world.

Moses thus uses comic folktales to teach the people valuable lessons. When he needs to illustrate why the Hebrews must win a crucial battle against the Amalekites, he says,

> "Right now these Israelites are just like a passel of rabbits. You know, Joshua, one time the rabbits all met together in a convention and decided to kill themselves because nothing looked up to them and nothing was scared of them. So they all headed for the river to drown themselves.... They ran over some frogs and the frogs hopped up crying, 'Quit it! Quit it!' So the rabbits said to one another, 'Those frogs are scared of us. We don't need to kill ourselves no more because something in the world is scared of us. Let's go on back home.' So they went on home happy again." (256)

The playful aspect of this sort of language might be viewed as a contradiction of Moses' more familiar role as stern agent of the law. A common ground emerges here, for as Huizinga tells us in his classic work, *Homo Ludens,* "Inside the play-ground an absolute and peculiar order reigns," for play

> creates order, *is* order. Into an imperfect world and into the confusion of life it brings a temporary, a limited perfection. Play demands order absolute and supreme.... The profound affinity between play and order is perhaps the reason why play... seems to lie to such a large extent in the field of aesthetics. Play has a tendency to be beautiful. It may be that this aesthetic factor is identical with the impulse to create orderly form, which animates play in all its aspects.... Play casts a spell over us; it is invested with the noblest qualities we are capable of perceiving in things: rhythm and harmony. (10)

Moses, in his mastery of folk speech and signifying in particular, thus seizes the powers of linguistic play, partly in an attempt to introduce the rule of law and ritual, paradoxically achieving at the same time a kind of "enchantment" in keeping with his hoodoo powers. Moreover, this acquisition through his apprenticeships with Jethro and the people of an alternative heritage differentiates him from the one that actually produced him, that of Egypt, and the law of the Pharaohs.

But Moses also uses his folk communication to confront Pharaoh, who responds with his own black dialect in scenes that punctuate the dramatic infliction of the ten plagues on Egypt. Pharaoh and Moses engage in a humor-infused verbal duel, publicly demonstrating their power through an activity equally focused on self-aggrandizement and put-downs. As Abrahams observes, the man of words strives to register as "egotistical, obnoxious, self-serving, and arrogant" ("Rapping" 142).

Pharaoh's language and the language of his court, though as powerful as Moses' and that of the Midianites, is distinctly different. The slang of the Egyptian court has a marked urban quality that reminds us of the hip language of Harlem Renaissance texts such as Claude McKay's *Home to Harlem* or Hurston's own short story "Muttsy." The tough-sounding talk fortunately provides no bars to comprehension and actually suggests a community of comprehension between the Hebrews and the Egyptians that is necessary for a joking relationship, thus enabling Moses and Pharaoh—who, after all, are nephew and uncle—to verbally spar. Although they don't play the dirty dozens (something Hurston's publishers would have censored), they certainly "play in the family."

Freedom's Dialectic

Moses' ability to answer in kind, in call and response, helps him become a great preacher and prophet and extends the message about humor and language that was sent out by *Their Eyes*. In some ways these two great novels constitute a dialectic. It seems important to emphasize this, for *Moses* frequently seems to erase some of the hard-won perceptions of the earlier book, which details the discovery of a woman's voice and the methods by which individualism may be wrested from the community while one is still part of it. In a larger sense, however, it delineates freedom's joy. *Moses*, by contrast, centers on freedom's law and the work needed in its establishment and maintenance. The complementary aspects of the two books, which find a common ground in the liminal state of wandering, might be diagrammed as follows:

Their Eyes	*Moses*
Matriarchy	Patriarchy
Freedom	Law
Spontaneity	Duty
Revolution	Obedience
The People	The Leader
Reality	Myth
Sex/Love	Abstinence/Work

Water	Fire
Talking	Writing
Leaving the Land	Returning to the Land
Rhythm/Ragtime	Melody/Spirituals

Seen this way, the apparent discrepancy between the thematics of the two books makes more sense, especially when we remember that although *Their Eyes* was written first, *Moses* ambitiously seeks to limn the contours of a much earlier, mythical time, a point of origins that must necessarily be opposed in many respects to the "New Testament" version of black folk culture.

Moses also critiques the state, which should be the guardian of freedom's law; all too often, it becomes corrupted. Hurston reveals this situation in her rendition of the Egyptian court, which obviously may be read as representative of contemporary legal injustices inflicted on American blacks. Moses, who could rule Egypt, sees the corruption of king and people and prefers to cast his lot with God's chosen, the Hebrews, which means a protracted struggle with their master, Pharaoh. Amazingly, Hurston succeeds in dramatizing this pitched battle through a series of comic verbal duels, mimicking the contests of champions that used to decide issues between medieval armies. Pharaoh, who publicly laughs at Moses' threats, hurling comic rejoinders at his requests, secretly wants to let the Hebrews go, thereby ridding himself of worry and humiliation—but he knows what the political consequences would be among his nobles. Held prisoner by a class structure modeled on slavery and also by a personal family tradition that has "preached and practiced hatred and vengeance for generations . . . Pharaoh was locked up in his own palace and inside himself" (207), thus ingeniously replicating the American South's dilemma of "having the wolf by the ears."

His helplessness before political conditions begins a great theme, the ironic thanklessness of leadership, even for those who seem to be enjoying great privilege. This leads forward and backward in the narrative; the subsequent postdeliverance ingratitude of the Hebrews emerges as a recurring theme that has a class aspect, a motif prefigured some time before the duels with Pharaoh, when Moses himself is a prince of Egypt. Sympathetic to their plight, Moses tries to help the Hebrew slaves, but they view him as just another boss: "'If what you are doing ain't bossing then there ain't a crocodile in the Nile!'" (95). Later this same man brags to another, "'Did I tell that Prince something? . . . I told his head a mess!'" This kind of talk verifies what Moses had already thought, and also a hidden commentary on the leveling aspect of humor: Moses "saw the gloating look on the face of the one who was talking, and a brother gloat on the face of several others. So! The will to humble a man more powerful than themselves was stronger than the emotion of gratitude. It was stronger than the wish for the common brotherhood of man. It was the cruelty of chickens—fleeing with great clamor before superior force but merciless towards the helpless. It made him feel cruel himself" (95). As Hemenway points out, in this early scene, Moses comes off as a white liberal, the type Hurston called "Negrotarians."[20] I would add that Moses also replicates, here and elsewhere, the dilemma of the racial leader, whose attempts to provide guidance lead to accusations of substituting himself for "the man." Scene after scene in this novel replays this issue. For despite Moses' folksy wiles, the tendency of the Hebrews to specify against their God-given leader, to complain about the blessings of liberty, reminds us of a character in *Mules and Men* who says, "'My people, my people, as the monkey said. You fool with Aunt Hagar's chillun and they'll sho discriminate you and put yo' name in the streets'" (161–62).

Although the attachment of the narrative line to Moses' character sometimes obscures the point, it seems clear that Hurston's sympathies were on both sides. As a writer who cared deeply about her culture and wanted to elevate it through her art, she saw herself as a leader and spokesperson and was all too aware of the resentment that her education and pronouncements frequently created in the community she wished to serve. These perceptions are prominent in Moses' lament on Mount Nebo in "The Fire and the Cloud."[21] On the other hand, she too chafed at any kind of paternalism; in a passage she ultimately omitted from her autobiography, she noted: "Neither do I have any taste for protests for the boss to provide me with a better hoe to chop cotton with. Why must I chop cotton at all? It seems to me not enough to demand that the boss put a little more stuffing in my bunk. I don't want a little better bunk. I want the boss' bed. I have been brought up under a system that has as its slogan your place and your class is where you make it, and I am going along those lines. I do not intend to nominate myself to any fixed class. . . . Because I have no Old World concepts, I cannot conceive of myself as a peasant" (10).

Yet Hurston will turn around and mock her characters who feel precisely this way when their desire for social status becomes material; bourgeois aspirations get needled through the grasping, scheming characters Miriam and Aaron, surely stand-ins for Du Bois's "talented tenth" and the emerging black bourgeoisie. "This Aaron was a short, squatty man who wanted things. First he wanted clothes like an Egyptian noble with ornaments. Then he wanted titles. Then Moses must recognize him as a brother. . . . Then he wanted things for his family, and then he wanted things for his tribe. He was a Levite and the Levites must lead in all things" (166). When Moses prays on Sinai for forty days, however, Aaron reverses his stance regarding his kinship with Moses: "'You can't put no dependence at all in no Egyptian, don't care who it is,'" and Miriam seconds him: "'Yes, that no-count Egyptian come with his mealy mouth and talk me and Aaron into bringing you off. We was the ones that done all the work because he ain't one of us sure enough'" (282).

Aaron reverts again, however, in a comic flip-flop that recalls the poses of wily slaves before an angry Ole Massa when Moses descends and finds the Israelites cavorting naked around the gold calf Aaron made them. Aaron's ingenious excuse offers an example of the contemporary phenomenon "shucking," talking one's way out of a troublesome situation (Kochman, "Toward" 150):

> "Lord, Moses, you're my bossman, and I know it. I wouldn't think of putting myself on an equal with you. You're a great big cockadoo and I ain't nothing. . . .
> "Know what they did? When you didn't come back right away they was going round behind your back running you down and scandalizing your name and. . . brought me all them ornaments. . . . And they shoved all them earrings and things in my hands and naturally I didn't want to be bothered with the things, so just to get 'em out of my hands I took and threw 'im in the fire and what you reckon, boss? . . . Out come that calf." (290)

This tale cleverly echoes the classic High John de Conquer story that Hurston would narrate herself, where John has stolen a young pig. Ole Massa smells it cooking and stops in John's hut, asking for food, prompting John to claim the pot contains a possum. When Massa demands some anyway, John replies, "'Well, Massa, I put this thing in here a possum, but if it comes out a pig, it ain't no fault of mine.'" In the High John tale Ole Massa has to laugh at the ingenious stratagem, and in fact lets his house slaves have roast pig regularly afterwards.[22] Aaron's apparent willingness to become abjectly submissive in order to escape punishment also aligns him with African folklore's Signifying Monkey, who frequently pleads for his life by playing humble to the larger animals (Abrahams, "Negro" 246).

The satire of Aaron comically underlines the real contrast between him and Moses; the latter represents the traditional aspects of the prophetic role of priesthood—an ascetic and solitary life, one demanded by God's call, leading to an association with the wilderness and the cosmic and kinship with the supernatural. Aaron, by contrast, represents the other pole of priestly orientation—that which gravitates toward aspects of kingship, namely hereditary office; communal, erotic, frequently urban life (Aaron yearns for Egypt's cities); fine dress; and sensual living (the feast/orgy of the Golden Calf).

Aaron provides us with another set of contradictory roles, for in his subversive attempts to "scandalize" Moses' name, in his identification with High John and in his obvious mastery of everyday signification (which Moses eventually acquires), Aaron represents a role of the man of words, one known for "broad talking," as opposed to the more formal "sweet talking" that Moses employs in exalted moments, and against Aaron's own "stiff" talking when he becomes pompous. Presumably, his language relaxes during the orgy, which he presides over in a capering and obviously clownlike manner. This episode represents a perfect example of Bakhtin's concept of carnivalization, when rite becomes overthrown by anti-rite. By puncturing Moses' rigid reign with a moment of classless liminality, Aaron offers a social extension of what Abrahams has termed the broad talker's gift of "a steam valve for antisocial community impulse" ("Training" 220). His comic pretensions, however, also relate him to Hurston's concept of contemporary "dicty" blacks. We understand that the calf scheme has ironically been undertaken by Aaron to undermine Moses' authority, only to insert his own after the moment of carnival passes. Humor makes this seeming paradox of linguistic and social behavior easily and visually comprehensible.

We should bear in mind, however, that despite this caricaturing of Aaron, Hurston sympathizes with the people, who in many ways he represents. Her divided loyalty to Moses and the opposed goals of the people he leads interestingly problematizes the book—Hurston obviously finds it difficult to wholly disapprove of the carnivalizing/democratic element of the Hebrews. Her description of their worship of the Golden Calf doesn't sound too negative: "A real old down home Egyptian ceremony getting ready to come off with Aaron at the altar. Just like old times back home. And they tell me a breakdown and stomp is going to follow. . . . They cast off clothes and they cast off care. Drums and cymbals and harps and voices singing loud and happy. . . . Maidens danced in ecstasy with closed eyes and nobody looked too closely at faces. Joy was the feeling, joy!" (284). This ancient equivalent of "getting happy" couldn't be more telling; their resentment of Moses' position puts them close to Hurston too. She said in her autobiography that "the people who founded this country, and the immigrants who came later, came here to get away from class distinctions and to keep their unborn children from knowing about them" (*Dust Tracks* 345).

In one version of her introduction to the unpublished novel "Herod the Great," Hurston lends further insight into why she was attracted to reinscribing the story in the first place and why we may justify our suspicion that her sympathies are divided between Moses' plight as a leader and the people's mule-headed independence:

> The Jews have produced a disproportionate amount of genius to their numbers. Individuals were bound to be born with intellectual curiosity, the inquiring mind, and the creative instinct. And since it is universally accepted that communication, the exchange of ideas is the very soul of civilization and progress, how could they have been expected to reject everything but the past? And even their earliest history shows the Jews to have been an individualistic and free-minded people, as even Moses found out to his annoyance. They followed no man blindly. (7)

Indeed, an excerpt from "The Elusive Goal: Brotherhood of Mankind," a late unpublished manuscript, demonstrates that her attitude toward Moses grew more severe over the years:

> It is strange that the Hebrews, celebrated for being peculiar and withdrawn, should have given so much for brotherhood. Let's look from Sinai to Saul—the era not glorious but tragic and crushing. Israel became a police state. For when the Dictator Moses descended the Mountain to read the ten sayings re-vamped Egyptian moral code to the Tribesmen he had already arranged to force their acceptance upon the people. The people looked around to find the Levites standing in the door of their tents with their swords at their sides ready to deal with dissenters. And it is to the eternal credit of the Hebrews that in spite of the armed Levites, some had the courage to object. Many were hacked down it is true, but they showed their mettle.
>
> The biassed recording priesthood was to set down many more instances of revolt and ruthless slaughter before Canaan was reached indicating that the independent free spirit was a par of those Tribesmen as with no other group the world has ever seen. Let the priesthood set them down as a stiff-necked people—ungrateful to a God who had brought them out of slavery, prone to sin and a generation of vipers, but they would and did show an inclination to practice the ties of brotherhood with the people they passed in their journey in spite of Moses— who had two non-Hebrew wives himself. But the nation must do as he said, Moses insisted—not as he did. . . . From Sinai the hour was represented as being so glorious, but in reality, it was very tragic. For at Sinai, Israel became a police state. (3–4)

We may see in these remarks rather detailed proof of how Hurston felt about the rights of the people and their collective spirit. Her ambivalence here presents yet another example of what John Dorst has called Hurston's "disruptive commentary" on bourgeois ideology. In a discus-

sion of her ethnography in *Mules,* he suggests that rather than replicating the type of fieldwork that seamlessly integrates the reader with
the cultural "Other" through an intermediary fieldworker, *Mules* actually raises unsettling questions about the efficacy of the participant
observer and the smug reader's easy acquisition of knowledge about
the "Other." He explains that the ending of *Their Eyes,* which demonstrates satisfactory closure and fulfillment (a debatable point), proves
quite different from that of *Mules,* where narrator Zora has to flee a
melee: "The elided text of *Mules and Men* reveals that ultimately even
to go there is not *really* to know there" (311).

I would agree with Dorst that Hurston offers more questions than
answers, but I would disagree—especially on the basis of *Jonah* and
Moses—with his assertion that the fiction, by contrast, provides closure.
As we have seen, *Jonah* refuses to attempt to do the impossible by finding resolution for the schism between John's soul and body, and *Moses*
similarly locates much of its tension (and its resultant humor, always a
by-product of incongruity) in the unresolved struggle between Moses
and the people—which seems, on the surface, to balance benevolent
dictatorship (modeled on that of God himself, the ultimate target) with
the libertarian impulses of individuals. Hurston's refusal to take Moses'
and God's line at face value demonstrates the validity of Dorst's claim
of her "disruptive" intent, which I would define here as creative blasphemy.[23]

On the other hand, her cited remarks against Moses need not be
viewed as the final word on how she actually felt about him, for of
course, she sympathizes with the plight of the racial leader as well, even
though she despises the potential in him for tyranny. Consequently,
out of this tension between benevolent dictatorship and the people's
will, the comedy of leveling humor emerges. In this she echoes Bakhtin, who saw all novels as having layers of "literary language . . . dialo-
gized, permeated with laughter, irony, humor, elements of self-parody" (*Dialogic* 7). For him, the novel's appropriation of a "polyglot"
language guarantees the end of "national languages, coexisting but
closed and deaf to each other" (12), thereby creating the conditions
for truly international humor in narrative, clearly one of Hurston's
aims. *Moses* is a book intent on melding numerous ethnic identities
(distinguished from each other here most often by linguistic means),
past and present, in the cauldron of socially conscious humor.

As a scholar necessarily writing in an oblique way in Stalinist society, Bakhtin would have appreciated the subtly coded trickster stories
and for-black-ears-only comic narratives embedded in *Moses.* Moreover,
Bakhtin saw the richest strand of novelistic material coming from the
long history of oral folklore. He theorized that the people's endless

desire to democratize culture produces a never-ending stream of parody and annihilating yet cheerful laughter. And yet this laughter does not erase; it merely levels. This theory finds rich application in moments of migration and social change, such as the immigration of southern blacks to northern cities, which the exodus in *Moses* replicates. For Bakhtin, subjects of struggle are dealt with comically, first by bringing them near, since at a distance subjects are not comical, but brought near they may be satirized, toppled, or transformed. "Laughter," he states, "demolishes fear and piety before an object, before a world, making of it an object of familiar contact. . . . Laughter delivers the object into the fearless hands of investigative experiment—both scientific and artistic—and into the hands of free experimental fantasy" (*Dialogic* 23).

We may see this attempt at uncrowning in yet another way in the pairing of Moses and Aaron, a character duo that forms a metonymy of the novel's pairing and overlapping of cultures. No genre or general character type lacks a parodying and travestying double, and throughout history, these doubles have themselves been sanctioned and canonized. As Bakhtin suggests, written, straightforward epic (the Exodus) or tragedy is one-sided, bounded, incapable of exhausting the object; parody forces us to confront those aspects of the object that are absent. In other words, we need the corrective of laughter to show us the true complexity of what had appeared to be a lofty but one-dimensional object or concept. "True ambivalent and universal laughter does not deny seriousness but purifies and completes it. . . . Laughter does not permit seriousness to atrophy and to be torn away from the one being, forever incomplete. It restores this ambivalent wholeness" (Bakhtin, *Rabelais* 123). In the pairing of Moses and Aaron, then, Hurston creates the formation of an image in pairs—top and bottom.

The classic comedic version of this is Don Quixote and Sancho Panza. In American versions we have had Mr. Dooley and his Mr. Hennessey and Langston Hughes's Simple and Boyd. In reality, Bakhtin would say, this replicates the dialogue of the face with the buttocks, and a knitting together of the whole person. This becomes not "kiss my ass," but a plea for the head to recognize the buttocks' equally vital role in their joint body. The dialogue ultimately suggests the messages "know thyself" and "become whole." Aaron's antics, which Hurston alternately seems to bemoan and applaud, functionally expand our view of Moses, as he either interacts with and "caps" Aaron or stands aloof in epic grandeur. We therefore see his strengths and weaknesses more clearly. Thus carnivalization and doubling Moses with Aaron serve as ways to problematize the biblical narrative, insert the will of the culture into patriarchal monologism, and to dismantle hegemony.

Hurston emphasizes humor's uncrowning ability when her characters say that people laughing at you is a disgrace. Prince Moses laughs at his royal uncle's threats, saying that somebody "might hear you and laugh at you. Then you will have to get a law passed that people can't laugh at Princes" (78). This is perhaps an ironic comment on the unwritten law that blacks can't laugh at white folks, because of humor's relationship to power, a point made wonderfully well in the poetry of Sterling Brown.[24] Many times in *Moses,* people give up things to avoid being the butt of laughter.

Herzen reminds us too that only equals may laugh together. "In church, in the palace, on parade, facing the department head, the police officer, the German administrator, nobody laughs. . . . If inferiors are permitted to laugh in front of their superiors . . . this would mean farewell to respect" (cited in Bakhtin, *Rabelais* 92n37).

We might note at this point that Moses, despite his regal position within the community, shares the people's desire to strip away phony trappings, and in fact, this becomes a hallmark of his identity and characterization. Moses, as Cheryl Wall has observed, rejecting the crown he could wear, has "as little use for class distinction as Janie and Tea Cake" ("Zora" 389). A key passage Hurston struck from the original manuscript deals with his acquisition of African "magic" in the courts of the Egyptian priest/conjurers:

> But most of all, he loved to linger in the sacred precincts of the priests. His awe soon wore away, seeing the priests stripped of their robes and about their duties of preparations for ceremonies. They were truly awesome figures before the altar, but he soon learned to distinguish between the office and the man. He began to ask to be shown how to produce the effects that so awed the multitudes at worship.
>
> "We have a smart one with us," one of the priests observed to his fellows. "He sees behind the scenes." (24)

Once again, Hurston presents Moses as a kind of deconstructionist who penetrates through layers of mystery to the underlying truth. Later his adaptation of Hebrew/black slang and comic folk language aids him in the linguistic sense, indeed, becoming part of his "magic" skills, thus making what Hurston liked to call "a Negro way of saying" but also, as the priests suggest here, a Negro way of *seeing*. Humor thus not only levels, but strips and reveals.

Humor and Gender

Unfortunately, humor designed to demonstrate admirable traits of the male figures in the novel often come at the expense of the female characters, as do points about color prejudice within the race. Whereas in *Their Eyes* Janie's quest synthesized the search for racial, sexual, and social justice, here, perhaps because of the overwhelmingly patriarchal material she must deal with, Hurston privileges the themes of class and race over gender. We might also wonder just who the narrator of *Moses* is here—Hurston or a biblical patriarchal voice that mimics and parodies patriarchal black narrators? Questions along these lines might usefully be framed by noting, as a feminist scholar has, that Moses' flight from Egypt into the desert and his sitting down by a well (both utilizing the same Hebrew verb "brh") echoes Hagar's flight from Abraham's household (Trible 31n22). Like her, he develops into the mythical "parent" of a nation—he the spiritual father of the Hebrews, she the physical mother of the Arabs. "Aunt Hagar's chillun" has always been a term used within the African American community to describe itself. Despite the multiple connections between male and female biblical narratives such as this, however, which seem to suggest possibilities for more variations from the "classic" narrative, Hurston seems to favor a more patriarchal approach.

We begin to see this when specific "readings" of female behavior emerge after Moses marries Zipporah, Jethro's daughter. During the Midianite years of their marriage, Zipporah wants Moses to put his Egyptian finery on again when a chief visits; Jethro says, "'Pay her no mind, Moses. . . . She is just like all the rest of the women. She wants to make out to the rest that you were some big high muck-de-muck back there in Egypt so she can put on side as Mrs. Muck-de-Muck, and earn some envy out of the rest of the women around here. She wants to make a Prince out of you so all the other women can suffer envy of the Princess Zipporah. Don't blame her for it. She's a woman, isn't she?'" (139). Later he tells his daughter, "'You are just like all the rest of the women—ready to upset the whole world to make an opportunity to dress yourself up in ornaments. That is all women around Kings are good for. . . . Fix it so you won't have no competition, then parade your swag in front of the others and let 'em look on and envy you. You make property grabbers out of otherwise good men'" (143). Later, Hurston herself comes down on her: "Time put tracks on Zipporah. . . . Her flowing body had taken to bulging here and there so she quit putting accent on her body and took pride in her two growing sons" (145). After freedom, when Zipporah joins Moses after a long separation, Jethro reports before she arrives: "'She all dressed up so till it would take a doctor to tell her how near she is dressed to death. . . . Zipporah always was sort of queeny-like in her ways. Just give her the least excuse and she'll put her trunk on her back and the lid on her

head.'" When Moses says he's got some ornaments for her, Jethro replies, "'I don't know where she's going to put it. She ain't got a finger
nor a toe left uncovered. If all them necklaces she got on don't choke
her to death I'd sure like to know the reason why. All her life, my daughter's been going around looking for a throne to sit on'" (266).

But Zipporah and Moses both signify on Miriam as an archetypal
old maid: "'Isn't that Miriam—that bitter-looking old woman over
there?'" Zipporah asks. Moses replies, "'That's right. She looks as if her
face had fallen into disuse years ago.' 'Oh, she has the look of never
having been loved. She has that terrible look of never having been
nuded by a man. I don't want her near me if I can help it. What on
earth is all that she's got on?'" (268). We then see Zipporah, however,
through the eyes of Miriam, producing a much more moving moment:
"She looked again and saw well-cared-for hands and feet of Zipporah,
and looked at her own gnarled fists and her square feet all twisted and
coarsened by slavery, and almost snarled out loud" (269), a moment
that reminds us of Charles Chesnutt's story "The Wife of His Youth"
and the contrast between the hero's young, freeborn fiance and his
dark, wizened, and slave-born wife.

Miriam ruptures our musings, however, by a comic tirade: "'Look
at the hussy! Look what is getting down off that camel, will you! Somebody to come queen it over us poor people and rob us. Look at her
trying to look like Mrs. Pharaoh! . . . Look at old Aunt Judy! Awring-
ing and atwisting herself and grinning like she was some young gal!
And she look like somebody slapped her in the face with a buzzard gut!
All of you look like you done gone crazy! Get on back to your tents!
Somebody in Israel got to have some sense'" (271). Remarkably, this
speech echoes Jody Starks's attacks on Janie's looks in *Their Eyes,* when
he seeks to deflect attention from his own illness and advancing age.
Here, however, Hurston follows with a picture of Miriam fingering
Zipporah's fine linen: "She looked down at her rough clothing and
work-twisted feet and hands and she became aware of class. This woman of Moses' had been oiled with something from birth that she lacked
and the futility of wishing for it made her more angry than ever" (273).
Thus even though the rivalry between Zipporah and Miriam has all the
earmarks of a comic catfight, played with verbal claws, teeth, and hiss-
es, with each signifying according to her background (Miriam as peasant, with her "buzzard gut" and "Aunt Judy" references, Zipporah with
her more sophisticated cattiness, the perfect female "talented tenth"),
the contrast in many ways makes the reader feel regret for the narrow
opportunities allotted both women by their cultures.

On the other hand, more often than not, the mockery of supposedly feminine traits lacks this deeper text and frequently relies on disparagement of bodily traits or the loss of physical beauty. When Moses has his first audience with Pharaoh Ta-Phar in his quest to set the Hebrews free, he sees his first wife, now married to Pharaoh: her "hips looked like they had moved round in front of her, or more like they had abdicated in favor of her stomach"; to be fair, Pharaoh's face seems to be "slipping down into his neck" (178). When the freed Israelites defeat the Amalekites, Hurston notes without comment that Moses spends the day counting up the spoils: "Horses, cows, mules, camels, women, wine and jewelry, and household vessels of gold and silver" (261).

Miriam, like Aaron, hungers for power and position and costly garments. Her insane jealousy of Zipporah, however, also has a viciously racial edge. When Zipporah arrives at the encampment, Miriam exclaims: "'Look at that dark complected woman he done brought and put up to be a Queen over the rest of us women. Why, it's awful. I never seen such a caper cut in all my born days'" (282). Later she refers to her as the "'black Mrs. Pharaoh . . . trying to make out she's a lordgod sitting on a bygod. All dressed up . . . like King Pharaoh's horse'" (296). Miriam eventually foments a revolt among the women against Zipporah that echoes the racism of the color-struck Mrs. Turner in *Their Eyes*: "'Get together as many women as you can and go stand around the tent of Moses and holler for him to get rid of that Ethiopian wife of his.' 'Thought you said she was a Midianite?' 'Oh, don't try to take me up on every little point. Even if she was born and raised in Midian her folks could still come from Ethiopia, couldn't they? Tell me! Look how dark her skin is. We don't want people like that among us mixing up our blood and all. That woman has got to go'" (297).

In this parody of various "blue-vein" societies in the United States, Hurston joins earlier critics of the genteel members of the race who replicated in their highly hierarchical social orders the biases of white America. She may have known Charles Chesnutt's treatment of this theme in "The Wife of His Youth" but she surely had read her friend Wallace Thurman's bitterly comic novel about color prejudice within the race, *The Blacker the Berry* (1929), and George Schuyler's biting satirical novel *Black No More* (1931). Moses' response to Miriam's vendetta was meant for these "dicty" blacks among Hurston's contemporaries as well, who found Hurston herself too black, in every way: "'Nobody here don't care anything about my wife's color. Haven't we had the mixed multitudes with us ever since we started from Egypt?'" (299). The rejection of a dark Midianite looms importantly here, for they are depicted as being closer to black Americans than even the Israelites.

Jethro lives in a black tent; Zipporah, after marrying Moses, is described for the first time in some detail, in highly sexual, repetitive, and definitely black terms.[25] Virtually everyone, in fact, minimizes Zipporah, even her father, but some of his comments clearly go beyond her to a warning against taking any woman too seriously. Early in the book, before Moses gets his "call," Jethro seems disturbed that his son-in-law's dreams have been reduced to the love of one woman; his dismay, however, finds humorous expression: "'Don't over-pull your belly on this love business and destroy it. Love some and think some. . . . You are an over-average man, Moses, and I hate to see you wasted on a woman'" (135–36). To be fair, he may mean merely that Moses shouldn't narrow his life to one strand, and the passage also reminds us of how Hurston, who clearly saw herself as an extraordinary woman and artist, gave up the love of her life when he insisted that she abandon her career. But most of all we see a negative view of Zipporah that works in tandem with Miriam's.

To be sure, one could say that Jethro, not Hurston, critiques Zipporah and that in the writer's earlier books, sexist commentators such as Sop-de-Bottom clearly aren't to be trusted. Unlike Janie in such situations, Zipporah never finds a defense except in terms of her color. Zipporah has been isolated and uneducated, which may account for some of her behavior, but Hurston doesn't dwell on these points. We're left believing in Miriam's assessment of Zipporah as trying to play Mrs. Pharaoh and seeing Hurston as changing the terms of an equation she had used in the past.

Hurston uses an actual event mentioned in the Bible to return to this female rivalry between these characters, seeking to ultimately squelch the color-struck element in Miriam. Hurston, of course, was signifying yet again on biblical precedent; here she accomplishes the feat by conflating two biblical narratives, for Miriam and Aaron speak against Moses in Numbers 12 because he marries an Ethiopian woman. In Hurston's novel, Moses does have an Ethiopian wife, but in Egypt, not in the wandering years.

Miriam's punishment results from her demand that "'that black Mrs. Pharaoh'" Zipporah be banished. Her attack actually aims at Moses too, as her subsequent charge makes clear: "'The Lord don't speak through your [Moses'] mouth alone. He speaks through my mouth and Aaron . . . just as much'" (300). God comes down in a cloud of anger and makes Miriam a leper, a punishment taken away when seven days pass, only because of the intercession of Moses. Hurston seems to botch the possibilities for enriching ambivalence here, however, for in Moses' personal condemnation of Miriam's color-struck spite, he uses a sexist stance; he rebukes her by saying "'Miss Miriam your case is pitiful. The trouble with you is that nobody ever married you. And when a woman ain't got no man to look after, she takes on the world in place of the man she missed. . . . You better keep my wife's name out of your mouth'" (300). And in fact, as a result of God's seven-day punishment, Hurston tells us, "All the rest of her days, Miriam was very silent" (301). This passage disturbs us, for Miriam's sin thus seems to be not only insubordination before God's agent or racism but the more common one of being an uppity woman who dares to talk back to a man, albeit in comic terms. Her penalty—divinely sanctioned silencing—appears to run directly counter to the seemingly feminist attitudes of *Their Eyes*. On the other hand, we would do well to ponder Mary Helen Washington's rereading of Janie's story, which persuasively argues Hurston's ambivalence about giving a powerful voice to a woman like Janie (*Invented*). *Moses* supports Washington's reading of Hurston's basic stance toward this issue.

Moses rethinks Miriam's case after she dies, however, for in her final moments she repents her real sin, which has been the people's too: not using freedom well. "'I reckon I done tackled something too big for me and it done throwed me like a bucking horse. . . . I been through living for years. I just ain't dead yet'" (319). Moses, in his eulogy, reminds the people—and acquaints us as readers for the first time—of the meetings Miriam arranged in Egypt to foster freedom and how she "changed weakness into resolution. Her dust weighed as much as all Israel" (323). Privately, Moses wonders at the strange movements of fate—for if it hadn't been for the young Miriam's original lie about his origins, would any of these historic events have come to pass? The scene makes us recall a telling moment in *Mules and Men;* George Thomas tells a folklore-gathering Zora, "'You come to de right place if lies is what you want. Ah'm gointer lie up a nation'" (21). Furthermore, in these musings, Moses performs an extremely important narrative function as well, one buttressed at several other moments in the text, by emphasizing how apparently insignificant acts by supposedly insignificant people—even a female slave—can cause gigantic historical events. His reflections here make us ponder whether the Almighty really masterminded this "sacral" history after all, but in effect Moses also "uncrowns" himself as the "great man of history." Once again we come to the ultimate kind of knowledge of the cosmic joke—for Hurston has made us rethink the foundational terms of the narrative she translates for us, as well as the origins of folklore and myth.

And yet, we should check our tendency to see in Miriam's lie proof of the power of "the little (wo)man" in the working out of history, for the power of her lie is commensurate with the people's need for myth. Myth provides a way of controlling and directing the world. And yet more may be found on the positive side of the ledger; Miriam in many ways reminds us of the tragic life of Nanny, Janie's grandmother in *Their Eyes,* because what Moses says of Miriam could be said of Nanny as well: "What with . . . her loveless life with one end sunk in slavery and the other twisted and snarled in freedom . . . he wondered which had hurt her most." And yet, unlike Nanny, "a mighty thing had happened in the world through the stumblings of a woman who couldn't see where she was going. She needed a big tomb so the generations that come after would know her and remember" (324). This passage partially transforms what has been a largely satirical and sexist portrayal, perhaps to soften the harshness of the earlier characterization, but possibly as well to laud the black clubwomen of Hurston's own time who did so much to help others, earning them the title "race women."[26]

We could also theorize that *Moses,* after all, like *Their Eyes,* constitutes at one level a *bildungsroman,* and Moses' final assessment of Miriam indicates both his personal growth and a new perspective for the reader. Still, Miriam's portrayal seems unfortunate, especially since Hurston could have strengthened the book significantly by providing a full expression of the early role Miriam played in liberation, a role merely hinted at here, and too late. Although we see her playing the cymbals and leading the people in dance when they are liberated (239), nothing more gets made of her important function as musician/priestess. We recall that Hurston has Janie say in *Their Eyes,* "'Sometimes God gits familiar wid us womenfolks too and talks His inside business'" (117), and surely Miriam could claim this as well. One could read the novel as a narrative about the substitute family, a constant theme in black literature, with the foundling Moses "raised" (after his metaphoric rebirth in the crossing scene) by the myth-mother Miriam and the conjure-father Jethro. This doesn't get stressed, however, as strongly as it could be. Hurston obviously took many liberties with the biblical text—why didn't she provide a more central role, not only for Zipporah and Miriam, but for the Jewish women in general?[27]

Domestic Folk Humor and Paternity

Women are similarly underplayed in domestic scenes, where most readers would expect them to star in prominent roles. We see little of the wonderful male-female humorous interchanges that characterize Hurston's other work. What we gain, however, is a better sense of Moses as a human being and his story as the narrative of a real person rather

than a mythical figure. The comic domestic scenes we do get, inter-
woven with the more serious and imposing major themes of the novel, serve to set up later moments when Moses functions as the paterfa-
milias of a nation rather than just of his own home. These sections of
the text make up the real center of the work, for Hurston understands
that it is ultimately in the quotidian and the local that the lofty principles of Moses' mountain must be tested, challenged, and finally accepted. Because of this, the humor in these domestic scenes focuses on the
men and especially on sibling and paternal relationships. As with
Hurston's domestic comedy in her other novels, these scenes often
feature food and folk culture.

Perhaps the most illustrative example of the complicated interplay
of all these issues is a scene involving Moses as a shepherd in Midian,
learning and practicing hoodoo. He has a chance to help his father-
in-law, Jethro, when fat and greedy cousin Zeppo descends for a visit
with his huge family. Zeppo goes straight to the cook tent to get "a little something to give him an appetite"; Moses, in an act we might call
"protective ecology" today, produces a rain of frogs that sends the visitors away screaming. The next day Zeppo sends a letter written in black
idiomatic English, initiating a comic epistolary duel with Jethro that
has shades of the Marx brothers (hence Zeppo's name):

> "DEAR COUSIN JETHRO:
>
> I take my seat and take my pen in hand to write you a letter. I want
> to know where is your raising that you ain't got no more manners than
> to let frogs be hopping all over people when they come to visit you? I
> have been a good and faithful cousin to you. I have always been kind
> enough to drop whatever I was doing and accept your invitation to bring
> my family and pass a few days with you and eat meat. But I know when
> I been insulted and I'll never accept another invitation. . . . But if you
> insist I will not refuse the meat you offer me. You can send it by my
> messenger when he comes.
>
> Your loving cousin,
> ZEPPO.
>
> P.S. I'll bound you all them frogs was the work of that son-in-law of
> yours, Moses. Nobody else could have have done it." (147)

Hurston thus lets the reader enjoy the pleasure of author-reader irony at the expense of the character, who ironically reveals his own true
greed unwittingly in a letter purportedly constructed as a lesson in
manners. We might note again here Victor Raskin's definition of the
classic comic ethnic "scripts" that we examined earlier; Zeppo and his
tribe clearly fit the stupid and dirty category, and the fact that they hail

from the other side of the mountain makes them a kind of ethnic "Other" too, in narrative terms, even though they are kin. This seems to echo the category of being a "cross-de-creek nigger" in *Jonah*. Hurston, in fact, pushes our reading of the letter by introducing it in a way hardly flattering to Zeppo's intellect: "He also sent back a note which obviously had taxed Zeppo's small education a lot to write" (147).

Jethro's blunt and comic response punctures the balloon of Zeppo's righteous indignation and speaks for the reader's reaction as well: "'All the manners I ever had you done et it up long ago. So I reckon there just ain't no more. You will have to refuse my offer of beef because I am not slaughtering today. All my cows have a bone in their legs. All of my beds are full of folks so you can't snore in my ears no more. . . . Yes, my son Moses is the finest hoodoo man in the world and my wife says that stopping you from eating somebody else's groceries is his greatest piece of work. But she may be wrong. Have you ever seen his sendings of snakes and lice?'" (147). The passage reminds us that joking relationships offer significant and revealing manifestations of kinship. Hurston is able to take this relationship one step farther by ingeniously extending it to similar relationships among all the Midianite and Hebrew peoples. She can then offer many varied definitions of what joking relationships are permissible in differing situations.

This episode serves as a comic analogue to scenes to come. The frogs and especially Jethro's semicomic warning prefigure the serious visitation of plagues on Egypt. Zeppo and his tribe, too, can be seen as forerunners of the plague of locusts. The frogs weave their own spell by allowing Hurston to introduce hoodoo into the narrative along with what today we might call magical realism, as Moses begins to work miracles. Hurston further tempers the humor by interjecting a serious note. Slavery emerges in the actions of this sponging relative. Although Zeppo's actions constitute only a mild form of despotism, the appropriation of one's food and one's bed (which physically extends into the appropriation of one's body) taken to an extreme becomes slavery. Clearly, despite its comic tone, this story changes the focus of the book from the realistic to the mythic.

At the same time Hurston uses creative anachronisms to help make her mythic ideas easier for readers to comprehend. In the Zeppo episode, we see contemporary references and objects, such as "take my pen in hand" and "groceries," which serve to move this mythic incident closer to home. We presume Moses sleeps in a tent, but when Miriam and Aaron call on him they come "knocking at Moses' door" (261). When Moses goes up the mountain to see God, the people's mouths stay shut in wonder, and "'they might just as well have had the lockjaw for all the use they made of their mouths'" (279). In perhaps the most effective use of this device, Moses, the father figure, lectures "son" Joshua, in an amusing but profound passage, about the nature of government which he compares to a moonshine still: "'I love liberty and I love freedom so I started off giving everybody a loose rein. But I soon found out that it wouldn't do. A great state is a well-blended mash of something of all of the people and all of none of the people. You understand. The liquor of statecraft is distilled from the mash you got'" (340), thereby mimicking the rural father's passing on of his moonshine business to his son. On the other hand, moonshine was also called "water of life," and liberty and freedom frequently find parallel expression.[28]

These anachronisms provide a link to the griot's art; telling stories of a historical nature, most often extemporaneously, makes such a habit inevitable (Okpewho 231). Indeed, *Moses* in many ways represents Hurston's most African-derived narrative in that griots too, in telling a story, are more intent on it registering on the audience at hand than in the details of the accepted facts or in providing a true history. Once again, we see parallels with the art of the translator, who must take into consideration the best way to relate another culture's meaning using the audience's frame of reference.

One of Hurston's most impressive griot acts in this novel comes when Moses begins his sojourn in Midian. En route in the desert he stays in a caravan rest stop, where black American culture becomes entertainment for the night. A man plays on a Middle Eastern instrument but sings, "'I had a good woman but the fool laid down and died,'" a classic blues lyric (107). Later two camel drivers signify on each other in a verbal comic duel. "'It is a good thing you didn't catch me. If you had they would have toted you across three yards—this yard, the church yard and the graveyard.' 'I don't beat up bums like you. I pass you up and call you Bad-eyed and Shorty, cause you'll look like all of them.'" This keeps up until they run out of inspiration; they then act the best of friends. As Moses observes, "'Here it is just like it is in Egypt—the scared people do all of the biggest talk'" (108), a trenchant comment on boasting in folk culture. Clearly, the scene represents a jook, the folk "place" that Hurston saw as central in her own culture, and a "text" to be read. It constitutes a cultural crossroads, where travelers and merchants meet and exchange information and stories. Its ancient counterpart significantly begins Moses' decades-long immersion in folk culture and hoodoo and the search for his identity.

Humor gets directed at other identity formulations as well, including the folkways of black culture in Hurston's America. When the Israelites yearn for their down-home comforts in Egypt, they complain about Moses' failure to feed them well: "'Here he done took and brought us out of Egypt where we was getting along just fine. We remember the nice fresh fish we used to get back there. . . . Nice sweet-tasting little pan-fish and a person could get all they could eat for five cents. Unhuhh! and didn't we used to eat 'em, too. And the nice fresh cucumbers, and the watermelons, and the leeks and the onions and plenty garlic for seasoning'" (308). This no doubt echoes the complaints of southern migrants to the North that Hurston knew, including the ubiquitous verbal punctuation frequently used in call-and-response patterns, "Unhuhh!" This scene also gives Moses the opportunity for a comic line, one designed to further his authority: "'Here I am struggling to make a great nation out of you and you are worrying about fried fish and cucumbers!'"; the people's sage reply, however, "'It's hard to love freedom if it keeps you hungry'" (309), constitutes an effective capping of the leader's supposed wisdom. The unstated but understood parallel of Moses' paternal responsibilities to that of the ordinary father's—feeding his children—creates more sympathy for the people.[29]

We would do well to remember at this juncture Hurston's own sense of exile from the South. In 1935 when she was working on *Moses* in New York, she wrote some letters to her Florida friend Dr. Edwin Grover of her longing for home: "O, to be down there in Florida beauty once more! I love the place. . . . I love my Florida. I am sick of these dull gray skies and what not. I want to be back home!"[30] This mood would obviously predispose her to look more indulgently on the Hebrew people's complaints in exile.

Hurston looks "back home" for sources of humor and ways to get readers to relate to her characters. She must have struggled with the paradox of utilizing the black folk expressions relating to pork and the Jewish prohibition against it. She clearly solved the problem by having Moses bring the laws against pork consumption into play only after he has received the commandments from God. This allows her to signify on the phrase in the earlier scenes, where hyperbole blends with folk expressions: "'Why, he's [Pharaoh] got a law about everything under the sun! Next thing you know he'll be saying cats can't have kittens. . . . He brags that him and the Egyptian nation is eating high on the hog now. . . . He's got us in the go-long'" (15–16). These complaints against unjust laws suggest that breaking them is permissible if they are compared with "natural law" and found wanting. Moses, however, works to establish an alternative, "official" law in biblical writ, which will then presumably expose error in secular law. Indeed, Hurston has Reverend Simms comically suggest this rather serious and subversive idea in "The Bone of Contention": "'Never mind bout dem white folks laws at O'landa, Brother Long. Dis is a colored town. Nohow we oughter run by de laws uh de Bible. Dem white folks laws dont go befo' whuts in dis sacred book'" (11).

Mentu, Moses' unofficial folklore tutor during his days as a prince, gets preferential treatment from his student, who brings him tidbits from the royal kitchens until "Mentu ceased to struggle with the other yard servants for bits of the hog head when roast pork was on the palace table. This was always an occasion with yard help. Roast pork at Pharaoh's table meant boiled hog head for the help. And old Mentu used to struggle mightily for such bits as he could get. But now he loftily stood aside from the struggle and explained to the others mysteriously, 'I am eating further back on the hog now'" (60–61). The passage ingeniously has its own logical context in the story, but also embeds an expression that originated in American slavery replicated in the midst of ancient Egypt. This phrase receives a final use when Jethro thanks Moses for all he has done: "'Why, we are eating high on the hog now'" (140). Because of the profusion of these early comic touches, we pay special attention when Moses states, in one of his first pronouncements to the Israelites, "'The god of the mountain detests the flesh of hogs. . . . No worshipper . . . may eat pork'" (175). Presumably, God gave Moses this command when he instructed him to go into Egypt.

The comic interchanges Moses has with the people help humanize him by extending our sense of his humorous side, initially most evident in his practical jokes on Zeppo. Near the end of his life, reminiscing with Joshua, he says the "'tussle I had with Balaam and that mule of his'" was "'the best time I had on the whole trip up to now'" (32), reminding us of the earlier episode with Zeppo and of Moses' rather endearing tendency to play the trickster. As he states, "'That was fun for me, outdoing Balaam like that. It was the first time since we left Egypt that I had a chance to strain against anybody that was trying to do something. It's good to sort of stretch yourself sometime. Power loves to meet power and strength loves strength.'"[31] Here, joking and horseplay become expressions of strength but are intimately tied to folk conjure, folk humor, verbal dueling, and practical jokes. Balaam's ass gets transformed into the southern mule.

These innocent-sounding episodes also undercut our sense of Moses' magic as something done by God through his human instrument, adding incrementally to our perception of Moses as hoodoo man. Indeed, other miracles get treated humorously too. The people call the magically produced bread "manna," "a word that didn't mean anything in particular anyhow, so they called the grains of bread by that name" (253); similarly, when Moses strikes the rock with his rod to produce water, He proclaims, "'From now on, the name of this place is Massah, which means a big fuss'" (255). Although biblical magic translates into hoodoo, Hurston seems to be interested in shifting our interest to the folk by demystifying God's miracles and the resultant narrative centering on them and him. Hurston and Moses overlap here, as both deconstruct the sacral and the mysterious.

Techniques such as these, which "decenter" God, provide space for Jethro, the earthly father figure who furthers Moses' career as a hoodoo man and worker of miracles. In contrast to the fear and wonder that characterize Moses' relation with I AM WHAT I AM, the deep love between Moses and his father-in-law finds oblique expression in the joking relationship they share, paralleling and extending the earlier joking relationship Moses had with Mentu.[32]

This type of repartee reappears years later in Moses' dealings with his surrogate son and successor as leader, Joshua. The Hebrew people similarly look on the latter as a mischievous favored son; the concept of verbal dueling so marked in Moses' scenes with Pharaoh reappears in the last chapters, when Joshua repeatedly kids with the people. They go back and forth with him, acting as a kind of comic chorus, calling him "Little Moses": "'Listen at that long, tall young one that ain't quit wetting his diapers yet, trying to tell us what to do with our own mouth. . . . Course, we did mention that we ain't had nothing decent to eat. . . . But that ain't talking about nobody. That's just saying . . . don't you be running up there putting out no lies on us no more, and we don't mean no Joe more, we mean no blamed More'" (249). One notices how this passage offers a gloss on black forms of expression, differentiating between "talking about" and "saying" and underlining the folk performances called "lying."

Similarly, Miriam complains about "'this Joshua who got his mouth stuck in everything. You got to put that young rooster in his place and make him stay in it. He's getting too biggity and sassy for any good use. Him giving orders to men with whiskers'" (262). These two passages offer some examples of the abundant signifying that goes on in the book, of the animal imagery that crops up everywhere, of the use of folk expressions, and of the use of humor in socialization, for both criticisms of Joshua indicate that he has overstepped boundaries of age and position and of joking relationships as well. At the same time, a degree of affection attends the teasing/comic complaining and a bit of approval, although the people know that eventually Joshua will have to establish more gravity in order to lead. It somewhat reminds one of Shakespeare's depiction of Prince Hal/King Henry, who seems to emerge a better king because of his boisterous days with Falstaff and the folk. Hurston, like Shakespeare, seems to be saying that humor can be used to secure power among the people but also that humor may be used to deflate authority.

The cumulative effect of these dramatic/comedic enactments of the domestic and the patriarchal is powerful, for here, more than anywhere else, Hurston illustrates the cosmic conundrums that the epic qualities of the narrative more overtly raise. The eternal issues that equate with the mountain can only find resolution in the structures of everyday life and familial, cultural interaction. Hurston, as usual, makes sure that her authorial ladder, as well as Moses' path to the mountaintop, is anchored in what Yeats called "the foul rag-and-bone shop of the heart."

The ending of the novel constitutes one of the major departures from the biblical story. Moses climbs Mount Nebo to view both the promised land and the spread of tents below that house his adopted people. He realizes he can't bring himself to go across the Jordan with them, where they'll force him to wear a crown. Dreaming of returning to Midian and his family, he suddenly realizes that he will have to fake his death, largely because the mythic figure the people have made of him seems necessary to protect the sanctity of his laws. Accordingly, he prepares a grave. "He would end in mystery as he had come. Then his laws would stand and he could spend those last years away" (349). In a magical but somehow realistic scene reminiscent of the mule's funeral led by buzzards in *Their Eyes*, Moses encounters an old talking lizard who knows another who lives on Sinai. This lizard bears the title "Keeper of memories" for all, a concept very like that of the African griot. Moses sets out to find the keeper immediately, saying farewell to the people below. This scene, apart from the anthropomorphism, notably devoid of humor, ends the book on a cosmic note. Moses, outlined against the red moon, illumines the seven suns of the universe that wheel above him amid lightning and thunder.

By refusing to end the book in death, a conversation with God, or a tearful farewell to Joshua, Hurston does several things. First, the talking lizard and the quest for one even wiser returns Moses to the world of hoodoo and Africa. The lizards, possibly reincarnated sages like him, may be predictive of his ultimate fate, an alternative to enthronement with I AM WHAT I AM. Finally, and perhaps most importantly, the refusal to provide closure ensures a more Afrocentric ending, where a new cycle seems to be beginning, not only for the Hebrew people below, but for Moses himself. In *Meridian*, Alice Walker's central figure murmurs to herself in despair, "The only new thing now would be the refusal of Christ to accept crucifixion. King should have refused. All those characters in all those novels that require death to end the book should refuse. All saints should walk away. Do their bit, then—just walk away. See Europe, visit Hawaii, become agronomists or raise Dalmatians" (151). At the end of the novel, Meridian herself does exactly that, leaving her hat/mantle of leadership to Truman Held. Moses, too, cedes leadership to Joshua, fakes his own death to preserve the myth the people unfortunately need, and goes on to a new life of his own. His farewell seems to apply to Yahweh as well, indicating that in his own life hoodoo—signifier of the African heritage—is enough.

As her treatments of duality, dialect, borders, bilingualism, and translation alone suggest, Hurston was immensely ambitious in attempting so much, and she inevitably came to feel that the novel was in some ways a failure. We can gauge Hurston's reaction to what she had wrought in a letter she wrote to Dr. Edwin Grover of Rollins College, the book's dedicatee:

> I hope that you will not be disappointed at the work. I have the feeling of disappointment about it. I don't think that I achieved all that I set out to do. I thought that in this book I would achieve my ideal, but it seems that I have not reached it yet but I shall keep trying as I know you want me to. . . . They [her British publishers] are asking for the manuscript of MOSES before it is published in America. My American publishers are very enthusiastic about the manuscript. I wish I shared their enthusiasm.
>
> Carl Van Vechten says it is the best thing I have done. Perhaps he is right but it still doesn't say all that I want it to say.[33]

Although we find an admission of dissatisfaction here, we shouldn't miss the equally important marks of pride as she notes Van Vechten's approval and the impatience of her publishers to get the book out. Indeed, throwing out these two facts could easily be seen as an effort to influence Grover's reading of the book.

Finally, Hurston had already admitted Moses was impossible to limn in *Mules and Men:* "No king has ever had the power of even one of Moses' ten words. Because Moses made a nation and a book, a thousand million leaves of ordinary men's writing couldn't tell what Moses said" (194). However, we would do well to remember Faulkner's dictum that all great novels fail in some way, for if the writer is any good, she will attempt more than she can do, in any case.[34]

The genius of *Moses, Man of the Mountain* lies in its comic and compelling revision of the Scriptures, which restores ritual sacral humor to a desiccated text, melding it subtly with the Eastern/African elements that originally inspired holy writ. Hurston could be seen as firing the first fictional volley of a scholarly quest for the Afro-Asian roots of human history, one that has taken on epic proportions today, especially in works like Martin Bernal's *Black Athena*. The brilliance of her characterizations stems from the creative and usually comic way the key figures speak—through their boisterous, contentious, interweaving voices we come to know them. The people of Israel, poised before their entry into the promised land, could well have exclaimed, as Martin Luther King did, "'We ain't what we ought to be and we ain't what we want to be and we ain't what we're going to be. But thank God, we ain't what we was'" (cited in Boskin, "'Black'" 145). Such voices lie at the heart of ritual restorative humor, where much improvisation and variation exists among individual entertainers, who display energy and originality as they participate in the communal dialogue. The separation from Egyptian hegemony and cultural dominance can only come through a form of ritual humor, one frequently associated with initiation rites. Ultimately, oppressed groups find identity and solidarity through self-parody, internal correction, caricature, burlesque, and parody of social institutions of dominant culture. Our failure to fully appreciate this all-important comic dimension of *Moses* has kept us from discerning its greatness. Hurston, in recognizing the comic possibilities of the Exodus story, saw the irony that is already there in the reversals of fortune, the whinings of the Israelites, their vacillations between the desire for freedom and material comfort. She dramatized the humanizing role humor plays in individual and national identity formation and consequently made the Scriptures come alive in an allegorical and contemporaneously relevant manner.[35]

Most profoundly perhaps, Hurston saw the value of signifying on God himself—at least on the white version of God's word. As Claudia Mitchell-Kernan notes, signifying plays on the folk perception that "dictionary entries for words are not always sufficient for interpreting meanings or messages, or that meaning goes beyond such interpretations" (166). The codified, dictionary sense of the Bible and the white monopoly on its interpretation gets exploded here, in a joyous but profoundly serious translation of sacred writ into folk discourse. Hurston thus gives God himself a long-needed remodeling job, by signifying on the Bible—at least the white version. In doing so she provides, for her culture and her age, that creative "re-accentuation" that Bakhtin identifies with cycles of literary renaissance. Her courageous experiments in *Moses*—and particularly those involving a creative use of folk-driven humor—bridge the gap between black and white, sign and utterance, humanity and God, illustrating what one character means when he says: "'Anybody depending on somebody else's gods is depending on a fox not to eat chickens'" (16).

Notes

1. See for example, Perry Miller's *Errand into the Wilderness*, Sacvan Bercovitch's *The Puritan Origins of the American Self* and *The American Jeremiad*, and Andrew Delbanco's *The Puritan Ordeal*.

2. For a brief history of references to Moses in black literature and culture, see Ruth Sheffey's insightful chapter "Hurston's *Moses, Man of the Mountain*" in her *Trajectory*.

3. An even better black "reading" of Genesis comes from the turn of the century: "Cain wuz an evil black man who wuz allus fightin' 'n' gamblin'. He killed his own brudda Abel in a fight ova a watermelon. De Lawd come behin' 'n ask Cain wheah his brudda wuz. Dat sassy nigger answer, 'Am I my brudda's keeper?' . . . Cain turn aroun', he sees it de Lawd speakin'. He got so scared his hairs stand right up straight an' his face turn pale. An dat weah de first white man come from" (Schechter 65).

4. Zora Neale Hurston to Jean Parker Westbury, Aug. 19, 1951, Hurston Collection, Rare Books and Manuscripts, University of Florida Library, Gainesville.

5. Robert Hemenway has carefully related her work with hoodoo and the *Moses* project; he has also suggested that she may well have known Freud's *Moses and Monotheism*, which similarly asserts that Moses was actually an Egyptian (*Zora* 257). However, as Ruth Sheffey has noted, Freud's text, written in 1937, wasn't published until 1939; Hurston began writing her novel in 1935 and it was published in the same year as Freud's work (166).

6. Later, at Fisk, Turner co-edited (with Cromwell and Dykes) one of the first anthologies of African American literature, *Readings from Negro Authors* (1931). Harper is not included among the forty-odd writers, but she and her major works, including *Moses*, are listed in an extensive bibliography (382). As Hurston was included (represented by "Drenched in Light") she quite likely would have seen the collection and possibly the reference.

7. As I noted in my discussion of *Jonah*, Hurston may have been influenced by yet another of Johnson's works, *God's Trombones* (1927), an imaginative setting of black sermons. Her *Moses* project could have been further influenced by the magnificent drawings Aaron Douglas did for Johnson; all the biblical figures are specifically black, including Christ.

8. It is fascinating to note that just after Faulkner informs the reader that Gavin has been engaged in this task for twenty-two years, old Molly Beauchamp demonstrates a profound and instinctual "translation" of sixteenth-century biblical words into African American past and present situations, as she demands Gavin help her rescue her grandson Butch, who is on death row in Illinois: "'Roth Edmonds sold my Benjamin. Sold him in Egypt. Pharaoh got him'" (341).

9. It also mimics the paradigm of a ubiquitous narrative form in black letters, the plight of the so-called "tragic" mulatto. Werner Sollors has demonstrated that the classic mulatto story in America has frequently relied on a national allegory, wherein white America becomes the father figure, black America the mother, and the offspring the "problematic, truly American heir who is denied his/her birthright and inheritance by his/her father," a tradition that is present, Sollors claims, in the title of *Native Son* ("Never" 305–6).

10. For traces of this friendship, see Bruce Kellner's *Carl Van Vechten and the Irreverent Decades* and *Letters of Carl Van Vechten.*

11. In "Girl Stalks Negro Lore," an interview with Zora by Joseph Mitchell, *New York World-Telegram* staff writer, she said *The Green Pastures* was "lousy as it can be. . . . It is good spectacle . . . but damned poor Negro" (*New York World Telegram* clipping, Hurston Collection, Rare Books and Manuscripts, University of Florida Library, Gainesville). Ironically, she was condemned to have her work compared to the play even in the publisher's blurb for her book, which read in part: "The play, *The Green Pastures,* had this same special feeling in its portrayal of the Negro conception of our Christian God—now Zora Neale Hurston, with her singular genius for interpreting her race, writes a book that is unique and unforgettable" (Hurston Collection, Rare Books and Manuscripts, University of Florida Library, Gainesville). Another shaft against the play was thrown as a subsidiary element of a comic diatribe against Alain Locke, an example of how her gift for mimicry could be used to devastating effect. "An instance of Dr. Locke's insincerity. I remember well at Howard University that he was one of the leaders in a hullabaloo against the singing of Negro spirituals. That was before so many people in high places had praised them. Now he tootches his lips all out and shivers with ecstasy when he speaks of 'those beautiful and sensitive things.' I remember his trembling with emotion over 'the faithfulness to Negro religion in *The Green Pastures,* which is anything you want to call it but the truth" ("The Chick with One Hen" 1–2).

12. Zora Neale Hurston to Carl Van Vechten, Jan. 22, 1934, James Weldon Johnson Collection, Yale Collection of American Literature, Beinecke Rare Book and Manuscript Library, Yale University, New Haven, Conn.

13. Later testimony to her interest in translating her novels to film is abundant; she spent four months as a story consultant at Paramount Studios in California, when she tried to interest them in her novels (Hemenway, *Zora* 276). We find additional proof that she related her writing on the Bible with the cinematic market in letters she wrote to her editor Jean Parker Westbury. She asks, "Have you an 'in' with Cecile B. DeMille? I know that I sound ambitious, but nothing ventured, nothing gained. I plan to try the LIFE OF HEROD THE GREAT as a drama, and it needs Hollywood. . . . Jack Kofoed, columnist in THE MIAMI HERALD, mentioned Orson Wells the other day, as moving from hotel to hotel, nearly all of his money gone, and doing nothing. I wished a great wish, that he could be induced to collaborate on Herod, but knowing him personally and his huge ego, I have been wondering whether to write him a letter. Yes, I'm ambitious, but don't count me out too soon. I might make it" (July 9, 1951, Hurston Collection, Rare Books and Manuscripts, Universi-

ty of Florida Library, Gainesville). She was even *dreaming* about biblical narrative: "I had a well-dreamed out story of David, Absalom and Bathsheba, but I see a movie has just been made on David and Bathsheba, so that's out, I suppose" (Aug. 19, 1951, Hurston Collection, Rare Books and Manuscripts, University of Florida Library, Gainesville). For an exhaustive and provocative survey of biblical films, consult Gerald E. Forshey, *American Religious and Biblical Spectaculars*, particular chapter 7, which deals with DeMille and *The Ten Commandments*.

14. For a detailed example of how folklore gets created, see Dance, *Long Gone*.

15. The phrase a "shape to fill a lack" is from the scene in *As I Lay Dying* where Addie comments on the meaningless nature of words such as love (164). For a varying view of Moses' crossing scene, consult Hemenway (*Zora* 270).

16. Mentu's folk imagination seems highly gender-oriented as well—man gets born in "the mothering Darkness" but the sun, "with his seven horns of flame is the father of life" (55). Similarly, man himself has a mind like a threshing floor to clean truth in, so becomes unhappy, seeing too clearly. Woman relieves his sorrow; her "'squint eyes' cause her to see only those things which please her. . . . She cannot separate the wheat from the chaff. But she achieves a harvest that makes her happy. When she sees man fleeing from his bowl in horror of himself, she feeds him from her own dish and he is blindly and divinely happy. As, yes, the female companion of man has the gift of the soothing-balm of lies" (56). There are many comic comments about women in the book, and most, like these, are somewhat sexist.

17. Still, we should remember that his African instruction—both in Egypt and at Koptos—comes first. And his Hebraic instruction is shown to us indirectly. Moses tells Jethro about reading the sacred book, but we never hear what is in it. Also, after Moses reads the sacred book, he returns it to the depths never to be read by anyone but him. Our only direct experience of a divine event thus comes when Moses meets God in the burning bush. The scene, virtually at the center of the book, features Jehovah's pronouncement, in all caps, I AM WHAT I AM, and his commandment to Moses to go down into Egypt to demand freedom for the Hebrews. Little humor appears here, and Moses speaks in standard English, although he does say, in the manner of a reluctant servant, "'Into Egypt? How come Lord? Egypt is no place for me to go'" (162). Humor returns though when he reports to Jethro: "'I can't do it, and that I AM WHAT I AM ought to know it'" (164), the impersonal pronoun operating as a signification and reduction of the ultimate "mouth Almighty."

18. For a full description of this process, see Stepto 163–69.

19. Late in the novel, for instance, Moses criticizes Aaron in hieroglyphic terms: "'You didn't think about service half as much as you did about getting served, Aaron. Your tiny horizon never did get no bigger, so you mistook a spotlight for the sun'" (333).

20. For Hurston's use of this term, see Hemenway, *Zora* 22–23, 37, 267.

21. Hurston commented on this problem sometime later in the fifties when she was working as a teacher at the Lincoln Park Academy in Fort Pierce; she

wrote a letter of complaint to M. Mitchell Ferguson, coordinator of the State Department of Education. "My name as an author is too big to be tolerated, lest it gather to itself the 'glory' of the school here. I have met that before. But perhaps it is natural. The mediocre have no importance except through appointment. They feel invaded and defeated by the presence of creative folk among them" (Mar. 7, 1958, Hurston Collection, Rare Books and Manuscripts, University of Florida Library, Gainesville). This reminds us of Deacon Hambo's description in *Jonah* of the black community as a basket of crabs, where anyone climbing higher than anyone else has to be pulled down, and of course, humor often does the trick.

22. For Hurston's earlier rendition of this story, see "Possum or Pig." Aaron's kinship in wiliness to High John makes us rethink Hurston's apparent attitude toward this complex character as well. We remember that the men on Jody's porch in *Their Eyes* speak highly of High John: "'He was uh man dat wuz more'n man. 'Tain't no mo' lak him. He wouldn't dig potatoes, and he wouldn't rake hay'" (104).

23. Albert Murray has shared Hurston's interest in Moses' ambivalent meanings. In *The Hero and the Blues* he wonders why blacks have oversimplified the Exodus story and points out that no one notes that "in U.S. terms, being half this, half that, [Moses] was a mulatto! Nor do they seem to have found anything significant in his role as lawgiver and utopian; and they seem completely oblivious to the confusion inherent in identifying with a nationalist who defines freedom and fulfillment in terms of leading his people out of the country of their actual birth and back across the sea to some exclusive territory" (60–61).

24. For a hilarious but ultimately disturbing poetic rendition of this syndrome, see Sterling Brown's great comic poem "Slim in Atlanta," where blacks are forbidden to laugh except in a telephone booth.

25. The fact that Moses marries outside the Hebrew community could also be Hurston's ironic inversion of a more usual pattern that Alice Walker has noted—the habit of prominent black men of marrying white or light-skinned women rather than "black black women," which Walker calls the "Dirty Little 'Secret' of Color in African American Life." She sees this pattern reflected in black literature as well, from *Clotelle* to well into the twentieth century ("Present" 302–3).

26. A useful but sometimes problematic overview of the club movement among African American women is offered in Wilson Jeremiah Moses' *The Golden Age of Black Nationalism, 1850–1925*. For a detailed description of these women's southern activities, consult Cynthia Neverdon-Morton, *Afro-American Women of the South and the Advancement of the Race, 1895–1925*.

27. A detailed feminist study of the Exodus story suggests that the biblical redactor also abridged Miriam's actual role, for in Micah 6:4 she appears as a national liberator: "For I brought thee up out of the land of Egypt, and redeemed thee out of the house of servants; and I sent before thee Moses, Aaron, and Miriam" (Pardes 11). Ilana Pardes also presents persuasive proof that Zipporah too was originally meant to be seen as a heroic figure, who fits into

a pattern of female saviors in the Bible. At one point she saves her husband's life. Although, like Miriam, Zipporah's story was edited by biblical authors, enough textual evidence remains to support this theory.

28. Hurston would later depict moonshining as an honorable way of supplementing an inadequate income in *Seraph,* perhaps following the example of her friend Marjorie Kinnan Rawlings's treatment of this issue in *South Moon Under* and *Cross Creek.*

29. We may also note Hurston's clever use and transformation of biblical facts here. Numbers 11:5 reads: "We remember the fish, which we did eat in Egypt freely; the cucumbers and the melons, and the leeks, and the onions, and the garlick." Here the fish are made into "Nice sweet-tasting little panfish" by the people and "fried fish" by Moses, who eliminates the leeks, onions, and garlic in favor of more familiar southern staples such as fish and cucumbers. He also adds the pleasure words "nice sweet-tasting little pan."

30. Zora Neale Hurston to Edwin Grover, Dec. 29, 1935, and May 14, 1935, Hurston Collection, Rare Books and Manuscripts, University of Florida Library, Gainesville.

31. Balaam, whose story is told in Numbers 22, is apparently a seer who is asked by the evil Moabite king Barak to curse the Hebrews. On his way his ass throws him against a wall after seeing God's angel standing in the way; after he smites the animal, it speaks to him (really an angel using the animal's shape) and he sees the angel himself. Finally, arriving at the Israelite camp, Balaam, now an agent of the Lord, blesses instead of curses them and prophesies a brilliant future for the people. Hurston makes Moses rather than the angel the instigator of the mule's speech through conjure, and it is Moses who tricks Balaam into the blessing as well. Furthermore, the magical narration employed here offers proof of the aforementioned connection between mastery of vernacular comic discourse and conjuration. Within the American slave system, conjurers provided a source of folk wisdom and power beyond the reach of the masters; as John Roberts notes, conjurers could therefore offer slaves "a focus for creating oral expressive traditions to transmit a conception of behaviors alternative to those fostered by existence under European domination" (94).

32. Like old Uncle Julius in Chesnutt's *The Conjure Woman,* old Mentu uses humor to get results from Moses and to make points in his moral tales. His parables about the old lizard who is too weak to catch flies or catch females contain nuggets of wisdom, which he specifically links to the human condition—"'It is sad but true that females seeking love do not wait for the weak and the aged. When the power to spring is gone—when you are older you will understand such things. A very trying period in a male thing's life'"—and the story also persuades Prince Moses to get some tidbits from the palace kitchen for Mentu (59). Ironic humor comes into the picture too, as Mentu warns Moses to take care no one finds out, for "the scraps from Pharaoh's table are set aside and dedicated to the stomachs of Pharaoh's dogs. Don't be caught in the misuse of the dog's dishes. Sacrilege is a terrible crime" (60). The link is thus made between slavery, where the master's horses got better treatment

than the slaves, and the concept of proper nutriment, physical and mental (the latter served by the tales). As Mentu says, "'Food makes people what they are. If the palace food makes a god out of high-born Pharaoh, it ought at least to make a man out of me'" (60). Hurston thus provides an anachronistic laugh that also explains to her largely white audience the origin of a still contemporary expression that was born in slavery. Jethro in many ways is an extension of Mentu; in one of his comic nuggets he reports that a raid to recover his own cows has netted some others. He then says, "'Well, I am not going to tote a casket in my pocket about it. . . . I don't expect to take to bed sick over it for even one day'" (126). Later he states, "'I have found out it is no more use to give advice to an old man than to give a tonic to a corpse'" (140). In both these last two utterances, he employs grim graveyard humor that is typical of the folk.

33. Zora Neale Hurston to Edwin Grover, Oct. 12, 1939, Hurston Collection, Rare Books and Manuscripts, University of Florida Library, Gainesville.

34. Faulkner's remarks came in response to a query: what was his favorite among his own books? He chose *The Sound and the Fury* because "it was the best failure. It was the one that I anguished the most over, that I worked the hardest at, that even when I knew I couldn't carry it off, I still worked at it. . . . That was the most gallant, the most magnificent failure" (Gwynn and Blotner 61). Hurston's remarks suggest a similar attitude.

35. The Exodus has long been the subject of allegory; as Dante pointed out, this biblical episode is an almost perfect allegorical narrative, for "if we inspect the letter alone the departure of the children of Israel from Egypt in the time of Moses is presented to us; if the allegory, our redemption wrought by Christ; if the moral sense, the conversion of the soul from the grief and misery of sin to the state of grace is presented to us; if the anagogical, the departure of the holy soul from the slavery of this corruption to the liberty of eternal glory is presented to us" (cited in Frye 221).

Part 3  Sunset

The storyteller: he is the man who could let the
wick of his life be consumed completely by the gentle
flame of his story.
  —*Walter Benjamin*

FIVE

Cuttin' the Cracker for the White Folks: *Seraph on the Suwanee*

And Abraham rose up early in the morning, and took bread, and a bottle of water, and gave it unto Hagar, putting it on her shoulder, and the child, and sent her away: and she departed, and wandered in the wilderness of Beersheba. . . . She said Let me not see the death of the child. And she sat over against him, and lift up her voice, and wept. And God heard the voice of the lad, and the angel of God called to Hagar out of heaven.
—*Genesis 21:14–17*

And Sarah said, God hath made me to laugh, so that all that hear will laugh with me.
—*Genesis 21:6*

Throughout Hurston's career, she tirelessly explored the role humor plays in life, especially in courtship and marriage. Most of the time her interest lay in its positive effects. In her last published novel, however, she seems to show that a lack of humor can poison the life of a character, and consequently, the people around her. Her laboratory became *Seraph on the Suwanee* (1948), her only published novel about white characters. Craig Werner, in a recent biographical essay on Hurston, argues that Hurston's least understood novel requires a special reading; an ability to understand the shifting, masked nature of black humorous traditions can reveal the novel's narrative strategy ("Zora"). Arvay, the heroine, lacks this quality and presumably so do many readers. Jim, Arvay's husband, appreciates black culture and knows how to "read" it, especially in his joking relationships with African Americans. This proves important, for as Werner points out, more than two dozen times Hurston has a character, usually Arvay, fail to understand a joke. In the few paragraphs he can devote to the book in his essay, Werner can't elaborate, but he is on to something.

Humor indeed lies at the heart of the book, and in more ways than Werner suggests. Arvay's psychological and emotional problems almost exclusively stem from a lifelong pattern of real and perceived rejection and a consequent stunting of her sense of humor. This results in a lack of identity, confidence, pride, and creativity. Her failure to communicate her real desires and feelings to others charts an opposite tack from Jim's joking, cross-racial fellowship, which makes him a favorite at all levels of southern society. He joyfully uses the exuberant resources of folk culture, black and white, to persuade, cajole, charm, instruct, and protect his family, friends, and employees. Because of these abilities, Hurston suggests, he becomes a successful businessman in varying fields and the most dynamic, compelling character in the novel, despite his unfortunate male chauvinism. Hurston was also writing *Seraph* as a variant of the American frontier novel, and Jim's rough edges, his ability to fight when he has to, and his sometimes crude but more often witty humor make him part of the lineage of frontier humorists that have added so much vitality to southern and American literature.

For all these reasons, I believe Werner is correct in his claim that "read with an emphasis on process and an awareness of the multiple levels of its humor, *Seraph on the Suwanee* metamorphoses into a comic masterpiece. Far from an artistic failure reflecting Hurston's declining powers, the concluding reconciliation between Jim and Arvay expresses the gospel impulse, the deeply Afrocentric belief that whatever the degree of their apparent discord, competing energies can be restored to harmony" ("Zora" 231).

The plot operates on two basic levels; on the one hand we share the tortured psychological struggles of Arvay Henson, a troubled Cracker mystic who withdraws into a private realm for years after her sister Larraine steals her preacher beau, Carl Middleton. A new man in town, the poor but well-born and energetic Jim Meserve, breaks through Arvay's resistance, marries her, and takes her away to orange country, where he starts a grove. When she gives birth to Earl, a retarded and deformed son, Arvay feels God still blames her for loving Larraine's husband all those years, and her inner gloom only darkens when Jim's attempt to use humor to bring her out of it seems merely mocking and based in his sense of social superiority. The devotion of her two subsequent children to Jim makes matters worse. Eventually, however, the tragic death of Earl forces Arvay to rethink things, and when Jim leaves her and her mother dies, Arvay finally breaks through to a personal sense of worth, symbolized when she torches her mother's rat-infested house, the scene of Arvay's psychological fixations during childhood and adolescence. She joins Jim at the coast, where his new shrimping fleet is about to set sail. Working beside him on the ocean, she boldly initiates a final and loving reunion. The other half of the narrative traces Jim's rise through various Florida industries, giving Hurston an opportunity to detail the beauty and energy of her beloved state, as it moved rapidly from near-frontier conditions into the modern age.

This bare outline cannot hope to do justice to a very ambitious narrative; among other achievements, it explores contemporary problems of race, class, and gender while providing a Freudian case study of the consequences of rejection. Humor's diagnostic and therapeutic role in dealing with all these issues proves considerable. Further, Hurston builds a mythical level into the psychic conundrums of her text by employing the biblical typology centered on the image of Hagar in the wilderness. All these issues do indeed get expressed as "competing energies" that are "restored to harmony" of a sort in the final chapter.

I shall argue that Hurston wrote her "white book" partly because removing race from her central field of interest made possible a more intense focus on gender but particularly class. On the other hand, although the black figures of the book certainly play a peripheral narrative role, their contribution proves crucial, in terms of Hurston's presentation of class and sass. Jim Meserve, though white, understands, and frequently uses, black performance styles, especially in his relationships with his "pet negroes," a subject of one of Hurston's most provocative essays and a surprisingly key concept in a book supposedly about white folks.

On another level, writing a book about white characters enables Hurston to explore some deeply personal feelings behind her most deceptive mask. The internalization of Arvay's hurt and anger and a resultant inferiority complex that damages her relations with others for years—especially her husband—offers a divergence from the facts of Hurston's life, but the overall pattern of rejection that she suffers matches them.

Finally, the novel constitutes Hurston's love song to Florida, her home, where she was to spend the rest of her life. She always hated the cold northern winters and gloried in telling her Harlem friends about her native state's warm weather, beautiful flowers, and fertile abundance. Her letters written in the North frequently express her longing for Florida, a sentiment shared by many of that state's citizens who had migrated to northern cities. Bessie Smith recorded "Florida Bound Blues" in 1925, which paralleled Hurston's state of mind as she began *Seraph:*

> Goodbye North, hello South
> It's so cold up here that the words freeze in your mouth.
> I'm going to Florida
> Where I can have my fun.

The backdrop to Arvay's story takes the reader through Florida's thriving economy, as the family successively moves from the Cracker boondocks and turpentine camps into the citrus industry, moonshining, swamp reclamation, real estate booms, and shrimping fleets on the coast. The raw energy of the changing frontier charges the narrative, and throughout, Hurston's nature imagery is lyrical and detailed, creating an ironically paradisic backdrop to Arvay's mental hell.

Florida on My Mind: The WPA, Rawlings, and Memory

One of the many problems of reading Hurston today is a side effect of the superb critical work that has been generated over the last few decades by scholars of African American and feminist schools of criticism. We have grown accustomed to *always* initially applying these types of critical mechanisms to Hurston's texts. Unfortunately, doing this with *Seraph* has led to misreadings of the book and to undervaluing its place in Hurston's oeuvre and the black and American literary canons.

Robert Hemenway, for instance, reads the book through a contemporary feminist lens and thereby misses its strengths. Arvay's reconciliation with Jim at the end, once she has become content with the roles of wife and mother, seems to Hemenway a descent "into the trap of her marriage forever"; his only question: did Hurston intend this "tragicomedy"? He flatly states that there is no hope for the marriage because Arvay has not achieved equality with Jim. By some (but certainly not all) contemporary feminist standards this might seem true. Hurston, however, publishing this book in the late forties, obviously thinks differently. As Hemenway sums the failure of the book up, "Just as Arvay begins to become interesting, she is lost again to domestic service" (314). His reading of the book thus depends on how we define "domestic service" and whether that is indeed an accurate way to describe how Jim and Arvay view her state. Hemenway seems to interpret the role of the housewife as slavery (never true for Arvay even in the early days of her marriage; even then she has servants to assist her, and in the later years, she and Jim are quite affluent) and ignores the fact that Arvay, hardly an artist or would-be businesswoman, has neither the aspiration, training, or inherent talent to be anything else.[1]

Other critics have focused on *Seraph*'s divergence from Hurston's other works, suggesting that it is inferior because of its very differences. Lillie Howard has usefully pointed out that Hurston had in fact not left her usual subject matter at all (*Zora* 135). Howard asserts that Hurston actually persists in writing about the folk and their culture and focusing on a woman's search for identity. Nor is Arvay's self-destructiveness new; Hurston's heroine Emmaline in the early play *Color-Struck* loses the man she loves because of her own lack of self-worth.

A critique that centers on modes of narration, patterns of joking relationships, psychological theories of rejection, class and economic issues, and realism actually proves much more useful for understanding this novel. Zora Neale Hurston, more than virtually any other black writer in American literary history, identified with the South, always considered herself a southerner, and was very loyal to the state that produced her. The first paragraph of her autobiography declares, "I have memories within that came out of the material that went to make me. Time and place have had their say" (*Dust Tracks* 3). That time and place was Florida, at the end of the nineteenth century and the beginning of the twentieth. More than any of her other books, *Seraph* is lovingly dedicated to the memory of an almost prelapsarian Florida. The dedication to Marjorie Kinnan Rawlings and Mrs. Spessard L. Holland (wife of Florida's U.S. senator) only deepens the sense of tribute to her home state already established.

There are many possible reasons Hurston decided to write about lower-class but upwardly mobile white characters and their black retainers. Doing so enabled her to more easily concentrate on simultaneously memorializing the land, its flora and fauna,[2] and the early days of Florida communities. And yet in Hurston's eyes, it was the dynamic Florida she was sketching, a beautiful frontier land moving powerfully into the modern age. Despite its limning of the passing of an era, *Seraph* hardly comprises an elegy, as, for example, Faulkner's *Go Down, Moses* does. No, Hurston instead lustily helps an awakening Florida sharpen its oyster knife.

Simultaneously, she added more background on the black folk culture she treated in her earlier books and therefore explained some other factors that had entered into making Zora, Zora. On the other hand, since blacks still had to take a back seat in the boom, writing about whites would give her more leeway in describing the dawn of a new entrepreneurial age for Florida, something that brought her much pride. The dialogics of her native state find a more diverse expression here as well, as Hurston, who always claimed to have "the map of Florida on my tongue" assembled a large chorus of diverse voices, moving from Cracker "teppentime" workers and preachers to affluent real estate moguls and beyond to the salty and truly motley crew of sailors on the Florida coast.

Without a doubt, this book grew out of the eighteen months Hurston spent on the payroll of the Florida Federal Writers' Project, a time that may have been one of the happiest of her life. This period has been little examined, but it is crucial to the proper understanding of this novel. Robert Hemenway devotes only three pages to this important moment in Hurston's second career as folklorist/anthropologist, and perhaps as a result, virtually dismisses *Seraph*.

Linguistically her most ambitious book and full of richly visual settings and situations, *Seraph* suggests a new interest in a more detailed kind of realism, inspired in part by a financial motive. Hazel Carby has noted that Hurston saw the book as an opportunity; she had had her agent at Scribner's approach MGM about filming the book in 1947, before it was published (Foreword x). Thinking about films of her works wasn't a new idea for Hurston, and her desire to write "white scripts" for the movies preceded her interest in writing *Seraph*. In a 1942 letter to Carl Van Vechten, Hurston discusses her recent work at Paramount Studios in Hollywood and her desire to be published in the *New Yorker*: "Having been on the writing staff at PARAMOUNT for several months, I have a tiny wedge in Hollywood, and I have hopes of breaking that old silly rule about Negroes not writing about white people. In fact, I have a sort of commitment from a producer at RKO that he will help me to do it."[3] Four years later, Hurston was no doubt encouraged to submit a movie project set in backwoods Florida after the enormous success of both the book (1938) and movie (1946) of Marjorie Kinnan Rawlings's *The Yearling*, a moving story of poor Florida Crackers, which won the Pulitzer Prize. Hurston admired Rawlings,[4] shared her deep love for Florida and its people, and, like her, looked to simple life in rural settings for inner peace.

There are strong parallels, in fact, between the work of Hurston and Rawlings in their descriptions of the land, the flora and fauna, the weather, and the larger-than-life figures they created to inhabit their cosmic landscapes. On the other hand, Rawlings employs almost no humor, deadpanning her way through almost every sort of scene;

displays a noted xenophobia in her fiction that also characterized her own personality; and savagely attacks the burgeoning industries that were transforming the face of her beloved adopted state. She seems intent on writing a hard-nosed narrative that unflinchingly matches the neo-naturalism of Hemingway, Steinbeck, and Dos Passos, but carefully avoids what she saw as the "filth" of more overtly Freudian writers such as Faulkner. One finds little affinity between her work and that of contemporary southern women writers, with the possible exception of Elizabeth Maddox Roberts. She more resembles such chroniclers of the folk as Conrad Richter, T. S. Stribling, and a subsequent female writer of the fifties, Harriette Arnow. The lives of her characters prove harsh, often tragic, but infused with natural beauty. These tough rural folk are virtually monosyllabic in their interpersonal communications, frequently violent, but more often passive and stoic. Hurston, by contrast, creates joking, innovative, ambitious, and constantly frenetic characters who are meant to be seen as dynamic exemplars of the New South, Florida version. Her own boosterism infuses everything that Jim Meserve does, and many of the signs of Arvay's moral and emotional progress are taken from the consumer's wishbook. Music, football, dancing, and many other pleasures of a rapidly learning, rural-to-suburbia set of characters are featured.

Through her realism Hurston primarily focuses on class and her notion of it originally developed in her own family, which she dramatized in *Jonah* through John Pearson's low standing with Lucy's family. His original, John Hurston, according to his daughter, was viewed with disdain by her mother's family: "Over-the-creek niggers lived from one white man's plantation to the other. Regular hand-to-mouth folks. Didn't own pots to pee in, nor beds to push 'em under. Didn't have no more pride than to let themselves be hired by poor-white trash. No more to 'em than the stuffings out of a zero" (*Dust Tracks* 13). Guests were ranked as well. The family used old newspapers in the privy house, but "fair to middling guests got sheets out of the old Sears, Roebuck catalogue. But Mama would sort over her old dress patterns when really fine company came, and the privy house was well scrubbed, lime thrown in, and the soft tissue paper pattern stuck on a nail inside the place for the comfort and pleasure of our guests" (26).

Although Hurston certainly knew some Crackers when she was growing up, her most intense scrutiny of this group came much later, after she had become both a practicing folklorist and novelist accustomed to noting the intricacies of sociological and anthropological detail as a member of the Florida Federal Writers' Project in

1938–39. Although Hurston worked on *The Florida Negro* (which was only recently published), she also had input into many of the publications that actually appeared and access to all the research materials the writers' team developed. Much of this found its way into the pages of *Seraph*.

In fact, the book opens with the kind of description Hurston had helped craft in *The Florida Negro* and *The Florida Guide,* but reworked so as to fit into her narrative plan. She points out that Stephen Foster made the Suwanee famous without having seen it, perhaps signaling the reader that the fabled stereotype of this region will be exploded by her narrative. Suggesting from the very beginning that folk culture proceeds out of peasant life and the land itself, Hurston asserts that culture here, bordered by "primitive forests . . . streams out from the sawmill and the 'teppentime 'still.'" We seem to have drifted back to her early fictional starting point, the world of the rural work of "Sweat" and "John Redding Goes to Sea." Here, however, there will be more of a sociological and historic bent: "Then too, there was ignorance and poverty, and the ever-present hookworm." Perhaps the most salient form of this "ignorance" is the fact that "few were concerned with the past. They had heard that the stubbornly resisting Indians had been there where they now lived, but they were dead and gone. Osceola, Miccanope, Billy Bow-Legs were nothing more than names that had even lost their bitter flavor. The conquering Spaniards had done their murdering, robbing, and raping and had long ago withdrawn from the Floridas. Few knew and nobody cared that the Hidalgos under De Soto had moved westward along this very route" (2). Although some critics presume this book is simply a whitewashing of black characters because the figures supposedly "speak black," Hurston in the preceding assertion makes crucial observations: the Crackers don't have a folk culture that memorializes actual events in history. Their stories and idioms bespeak a repository of folk wisdom, but one unconnected with history. Obviously, African Americans would have more cultural strength in this connection, as so much of their oral tradition is tied to history. How this would affect Arvay remains unclear—but her family in Sawley seems adrift in time, much like the Lesters of Caldwell's *Tobacco Road,* with disastrous results.

Hurting Jokes and Guilty Dreams

The narrative proper begins with a moment of unusual demarcation between the racial communities, a Sunday morning, for of course the races do not worship together: "This was a Sunday. . . . The Negroes were about their own doings in their own part of town, and white Sawley was either in church or on the way." Hurston describes the big turnout at the white church comically, with an animal analogy: "Sawley was boiling like a big red ants' nest that had been ploughed up. . . . Arvay was . . . being courted." Their interest stems from the oddity of Arvay's renunciation of the world five years earlier, which we learn was actually caused by her pain over her sister Larraine's marriage to the man Arvay still thinks she loves, the Reverend Carl Middleton. Indeed, Hurston tells us waggishly through a local wit that such religious fervor has no precedent here: "Sawley wore out the knees of its britches crawling to the Cross and wore out the seat of its pants back-sliding. Excessive ceremonies were things that the Negroes went in for. White folks just didn't go on like that" (3). The narrator's description of Arvay comes from an expurgated version of the repertoire of male desire:

> No heavy-hipped girl below that extremely small waist, and her legs were long and slim-made instead of the much-admired "whiskey-keg" look to her legs that was common. . . . Arvay had a fine-made kind of a nose and mouth and a face shaped like an egg laid by a Leghorn pullet. . . . She was said to be so slim that a man would have to shake the sheets to find her in bed, but there were many around Sawley who were willing to put themselves to the trouble of making a thorough search of the bed every night. Many a man felt that given the chance, he could put plenty of meat on Arvay's bones. So there was a feeling of shock and loss when Arvay gave up the world. It brought on plenty of talk. (4)

The robust physicality of the description and the double entendres are typical of the tenor and tone of the narrator's remarks; the fact that Hurston speaks at times more in the nature of a typical male narrator makes the reader unconsciously tilt toward Jim Meserve rather than Arvay when their stories converge. The metaphors of eating and drinking, used here to figure the body—whiskey/egg/pullet/meat/bones—provide a Rabelaisian/folk context that sometimes seems masculinist, sometimes simply human.

Hurston gives us an affectionately detailed view of the community's level of education, and also their wit, by letting them speak jointly, casually chauvinistically, and anonymously, as in this analysis of Arvay's speech of renunciation to the church, five years prior: "Everybody said it was just fine. There had been nothing about the heathens of China, India and Africa wallowing around on the heavenly chairs nor ankling up and down the golden streets. None of her hearers could have imagined such a thing. Fancy meeting a Hindu, with his middle tied up in a dhoti and with white head-rag on, around the Throne, or singing in the Choir! It was too much, and nobody tried to imagine any such thing. He ought to consider himself pretty lucky to get saved from Hell" (4–5). Hurston astutely lets the xenophobia, racism, and ignorance expressed here speak for itself, but she probably enjoys the humorous way it gets expressed. The vision of the Hindu around the Throne proves "too much" for the commentators because that locale so obviously gets imagined as a gilded version of Sawley-America, thereby setting up the incongruous juxtaposition that Freud posits as the foundation of humor. A more careful reader, however, will observe how Arvay herself slips further and further away from the center of the communal consciousness as this train of thought gets developed.

Carl, her brother-in-law and the minister, matches Arvay's statement by offering to become a missionary, knowing his flock will object, and indeed, "to compensate for this denial, the parsonage was re-painted, and five dollars a month was added to his salary, bringing the total to an even seventy dollars a month" (5). We see we are back in the realm of the hypocrite preacher, but this one's sins are pecuniary rather than venal—perhaps a subtle comment on white culture. Later, Brock Henson derisively signifies on his son-in-law and his bogus "call": "Dodging honest work . . . Carl Middleton up in a pulpit beating on a Bible and hollering was nothing but a first-class teppentime-still hand going to waste" (9).

Arvay's strange "fits," later revealed by Jim to be self-induced whenever a suitor threatens her solitude, are shrugged off by the community, as they assume that "marriage would straighten her out," an indication the community accepts the process of "breaking a woman" as an ordinary part of this commitment. As these few excerpts suggest, the entire first chapter comes through the perspective of the town, and thus echoes the method of the first chapter of *Their Eyes*.

Hurston establishes the class differential between Arvay and Jim quite early, by pointing out that his ancestors had owned plantations on the Alabama River before the war. His supposed social superiority accentuates Arvay's sense of social vulnerability and makes her overly sensitive to Jim's jokes. Although he now has nothing and "had come to town three months ago with only a small bundle, containing his changing clothes, he has a flavor about him. He was like a ham-string. He was not meat any longer, but he smelled of what he had once been associated with." This fits in with the town's assumption that a husband will provide "meat" for Arvay's "bones." Handsome black Irish Jim has "dimples in his lean cheeks, white strong teeth set in a chaffing mouth," markers of his gift for gab and laughter that help him into a woodsman job at the turpentine camp. Hurston obviously wanted to use her extensive fieldwork during her FWP days in this piece, and she lets her narrator demonstrate that knowledge early on: "'Teppentime' folks are born, not made, and certainly not over-night'" (7).

Arvay's father, Brock Henson, hires Jim at the camp, no doubt because he identifies with him: "Brock Henson was a Cracker from way back. Life had not been easy for him, and he had cutting edges on his spirits, in spite of his love of jokes" (7). Since Hurston herself at this point in her career could well have been looking in the mirror as she wrote this, and because she indicates throughout the novel that Arvay suffers by lacking a healthy sense of of humor, this line proves very interesting. Adding to Brock's depiction as a "poor white," Hurston's description of the dilapidated Henson house leans a bit in the direction of Caldwell's home of the Lesters in *Tobacco Road,* a book with much rough teasing humor that possibly influenced this one in a number of ways: "The privyhouse leaned a little to one side less than fifty feet from the kitchen door" (8).

Poor whites have always been the subject of African American humor; Ralph Ellison speaks of this in remembering seeing avatars of Jeeter Lester and his family in Alabama, near Tuskeegee:

> But in that setting their capacity for racial violence would have been far more over-whelming than their comical wrong-headedness. Indeed, in look, gesture, and deed they had crowded me so continuously that I had been tempted to armor myself against their threat by denying them *their* humanity as they sought to deny me mine . . . an attitude given expression in the child's jingle
>
> > My name is Ran
> > I work in the sand,
> > but I'd rather be a *nigger*
> > Than a poor white man. . . .
>
> But while such boasting brags—and there were others (*These white folks think they so fine / But their raggedy drawers / Stink just like mine* is another)—provided a release of steam they were not only childish but ultimately frustrating. . . . The necessity for keeping one's negative opinions of whites within one's own group became a life-preserving discipline. (*Going* 166)

Ellison's comments indicate why many black writers had hesitated to write about this group. Hurston solved the problem by presenting them less as caricatures and more as human beings. The Sawley community may be crude, but Hurston allows it its own folk vigor and salty expression and allows the people to demonstrate their humanity, frequently through humor.

On the other hand, much of this, while amusing, has a cruel edge. Brock teases Arvay throughout her formative years, and Jim's joking uncomfortably echoes the father's. Jim's jokes have an extra edge, however, because of Arvay's perception of his superior social class, which makes his teasing seem condescending and sometimes ugly. She links this to the rejection she obviously feels she suffered in her family, where her oddities received merciless ribbing. She thinks her family and the community prefer her elder sister and rival, Larraine, over her and that's why she is so teased.

A man with "the nerve of a brass monkey," Jim judges Arvay worth the trouble of courting and breaking in and laughs off her vow to renounce the world and love. "The doings were something like a well-trained hound dog tackling a bob-cat, and everybody wanted to be in on the fun. So they were all on the way to church that Sunday morning, walking, in buggies, riding horse-back and some even straddling grass-gut mules or in double wagons pulled by mules" (7–8). This suggests the bobtailed community going to a circus rather than church, thereby setting readers up to feel a certain initial degree of sympathy for Arvay.

Hurston continues to develop character via the town, occasionally by saying what the people don't know: "They did not suspect that the general preference for Larraine, Arvay's more robust and aggressive sister, had done something to Arvay's soul across the years. They could not know, because Arvay had never told anyone how she felt and why" (9). Through this one sentence she is able to introduce the themes of sibling rivalry, hidden and forbidden love, and the resurgence of *Their Eyes* material, a woman's lack of voice. Arvay's role as one of two daughters sets up the biblical theme of the younger eventually overtaking the elder and securing the parental blessing and inheritance (which Arvay does by the end of the book). Of key importance: Carl had in fact called on Arvay for months before apparently jilting her for Larraine, who "snakes" her own sister. Hurston makes a sexual joke out of the courtship (which she renders via a flashback), for Carl habitually "consults" with Arvay (supposedly about hymn selection) while she sits at the organ, which she plays for the church: "Leaning over her shoulder . . . little touches of his hand seemingly by accident, softness in his voice, and telling her that she was an exceptional young girl" (10).

Arvay feels painfully guilty from having pleasurable sexual dreams about Carl during the early years of his marriage to Larraine. Losing Carl seems to begin a series of losses in her life, but could relate retrospectively to her childhood perception that she had lost her parents' love to Larraine. Later, her son Earl's death causes a similarly protracted period of mourning, and bit by bit her life gets swallowed up by melancholia. In the case of Carl (and later, Jim, often perceived as "lost" to her), we have an example of Freud's definition of melancholia: "The object has not perhaps actually died, but has been lost as an object of love (e.g. in the case of a betrothed girl who has been jilted). . . . The distinguishing mental features of melancholia are a profoundly painful dejection, cessation of interest in the outside world, loss of the capacity to love . . . and a lowering of the self-regarding feelings to a degree that finds utterance in self-reproaches and self-revilings, and culminates in a delusional expectation of punishment" ("Mourning" 244–45). Freud distinguished between mourning and melancholia by noting that disturbance of self-regard is present only in the latter.

Arvay's situation throughout the novel so closely fits this description that one supposes Hurston knew Freud's essay. She would of course have been exposed to Freud's theories much earlier, first at Columbia, where her mentor, Franz Boas, went so far as to say that folktales were the result of an interchange between daydreams and "ardent desires" engendered by the mind (Boas 610).[5]

The Freudian nature of Hurston's material was picked up immediately by Frank G. Slaughter, who reviewed the book for the *New York Times* under the heading "Freud in Turpentine." Unfortunately, his short, dismissive analysis indicates a cursory reading (he describes Arvay's first tryst with Jim as taking place under "the turpentine trees," and refers to Carl as a "visiting minister"). Worse, Slaughter condescendingly speculates that Hurston "took a textbook on Freudian psychology and adapted it to her needs, perhaps with her tongue in her cheek"; he reveals his own ignorance of Freud, however, by claiming that the book is about a "hysterical neurotic" (24).

Hurston's careful working out of Arvay's psychology suggests her deeper knowledge of psychoanalytic theory. Freud was a favorite topic during the Harlem Renaissance and in New York intellectual society in general during the twenties and thirties, especially his interpretation of dreams, a subject that Hurston must have found intriguing for several reasons. Dreams have traditionally played a large role in black sermons and in the "travels" of recent converts who have "come through." Dreams play key roles in conjuring and rootwork and in the widespread habit in black urban neighborhoods of poring over dreams for destined numbers to play in neighborhood rackets. Hurston's mentor Boas no doubt introduced her to Freud as early as the twenties, but other friends like Van Vechten were aficionados as well. Whatever the source, Hurston certainly saw the immense potential of Freud's theories for *Seraph,* where they would work in tandem with backwoods religion. Arvay's dreams, for instance, are both typological and Freudian: "Some imp of Satan seemed to grab hold of her and drag her right into the darkened bedroom where Carl and 'Raine were, and made her look and see and hear from beginning to the end" (11). She also dreams of Larraine dying and Carl begging for her love, and the dreaded discovery of these evil thoughts not only fills her with terror of divine retribution but also public ridicule: "Not a soul in Sawley suspected this secret life of Arvay's. Most of them would have laughed at her if they had known about it," a key observation that explains much about her inability to laugh at herself or with others (11).

Ridicule seems tantamount to hellfire itself to Arvay. And indeed, Hurston almost immediately shows how those propped up high can quickly fall through communal joking: when the community decides Carl isn't much of a preacher (no creativity), or a singer (no voice), both qualities that the very black John Pearson had in abundance in *Jonah,* "some wag went so far as to say that Reverend Middleton couldn't even raise a tune if you put a wagon-load of good compost under him and ten sacks of commercial fertilizer" (11). This blast offers a classic example of what Bakhtin describes as the typical leveling joke, one that unites the intellect and the buttocks.

Arvay's marital struggles with these problems are preceded by a stormy and hilarious courtship. Arvay's father, anything but subtle, punctures her romantic dithering by going directly, if cruelly, to the point: "'Ain't you never going to have sense enough to get yourself a husband? You intend to lay round here on me for the rest of your days and moan and pray?'" Her mother, Maria, makes it a comic duet: "'Here all these gals around here 'bout to bust they guts trying to git to him, and Arvay, that seems like she got the preference with him, trying to cut the tom fool'" (13). Hurston as narrator is hardly gentler with her authorial "hurtful humor": "Arvay . . . stood grim and panting before the looking-glass, her eyes stretched wide in fear like a colt that has been saddled for the first time" (13). Her thoughts, however, if not her utterances, indicate an interior sense of comic scorn; seeing her parents talking with Jim, "Arvay mentally scorned them, and acting two glad dogs in a meat-house!" (13). As we see, although her parents accuse her of acting the "fool," Arvay believes the town wants to make her their fool in the spectacle of Jim romancing her. Moreover, her parents' and the town's interest in "marrying her off" looks like more rejection and abandonment and demonstrates the sexist habit of regarding women as chattel.

As she leaves for church, she hears a "suppressed guffaw from her father and her face flamed" (14), which thus strikes the first note of her relationship with Jim, and naturally segues into the first verbal duel in the narrative:

> "What you grinning all over yourself like a chessy-cat for? You act like you found a mare's nest and can't count the eggs." Jim . . . laughed some more. "Grinning just like the Devil's doll-baby!" Arvay added as a further insult.
>
> "Wouldn't hurt your face to grin a little, would it, Miss Arvay? You got yours all tied up in a winter-knot, or like you been feasting off of green persimmons. . . ."
>
> "You'se doing enough grinning and skinning back your gums for the two of us. I'd give a whoop and a holler, though, if you was to go on about your business and leave me be. . . ."
>
> "Go ahead and tell me something that I can understand. I might be sort of chuckle-headed, so don't chunk the whole pan of bread at me; crumble it up fine so I can handle it. . . ."
>
> "Why do you want to come a'pestering and a'picking at me for? You know that you just want to make game of me! . . . I never done nothin' to you for you to come taking me for a figure of fun, and making a laughing-stock out of me for folks to poke fun at." The laughter died off out of Jim Meserve's face, and he stopped and stood looking down into her tortured eyes for a full minute. (15)

This passage illustrates how hurtful Arvay finds both Jim's humor and the pain acting out her courtship before the community causes her. It also points to the continuing problem she and Jim will have communicating their most basic concerns. Nevertheless, Cracker folklore gives her tools for the duel; she's hardly a passive victim—but most of her defensive maneuvers in the course of the book wind up hurting her. Indeed, after Arvay goes so far as to slap him, Jim declares, in a demonstration of both his love and his insight, "'I have to stay with you and stand by you and give my good protection to keep you from hurting your ownself too much'" (15).

We are permitted access to Arvay's typically dread-filled projection into the future: "Folks would be coming along this road and see her in the company of Jim, and she pictured them grinning slyly and making jokes about her. . . . After Jim had made a public show of her, he would naturally get himself a regular girl, and they would all laugh at her, Arvay, and say how Jim Meserve and whoever his wife might be had made her look like a fool at a funeral" (16). And indeed, it seems she's right; a wagon comes along: "Old Lady Minnie Brawley was so scared that her wrinkled-around old eyes might miss something that she reached up a freckled old claw and flung back the bib part of her floppy calico bonnet the better to gaze and to peer. Grins and giggles broke out among the younger members of the clan." Her suspicions confirmed, Arvay voices her concern: "'Making a fool out of me right out here on the Big Road. Acting just like the Devil!'" (17).

To Arvay's surprise, however, she enjoys the envious looks from "single women and courting girls" at church. "Her vanity put on a little flesh"—an echo of the marriage as meat for the bone analogy. We overhear an envious girl's witticism: "'Can you imagine them married and in the bed together? I bet they would sound like a big dish-pan of crockery rattling together'" (19).[6] Clearly, we are back in the realm of female rivalry and signifying that we saw in the courtship days of John and Lucy in *Jonah*. The men contribute here too. Arvay overhears them discussing her; someone says, "'Go, gator, and muddy the water!'" "'I'd give a spot cash one hundred dollars if Jim would up and buss her.'" "'Arvay would throw a acre of fits.'" Arvay's anger at this laughter, however, becomes offset by seeing Larraine's jealousy: "She had Carl Middleton, and she had three children to boot. Let her pout and crave! . . . Jim Meserve, placed beside Carl Middleton, was like a slick race-horse beside a grass-gut mule" (20– 21). Like Janie, it seems, she has an inside and an outside, and in fact, is capable, at least internally, of quite creative signification.

In one of the book's more infamous passages, Arvay responds to Jim's proposal of marriage by saying, "'I'd have to take time to make up my mind.'" Jim replies,

> "So far as making up your mind is concerned, that matters a difference. Women folks don't have no mind to make up nohow. They wasn't made for that. Lady folks were just made to laugh and act loving and kind and have a good man to do for them all he's able, and have him as many boy-children as he figgers he'd like to have, and make him so happy that he's willing to work and fetch in every dad-blamed thing that his wife thinks she would like to have. That's what women are made for. . . . Since I been here in Sawley, I done got in the notion that I'd like to get hold of one of the useless things to keep for a play-pretty." (23)

This speech sounds very like Jody Starks's pronouncement about women and chickens needing someone to do their thinking for them, but it adds quite a number of important qualities, especially the phrase "laugh and act loving and kind." Moreover, Jim's comic exaggeration of male attitudinizing suggests he's perceptive enough to parody the tradition. But Arvay can't take faith in his love: "Now, was she to believe that this very pretty man clothed in all the joys of Heaven and earth was for *her*, and all that she had to do was to part her lips and say 'yes' to have him all for herself for life? Oh, no, this was just another hurting joke being played on her" (23). In another echo of *Their Eyes,* Jim claims, "'I'm too tough for you to get shed of like you seem to be trying to do'"; Arvay responds, "'You figger that you'se all that tough, Mister Meserve?'"—but feels his arm tremble (24). This dichotomy of outer bombast and inner trembling should alert us as readers to the possibility that Jim's language contains a good deal of bluster that must be discounted if we are to really understand the man within. As so often in Hurston, a question asked by a character becomes a central concern for the reader. Throughout the book we are forced to question Jim's "toughness," particularly what at first seems to be a rigid male chauvinism. Arvay's question also echoes Janie's of Tea Cake: "'You all that Sweet?'"

Jim's answer encapsulates a typical tall-tale tradition; he claims he routinely catches lightning and hurls it back. When he was struck once, he says, "'Was I mad! Just as hot as Tucker when the mule kicked his Mammy. All them colored men that was working under me come running to see if I was killed. . . . Told 'em they might as well go on back to work. I wasn't hurt at all, but that sneaking bolt of lightning was done up pretty bad. Yes, Ma'am! Last I seen of it, it was going off through the woods a'limping.' Jim's face brimmed over with laughter like an orange being squeezed, and he stood with one hand resting on the jamb of the door holding back the explosion until Arvay joined him in it." But later her mood darkens: "'Why, Mister Meserve!' Arvay flashed angry eyes up. . . . 'Telling that big old something-ain't-so, and on the Sabbath Day at that! . . . Nobody with any sense would put a bit of dependence in anything that you say. Always trying to make light of folks.' 'You mean that you didn't see the joke in that tale, Miss Arvay?' Jim asked. 'Oh, so that was supposed to be a joke? I don't favor so many jokes, Mister Meserve. I don't like to be took for a fool. I admire for folks to talk plain and say just what they mean'" (24–25). This passage proves crucial for understanding the rest of the book. Arvay refuses to enter into a joking relationship, a necessary component of both courtship and marriage according to Hurston. Her wounded sense of self cannot imagine a joke that doesn't "hurt," thus aligning her with those who insist on misreading Freud and labeling all humor aggressive.

Arvay cannot appreciate anything that is double coded, and this helps explain why Jim is sympathetic to and sympatico with the blacks in the book, while Arvay often stands aloof.

This scene provides a paradigm of Arvay's mental problems and the tangled relation she shares with Jim. As Freud asserted, a person with low self-regard might not get an ego boost from falling in love, for "a person in love is humble. A person who loves has, so to speak, forfeited a part of his narcissism, and it can only be replaced by his being loved" ("Narcissism" 550). Although we understand Jim loves Arvay, she can't understand how he could love such a worthless person as she. At low moments, she withdraws her love. Freud observes, "When libido is repressed . . . the satisfaction of love is impossible, and the re-enrichment of the ego can be effected only by a withdrawal of libido from its objects" (560–61). This may be traced back, of course, to the pattern of rejection she experienced in her youth within her family and in the town, but more importantly, to the "death" of Carl in his marriage to Larraine and Arvay's self-imposed period of "mourning" and withdrawal of five years. In this she resembles the classic pattern of melancholia, and again Freud helps us: "The melancholic displays . . . an extraordinary diminution in his self-regard, an impoverishment of his ego on a grand scale. The patient represents his ego to us as worthless, incapable of any achievement and morally despicable; he reproaches himself, vilifies himself and expects to be cast out and punished. He abases himself before everyone and commiserates with his own relatives for being connected with anyone so unworthy. . . . This picture of a delusion (mainly moral) inferiority is completed by sleeplessness and refusal to take nourishment" ("Mourning" 246).

Hurston follows this weighty moment, however, with a comic scene. Hurston's inventory of the Hensons' living room through Jim's eyes provides a detailed satire of lower-class vulgarity, equivalent in effect to Huck Finn's surveyal of the Grangerford parlor. In addition to skewering Cracker taste, Hurston satirizes the pious myths of the lost cause and the church values that parallel it. We see a picture of

> some artist's concept of General Robert E. Lee at Manassas. . . . Though the enemy was always right up under the feet of the general's horse, he assumed that the men he led could not see them. Generals always pointed either their swords or their fingers to show his men the enemy. . . . Peter was there in his unfortunate attempt to walk the waters like Christ. Acknowledging his lack of faith and his failure, he was pictured as squatting on the surface of the water, looking up guiltily into the face of his Master. . . . It struck Jim that if Peter could squat

like that without sinking, he could walk, and he started to comment on it, but remembered and held his peace. (27)[7]

Jim's sardonic mental puncturing of the Hensons' pretensions finds an immediate parallel in his loaded question for Arvay: why did Larraine marry Carl? "'I just had the notion that your sister wasn't so full of religion as all that, and neither your pastor, so far as that is concerned. He looks like nothing but a big old humbug to me, and I wondered how she happened to get took in by something like that'" (28). This comic bull's-eye skewers Larraine and Carl, but also, unknown to Jim, Arvay (thus creating some author/reader irony). This joke, in fact, snowballs, for it causes one of Arvay's famous "fits," from which Jim rouses her by a judicious oral application of turpentine, some of which he spills into her eye, causing her to drop her faked pose and to rage around the room. Brock's delighted response hardly helps: "'Quickest cure for spasm-fits I ever did see. Yessiree!'" and Arvay screams, "'You long-legged scoundrel-beast, you! You and your no-count jokes. I got a good notion to take me a gun and kill you! . . . Pouring teppentime in my eye for a joke. Git! Light a shuck offen this place!'" (30).

This seemingly minor incident and the name of the central figure, Jim Meserve, apparently come from Eatonville lore, for in sketch two of "The Eatonville Anthology," "Turpentine Love," Jim Merchant stays in good humor, "even with his wife" (implying he has reason not to be). Though Mrs. Merchant "has had all her teeth pulled out . . . they still get along splendidly" (178). Like Jim, Merchant fell in love at first sight and didn't give up on his beloved even though she had several fits in his presence. One Sunday, the most appropriate day for a miracle, his unnamed intended again has a fit in front of him. Her mother gives her a dose of turpentine to stop it and accidentally spills it in her eye and "cures" her of fits for life. Although some might seize on this to say this proves the Meserves really are black characters in whiteface, a charge I hope I have disproved, it does indeed demonstrate that even in a book about white characters, Hurston was once again recycling and rethinking human stories in her past that had significance beyond their mere details. We are especially struck by the ending of the sketch: "She never had another fit, so they got married and have kept each other in *good humor,* ever since" (178; my emphasis).

Hurston's refiguration of this ten-line sketch reveals much. The text suggests Jim's spill was no accident, that he purposefully seeks to remove what has been until now Arvay's last and best stratagem for repelling suitors, a claim of being "tetched" or "marked." Hurston here replicates a device from a fairy tale, like that in Puccini's *Turandot,* which was based on a Chinese fairy tale set by Gozzi (Kobbe 1200). A cruel Princess Turandot kills those who love her. At the cost of his life, the prince must guess the princess's name, a test, akin to a riddle, of love, persistence, and worth.

Hurston's revision of her own fairy tale, in fact, exactly replicates the device Stephen Sondheim and James Lapine employ in their brilliant musical *Into the Woods.* In the first act they conflate the stories of three traditional fairy tales; they are played with plenty of contemporary laughs thrown in, but conclude traditionally. The second act, however, shows they didn't live happily ever after, as tragedy strikes all three sets of characters; the survivors have to cross the lines of the stories and help each other, binding together to form a new, surrogate family.

Similarly, in Hurston's conceit, Arvay, like Cinderella, finds her handsome prince, who whisks her away from her unhappy home (replete with a wicked sister) and installs her in what eventually is described as a veritable central Florida "castle." Like the characters in Sondheim's second act, however, she too isn't "out of the woods," here the swamp of her unconscious. Most of *Seraph,* accordingly, details why they don't live "happily ever after," or tellingly, like the Merchants, "in good humor" ever after. The difference in these two phrases tells us much about Hurston's formula for personal and marital bliss; without humor, one can have neither. We finally get a happy—or should we say "good humored"?—ending here, but only after the central characters have struggled with internal problems for years.

Although Arvay misses the point of jokes, Jim's humorous folk-inspired declaration of love impresses her: "'Fact is, I'd rather all the rest of the women in the world to be dead than for you to even have the toothache'" (31). But in one of her emotional flip-flops that often keep the reader from developing real rapport with her, Arvay the melancholic now feels guilty—unworthy of Jim because of mental adultery with Carl. Her reading of his attitude, however, does not necessarily represent what he or Hurston think about the situation:

> He had just as good as excused the woman he married from all worry and bother. In so many words he had said, "Love and marry me and sleep with me. That is all I need you for. Your brains are not sufficient to help me with my work; you can't think with me. Let's get this thing straight in the beginning. Putting your head on the same pillow with mine is not the same thing as mingling your brains with mine anymore than crying when I cry is giving you the power to feel my sorrow. You

can feel my sympathy but not my sorrow." . . . Being of high family, and having more book learning than she had, and being all that handsome, he could be as choosey as he pleased. (33)

This important passage tells us almost clinically the origins of Arvay's psychological problems. She "reads" Jim stereotypically, assigns motives accordingly, and damns herself as being both unworthy of his presumed expectations of a wife but also of his "class's" traditional standards, largely because she couldn't get the joke in his proposal. Her alternating rage at not being worthy—much of it self-directed, but expressed against Jim—and abject humility at being accepted nonetheless, reminds us in some ways of the relation of Lucy and John in *Jonah*, where class roles were reversed.

Moments of humility always cause Arvay to eventually sign forgiveness; at this point, she takes Jim to her sacred place, the mulberry tree: "She wanted Carl and all her thoughts about him to be gone from under that mulberry tree. She wanted to feel that the temple was cleansed, and that she herself was clean and worthy of what she was about to receive" (34). The bell-like enclosure, so clearly female, has found its "clapper," which will soon cause Arvay and her "temple" to reverberate with life.

Readers of *Their Eyes* will recognize yet another tree symbol, and there is reason to believe that Hurston was once again utilizing the lore of *The Golden Bough*. We saw how Tea Cake and Janie are related to the Grove at Nemi. The same volume of Frazer contains a reference to the only classical source that suggests Arvay's name (203). The Arval brothers were priests of a fertility goddess who met in a grove. They performed expiatory sacrifices there if any bough had been damaged or any labor had been done inside it. They also had to offer solemn vows on behalf of the Imperial House on Janus's holy days of January 1 and 3 (Seyffert, Nettleship, and Sandys 74), dates, as we have seen, "sacred" to Hurston as well.

Language, Class, and Sass

Any consideration of the charge that *Seraph* puts white masks on black characters must confront the language of the book, which several critics claim is not that of poor white Floridians. The complexity of this issue deepens when one factors in the racist nature of early scholarship devoted to the origins of black speech. In the 1930s and 1940s, eminent linguists—chief among them, George Krapp—mounted the argument that black rural speech was in fact language that originated with poor whites; blacks, however, unlike that group, had failed to "progress," so that differences between the speech patterns of poor whites and blacks were actually evidence of "white archaic" speech predominating in the black community. Obviously, this has much in common with the school of social thought that viewed overall black culture as a shabby copy of white culture, rather than something distinct, with a cultural ambiance all its own. More recently, however, Joey Lee Dillard has demonstrated the very significant effect black dialect has had on white southern speech for more than three centuries and lists the considerable scholarship that has always documented it.[8] As he points out, even the habit racist white southerners have of parodying black dialect shows their familiarity with it (215).

In any case, as in her prior works, Hurston attempts to dramatize the issues that concern her here through folk speech, which sometimes may be earmarked "Cracker" and at other times "black." Both modes are warmed by idiom, folk expression, embedded narrative, animal imagery, repetition, rhythm, and dialect. The use of free indirect discourse by the narrator to tell us Arvay's thoughts frequently becomes "speakerly" of the culture too; Arvay, for instance, on her first trip back to her humble hometown asks herself, "'What awful gang of Crackers is that?'" before realizing they're her relatives. The authorial voice continues, "Common in the flesh and common in what they had on . . . so common-cladded, and their poor-looking skins, and unbred feet and legs, and the whole make of them . . . it made her feel to be cruel" (118). The irregular syntax and odd modifiers used here and elsewhere resemble that of the Cracker characters Marjorie Kinnan Rawlings immortalized. At many other times, however, the Hensons do sound like Hurston's other characters. Those who expect these characters to speak in a radically different way from John Buddy, Lucy, Janie, Tea Cake, Moses, and Jethro will be surprised, for in many ways their speech is similar.

Hazel Carby, in her thoughtful but uncharacteristically tentative introduction warns readers that Hurston, who has been lauded by many critics for preserving the black linguistic heritage in her works, actually went on record when writing about *Seraph* that there was no such thing as "Negro dialect in the South." Hurston indeed went on to say that southern speech contains relics of old English folk speech, which is rich in simile and metaphor, that black and white both talk for talk's sake, and that white southern orators excel. Furthermore, these orators "did *not* get it from the Negroes. The Africans coming to America got it from them. If it were African, then why is it not in evidence among all Negroes in the western world? No, the agrarian system stabilized in the South by slavery slowed down change . . . and so the tendency to colorful language that characterized Shakespeare and his contemporaries and made possible the beautiful and poetic language of the King James Bible got left over to an extent in the rural South" (viii–ix). Obviously, Carby disagrees with this assertion, but she fails to mention that Hurston was actually merely endorsing what was overwhelmingly accepted as fact at this time by linguists and folklorists.

Carby also claims that whole phrases are "lifted from the mouth of a black character in an earlier novel and inserted into the mouth of a member of the white Meserve family. The rhythm and syntax of Hurston's black folk haunt the reader throughout the novel" (ix). Although she never says so, the trope of words lifted from black mouths and inserted into white ones clearly suggests that Carby feels Hurston has merely switched the skin colors of her characters, maintaining the same voices.

However, as work such as Dillard's demonstrates, many of the expressions that the white characters use here actually were common parlance for both poor whites and blacks of the period. Which group generated them first or not is quite another question. Indeed, if one grants areas of linguistic congruence to the two groups, it quickly becomes obvious that the paucity of linguistic evidence from these largely illiterate communities of discourse makes it impossible to decide which group originated which word or phrase or to claim that any one version of "pure" speech indeed exists. Nothing in the United States is "pure," and the idea that there has been some magic wall of separation between the linguistic systems of black and white southerners simply cannot be supported.

On the other hand, certain expressions that have a specifically black frame of reference certainly can and should be earmarked as unique to that group. The idioms and expressions of *Seraph*, however, by and large are not of that type. I would argue, in fact, that although readers of Hurston's other books (particularly nonsoutherners, black or white) who have not studied the language of the American South of the period the way Hurston did might very well feel that she has simply replicated black speech in white mouths. Hurston in fact had done quite a bit of research into the materials that became *Seraph*. We know quite a bit about her work collecting black folklore in the twenties and early thirties for what became *Mules and Men*, and still later, the Haitian and Jamaican research that resulted in *Tell My Horse*. Hurston similarly spent eighteen months as an editor for the Florida Federal Writers' Project, joining the team on April 25, 1938; in the following months she learned a great deal about poor backwoods white Floridians. Finally, and conclusively, Hurston wrote Marjorie Kinnan Rawlings in December 1948:

> About the idiom of the book, I too thought that when I went out to dwell among the poor white in Dixie County that they were copying us. But I found their colorful speech so general that I began to see that it belonged to them. After my fit of jealousy was cooled off, I realized that Negroes introduced into N. America spoke *no* English at all, and learned from the whites. Our sense of rhythm points it up a bit, but the expressions for the most part are English held over from the Colonial period. I began to read English literature and found much of the picture talk in there. The black face minstrels of the past sold America on the notion that all colorful idioms originated with Negroes. Just stand around where poor whites work, or around the village stores of Saturday nights and listen and you will hear something.[9]

This letter confirms that Hurston had made a study of poor white speech and echoes the statement Carby cites. Although it contains mistaken ideas, they were shared by most linguists of the time.

In a scene destined to receive much attention from readers, Arvay takes Jim inside her sacred tree and tells him how she used to "pretend": "'And that's when I found out that Heaven was so far off. . . . I looked and I looked as hard as I could through the top of the tree, and I never could make out a thing. No angels moving around or nothing. I never could see a thing, so I knowed that Heaven was further away than folks made out it was'" (45). Swinging on the lower limbs, her skirt lifts and reveals her legs, and Jim seizes her and bears her to the ground, tearing at her tight-legged drawers. The text reads, "Arvay opened her mouth to scream, but no sound emerged. Her mouth was closed by Jim's passionate kisses, and in a moment more, despite her struggles, Arvay knew a pain remorseless sweet." Her first thought afterward, however, is not that she has been raped, but rather "taken for a fool," an object for cruel joking. Jim's assertions of love, however, reassure her, "Some unknown power" causes her to press herself "tightly against [him]. . . . A terrible fear came over her that he might somehow vanish away from her arms, and she sought to hold him by the tightness of her embrace and her flood of kisses." She thus initiates another sexual embrace, but "even then she was not satisfied" (47).

The text seems clear enough that the desire is mutual, but readers could well still see this as a rape largely because of Jim's adolescently crude analysis of the tenderness that has passed; however, Arvay herself inspires his rhetoric. As he whips the buggy team toward town and a precipitous marriage, he laughs at the irony of the situation. "'Arvay Henson! . . . The apostle to the heathens!' Then he chuckled some more. Arvay looked at him with quickly troubled eyes. Look like Jim was making fun of her. Something closed up inside of her'" (50). This section crucially underlines Arvay's psychological problem. Morbidly aware of her unworthy status as a Cracker, guilty of lusting after her sister's husband, afraid of being an object of ridicule, and thus largely devoid of a sense of humor, she reads all humor as suspect, aggressive, and threatening; interpreting it in this pseudo-Freudian way causes her to be "Freudianly" troubled throughout the book. We should remember, however, that Jim's parallel inability to express his emotions verbally lies behind their failure to communicate fully, except through their bodies. But even this mode fails them at times.

Arvay's chronic "closing up inside" shuts off Jim, her children, other people, and her own better self, and her inability to appreciate humor plays a central part in the procedure. Hurston underlines this by setting her up as an innocent "straight (wo)man" to Joe's comedic role.

> "No need for you to go proaging clean around the world no more looking for no heathens to save, though."
> "Why, Jim? Is they all done saved or died off?"
> "Naw, indeed. . . . But their case don't come up in your court no more." . . .
> So after what went on under the mulberry tree, Jim figgers that I ain't fitten no more to tote the Word, Arvay thought. . . .
> "You're married, Arvay. Under that mulberry tree."
> "All I know is that I been raped."
> "You sure was, and the job was done up brown. . . . You're going to keep on getting raped. . . . No more missionarying around for you. You done caught your heathen, baby. You got one all by yourself. And I'm here to tell you that you done brought him through religion and absolutely converted his soul. He been hanging around the mourner's bench for quite some time, but you done brought him through religion, and saved him from a burning shell. You are a wonderful woman, Arvay." (51)

Clearly, this speech offends many contemporary readers for obvious reasons. We must keep in mind the details of the scene and the fact that Arvay calls it rape only after she decides Jim will think her cheap and abandon her if he thinks he has satisfied her desire. Jim deflects her charge by accepting it as a joke, exaggerating it, and making it a prelude to a declaration of total love and devotion, as he beats the horses to get them to town for a sudden elopement. The references to a missionary Arvay "bringing through" a heathen to religion provides further comic ornamentation, but also offers a guilt-ridden Arvay an out. Jim obviously thinks he's pulled Arvay off a preposterous, pompous, and self-damaging throne of religious hypocrisy, that he has in effect "brought her through" and "saved her."

Those who still read Jim's actions as a rape might consider the following passage from the novel's manuscript that Hurston struck: "As the triumphat [*sic*] Arvay came down the steps of the old red brick courthouse holding on to Jim's arm, she had a wild impulse. She felt to go back home and take those torn drawers and nail them to a flagpole and let them wave from the courhouse [*sic*] dome. Under their sign she had conquered! But, no, she reckoned that would look too brazen. She would take them with the rumpled blue dress and fold them away for remembrance" (70). This is hardly the expression of a rape victim. Furthermore, the passage may be read as an explanation of why Arvay has no sense of humor. As she sees it, the nexus of humor/power/sex can only act against her. Their ensuing love and marriage certainly argue against a simplistic presentist equation with date rape.

Hurston makes exaggerated and comic use of rape later in the narrative, when Arvay overhears her lovestruck daughter in conversation with her beau, Hatton; the latter says, "'Angie! Do that again, and so help me, I'll rape you!'" to which she replies, to Arvay's horror, "'So rape me, and I'll help you!'" This leads Arvay to grab Jim's revolver and declare, stereotypically, "'I'll kill him dead and then stomp his head, the Yankee scamp, the dirty Carpetbagger! Done burnt out and robbed and murdered all over the South, and now come back to take the under-currents of my child!'" Jim comes in, however, and laughs at her. "'Nothing to laugh over, Jim Meserve. While you set here sniggling and giggling, that scamp is liable to be over there raping our child.' 'You mean our child is liable to be over there raping Hatton, don't you?' He laughed some more. 'If I know my daughter, this is one battle that the Yankees will never win'" (156). Nevertheless, he starts an investigation of Hatton's background.

Hurston's repetition and signification on the joking use of a very serious term, by two generations, demonstrates her interest in the comedic use of hyperbole in human relationships and the falsity of romantic language that this language of parody reveals. Arvay's association of rape with Yankees and lost cause mythology suggests Hurston's intent to signify on that as well, particularly on the foolish way stereotypes work and the danger they pose to actual situations.

On another level, the jokes about rape masking deeper feelings of true love speak as well to an impoverished set of linguistic options for men, who are taught to hide their emotional needs. As so often happens in Hurston, she resorts to comic folklore and expression to provide an oblique way of reading a sensitive situation.

The Souls and Roles of Black Folk

Arvay's young marriage becomes more viable and more accessible to us through the introduction of black characters and black life. One day, Jim hears somebody singing blues at a distance. Joe Kelsey, Jim's black friend, owns the voice—but the fact that a disembodied blues voice represents him initially makes him representative of black folk culture.[10] Hurston immediately links him with the comedic mode and in a nonstereotypical way:

> Joe Kelsey was a reddy brown Negro, ugly as sin, but with the best-looking smile that Jim had ever seen on a man. It always lit him right up. It always made Jim feel like playing and joking. Just seeing Joe put him into a playful mood and he decided at once to slip up on Joe and play some practical joke. . . . Jim got up close to Joe's back and made a sudden howl like an angry bob-cat on the kill. At the same time, he clawed his fingers and stuck them into Joe's broad back. Joe jumped around, pretending great fright. . . . Then they both broke into loud laughter. (39)

Here, as in the following exchange, Hurston has the men play with comic stereotypes, such as the fear of the supernatural that blacks supposedly have, but in virtually every case she explodes it and makes it clear that both men respect each other and are talking around traditional motifs. Jim tells Joe, "'It's Saturday nights that's your trouble Joe. Saturday pay-night, you spend all you got on likker and women. . . . Look like that's all you colored folks live for on this camp, Saturday night.'" Joe "scratched his head and seemed to reach a conclusion. 'I speck youse right about that Saturday night business, Mister Jim. Fact of the matter is, I knows youse dead right. But if you ever was to be a Negro just *one* Saturday night, you'd never want to be white no more'" (40). This exchange constitutes a variation on a classic joke (which African Americans still tell) to explode the stereotype that Jim has offered, and Jim's laughter at it indicates he knows it.[11]

As this scene prefigures, Joe, his wife, Dessie, and their family and friends over the years bring laughter, rich folk culture, and a sense of community to Jim and Arvay. Jim, and eventually Arvay as well,

find social fulfillment and companionship through their relationships with the Kelseys, especially through verbal joking and dueling and humor-infused gossip and tale-telling. Once the newlyweds
make their new home in a turpentine camp, for instance, Joe brings
black musicians to serenade the couple; Arvay responds with new
feelings toward the singers and nature itself as her soul seems to
flower. Humor sparks the scene; Jim, as usual, is unable to express
his own feelings and masks them with humor. The crowd outside
begins to jeer and scream with laughter, in typical shivaree fashion:
"'That'll do, Joe Kelsey,'" Jim cries, with pretend seriousness. "'You
done lied enough for one time. Here, take this jug of moonshine
and see that everybody gets some. Now, don't go on off and drink
it all up you ownself, you buzzard, you! You know I know you, Joe.'
There was loud laughter at this back-handed caress, and the crowd
hurried off to the Jook to have themselves a time'" (53–54). In this
passage and others, we suspect Joe and Arvay as well find vicarious
pleasure in black modes of expression they themselves are unable
to master. Indeed, Hurston seems to suggest, here and elsewhere,
that American men, operating in a homophobic, macho setting,
must use the same comic language of indirection that African
Americans must use, for different reasons.[12]

These earlier scenes also demonstrate subtleties of Jim's appreciation of black people and their culture. When he speaks to Arvay of
his trust in Joe and Dessie, "two nicest folks it has ever been my pleasure to meet," we notice he doesn't include the qualifier "colored"
to "folks." Hurston seizes the occasion to show us Arvay's feelings
toward blacks:

> Arvay was a daughter of the South. She knew exactly what to think from
> that. "Joe is your pet, I'll bound you."
>
> "Kee-reck! Different from every other Negro I ever did see. He's re-
> markable. Honest as the day is long. Just mighty damn fine, that's all."
>
> Arvay sympathized and understood. Every Southern white man has
> his pet Negro. His Negro is always fine, honest, faithful to him unto
> death, and most remarkable. Indeed, no other Negro on earth is fitten
> to hold him a light, and few white people. He never lies, and in fact
> can do no wrong. If he happens to do what other people might con-
> sider wrong, it is never his Negro's fault. He was pushed and shoved
> into it by some unworthy varmint. If he kills somebody else, the dead
> varmint took and run into the pet's knife or bullet and practically
> committed suicide just to put the pet in wrong, the low-life-ted scoun-
> drel-beast! If the white patron has his way, the pet will never serve a

day in jail for it. The utmost of his influence will be invoked to balk the law. Turn go *his* Negro from that jail! (55)[13]

This clever passage, rattling with obvious ironies, reiterates Hurston's 1942 *American Mercury* piece "The 'Pet Negro' System," a semicomic treatment of a serious subject that begins in mock biblical tone: "Brothers and Sisters, I take my text this morning from the Book of Dixie. I take my text and I take my time" (593). Mock-preaching as a southern insider to northern outsiders, she explains,

> The North has no interest in the particular Negro, but talks of justice for the whole. The South has no interest, and pretends none, in the mass of Negroes but is very much concerned about the individual. So that brings us to the pet Negro, because to me at least it symbolizes the web of feelings and mutual dependencies spun by generations and generations of living together and natural adjustment. It isn't half as pretty as the ideal adjustment of theorizers, but it's a lot more real and durable, and a lot of black folk, I'm afraid, find it mighty cozy. (594)

This qualifying last sentence should alert us to the fact that Hurston plays a doubled game here, and what follows soon confirms it. In a brilliant passage, Hurston talks about an outsider driving through a black southern neighborhood of well-kept homes and fine cars in amazement, for of course the Yankee expected shacks and misery. "But the other side is talked about by the champions of white supremacy, because it makes their stand, and their stated reasons for keeping the Negro down look a bit foolish. The Negro crusaders and their white adherents can't talk about it because it is obviously bad strategy. The worst aspects must be kept before the public to force action" (596). We might wince at this analysis, especially if we yield to the tendency to class it as another reflection of Hurston's notorious late-career "reactionism"; but Hurston cleverly puts liberals between a rock and a hard place, for if you object to her reasoning you are clearly in one of the two camps. Moreover, her point in the essay seems to be to display the error in always thinking of black people as victims, for this inevitably involves shrouding the race's glories and achievements.

Hurston protects herself, however; she's not here to "pass judgment": "I am not defending the system, belov-ed, but trying to explain it. . . . It works to prevent hasty explosions. . . . It may be the proof that this race situation in America is not entirely hopeless and may even be worked out eventually." And yet both sides, out of fear of the labels "white man's nigger" or "nigger lover," keep the thing secret.

Hurston ends the "sermon" with a moral, rounded off by a comic fillip: "In a way, it is a great and heartening tribute to human nature. It will be bound by nothing. . . . And no man shall seek to deprive a man of his Pet Negro. It shall be unwritten-lawful for any to seek to prevent him in his pleasure thereof. Thus spoke the Prophet of Dixie. *SELAH*" (600).

This essay can be read another way, as well, for if we examine the unstated but obvious role humor plays in this complex set of relationships, we may understand how Hurston uses it in *Seraph* and elsewhere. Positive forms of humor may only exist in privileged joking relationships, the kind permitted by the "pet" system. There are obvious human benefits here, but dangers as well, as Hurston acknowledges. Humor can mask the fact that things are not as they should be, and in fact, if we interpolate Hurston's statement that "pet systems" can prevent racial blow-ups into a statement about humor, we may see another danger of the system that Hurston ignores, at least here. Rose Coser has studied the humor of hospital patients, whose rage at the inhumanity of doctors, nurses, and their helpless condition in general generates "hospital humor." Although such joking clearly helps patients recover, avoids confrontations, and provides several other benefits, humor generated in this manner lances the boil of anger, a source of energy that if allowed to build momentum could erupt into a productive revolution against oppression. A patient can thus transform what would have been a complaint, such as "Dinner was no good, what I cook is better," to a joke, when in conversation with other patients: "Those hamburgers today were as hard as rocks, if I'd bounced them against the wall they'd come right back" (Coser 176). Order may be preserved, but injustice may be as well. We might reflect here how completely humorless most earnest revolutionaries in the early stages of virtually all great causes have been, for they correctly see humor as an impediment to the initial stages of revolt.[14]

Sometime later, Jim, seeking advancement and wishing to honor Arvay's request to leave Sawley, leaves the turpentine trade and moves the family to Citrabelle, where he struggles to break into the citrus industry. His rapport with the black workers, who teach him the trade, saves him: "He had taken up around the jooks and gathering places in Colored Town, and swapped stories, and stood treats, and eased in questions in desperate hope, wondering if his money would hold out until he could get a footing, and how he had finally gotten information which landed him his job" (66). As foreman, he hires the best cutters and gets the men working well, using the spirit of competition, decent wages, and a black performing/joking style that creates harmony: "They were the highest-paid men in that part of the state and getting known" (67). When Jim rewards his black crew with a lavish barbeque, they clean up his property while they're there. Hurston slyly underscores the fact that Jim's calculated kindness also costs possibly racist white merchants:

> Monday, downtown, the markets which usually got the colored trade were wondering what on earth had become of the colored folks. They had more than four hundred pounds of unsold meat on hand. His crew brought him many compliments and assured him that anytime he needed any further help, why all he needed to do was to let them know. He was a perfect gentleman, and they were only too glad to oblige him. It was the same every way he turned. Negroes whom he had never seen before were saying the same thing. Jim was laughing up his sleeve and wanted to take Arvay into the joke, then decided against it. (72–73)

Clearly, Jim has become a "pet" white, in an inversion of the system Hurston outlined in her article. Arvay, however, typically fails to see the inner workings of the arrangement and complains that the men who built their house for a reasonable fee have taken off all the scrap lumber she could have used for kindling. Jim responds, "'If I act like I don't notice it, I got a lot of willing friends, and nobody will ever steal a thing off this place. I got this house built way under the regular figure anyhow. All of 'em would feel hard towards me if I went around asking about those scraps of wood. Leave it be'" (73). Obviously blind to the contributions of Jim's friends, she knows nothing about his doings either, "his twisting and turning and conniving to make life pleasant for her sake" (74). This section points in several ways to the way humor can bridge gaps, create goodwill, and ease racial relationships. By making Jim's performing style specifically black, Hurston indicates whites can learn from her people, and that this in turn can turn economic profits for all concerned.

Biblical Jokes/Biblical Nightmares

Hurston's biblical imagination had turned out to be vital for her art, just as it had always been for the community that inspired her. Clearly, she saw biblical myth as central for the Cracker community as well, but in a more limited and ominous way. Arvay's deep religiosity, inherited from her mother, leans toward a terror-ridden biblical hermeneutic; she tends to think typologically. We should not lose sight of the fact here that Arvay's melancholia, as was true of many great writers of the renaissance and beyond, often inspires fantastic scenarios in her mind, albeit ones that have no artistic sequel, and these imagined scenes of doom and sin often have their base in the images of Revelation. Jim, by contrast, obviously more in line with Hurston's skepticism and irreverence, brims over with humorous interpretive insight. His apparent blasphemy frightens Arvay, so religion becomes yet another area of comic disjuncture for her and Jim, but one with tragic consequences.

For instance, one would think that Arvay would be happy about her pregnancy, but the family still lives in Sawley at that point. Her jealousy of Larraine's excessive attention to Jim and her fear that Larraine will tell him of her former love for Carl cause her to dream of seeing Larraine's neck cut; the knife appears in her own hands. Fearing her Cain-like hidden rages, she vainly begs Jim to take her away.

She has the superstitious backwoods habit of letting the Bible fall open on its own as a sort of divine message each night. When it opens to the killing of Abel by Cain, Arvay becomes horrified. Jim comments pungently,

> "I don't blame God. . . . I'd turn against a man that didn't have no better sense than to burn a stinking cabbage right under my nose. . . . Cain's first crime was not killing his brother Abel, but in not having no sense of humor. The man was so chuckle-headed that he couldn't even take a joke. . . . Common sense ought to have told him God wouldn't stand for him stinking up Heaven and all like that. How come he couldn't have made God a nice cool salad and took it to Him? That would have been something out of his garden too, wouldn't it? Tell me!"

An outraged Arvay thinks Jim is "crazy or awful wicked one, to be looking for jokes in the Bible" and doesn't listen as he sagely remarks, "'Well, if it's about the doings of people, it must be plenty jokes in there'" (59). Arvay's horror at the intrusion of this passage stems, at least unconsciously, from her nocturnal dreams of Larraine's death. We readers, however, notice the more important and accompanying idea of the saving grace of a sense of humor and Jim's valuable ability to read humorous—and therefore deeper—meanings in the holy writ. For Arvay, however, the idea of dealing with such horrific personal matters with humor is inconceivable.

On another level, Hurston seems to be rehearsing in this bedtime quarrel the issues she had to face in writing *Moses* and her own comic stance, which Jim clearly sanctions. "The sacred quality of the Bible, sinner-people who could make mock of holy things. Folks given to jokes and the dumbness of those who couldn't see a joke, and on and on. Jim was not really annoyed at first, he just enjoyed teasing Arvay, but Arvay went further than Jim thought necessary, and he stung her somewhat with ridicule" (59). The pattern of the marriage is set; Jim, a habitual joker who salts his every expression with humor, feels condemned by Arvay as a "sinner and a scoffer," while Arvay "found out that Jim thought her a trifle dumb" (60). She refuses to associate humor in any form with the Bible and thus proves the point about revolutionaries, another kind of "true believer." Humor thus signals opposite things to both Arvay and Jim and plays havoc with their marriage. Arvay's inability to create intimacy or accept it through humor tragically connects to her association of it with her sense of the sacral, class ridicule, and her melancholic self-hatred; her sense of social inferiority becomes heightened by reading attempts to bridge gaps on Jim's part by humor as superior put-downs. The argument over the Bible significantly takes place in bed and ultimately affects the couple's sex life. A vicious circle solidifies around them.

Jim's teasing of Arvay should not pass unnoticed. Psychologists have noted the frequent inability of American men, particularly those living in rural settings, to articulate their more tender feelings. Such men use practical jokes, roughhousing, and general forms of teasing to hide the supposedly "feminine" side that emotions represent (Sperling 472). Other southern writers, including Marjorie Kinnan Rawlings, emphasize this quality in many male characters. Frequently these forbidden emotions find an outlet in teasing. Earlier scenes demonstrate how Jim's obvious concern for and love of Arvay often finds inadequate, even chauvinistic expression that is at odds with his actual behavior. The whole syndrome of teasing proves crucial, however, to his interaction with Arvay, for although we see this as a desperate bridge thrown across to her, part of his male world, Arvay has had little positive experience with this type of discourse but even less communication with male forms of linguistic intimacy (she has no brothers). She tends to interpret teasing encounters with aggression and as signs of her unworthiness to join whatever group is represented.

The subtle links between verbal teasing and patterns of withdrawal and rejection provide some insight here. The parent who teases excessively, in patterns associated with giving and withdrawing, accepting and rejecting, encouraging and thwarting, can psychically damage a child. When such a child grows up without the ability to engage in successful bantering and humorous social exchanges which constitute responses to teasing, that adult frequently becomes embarrassed in social situations and has difficulty reading the degree and type of teasing, which can vary considerably from sadism to loving play (Sperling 458–62). Moreover, the insecurity about responses to teasing may be magnified when coupled with perceptions of class inferiority, as with Arvay. We notice her vacillation between loving attentiveness and withdrawal in her responses to Jim, thereby setting up a mirror image of her rejection and establishing another vicious circle in the marriage.

Class distinctions again emerge when Arvay, pregnant, develops "strange moods and appetites. A great craving for meat, and for . . . that fine, cream-colored clay which she had seen her mother eating all her life" (58). Her behavior introduces a class barrier between her and the horrified Jim, who nevertheless expresses it in folk humor reminiscent of Big Sweet in *Mules and Men,* which has a biblical edge to it: "He had better not find any more of the goddamned filthy, dirty stuff around the place. If he did, he was going around the ham-bone looking for meat! That was *the word* with the bark on it" (58; my emphasis). Although the reader presumably shares Jim's horror, this scene shows him incapable of accepting class differences.

Soon afterward, when Jim moves the family to Citrabelle, "a bright-looking flowery town on the Florida ridge south of Polk County," Arvay's Puritan values again rear their ugly head, and the narrator's free indirect commentary on Arvay's thoughts has a sharply sarcastic edge: "Things had a picknicky, pleasury look that, while it was pretty, made Arvay wonder if folks were not taking things too easy down in here. Heaven wasn't going to be any refreshment to folks if they got along with no more trouble than this. As far as she could see, the place was plumb given over to pleasure. . . . It was the duty of man to suffer in this world, and these people round down here in south Florida were plainly shirking their duty" (64). The passage proves doubly ironic, for following it we learn Jim is going through a struggle for their very existence. "She did not know about those terrible three weeks when Jim, knowing nothing about citrus-fruit production, had stood around with his hands in his pockets feeling and turning over the little money he had, and casting about for some way to get into the work" (65). But Jim's attitude here might be read as patriarchal in that he wants to keep her in "domestic Heaven" while he works "outside the gates." But hiding his plight from her, while ostensibly kind, also creates false images and weakens the marriage.

Hagar Henson and Hagar Hurston

That scene of both refuge and horror so frequently found in the slave narrative, the swamp, intrudes when Jim buys property near one. Arvay's fear of it clearly links it with her murky unconscious. Her fear of her son getting lost in it evokes an "ugly" and revealing guffaw from the boy's father: "'Earl?' . . . Jim laughed harshly. 'That scary thing ain't apt to stray nowhere at all. If that's all you got to worry about, you can put your mind at rest. He's scared to death of even a baby chick, and then he ain't all that active'" (71). This apparently meaningless exchange sets up Arvay's greatest test, the death of her deformed, retarded son Earl in the swamp years later, after he attacks a young Portuguese girl, fulfilling his typological position as Ishmael, the "wild man; his hand will be against every man, and every man's hand against him" (Gen. 16:12).

This similarly sets up Arvay to be Hagar, a figure of special significance in African American culture. Hagar is the archetypal strong black mother who struggles heroically to survive the patriarchal and tribal rejection of her and her son in one of several biblical myths supposedly explaining the existence of the black race. Hurston had recorded many stories and expressions during her folklore collecting days about the tendencies of "Aunt Hagar's children" and obviously was intrigued by these tales. Interestingly enough, the name means "wandering," a term Hurston circles back to again and again in both her fiction and her autobiography.[15]

Arvay constantly thinks of herself as a Hagar figure, and not just in connection with Earl. Born deformed, he looks like Arvay's Uncle Chester, her mother's "queer in the head" brother. But when the tiny mouth goes for her breast, "Arvay had to laugh at his eagerness." His defects increase her love and her pity. She shuts herself up with the baby so no one can hear her tell him "'Mam is going to love you, don't care who else don't care. . . . This is the punishment for the way I used to be. . . . It must be the chastisement I been looking for. You're Mama's precious honey'" (62). This scene clearly demonstrates both Arvay's negative self-image and the way in which Earl tends to prolong rather than cure it. As Kathryn Rabuzzi notes, some mothers may find that a child may seem more like an amputation than a gain (56), and Arvay goes further; this child constitutes her punishment.

And in fact, Earl's entry into the novel sets up a lengthy pattern of allegory. Years later, pregnant with her third child, Arvay takes one of Jim's jokes seriously when he pretends he doesn't want another daughter (echoing the actual sentiments of Hurston's father when *she* was born). "Arvay crept into the Bible and pulled down the lid. She made herself into parables and identified herself with Hannah before the conception of Samuel, and with Hagar, driven out into the desert by Abraham, and other sorrowful women. All day long during the hours that Jim was absent, Arvay went around muttering prayers for deliverance from her fancied danger" (87–88). A sexual and typological joke gets embedded here; Arvay's reaction and dreadful speculations find expression in Hagar and Hannah. Hagar was cast out; Hannah, however, although beloved by her husband, was barren, for "the Lord had shut up her womb" (1 Sam. 5). Arvay's fear of losing Jim, all through the book, causes her to withdraw within herself; as Janie said about her relationship to Jody, "She wasn't petal-open anymore with him" (*Eyes* 111), and Janie, we remember, was barren.

Arvay's identification with Hagar offers a key to the novel, for it suggests an abandonment of a dutiful wife because of class differences and because her son, like her, merits rejection. Earl clearly represents Ishmael; although he doesn't live to father a nation, he signifies the darker side of Arvay that lives on until her reconciliation with Jim. Hurston always links Earl to Arvay's side of the family, never to Jim's, and Arvay repeatedly feels that the Meserves never stop thinking of her as a despised, Cracker "Henson." Earl develops into the physical projection of her own repressed "Other" into the world, the physical manifestation of her "sin" of loving her sister's husband.

St. Paul gave an allegorical, New Testament exegesis of Hagar's myth: "Nevertheless what saith the scripture? Cast out the bondwoman and her son: for the son of the bondwoman shall not be heir with the son of the freewoman" (Gal. 4:30). The two women represent the two Arvays—the cowering, asocial misfit and the vibrant "free woman" who comes to the fore intermittently, but most prominently in the last pages. In this way, Earl as a sign of the "bondwoman" resembles Hester's daughter Pearl (in fact, his name is embedded in hers) in *The Scarlet Letter.* Arvay, however, calls out and finds comfort, eventually, from the angel within; her marriage, in fact, seems secure once she gives birth to an angel (Angeline). Thus the title *Seraph on the Suwanee* could refer not to Arvay or Jim but to the rebirth of Arvay (a multistage development), when she lets her better side conquer her dark id. This rebirth becomes symbolized through laughter, which transforms her, finally, into a different biblical character.

Sarah, Abraham's wife, is barren, so God tells her to let Abraham cohabit with her servant Hagar. In ancient society, a woman who elected this option would have the servant give birth between her knees, thereby transferring maternity to her. After Hagar gives birth to Ishmael, however, God works a miracle and the ancient Sarah conceives, causing her to laugh. Subsequent to the birth of her son Isaac, her jealousy causes her to demand Hagar and Ishmael's ouster from the household. Sarah and Hagar, however, are both progenitors of nations (Jews and Arabs, respectively), whose progeny become the "chosen people" of competing religions. Sarah's identity as the ancestor of the favored group and her late conception/laughter indicate a final wholeness that ancient societies assumed a barren woman lacked.

Arvay seeks this kind of wholeness throughout the novel, searching desperately for what Sarah finds she had all along. Although Arvay isn't barren like Sarah she is estranged from her husband and resents her two normal children. To her Earl is a part of herself, a part that if she accepts she can become whole, for his deformity seems a projection of her inner torment. Hurston signals his symbolic importance to the book by inserting one of only two dates in the novel; Arvay significantly records the birth of Earl David Meserve, "*July 26th, 1906*" (63). Earl is not Isaac, however, and instead fulfills the Bible's prophecy of Ishmael's wildness when he attempts to kill both his mother and father. He is finally slain by a vigilante posse that includes his father. Like Ishmael, his "mockery" of social decorum and law (the attempted rape of Lucy Ann Corregio) dictates his removal, and he finds shelter in the wilderness (the swamp) to which the patriarchs drive him.

The pain Arvay feels during Earl's infancy isn't assuaged when she gives birth to a healthy girl, since it's not the boy Jim wanted, and to her, Angeline resembles Larraine, a revealing perception that should signal to us the way Arvay will see her own daughter as a rival for her husband's affection. This idea expands in a different direction when Jim snorts scornfully, "'In the pig's eye! My child don't look like Larraine. . . . She takes right after my mother, as you would know if you had ever seen her. I'm naming her Angeline, after my mother, too'" (75). Jim now becomes a doting father. Jim's preference for Angeline appears in the loving, joking tone he adopts toward her; this joking never characterizes his relationship with Earl. When he buys an engraved ring for baby Angeline, Arvay bitterly reflects, "There had been no little ring nor anything for poor Earl. Already, she could see the pattern opening out. Her own childhood all over again, with Angeline favored like Raine always had been, and she made ready to resist. The lines were drawn, and she had become a partisan" (77).

Even the infant Angeline, in fact, seems to have a more impish sense of humor than her mother, as a comic scene demonstrates. Partial to her father, Angeline cries when he's late returning home. "'Shut up!' Arvay scolded as she jerked the baby into her clothes. 'I'm the one that's doing for you, and you squalling after Jim. Hush!' Jim overheard her and flew into the room and snatched Angeline up in his arms. The little devil immediately behaved as if she had just been rescued from mortal danger. She snuggled her head up under Jim's chin and looked out at her mother in a most accusing way" (77). Instead of laughing, the way readers do, Arvay sees this as yet another sign of her insignificance. "'This is my first time to see a man cut the crazy over a child to that extent. Look like I done borned somebody to be over me in my own house. I don't count for nothing no more around here, I see'" (78).

We might sense a more complicated scenario, for Hurston obviously rehearses here her sibling rivalry with her sister Sarah, her father's favorite and firstborn daughter, but also the far more extensive pattern of rejection that seemed in many ways to dog Hurston throughout her life. Earl, Arvay's child, withdrawn, inarticulate, deformed, pale, and humorless, in many ways functions as a projection of her unconscious; Angeline and Kenny, by contrast, become healthy, well-adjusted children who both have a strong sense of individual worth and integrity. They excel at joking and mischievous pranks, attributes easily traced to their fun-loving father. And in fact, the only other date inserted into the book is that of Angeline's birth, January 7, 1909. January 7 was the date Hurston always gave as her own birthdate, so she obviously sees Angie as a kindred spirit. Earl, coddled by Arvay, gets shuttled into a pattern of withdrawal and womblike existence. Juliet Mitchell, in *Psychoanalysis and Feminism,* points to the way early mother-child bonding creates a kind of nonsocial world for the child, which the father ruptures; he thus stands for society and culture. As Nancy Chodorow notes, however, the mother must "know when and how to begin to allow the child to differentiate from her. . . . She must guide her child's separation from her" (83). Arvay never initiates this with Earl, and indeed, seems to think it biblically right that the sins of the mother be visited upon the child.

Dust Tracks by the Suwanee?

Because *Seraph* seems to rehearse elements of Hurston's early familial life, a brief review of this pattern as it appears in *Dust Tracks* seems in order. When Zora was born, John Hurston reportedly threatened to cut his throat: "One girl was enough. . . . I don't think he ever got over the trick he felt that I played on him by getting born a girl. . . . He was nice about it in a way. He didn't tie me in a sack and drop me in the lake, as he probably felt like doing" (28). As the children aged, Sarah "had music lessons on the piano. It did not matter that she was not interested in music, it was part of his pride. . . . She had a gold ring for her finger, and gold earrings. When I begged for music lessons, I was told to dry up before he bust the hide on my back" (99).

The intensity and importance of her father's feelings is worth tracing in some detail, for obviously, she differs dramatically from Arvay in the way she handled rejection. Indeed, Hurston's sense of not belonging to her family was both exhilarating and depressing. Her sense of exceptionalism and unity with the cosmic gods contrasted with the bitter sense of her father's rejection and scorn. *Dust Tracks* recounts a dinner table scene before Christmas, where Zora's wish for a riding horse sparks an angry outburst from her father. He informs her she isn't white, that she's always "'trying to wear de big hat. . . . Don't know how you got in this family nohow. You ain't like none of de rest of my young 'uns'" (38).[16]

This animus gets manifested in other ways; Hurston refers to the way adults object to the disconcerting questions children formulate, as when they ask how adults know what they know: "There must be something wrong with a child that questions the gods of the pigeonholes. I was always asking and making myself a crow in a pigeon's nest" (33–34). Obviously, we may read this another way in light of her father's comments above, and still another when we factor in her relatively dark skin. Even her grandmother, clearly the model for the whiskered granny in "Drenched in Light," the "nicey-nasty" Emmeline Potts, and the more foreboding figure of Nanny in *Their Eyes,* seems to have rejected her: "Git down offa dat gate-post! You li'l sow. . . . They's gwine to lynch you, yet. . . . Youse too brazen to live long" (46). At school, too, Zora seems to have had enemies; when the teacher appears determined to whip her, snickers erupt; "The smart-aleck was going to get it" (49).

In Hurston's celebrated childhood "visions" of the future, she sees she will be alone and wander. "I studied people all around me, searching for someone to fend it off. But I was told inside myself that there was no one. It gave me a feeling of terrible aloneness. I stood in a world of vanished communion with my kind, which is worse than if it had never been. Nothing is so desolate as a place where life has been and gone. I stood on a soundless island in a tideless sea. Time was to prove the truth of my visions, for one by one they came to pass"

(59). Leaving Eatonville after her mother's funeral, she states, "I was on my way from the village, never to return to it as a real part of the town. Jacksonville made me know that I was a little colored girl. . . . Girls complained that they couldn't get a chance to talk without me turning up somewhere to be in the way. I broke up many good 'He said' conferences just by showing up" (94). Her heartfelt summary: "Just a jagged hole where my home used to be" (95). In fact, *Dust Tracks* indicates that Hurston never did find a "home" to replace that of her childhood.

Her father neglects to pay her boarding school bill, doesn't send for her at the end of the term, and eventually tells the school they can adopt her. Although her way home gets paid, Hurston claims her stepmother farms her out to relatives along with the other remaining children. Hurston's feared "vision" of being "homeless and uncared for" had come to pass: "I had always thought I would be in some lone, arctic wasteland with no one under the sound of my voice. I found the cold, the desolate solitude, and earless silences, but I discovered that all that geography was within me" (115).

How did Hurston handle all this rejection? Primarily through humor. Her ability to "talk that talk" and tell tales made her an ideal companion for white children, mitigating her definite lack of interest in household chores. After bouncing around for years, she finally landed a job with a traveling Gilbert and Sullivan troupe as a lady's maid.

"I was young and green, so the baritone started out teasing me the first day. I jumped up and told him to stop trying to run the hog over me! That set everybody off. They teased me all the time just to hear me talk. But there was no malice in it. If I got mad and spoke my piece, they liked it even better" (136). The pattern of rejection reappears here, too; her employer, Miss M., will play all manner of games with Zora for hours, but the next day will say hardly a word (140). Still, Zora gets along much better than an Arvay would in this and other joking situations because she counters her sense of rejection with an even stronger and creative sense of fun and self-worth, despite what the world dishes out. Significantly, she can stand, and even relish, teasing.

Nellie McKay has written on the autobiographical nature of *Their Eyes* and points to episodes in the novel that are similar to ones in *Dust Tracks* (68). This is a surface pattern in the life as lived, however, and Hurston's brilliant success along the lines McKay suggests also stems from a darker pattern of isolation centered on moments of rejection, intense rivalry with her sister, and the decision to challenge men for a literary place in the sun. Thus while I agree completely with McKay's astute analysis, *Seraph* provides an equally compelling case for the autobiographical nature of Hurston's work. This novel grows out of very different, and hidden, images of the self that we ordinarily don't associate with her.

Later in her life, once she had become a successful and ambitious writer, Hurston fell in love with "A.W.P." Jim Meserve may seem distasteful to contemporary women, but Hurston seems to have liked a man much like him just fine until he threatened her career. Consider her description of A.W.P, the "love of her life," in *Dust Tracks*, when he tells her, "'You've got a real man on your hands. You've got somebody to do for you. I'm tired of seeing you work so hard. I wouldn't want *my* wife to do anything but look after me. Be home looking like Skookums when I get there'"; she remarks, "With those words he endowed me with Radio City, the General Motors Corporation, the United States, Europe, Asia and some outlying continents. I had everything!" (255). Moreover, her fear of desertion causes her to live "in terrible fear lest women camp on his doorstep in droves and take him away from me" (256), an echo of Arvay's distrust of the Corregio women.

Robert Hemenway has read A.W.P. as a version of Arvay, for as Hurston says, he feels that he doesn't matter enough to her. A.W.P.'s contrasting self-confidence, however, and his lack of the melancholic's characteristics, coupled with Hurston's life-long fear of rejection makes this speculation seem rather dubious. The real parallel comes in her admission, "The terrible thing was that we could neither leave each other alone, nor compromise. . . . We were alternately the happiest people in the world, and the most miserable. I suddenly decided to go away to see if I could live without him. I did not even tell him that I was going. But I wired him from some town. . . . Six weeks later I was back in New York and just as much his slave as ever. Really, I never had occasion to doubt his sincerity, but I used to drag my heart over hot coals by supposing" (257–59). Thus the love affair that supposedly prompted the scenario for *Their Eyes* perhaps played a larger role in shaping *Seraph*, for Zora and A.W.P. epitomize Strindberg's version of Hell—a man and woman desperately unhappy together who are yet unable to part.

Another possible way to read this scenario lies in admitting that Hurston to a large degree accepted stereotyped gender roles. In her relationship with A.W.P. she had a "man's role" (a profession) but also wanted to be a "real woman." One reading of the Meserve marriage and its final apparent harmony at novel's end thus might be that only in fiction can Hurston play both roles and thus have her ideal romance.[17]

Although a careful reading of *Dust Tracks* thus suggests a pattern of rejection in Hurston's life, the clues sent out by this notoriously "frustrating" text come out in an intermittent and fragmentary way. But we find further evidence of rejection in Hurston's letters, particularly those sent to Langston Hughes and Carl Van Vechten. The notorious split with Hughes over their collaboration on *Mule Bone* has been well documented in the HarperCollins edition of the play. What that book doesn't include, however, are the tender, extravagantly worded letters that Hurston wrote to Hughes before the secretary/writer Louise Thompson came into the picture, with Hughes supposedly proposing that the duo become an artistic trio. When we remember the long trip across the South that he and Zora took together in the summer of 1927 and the extreme reaction Hurston had to Hughes' "betrayal," one has to suspect she loved Langston and resented Thompson, a sophisticated, lighter-skinned woman from Chicago, not so much as an artistic rival but as a threat to either a treasured and deep friendship or a budding romance or both. Thompson's "betrayal" likewise would have hurt, as she too had been a beloved friend and almost like a sister to Zora. Louise seemingly was playing a part in casting Zora into the wilderness, just as her own sister Sarah had.

Hurston also wrote adoring letters to Carl Van Vechten and she dedicated *Tell My Horse* to him. She most often addressed him as "Darling Carlo," and in 1937, and then again in 1943, she wrote him that she had no closer friend than he. Getting his permission to write his biography was a goal she pursued fruitlessly for years. Although Van Vechten certainly cared for her as well, he sometimes joked about her with Hughes, Fannie Hurst, and others behind her back (Kellner, *Letters* 186, 275). When she died in 1960 he hadn't been in touch with Zora for at least fifteen years.

One could even suspect that a short and passionate letter Hurston wrote to Van Vechten in 1944, seemingly at a low point in her life, became the controlling thematic of *Seraph:*

> What can I say to put form to my feelings? I have thought and thought. I love you very dearly. If in my struggle with life and the press of the moment, I seemed to be indifferent to you, it was less than a mist upon the surface of things. I have learned to know that the thing we call misunderstanding—that blind bumping of one vessel against the other as they grope for nearness, is the greatest tragedy of humanity. Of all animate life. This cosmic blindness that prevents even the very near

from being clearly seen. That is when it hurts most. One feels the futility of life when even those closest to one cannot be clearly seen.[18]

This poignant lament would seem to have relevance beyond her connection with Van Vechten, encompassing Hughes, Wallace Thurman, Alain Locke, Sterling Brown, and others. Throughout her life, people she cared for deeply—Fannie Hurst, Ethel Waters, Jane Belo, to name just three others—often criticized her, underestimated her, or just drifted away from her, for whatever reason, and although some were no doubt shocked to read about her "pauper's death" in 1960, she in fact had been forgotten by many of them for years at that point. Hurston devoted a whole chapter in her autobiography to Hurst and Waters; she isn't even mentioned in their life stories.

We of course prefer to think of Zora Neale Hurston as an exuberant, never-conquered, beloved, and joyous person, and in many ways she was, but her last published book suggests her moments "on the mountain" alternated with stretches of isolation, rejection, and despair. The nature of her writing, especially its humor, frequently masks this other aspect. Writing a "white novel" offered another kind of masking.

Versions of "Gendered" Humor

The Meserves' marital problems become underlined by Jim's increasing nights out, spent drinking and fighting, suggesting the toll on his soul that his frustrating link to a humorless and insecure woman exacts. Arvay, sensing a solution without seeing the obvious way she could contribute to it personally, has Jim send for Joe, knowing that the joking, tale–telling black buddy Jim loves will help right things. Once again, an impasse in this white marriage dissolves via an infusion of joking warmth from the black characters. But before Joe arrives, Jim gets in an epic fight called "the Battle of the Horse's Behind," a scene that reveals much about the role of humor in the book.

Hawley Pitts, the ugliest man in the county, envies Jim's good looks but cowardly finds satisfaction in teasing little Pearly Snead, whose wife left him for another man. "Hawley was too big for Pearly to fight to any advantage, and so he tried to make a laugh and leave the place, like he was humoring the joke. . . . Pearly wanted to fight. . . . But . . . it would not pay. . . . [He] tried to turn it off in a grin" (80). Jim, a joker who nevertheless eschews cruel humor, indirectly takes up for Pearly by attacking Hawley in a broadly comic *ad hominum* way, accusing him of "'offering Mrs. Meserve the dirtiest kind of a disrespect.

. . . She could come along and see you with a face like that. . . . Why, I'd just as soon for her to see you without your pants on as that face . . . that mouth of yours. . . . It's a horse's behind, and a female horse at that.' Spontaneous and raucous laughter broke out instantly. Even Pearly could take a part" (81). This corrective, courageous, democratizing humor obviously resembles the famous exchange between Janie and Joe Starks in *Their Eyes*, in its devastating exposure/ feminization of a bully, but also in its "capping" quality—no response except violence will do. Although Jim's comic taunts seem to merely precipitate violence, after the fight Jim toasts Hawley as "'a fair fighter and a true friend.' . . . Hawley swelled like a pouter pigeon. . . . He had room inside for a big gesture. So he reached and got Pearly and placed his big arm around the little man's shoulder. 'Say, Pearly, you being luckier than the rest of us, not having no old hen to bother with, how about us all going over to your house and finishing off this thing?'" (83). With everyone buoyed by this anti-woman humor, they do.

Typically, Arvay can't understand. Jim excuses it ethnically: "'Just put it down to me being a man and part Irish and let it go at that. You get so at times that you got to give vent to your muscles'" (84). The question of why one "gets so" receives no answer, but Jim's relief at finding a problem he can solve through humor and violence offers him a release from the domestic conundrum.

Appropriately, this scene's sequel concentrates on female humor and relationships. When Dessie arrives, Arvay feels "it was just as good as a visit to west Florida to hear Dessie talk. . . . Whose babies Dessie had caught, and who were supposed to be the fathers, but who they really favored, and so on and on as they set hens, being careful to put all the eggs but two of a setting in with the right hand to hatch out pullets and only two roosters to a batch" (85). Obviously, the women's activities as they talk constitute a doubled joke, duplicating as it does their subject and the men's preceding references to "hens." The humor doubles yet again when we learn of Arvay's pregnancy.

This happy news, however, provokes yet another quarrel with her intoxicated husband: "Jim was in a mood for wit and laughter, and Arvay's solemn eyes provoked him more. . . . Jim just could not resist pulling Arvay's leg a bit. So he stood straddled legged, put on a stern face and pontificated. 'I'm agreeable, providing you promise me one thing. . . . You can have that baby, providing that you swear and promise to bring it here a boy.'" He teases her, saying he never wanted any girls. "'Look how nice I acted when you up and had Angie on me. If I had of been cruel, I could of made you tie her up in a sack and chunk her into the lake, but I didn't do it'" (86). Arvay foolishly lies awake all night, trembling, victimizing herself because she fails to get the joke. By misreading his cues, Arvay increasingly thinks he doesn't love her. As readers, we know better—but we should remember how Jim's joking admonition echoes a profoundly serious one Hurston's father made to her mother before Zora's birth. By casting it in a comic light, Hurston rights the wrong done her.

Months later, Arvay finally tells Jim of the months of agony she has suffered fearing his desertion if she bears a girl; she in fact has prayed for a miscarriage. This prompts him to say he was joking.

> "A joke! A joke and here I been suffering all this time! Jim, I'm never going to forget you for this thing."
>
> Jim did not laugh it off . . . and apologized to Arvay most humbly. . . . "I thought that anybody at all would see through a joke like that. Anybody with even a teaspoonful of sense knows that you can't tell what a child'll turn out to be until it gets born. . . . I'd go to Hell for my daughter. . . . I'd be bound to love any child that you had for me. . . . Where is your common, ordinary sense? Why did you want to twist a joke around like that?" (91–92)

He privately thinks "there was not sufficient understanding in his marriage" and he walks away, the only solution he can typically find, thus actualizing Arvay's fears that caused the situation in the first place, yet another vicious circle. He cops out and blames it on her sex: "She was a woman and women folks were not given to thinking nohow. . . . He had played the fool, not Arvay. . . . There was something about Arvay that put him in mind of his mother. . . . All the agony of his lost mother was gone when he could rest his head on Arvay's bosom and go to sleep of nights. . . . He placed Arvay as having powers. . . . She did not know her own strength. . . . Twenty to twenty-five years later on, he could afford to let her know. No sense in crowding his luck" (94). They achieve a reconciliation through sexual language, but once again their problems prove insoluble through discussion. They remain in this same situation until the end of the novel, for only then does Arvay come to understand the full extent of her female "power" while she is in the bosom of the sea as she cradles a sleeping Jim's head in her lap.

Their exchange here demonstrates in comic fashion the tragic consequences of thinking stereotypically. Jim grants Arvay's "power" but claims she doesn't think; at the same time, however, he compares her with his mother, a woman he worshipped. We see his need for mothering emerge, which helps us to understand the end of the novel. He also feels he played the fool but doesn't know how to atone for it. But at the same time Arvay feels like a fool for having suffered all those months so needlessly; instead of facing her lack of humor, she blames Jim for making a fool of her.

An extended analysis of a piece Hurston composed while working on *Seraph*, which until now has not been noted by Hurston scholars, helps explain these issues. "The Lost Keys of Glory" offers a much expanded version of "Why Women Take Advantage of Men," collected in *Mules and Men* and central to Tea Cake and Janie's relationship in *Their Eyes* (33–38). In the beginning, the tale relates, men and women were of equal strength; when quarreling, they "would stop changing words, and get to changing licks," but neither could win. Man, upset, asks God for more strength and gets it, on the condition that he "not take advantage of Woman, and mistreat her in any form nor fashion. You must be good to her, and kind, and take care of her." Man doesn't honor this and beats Woman. She, angry, demands justice, but God refuses. Fortunately, "the Devil and the Woman had always been the best of friends." He instructs her to go back and meekly ask God for the bunch of keys hanging from a silver nail on Heaven's mantel. She does, and thus gets power over the cradle, the bedroom, and the kitchen. Man, shut out, offers to give woman strength again, but the Devil counsels against it. "You have the best of the bargain. Tell him to keep his strength and you keep your keys. . . . You will always have the advantage of man" (6).

Up until this point, the folktale matches the one in *Mules*. Hurston's 1947 version, however, then inserts a quarrel between Woman and the Devil, which results in her losing the keys. She then goes out into the field and tells Man she will match him in row for row work. Here Hurston breaks in:

> In 1947, women have entered every profession and skill that . . . men follow for a living. There is no doubt that women are taking themselves quite seriously as the equal of men in all of these pursuits. It is obvious, however, that women are not adequate to the struggle. . . . They are still to be convinced that God has given men the upper hand in certain ways. . . . Except for the fields of literature and the theatre, the very best women in any particular field have never been able to come up to a standard of excellency equal to the best men in that same profession . . . even Dress-Design and Cooking, the men are the top. . . . Men even invent the very tools with which women do their housework. (9)

Hurston, however, isn't upset by this, for "our very frailty becomes us. . . . We are the pigments on the pallet after men have sketched in the figure" (9). She also claims women's intellect never gets valued in the professions as much as their femininity, as evidenced when women try to "muscle" men down by "sheer mental strength," bringing on iron opposition or the ire of male groups. "But let us ask that same thing as a favor, and those same men will outdo themselves to help us on our way." Hurston then cites the example of Clare Boothe Luce: "She owes a great deal more to her beauty and her female charm than she does to her brains. . . . The brains are there, but if they had been in an ugly head, the men would have taken pleasyre [*sic*] in beating them out" (10).

Nor is this all. Hurston admits women make equally good grades in school, but they then fail to achieve commensurately in the working world. Motherhood can't furnish an alibi either: "It is a notorious fact that most career women do not become mothers, even if they marry." She feels women suffer from a "high rate of neurasthenics," for they lack "detachment in . . . emotions" (10). The term "neurasthenics" of course had more currency in 1947; *Webster's Dictionary* defined it then as "an emotional and psychic disorder that is characterized by impaired functioning in interpersonal relationships, and often by fatigue, depression, feelings of inadequacy, headaches, hypersensitivity to sensory stimulation (as by light or noise), and psychosomatic symptoms (as disturbances of digestion and circulation)." Obviously, this description fits Arvay perfectly, but Hurston claims here that "the nation is strewn with female neurotics from end to end," so Arvay seems broadly representative (11). Obviously, a more complex psychoanalytical construct may have been on Hurston's mind, depending on whether or not she had read Freud. Whether Hurston means this as a criticism of Arvay or a statement of her helplessness (or both) seems unclear.

What does Hurston see as the result of all this? "Inter-sexual tragedies," like the beautiful female dental student who thinks of herself as a great dentist because her peers and instructors cater to her, causing her to turn down offers of marriage. Once in practice, however, few men trust her skill, while women stay away "in droves." After six years, she marries a shipping clerk, becomes a "humble housewife," has a nervous breakdown, and divorces. A life of licentiousness follows, and then two more disastrous marriages. A broken woman, she talks constantly about the man she could have married.

Hurston's second example, Winifred B., "luckily" marries a doctor, but foolishly becomes jealous of a female journalist he admires. Consequently, she returns to school and becomes a sociologist. Nine years later, her extremely successful husband has no use for his career-obsessed wife, especially since her good looks have faded. She has to live alone on a meager stipend in a small apartment. The journalist who was her model, however, has given up her career for the most part in favor of devoted service to another doctor. "*Her* husband got steak and potatoes and apple pie on demand, his slippers brought to him wherever he might choose to flop down and wallow in the house, and his cigar ashes brought no protest from the erstwhile woman of affairs" (14).

Winifred, disillusioned and broken, becomes a "rabid Communist, and took to speaking in Union Square" (14). Women like these, Hurston says, mistakenly take models like Dorothy Thompson, when in fact, "Miss Thompson is dependent on a man for her happiness and recognizes the fact only too well."[19] Hurston goes on to condemn women who seek sexual freedom; if they do marry, their sexual record precludes "that springtime ecsatsy [*sic*] of the intimacies with the one-possible man for her. . . . Too much pre-marital affairs kill off the mystery that men used to feel, and make marriage less binding on them. . . . She knows how to take care of herself, he concludes, and lets the marriage slide." This sermon ends with the question, "Are not the unknown women, [*sic*] bossing the man of her choice really happier than the career-woman, however, famous outside her natural sphere?" (15). "The Lost Keys" demonstrates Hurston's increasingly conservative attitudes toward women's roles but may have been inspired more by a sense of frustration than by a sense of the way things should be. The piece indicates women like Arvay, who lack Hurston's special talents and ambitions, obviously must take a different road in life and make the best of their situations. Knowing how to use humor as a fourth "key" obviously helps considerably.

After all the fuss over Jim's joking about the unborn baby's sex, Arvay gives birth to Kenny; eight years later, he takes his best friend, Belinda, Dessie's child, to watch the train come into the station. In a comic rendition of the "primitive" responses of children, Hurston intones, "Kenny was so overcome that . . . he wanted to do something in worship of the train. But What?" (97). Inspired, he has Belinda turn some of her famous cartwheels, not realizing she has no underpants on; a horrified woman tells them to stop. "Kenny was surprised. . . . Here was the greatest artist of her time, and some fool hollering to turn her down. . . . There were smothered chuckles, and some unsmothered, running the whole length of the train" (97–98). When a white man throws "two-bits" down (the proverbial fee for a cheap whore), Kenny's innocence permits delightful irony: "But the nice man had given him a quarter to turn Belinda up. 'Fifty cents to turn her down!' Kenny shouted, clothed in innocence and arrogance. The audience roared with laughter at this turn of affairs. The heckler became more furious at being opposed, and then made the butt of laughter by the dirty-faced little imp." Later, counting the money, the children still don't know why the woman was mad: "Tetched in the head," they agree, as they go down the road eating the bananas they bought (99). Obviously, Hurston has some anthropological fun here, sending up a fieldworker's description of a phallic God (the train) being saluted ritualistically with the pudenda of a young virgin; the "sacramental" food of bananas makes it even better.

The townspeople are amused: "That Kenny Meserve! He took after his Pappy all right. . . . Jim . . . was joshed and teased, and he laughed . . . proud of Kenny. So Jim was put out when . . . he . . . found Arvay all upset over the incident. Kenny and Belinda had been whipped. . . . 'What is it to be lawing and jawing about, Arvay? It was nothing but children's doings. . . . Belinda leading Kenny! That's a joke. . . . He's too much like his old man.'" Arvay responds, "'Belinda being that no-count Joe's young'un, I reckon any caper that she might up and cut just have to be put up with. Look like Joe is the boss on this place.' He gave a big, clapping laugh and picked Arvay up and sat down with her in his lap. 'This baby-wife I got can't stand for her husband to think well of nobody but her'" (100). This episode offers yet another example of Arvay's lack of humor, Puritanism, and apparent racism, but her antipathy for Belinda's father seems to stem from the fact that Jim spends so much time with him.[20]

When Arvay learns that Jim and Joe are moonshining,[21] however, she blames Joe, giving him an excuse to move away. Hurston isn't above making a little fun of Joe, as one of "My People! My People!": "Joe bought himself a car and announced that he had got to be people in Citrabelle. Doing this on a high-toned scale. Heavy-set Daddy. If a woman asked him for a nickel, he gave her a ten-dollar bill. Ask him for a drink of likker, and he bought her a whiskey-still" (105), but his new house goes unfinished.

After introducing moonshining, Hurston gives Jim and Arvay new tenants, the Portuguese Corregios, to make this novel speak to the diversity of Florida. Their Portuguese heritage "made them foreigners, and no foreigners were ever quite white to Arvay. Real white people talked English and without any funny sounds to it. The fact that his wife was a Georgia-born girl that he had married up around Savannah did not help the case one bit, so far as Arvay could see. The woman had gone back on her kind and fallen from grace." Besides, more importantly, "This was not *laughing*, obliging Dessie. There were two separate families now on the place" (107; my emphasis). This passage returns us again to the "Pet Negro" syndrome, to the point that Arvay almost consciously admits that the Kelseys were "part of the family"; Mrs. Corregio, Arvay's social equal, can't be as amusing because she constitutes more of a threat than Dessie.

In fact, Arvay appears more racist toward the new arrivals; she calls Mr. Corregio "the Gee" and his wife "The Georgia Cracker," obviously forgetting her own origins. Besides, Mrs. Corregio, a handsome woman, "bright-eyed, a trifle full-bodied and full of laughs and jokes," and her two lovely daughters possess what Arvay doesn't have—a sense of fun and exuberance. She resents them, and when the wife cooks seafood, Arvay won't eat it, calling the food "Geechy messes," which would apply to the Geechee blacks of the Atlantic tidewater, as well as the "Gees," thereby creating a pun. Hurston brilliantly heightens the building tensions by interweaving Arvay's jealousy of the Corregio women with her growing protectiveness toward Earl, now approaching adulthood and clearly a mentally disturbed young man. She won't hear of him being sent to an asylum and sees Jim's "plots" to send Earl away as a sign of class superiority:

> He was that same James Kenneth Meserve of the great plantations, and looked down on her as the backwoods Cracker, the piney-woods rooter, and thought that he could just run the hog over her in anyway that he pleased. He could tell her to her face that those Gees were there to stay and she couldn't help herself. He could snatch her son from her, to accommodate those Gees, and stick her child in a crazyhouse. Well, she might not come from no high muck-de-mucks, but she would show him a thing or two. She was Little David to his mighty Goliath. He might go for a big cigar, but she would smoke him! (115)

This important passage rehearses the issues that have always been central to the marriage, but registers them in a new, heightened key. Earl's middle name, David, suggests that Arvay's relation to Jim is a mockery replacement for Earl's oedipal configuration with Jim. Earl lacks the wit to pursue this relationship, but paradoxically and ironically he dies from it when he attempts to shoot Jim. Furthermore, with her "womanly" competitive spirit roused, Arvay finally proves capable (at least in her mind) of feisty, semi-comic, folk-derived expressions of resolve, combining barnyard, biblical, ethnic, and class phrases.

Appropriately, at this first sign of independence and possible growth, Arvay leaves Jim, supposedly for a visit to Sawley, which seems shabby, seedy, and infested with rats, roaches, and flies. Playing the big shot, just as Joe did earlier in his way, she gives Earl five dollars to go to town to treat cousins and shows off her dresses to Raine: "It did her good to see the look of gloating pride on her mother's face. Maria gave Larraine a cut-eye look as much as to say, 'Now, how do like that come stepping up to you?' Arvay was not bringing up the tail end of things any more" (119). This scene begins the biblical reversal of younger-elder siblings that will climax in Arvay's second visit home when her mother lies dying. During the earlier visit, however, Arvay steps inside her "green temple" of the mulberry tree, only to read it as a mirror of a changed self. Although the tree retains its power and mystery, a small owl sleeping in its branches seems to be her old self, which had cried out for someone to rescue it by driving away "the lonesome feeling from its heart" (119).

Tragic Rupture/Humorous Bonding

The happy, normal development of "Jim's children" Kenny and Angie finds a tragic contrast when "Arvay's child" Earl tries to rape Lucy Ann Corregio. Arvay refuses to accept it, even when Jim offers incontrovertible proof. A terrible drama mounts as we find Earl has Jim's gun and has fled a posse, only to be trapped in the swamp. Jim tries to save his son, but Earl fires on him, and as a result the other men kill him.

Why did Hurston include this powerful and grim episode? Possibly she wanted to demonstrate to white people what a lynching might be like for a white mother if her son were accused of rape. Certainly the swamp functions as refuge in many slave narratives and stories concerning lynch mobs. More importantly, however, Earl always gets associated with Arvay's dark, hidden self; his death becomes a punishment for her mental sexual "crimes" with her sister's husband. His final flight into the swamp equals her frantic repression of the truth. His retarded, disturbed, almost animal-like nature, whimpering but dangerous, speaks to her soul and ours.

The fact that he tries to kill his own father forces into deeper expression Arvay's rages against the same man. Perhaps even more significantly, earlier, just after the attempted rape, he tries to kill Arvay too; hiding under the kitchen table with an axe, he emerges and goes for his mother's throat. She fends him off with great difficulty and persuades him to flee. Later, after it's all over, Arvay pretends he thought she was somebody else. Still, the horror of attempted matricide and patricide (the axe underlining this in its association with both *The Oresteia* and Lizzie Borden) seems more significantly symbolic of her ability to inflict pain unconsciously on others and, tellingly, on herself.

In fact, Earl's link with her repressed fears surfaces in a new way after his death, for Arvay has no sex with Jim for a month. When she finally submits, she realizes she is relieved Earl is dead. We may now extend further our discussion of Arvay's "melancholy" over losing Carl, which was projected onto Earl at the scene of his birth when his deformity was revealed. Now that her son's death offers an actual occasion for mourning and melancholy, rather than a purely mental one, she finds a way to work through a separation of the libido from the lost object. The last link with Carl's representation in her unconscious (not Carl himself) has now been destroyed. Until this fixation of Arvay's melancholia is removed, any hope for her renaissance through love and laughter must remain moot. As Hurston states, "A great, great burden *had* been wrenched off her shoulders, something that stood between her and Jim" (137).

The intersection of love and laughter finds humorous expression one month after Earl's death, when Arvay sees Jim outside the gate talking with Fast Mary, "a young woman whom folks made lots of jokes about." Mary tells Jim that Kenny "'and his sister come along, and . . . begin to giggle and poke fun at me. . . . That Kenny is a little limb of Satan.'" She claims the boy looked up under her clothes; "'It's kind of hot today, and I was kind of thin-cladded. . . . He said that it looked like a mulberry pie.'"[22] A perceptive reader might remember that the child's euphemism for Mary's sexual organs replicates the fruit of the tree under which Arvay and Jim consummated their love.

> Arvay saw Jim choking down a laugh. . . . What do Jim mean by listening to all that rigmarole from that fan-foot, that street-walker, that brick-bat for? . . . They say any man can have her for a fish sandwich and a drink of gin. They claims that she takes men right up on the court-house lawn on dark nights, asks 'em for a dime apiece, lays down, grabs hold of the grass and tells 'em, "Let's go!"
>
> "Well, Mary," Jim was saying with a half-hidden grin on his face, "you realize that Kenny ain't hardly twelve years old as yet. . . . It would take a man . . . to give you a sound opinion."
>
> "That's right, Mister Jim . . . a man like you." (141)

Arvay jumps out on the porch as if to clean it, exclaiming, "'Don't you worry, Mary, I'll really tend to him for meddling with *you*. . . . I'll mighty nigh beat him to death.'" Mary can't resist responding:

> "Humph! Some of these old nice-nasty folks make me sick of my stomach. Putting on all them holy airs, and trying to slur at me.". . .
> [Arvay] washed the face, the thin body, the cheap dress and the run-

over high-heeled shoes with a look that was as good as hurling a bucket of solid sewage over the girl.

"Don't you be looking at me with your scorn like that!" Mary bellowed. . . . "With your cold acting ways, nobody in town can't tell whether you're a man or a woman."

. . . Arvay favored Mary with another scornful look, dropped the brush in the bucket, dipped her cloth, wrung it out with great deliberation, then said cooly, "That ain't *Your* trouble, honey. They all know about *you . . . exactly.*" Arvay heard a smothered chuckle from Jim. He was in the bedroom." (143)

Mary says she'll pray for Arvay, who replies, "'*You* praying to God against anybody? Humph! . . . I'll bet you when you get down on them rusty knees and get to worrying God, He goes in His privy-house and slams the door.'. . . [What hurt Mary was] that loud cackle. . . . Jim was in there roaring with laughter" (143–44). When Arvay's continuing tirade makes Mary flee, Jim declares, "'You sure did give poor Mary a reading, honey.'" Arvay responds, "'I don't reckon you told that heifer to come racking up here to grin up in your face. . . . That fan-foot . . . setting in public with her no-count, trashy legs gapped open . . . run to you hoping to get a trade out of the thing before it was over, the hongry-gut sow!'" (145).

I quote this scene at length, for it shows Arvay truly transformed, signifying to beat the band. Her specifying significantly takes place on the porch, locus of verbal dueling in Hurston's earlier works, and especially echoes Big Sweet of *Mules;* her pretend "washing" comically signifies on the cleansing/purging of filth images she uses, which are paralleled by Hurston's authorial voice. Jim's laughter symbolizes more than amusement—some might say it's typically male humor over dividing and conquering women—we see him full of joy at Arvay's comic creativity finally coming into fruition, causing him to laugh, something new that the tragedy with Earl has possibly permitted. On the other hand, we note that the use of competitive humor over a man has a negative side too and represents only a step toward the truly healthy humor that characterizes Arvay at the end of the book.

The Humor of Courtship Revisited

Sexuality acquires a new expression when Angie becomes a teenage beauty; we see her pose nude before the mirror and then idiomatically demand a long dress: "'Beat me if you want to, you can't kill me, and if you kill me, you sure Lord can't eat me. I'm not going to wear no short dress.'"[23] Her brazen self-confidence, epitomized by both her open narcissism and her boisterous sense of humor, sets her off from Arvay and proceeds from her status as "Daddy's girl," in more ways than one. Again, Arvay seems to have developed more of a sense of humor, at least in her dealings with her daughter, for she responds, "'Call youself hitting a straight lick with a crooked stick, I take it. . . . The main idea you want understood is that you smell youself and wants to take company'" (150). This particular comic expression—which means the person has passed through puberty—really does seem to be unique to black groups; I have found no mention of its adoption by white southerners. Jim, obviously the chief social (and therefore, linguistic) role model for the children, consistently seems fascinated by black culture and linguistically adept at using black southern language. Since Angie dotes on her father, she naturally and frequently uses black expressions. Another example of this comes when Arvay objects to Angie's beau, Hatton Howland, because he's a Yankee, but Angie shouts, in a scene that perhaps expresses Hurston's amused contempt for the fabled "Lost Cause/Daughters of the Confederacy Syndrome" yet again, "'I don't care if he even come from Diddy-Wah-Diddy! I don't care nothing at all about no old Civil War. I don't care nothing about Jeff Davis nor Abraham Lincoln nor Lee nor nobody else if it's got to come between me and Hatton Howland. Compared with him, it comes before me just like a gnat in a whirlwind'" (151).[24]

Angie obviously has the spirit and self-confidence that Arvay often lacks and the comic rejoinders to go with it. She demonstrated this when she earlier pounced on Hatton at the Easter Prom, asked him to dance, and kissed him, shocking Arvay. In knowing exactly what she wants and being willing to do what it takes to get it, Angie resembles Lucy Potts, who similarly stands up to her mother, Emmeline; Arvay appears to be the latter's avatar in these scenes, and thus takes on a new generational role in the comic courtship scenario. Angie represents what Arvay should have been and isn't; the similarity between their names seems telling, and Angeline's moves closer to the seraph of the book's title. Ultimately, however, Arvay could be said to have become the seraph through the hard-won acquisition of virtues that seem to be Angie's innately.

Angie's romance leads Jim to epitomize his feelings on love, which also sums up a key aspect of the plot: "'Love is a funny thing, Little-Bits. Seems like that one person gets next to your heart, and you can't shake 'em loose no matter which way you twist and turn. You just got to go on serving 'em all your born days.'" The idea of service gets taken further too, as Arvay says she doesn't want Angie to be such a slave to a man that he can "'handle her anyway they will or may, and she be so under the influence that she can't help herself,'" to which Jim replies, "'That is the only way to be in love. It ain't really love when you gamble with your stuff out the window. Leave all you best things outside and come in and get in the game, and soon as you win a little something, jump and run'" (154). This scene should put to rest what Hurston meant by naming Jim Me-serve; instead of reading him entirely as a demanding male chauvinist, we should start seeing that in his own way (which sometimes means through his inarticulateness and overtly, but often empty, male chauvinist language), he loves Arvay deeply, and indeed can say "I serve," "I have served," and "I will serve."

The question of the book, however, is whether Arvay can learn to serve herself by loving herself, and therefore be capable of loving and serving Jim as he has her over the years. Until then, as in Hurston's letter to Van Vechten, her ship will "blindly bump" against his in a failure of connection. Obviously, these sentiments link Jim to Janie and Tea Cake in *Their Eyes;* Janie's insistence to Pheoby that her love for Tea Cake is no "business proposition," but rather a "love game" where one gambles all, finds an echo in Jim. The idea of service here, which must be borne in mind in reading *Seraph*'s final scene, also brings up the biblical idea of service and its connection to love.

Arvay's maturity receives comic emphasis when she eavesdrops on Angie and Hatton apparently talking, jokingly, about having sex. Outraged, she runs for Jim's revolver, determined to get rid of Hatton forever, but Jim arrives, laughs, and calms her down. In the parlor, the lovers now sit primly on either end of the sofa, Angie as if under a laudanum spell, while Hatton, "flushed in the face, was fidgeting like he had a hot stove lid in the seat of his pants" (157), thus casting Arvay into the comic role of Mrs. Potts in *Jonah*. Hurston's use of bawdy body humor leads us to smile, and even Arvay is amused by the scene: "Hatton further betrayed his condition by throwing one arm about a pillow and patting and petting it with the fingers of his long, strong hand. Arvay smiled inwardly with a feeling of morbid triumph. . . . This romance . . . was not all one-sided. . . . Angeline was giving this long tall boy just as good as he sent." Furthermore, she learns the utility of a casual, humorous attitude in such a situation: "Jim, with the aid of a lot of jokes and sayings, skillfully led Hatton to talk about himself and his plans." Jim laughs and says,

"I have to hand it to you. You really know how to hustle."

Hatton laughed with Jim. "Well, you know what they say about us Damnyankees down here. Come down with a dirty shirt and five dollars and never change either one and still manage to end up rich. . . . I want it so that my wife can toss a ten dollar bill in the penny collection in church, and if the usher looks surprised at her and frowns, take her finger and beckon him back and fling in a hundred and tell him to go with that. If she catches him frowning any more, she'll call him back and fling in a thousand."

When the laughter dies down, Jim says: "'Spoken like a man, Howland'" (158–60).

This richly detailed scene offers comic commentary on the continuing difference in comic attitude between Jim and Arvay, on the way humor establishes intimacy and a relaxed mood between the men, but also, and perhaps most importantly, on the way humor was being used by both invading Yankees and host southerners to bridge the sometimes unpleasant gap between them. In this sense the Angie-Hatton affair comically echoes the standard love plot of Reconstruction era novels, such as Thomas Nelson Page's *Red Rock* (1898). Arvay's aforementioned willingness to play the outraged southern belle mother stands in contrast to Hatton's relaxed, self-reflexive joking and to Jim's genial but actually concerned inquiries.

Hatton's parallel to Jim in these scenes should be mentioned too. Notice the comment about the church collection plate, which reminds us of the scene at church during Arvay's courtship. We also soon learn that Hatton runs numbers, in addition to plying a mechanic's trade, something parallel to Jim's twin activities of citrus farming and moonshining. Hurston always seems to feel (along with her friend Marjorie Kinnan Rawlings) that such illicit trades are fine in hard times, and indeed, a man's flexibility makes him similar to the kind of man Emerson wanted the American to be, well-versed in many trades. Hatton also learns easily, and later, he'll follow Jim's advice to quit the numbers and to use those profits to get into the Florida real estate business, where he's very successful. At this point, however, Hatton, again like Jim, can't wait for a wedding, so the couple elopes.

Jim has a typically humorous reaction when they return:

"Drag it on in here and get your whipping! . . . Come in with your britches down!"

Angeline . . . led the others in with a laugh. Jim grabbed Hatton and wrestled him around boisterously and hollered over his shoulder to Arvay. "I got this one, you grab the other one and frail her good! We'll show 'em how to run off and marry on us."

Arvay . . . hugged her first lest the fiery temper of Angeline prompt her to say the things that Arvay feared, then slapped her two or three times playfully across the buttocks.

"Now, Madam, get in that kitchen and taste that egg-nog I fixed for you. Git!"

Angeline looked at Arvay in astonishment for a minute, then ran for the kitchen pretending to cry loudly into the crook of her elbow. Arvay followed as if in pursuit. (164)

For once Arvay can take part in communal/familial comic ritual, perhaps because Angie's elopement echoes happier earlier days of her own. Her sense of fun here runs counter to her past, so much so that her own daughter is "astonished." Obviously, all the figures are involved in a parody of "genteel" behavior, and the scene appropriately shifts from the conventional/parlor to the festive/kitchen.

Angie's transformation into what would today be called a Yuppie feeds Arvay's inferiority complex, however, as her daughter easily excels in society: "Hatton and Angie had one of the choicest sites on the big lake that was now known as Lake Charm. . . . She saw her daughter friending with people whom she herself had never dreamed of associating with," and Arvay wonders if she's needed anymore. Contractor Howland drains the swamp to build his development; it seems "infinitely more threatening" to Arvay than "the dark gloom of the swamp had been" (172), because it symbolizes the end of her parenting stage; now she has to face the fact that the real swamp exists within her psyche.

Her paranoia increases when she learns Jim was present to give consent the day Angie eloped. "Why, she asked herself, should she be surprised at being ignored like this? It had always been that way as long as she could remember. She had never been counted or necessary." Reading her Bible (never a positive contribution to her mental state), she reflects, "so far as they were concerned, she was still a Henson. . . . A handmaiden like Hagar, who had found favor in the master's sight . . . took her for dumb and ignorant, and so narrow in her mind that she couldn't be expected to see that Hatton was a fine boy" (174). In Arvay's tortured reading, her daughter's marriage and the upward mobility it symbolizes displaces her own, making her a Henson (and therefore a Cracker) again. In apparent "relapses" like this, Arvay's brooding over imagined slights and projected awareness on the part of her family and others of the inferiority she tries to mask makes her throw herself into the wilderness—and these recurring moments of the novel prove tedious—an equivalent wasteland for the reader.

The Humor of the Melting Pot

Yet another marker of the influence of black culture emerges when Kenny becomes a bandleader whose group specializes in "black" music, one of many aspects of the book that reflect a "melting pot" motif. Years earlier, white/black overlays were stressed when Kenny began to play the piano (taught by Arvay) and simultaneously to learn black music from his mentor Joe, even creating tunes with bottle-necks. He and Angie love to sing "Charleston!" and "Shake That Thing" by "some Ethel Waters, who Kenny and Angeline thought was great" (123).

Kenny develops his adaptations of black music at college, where he leads the band. Kenny, Jim reports, "'claims that white bands up North and in different places like New Orleans are taking over darky music and making more money at it than the darkies used to. Singers and musicians and all. You do hear it over the radio at times, Arvay.'" Kenny says that eventually white artists will take it all over: "'Getting so it's not considered just darky music and dancing nowadays. It's American, and belongs to everybody'" (176). One hears Hurston's pride in the recognition of black culture and its salutary effect in the "melting" and recombining of cultural elements, but between the lines and beyond her anger at white appropriation, northern hypocrisy, and the lack of black profits, there's also nostalgia over the end of an era in black folk culture that this signifies.[25] The music, however, thematically unites an assembly of Florida's mixed inhabitants at a football game in Gainesville. Jim plays a part in this by arranging for Felicia Corregio to be Kenny's date. Arvay, ever prejudiced (as she was initially with "Yankee" Hatton), disapproves of this Catholic "foreigner," whose name "means sorrow" to Arvay. Actually, "Corregio" means "magistrate" or "judge" in Portuguese, perhaps pointing to the way Arvay herself is ironically judged by the reader here; moreover, "Felicia" means "fruitful/happy." Earlier, Arvay has suspected Jim was interested in either Felicia or her mother. Now her paranoid sexual fantasies multiply: "Was it the mother or the daughter? Oh, that was too awful to think about. Laying around with the father and running after the son" (183). Both of Arvay's children, however, in their romantic choices, cancel their mother's prejudices and exemplify Hurston's belief in the virtues of an integrationist melting pot Americanism.

Ironically, Arvay's pain comes from not "melting" herself: "Listening to the people . . . she became terribly conscious of her way of speech," fearing the cruel, mocking, corrective humor it might inspire. "She hated to open her mouth for fear of making a balk, and putting her children to shame" (183). Arvay thus pathetically reminds us of immigrant mothers unfamiliar with English who see their children bypass them in acculturation. Here, however, the mother doesn't "melt" because of insecurities caused by her social, psychic, and marital history and because her lack of humor contributes to her inability to "mix" in any way.

By contrast, at the dance, the lushly dressed Angeline and Felicia do exactly that and cause some male drollery; Jim tells an admiring banker Angeline and Felicia are "'town girls . . . about the ugliest. . . . Fact is, they were run out of Citrabelle for the day so . . . folks could enjoy their Thanksgiving dinner.' The three men chuckled, and Jim went one better. 'Just a couple of culls off of my place.' 'I'll take your culls off of your hands and take 'em to Leesburg to ugly up the place'" (184). These jokes are cousin to the "he/she's so ugly that" jokes in black culture (see *Mules and Men* 73), and offer more testimony to male joking conventions that mask tender, loving feelings.

Strindberg on the Suwanee

Arvay stops the fun, accusing Jim of "gapping" at Felicia. She's haunted by the Corregios' association with Earl's death, but doesn't explain this in demanding that Jim take her home, ruining the scene of his greatest triumph. Kenny led bands at both the football game and the dance, with lovely Felicia as his date; simultaneously, Angie reigned as the gorgeous wife of a prominent developer. Thus although we see Jim's ensuing actions and words as tantamount to a rape, he intends his "lesson" to make Arvay see how she has blindly made him "serve Me"; he snarls, "'Where I made my big mistake was in not starting you off with a good beating. . . . I have never laid the weight of my hand on you in malice, and you done got beside yourself'" (189). He rips her dress off, forces her to kiss him, but then refuses to respond. Disturbingly, he asserts, "'You're my damn property, and I want you right where you are, and I want you naked.'" Arvay cries out, "'I can't stand this bondage. . . . I can't never feel satisfied that I got you tied to me, and I can't leave you, and I can't kill you nor hurt you. . . . I'm tied and bound down in a burning Hell and no way out. . . . I can't see never no peace of mind. It's a sure enough hard game when you got to die to beat it, but that's just what I aim to do—kill myself!'" A careful reader, while appalled by Jim's words and method, will see that what Arvay says of her own plight actually reflects his. Her insistence on possession of Jim and blindness to his needs, amply displayed throughout the novel, makes us see that the position Jim has purpose-fully placed her in—naked, vulnerable, doing all the real loving, "'ain't acting mutual'" (191)—characterizes her. The scene, evoca-tive of Strindberg's *Dance of Death,* appropriately plays out without hu-morous touches; Hurston thereby signals the sickness of the marriage.

Still, Arvay has "peaks" too, especially of "class" triumph. When Jim builds her a sleeping porch with French doors, she reflects, "'For the used-to-be Arvay Henson, that kind of a thing was a mighty high kick for a low cow.' . . . Arvay joked and laughed with Jim and they had a great deal of fun these days" (204–5). Clearly, owning things and having others envy them makes Arvay more confident and helps her handle her son's death. Laughter and joking, as always in Hurston, offers a barometric reading of mental health.

The Hensons' increasing material wealth, however, has another side to it. Melanie Klein, in her study of mourning, shows how be-reaved people will often take an interest in a new house (here, a sleep-ing porch and its furnishings) in an effort to reorganize their inter-nal psychological "good things," including the recreation of the departed beloved (328). Arvay seems to be doing that: "She was as near to complete happiness as she had ever been in her life. The porch told her that she belonged" (207).

However, a phone call from Kenny saying he's left college to take a job in New York with a band casts Arvay into Hagar's wilderness alone: "'All the little family I done got together is gone and done left me in one way or another.'" She coldly ignores Jim's reminder that she has him. The porch no longer enchants: "She saw it as from afar and in a vision. Like John on the island of Patmos. A golden land of refuge where all would be peace, but from which she was now ex-pelled. Her power seemed broken . . . 'Just like I always thought and feared . . . they all done turned from me and gone.' . . . Behind the closed door . . . she went forth to face the demon of waste and desert places and take him for her company" (211). She feels people are indifferent to her, a shift not unusual in mourning. As Klein states, in such a case "the frightening indifference of . . . people was reflect-ed from . . . internal objects, who . . . had turned into a multitude of 'bad' persecuting objects" (329). We note too the doubled typology; Hagar's wilderness now equates with St. John's Patmos, the John of harsh judgment that Arvay frequently becomes with Jim. Significantly, Arvay in these moods more often loses her voice, for Hagar's banish-ment to the wilderness also silences her; indeed, she disappears from the story of Abraham. Moreover, Sarah thinks of her rival as "Hagar the Egyptian." We have already seen Hurston's figuration of Egyptians as black; thus the parallel between Cracker Arvay/Egyptian Hagar would seem to suggest the equation, in terms of "undesirable Other," of Cracker/black. Indeed, one critic who obviously skimmed the book and thought of it in terms of Hurston's other works claimed that the story was "the moving story of Arvay, a Mulatto, and Jim the son of an aristocratic family" (Blake 150). One can see the mistake, for the liminal condition of Hagar/Arvay, moving back and forth from the wilderness of isolation and self-doubt to the promised land of acceptance and love, mimics the tragic mulatta and passing novels of the nineteenth century.

Arvay recovers for a moment but looks for a scapegoat and finds it in the Corregios. Her formulations should be linked to her conception of herself as St. John on Patmos, the saint of damnation, judgment, and destruction:

> Then they could turn and twist his [Kenny's] poor young mind . . . skull-drag him into marrying Felicia. . . . Arvay had thought of herself since childhood as a soldier in the army of her Lord . . . a follower of the Meek and Lowly Lamb, never once, in all these years, and hearing the expression as often as she had, the contradiction in the term [*sic*]. Who was the enemy to be assaulted without mercy and exterminated? . . . Felicia and her mother were nothing but heathen idolaters. . . . Arvay proceeded to set up images of them among the African savages and heathen Chinee. . . . They were no different from that awful Herodias and her daughter Salome who had got John the Baptist killed . . . like that Salome, dressed in nothing but veils to tempt the poor boy. . . . Arvay shook and shuddered at her home-made picture . . . but [it] . . . strangely brought her comfort. God didn't like ugly, and neither did God eat okra. . . . Felicia and her Maw would catch it and catch it good! . . . She was inclined to feel sorry for them. They didn't count as her enemies anymore. (211–13)

This extraordinary piece of illogical fundamentalism has the effect of making the reader laugh yet again at Arvay's ignorance, while marveling at Hurston's impressive rendering of lower-class white speech, punctuated by expressions Arvay has gleaned from Dessie (i.e., the idiom "God don't eat okra" [which is slick]). It also points to a fundamental problem of the book: Hurston makes so light of both Arvay's intelligence and her narrow-mindedness that we sometimes find it hard to sympathize with her. In this scene in particular she comes off as a kind of Cracker Archie Bunker. This creates rich possibilities for author/reader ironic laughter (especially at such extravagant constructions as the image of Felicia dancing Salome's "Seven Veils" number in Manhattan), but it undermines the human tie we need to feel. On the other hand, the comic figuration of Salome and Herodias as Florida rustics offers a comic flip side to the somber metaphysics of the Hagar-Ishmael iconology. Finally, the passage demonstrates Arvay's continual fear of rivals and accompanying rejection of friends she desperately needs. Joe and Dessie's replacements, the Corregios, delight everyone but her. The fact that Mrs. Corregio also has Cracker roots makes her even more demonic, a pagan double.

The unhappy hate to hear others are happy; Arvay becomes irritated when she hears Jim and Jeff, Joe and Dessie's son, laughing one morning:

> What in the world did they find to skin back their gums and sniggle over to all of that. . . . Giggle! Sniggle! . . . Must of found a mare's nest and couldn't count the eggs. . . . She made up her mind to go out in the kitchen, and by the way she acted, put a damper on all that. . . . Then she caught herself. . . . It would be better if she let on that they themselves had got her out of humor. . . . She would wait till somebody said or did something that she could take exception to, and turn their dampers down for 'em good and proper. (214)

And indeed, she's horrible to them. Jeff's coded response comes right out of slavery: "'Look like Ole Miss got up on the wrong side of the bed this mawning'" (215). Won over by their humor, Arvay invites them and Joe in; her thaw into jocular humor leads to a reward, for Joe tells her she deserves credit for transmitting her musical talent to Kenny, something that's never occurred to her before. Kenny's music thus get figured as bicultural (from Joe and Arvay), while his humor similarly comes from Jim and Joe. This discussion leads to an awareness that the children have been blessed by growing up in a biracial setting, and indeed, Joe tells Arvay, "'We Meserves'll look after one another'" (221).

Soon after, Jim calls her outside—laughing, he has a giant rattler by its neck. "Arvay had a deep-seated fear and dislike of snakes. Any kind of a snake. She shrank from worms even because they reminded her of snakes. . . . Jim looked at her fright and chuckled" (222). The snake begins to gain control, yet Arvay remains paralyzed with fear and cannot move to help her husband. Jeff saves Jim but gives Arvay a look that condemns her. Significantly, Jim lets the snake go because he fought fair but turns on Arvay in one of his key pronouncements in the book, accusing her of the wrong kind of love:

> "I'm just as hungry as a dog for a knowing and a doing kind of love.[26]
> You love like a coward. Don't take no steps at all. Just stand around

and hope for things to happen out right. Unthankful and unknowing like a hog under a acorn tree. Eating and grunting with your ears hanging over your eyes, and never even looking up to see where the acorns are coming from. What satisfaction can I get. . . . Ain't you never stopped to consider at all? . . . All I ever wanted to hear from you was that you realized that I was doing out of love, and thought of you so high, that I wanted to see you pomped away up there. I never have seen you as a teppentime Cracker like you have thrown in my face time and again. I saw you like a king's daughter out of a story-book with your long, soft golden hair." (231)

By contemporary standards, this speech sounds suspiciously like those of Jody Starks; but a crucial difference lies in the fact that unlike Jody, Jim objects to Arvay's lack of a voice and her failure to relate to others, as well as to him. He leaves her for a life on the coast, casting her back into Hagar's wasteland.

This recurring focus on a search for a voice constitutes one of Hurston's most enduring themes, perhaps her central theme. With the help of family and friends, John, Janie, Moses, and Arvay all emerge from a crucible of initiation, tragedy, and trial with an arsenal of dialogic skills, and like the African diaspora they represent, the comic dimension of voice proves crucial in social interaction and intimacy and the achievement of individual and group identity.

The Comic Conflagration of Nostalgia

When Arvay learns her mother lies dying, she takes it as a sign from God. Now that she's lost her immediate family, she nostalgically and comically valorizes her formerly scorned Cracker background: "Arvay tossed her head defiantly and rhymed out that she was a Cracker bred and a Cracker born, and when she was dead there'd be a Cracker gone. . . . She was going *home!* Home to the good old times and simple, honest things, where greed after money and power had no place." Ironically, she thinks these thoughts as she packs her expensive clothes in Mark Cross luggage, which as Hurston tells us, "cost more than a turpentine worker ever handled in a year. That the people whom she was now gilding up had not the means to produce a son like Kenny. That the kind of father that they had had something to do with her children's good looks, and that beauty that everybody gave Angeline credit for was enhanced and made evident by her self-confidence which arose out of assurance brought on by means which Jim had provided . . . Arvay was not analyzing" (239).

All is changed at home: a new Stephen Foster hotel and tourist camps have replaced the sawmills and turpentine woods. Her taxi driver brags: "'Since the Old Gentleman died and Young Brad Cary took hold of things, some good changes have been made, but a lot of these old fogies and dumb peckerwoods don't like it.' Arvay took sides with the peckerwoods in a timid way. 'Still and all, in the good old days, the folks in Sawley was good and kind and neighborly. I'd hate to see all that done away with.'" The driver responds: "'I hauled the mud to make some of 'em. . . . They hate like sin to take a forward step . . . like they was took out their cradles, they'll be screwed down in their coffins'" (240), comically echoing Hurston's New South creed.

The old cabin and her family seem equally decayed: "And people who held to old ideas shocked her most unpleasantly in the person of her own sister, whom she identified in that ton of coarse-looking flesh sitting on the dilapidated old steps in a faded cheap cotton dress and dirty white cotton stockings. Larraine was taking a dip of snuff" (241). Carl, Arvay's fantasy lover, looks even worse: "A soiled, heavy-set man jerked his head out from under the hood of an unbelievably battered old Model T and flung his heavy features towards Arvay, standing beside the taxi. No! This drab creature could not be the once neat and self-assured Carl Middleton" (241). Hurston brings out some strongly naturalistic imagery here, straight out of *Tobacco Road:* Arvay hears "the squeak and patter of rats in the walls" (242). Her pathetically wasted mother cries out, in a wrenching yet comically signifying diatribe: "'I winned! I winned! . . . I lasted out until my baby child got to me. . . . Carl and Larraine was using me, hanging around just like turkey buzzards. . . . I wanted you to have the place when I was gone. . . . Disfurnishing me of the little money you sent me, and piling in here and destroying up the groceries I buy . . . stuff they trashy guts and lay 'round like gators in the sun. . . . I wouldn't even give 'em air if they was stopped up in a jug, the no-manners way that they have treated me'" (244–45). Under her mattress are pictures of Kenny, with a money order; Angie has sent her things too. She asks for a nice funeral and a look of triumph appears on her face when Arvay promises to provide one.

This extended scene offers tremendous internal satisfaction for Arvay, for the transfiguration of the formerly admired Larraine and her family not only into actual grotesques but satiric targets for her mother's down-home comic contempt literally and figuratively gives Arvay the last laugh, a motif exponentially developed in these final Sawley scenes. It also fulfills the biblical pattern we noticed building in the opening chapters, for here, in the classic pattern of Esau-Jacob,

Leah-Rachel, the younger child surpasses the elder and receives the parental blessing and inheritance. This magnifies through the implied extension of Arvay into her benevolent children. Finally, receiving the unqualified love of her mother surely operates powerfully in terms of Arvay finally possessing a full understanding of her own maternal function, one completely realized at the end of the novel.

In a scene reminiscent of Jody's humiliation by Janie in front of his friends, Carl demands one thousand dollars from Arvay at her fancy hotel, saying she owes him for an injury suffered at the old home. Although the clerk assures her Carl has no case, Arvay's memory of the man he once was makes her try to find a way to give him a small sum, but his rudeness makes her demand he say where he was injured. The scene develops real comic momentum, because like Gracie Allen, Arvay's ignorance of the humor of her remarks or how Carl and the other men are taking them increases the reader/author/minor character irony. "'Well, if you'se determined for me to get common with you . . . it's my behind. . . . I guess now you want me to show it to you.'" Arvay seriously replies, "'I can tell you something mighty good for a case like that. Get hold of some mutton tallow, then melt it and mix it together with some teppen-time and grease yourself good back there.' The manager, the bell-hops, and three male guests who were seated in the lobby sniggered." She makes it worse: "'Yeah, it's mighty healing and dependable. . . . If it was a burn, you would need some baking soda and mix it good with some wet Octagon soap, and you take' . . . The laughter was more public this time. Nobody was pretending to hide it. . . . 'But I ain't joking.' . . . The howls of laughter drowned her out." Carl: "'I didn't come here for you to teach and tell me how to grease my behind!'" (258).

Why does Hurston refuse to give Arvay a "whip hand" here like the one she bestows on Janie in her parallel showdown with Jody in *Their Eyes?* One answer might be that her unwittingly sexual and Rabelaisian humor erases any idea we might have that she continues to feel anything for Carl. Further, what follows gets set up better this way, with an innocent Arvay. In a shocking revelation, the manager tells her that Carl's sweet on her, that he was telling them about courting her. Apparently the young Larraine, like Scarlett O'Hara, snaked her sister's beau. She told Carl Arvay didn't love him; this crushed his ambitions and ruined his life.

Arvay's reaction is strange, but fitting, for knowledge of her power generates therapeutic, possibly victorious laughter. "Arvay fell on her face across the bed and laughed hysterically. It was too funny.

Weak as she was, Carl believing that she could prop him up . . .
Larraine . . . feeling so frail of her chances that she needed to steal
herself a husband from Arvay. Then both Carl and Larraine felt themselves less than she was. Maybe there were a lot of weak-feeling folks
in the world. . . . Poor, poor Larraine! Poor Carl too. Life had funny
ways" (260).

Paying for the dignified funeral makes her realize she is a woman
of substance. But later, at the old home, everything has been stolen
except pictures of the Meserves, which have been stomped and mu-
tilated. Even the porch boards have been scavenged. Trash piled up
around a pear tree indicates a plan to burn it, perhaps Hurston's
private link with *Their Eyes* and what the pear tree means there; Arvay's special tree, a mulberry, has likewise been prepared for destruction. Alone, Arvay goes to that tree, now in February bare of leaves
but full of buds. "Here had been her dreams since early childhood.
Here, in violent ecstasy, had begun her real life. Like her Mama's
keep-sakes, this mulberry tree was her memory-thing. . . . This tree was
a sacred symbol. She wished that she could use it like a badge and
pin it like a bouquet over her heart." She looks at the dilapidated
house of her father from this vibrant spiritual one: "It was an evil, ill-
deformed monstropolous accumulation of time and scum. It had
soaked in so much of doing-without, of soul-starvation, of brutish
vacancy of aim, of absent dreams, envy of trifles, ambitions for little-
ness, smothered cries and trampled love, that it was a sanctuary of
tiny and sanctioned vices." She sets the house on fire and watches it
burn from the mulberry tree. "Exultation swept over her followed by
a peaceful calm. It was the first time in her life that she was conscious
of feeling that way. . . . She had made a peace and was in harmony
with her life. The physical sign of her disturbance was consuming
down in flames, and she was under her tree of life" (270).

This important scene offers a progression of the purging of her
dark repressed self that began with Earl's death, which frees her to a
certain extent; there, however, she was passive; here, in a progression,
she actively destroys yet another, and in some ways more primal (because of its identification with the father) psychic shadow. The shack's
immolation further symbolizes her new freedom from social deter-
minism and the shadows of class that have dogged her and echoes
the draining of the swamp, another psychic symbol.[27]

The fire brings us to a further consideration of the book's title.
Frank Slaughter, reviewing the novel in 1948, assumed that Arvay was
the seraph of the title, a word defined by *Webster's Dictionary* as "one
of an order of celestial beings conceived as fiery and purifying min-

isters of Jehovah" (Slaughter 24). Seraphs only appear once in the Bible; Isaiah is privileged to see God on a throne, under hovering seraphim:

> And one cried unto another, and said, "Holy, holy, holy, *is* the Lord of hosts: the whole earth *is* full of his glory." And the posts of the door moved at the voice of him that cried, and the house was filled with smoke. Then said I, "Woe *is* me! for I am undone; because I am a man of unclean lips, and I dwell in the midst of a people of unclean lips: for mine eyes have seen the King, the Lord of hosts." Then flew one of the seraphims unto me, having a live coal in his hand, which he had taken with the tongs from off the altar: And he laid *it* upon my mouth, and said, "Lo, this hath touched thy lips; and thine iniquity is taken away, and thy sin purged." (Isa. 6:3–7)

One could argue that Arvay's awareness of the true nature of Jim's love finally burns away her sin/guilt/"unworthiness" while "dwelling in the midst of a people of unclean lips" (Crackers), where she lusted after her sister's husband. In this reading, Jim would be the seraph. On the other hand, Arvay, by setting fire to the house that symbolizes her old self, replicates the action of the angel and thus frees her own lips, so she may be the seraph herself. Regardless, the true psychological breakthrough here lies in Arvay's understanding that all these years when she thought the mulberry tree was her "sign," the ramshackle cabin of her familial and personal past has ruled in its place. Burning it clears a psychic space, and as with Isaiah, purifies Arvay's voice, which henceforth will be confident, loving, and laughing.

She tells Miss Hettie she's going home. "'My last string has done been loosed'"; she adds staying "'would be a turning back on my travels,'" which has a spiritual ring (272). As a sign of her liberation, Arvay decides to donate the farm to the people of Sawley as a park, with only one stipulation: save the mulberry tree. We should read this as the literal and figurative transformation of the scene of her early, psychic pain into a communal ground for play and humor, which she will eventually attempt to do, on the individual level, with her marriage.

When Arvay comes home her warmth and humor astonish Jeff and Janie, Joe and Dessie's son and his wife. Janie declares Arvay "'sure is folks,'" and Jeff adds, "'Just like Mister Jim, ain't she Janie! . . . Miss Arvay's done come to be just like him'" (275). Arvay decides to have Jeff drive her to Jim on the coast and invites Janie along. As they pass the Indian River, Jeff points out ancient Indian Turtle Mounds, rusting iron pots left from the indigo industry of the Minorcans, and foundations of a fort "left by the Spaniards," proving yet again Hurston's assertion that blacks know history better than poor whites and making good use of the research she did for an article on the Indian River ("Lawrence").

They arrive at New Smyrna, where Jim's factory is run by the Toomers. When Jim enters, he's very controlled, like Arvay. She sends Jeff and Janie off to see the town and suggests they take most of the lunch she's prepared. Jim objects; he wants some and says, "'That's enough for Jeff and Janie. They're going straight back home where there's plenty more. Give a man that needs it a chance'" (282). This deceptive passage does a number of things. First, Jim's "hunger for love" finds a symbol in the lunch. Jeff and Janie don't need a large portion for they have abundant love already. Finally, by sending Jeff back, Arvay has to stay.

Laughter and Rebirth on the Sea

These final scenes on the coast are prepared for earlier, in Citrabelle, when Jim has only begun to set up his maritime industry. He and Arvay continue to fail to connect, this time because Jim has absorbed yet another business's "language," which as usual, causes comic misunderstanding. Reporting on Alfredo's shrimping operations, Jim remarks, "'The last time, he took that boat out and sunk her!'" causing Arvay's dismay. "Jim laughed gaily. 'Naw, indeed. When a shrimper says that, he means that he come in loaded . . . riding low down to the water. Fishermen got their own way of saying things. Got their own way of talking by signs too and a whole lot of crazy things. You really ought to be along with me some times. They'd make you laugh yourself to death'" (177). This comment prophesies the death of Arvay's old, cringing self, the self she "laughs to death" at the Sawley hotel, and the scene's sequel, when she joins Jim and the fleet. At sea, her natural laughter, now based in confidence, does indeed signal her birth into a new life.

Hurston prefigures the buoyant psychological health symbolized by the sea much earlier, when Hatton Development drains the swamp to make way for new homes. As Arvay watches gangs of husky black roustabouts felling the giant trees, she's surprised to feel sympathy: "She had hated and feared the swamp, but long association had changed her without her realizing it. . . . The swamp monster retreated before the magic of man. Arvay watched the conquest of her old enemy with the utmost fascination. It was very personal" (171). Her nostalgia, however, has an unhealthy side, for this "draining" mirrors the healthy shrinking of Arvay's psychological problems, which permits the final joyous scenes on the sea. Her feeling here reminds us of the Prisoner of Chillon's meditation:

> My very chains and I grew friends
> So much a long communion tends
> To make us what we are: even I
> Regain'd my freedom with a sigh.
>   (Byron 49)

The unhealthy gloom of the swamp waters gets replaced by the sweep and purity of the sea when the novel shifts to Jim's coastal shrimping business. He has signaled his love for his women by naming the boats *Angeline* and *Arvay Henson*. His easy rapport and joking with the sailors, as usual, helps account for his success. These coastal chapters appropriately contain ribald, salty humor: Stumpy the sailor says he'll never own a boat: "'Too much good likker that needs drinking up, and everytime I see a pretty woman switching along, I got to stop and drop a flag on it'" (194). This sexual double entendre would hardly have made it into Hurston's earlier books.

Male initiatory humor gets rendered in the story of the mythical Bozo and how to find him. "Before the Third Man got through with his fantastic directions, Jim caught on that was some joke. . . . 'Much obliged for the information,' Jim said. 'And now that I know about Bozo, I take it that I'm initiated.' 'Kee-rect, My Captain,' the Third Man grinned. 'Reckon I'd better go finish off breakfast. Old Bozo is liable to board us any time and we ought to be in shape to tackle him'" (195–96). Obviously, this orally initiates the new sailor, something like the "snipe hunt" green campers must endure. Humor's role in liminality and the establishment of communitas finds another expression here. The tale of course belongs to the American standard repertory of tall tales as well.

Alfredo Corregio reappears as the captain of the *Angeline*, and a black man captains the *Kenny Meserve* (appropriately, since Kenny's life has been shaped by black culture). Jim plans to name other boats after son-in-law Hatton; a soon-to-be-born grandchild (news to the reader); and finally, he'll name the last one *Big Jim*. This reaffirms that Jim always thinks of others before himself and that his ruling impulse has always been to "launch" his family and "keep it afloat." The metaphors here remind us of the magnificent opening line of *Their Eyes*: "Ships at a distance have every man's wish on board" (9). They also provide a literalization of Hurston's metaphor of people/ ships who can only "bump" against each other's hulls sometimes, rather than really connect. Now those ships have been boarded, launched, and work together. They are, moreover, Hurston's ships, ships that speak of an integrated, laughing world. "Some boats had mixed crews. They all talked about the same things, and they all cursed out the owners. . . . 'Cussing the boss out behind his back is a lot of pleasure. I forget that I'm the owner and cuss my ownself out at times.' Jim laughed and Arvay joined in with him" (285). This surely is one of the most significant lines in the book. In a purposeful creation of sexual tension and suspense, however, Hurston delays the longed-for resumption of their marital love; Arvay sleeps alone in Jim's cabin.

The next day, stripped to the waist, Jim appears as the heroic captain, getting the ship over the bar after a titanic struggle with the waves. Arvay appears by his side, dressed in the new clothes Jim has bought her, blue jeans, blue shirt, and sea boots.[28] Arvay's "rebirth" thus resembles Janie's on the muck, where Tea Cake dresses her in overalls; stepping over gendered dress lines signifies equality, freedom, and intimacy.

The terrified mate cries out, in an ironic, inverting echo of Whitman, "'Captain! My Captain! You gone crazy? Turn back! This bar is too rough to cross right now. Oh, Captain!'" In a dramatic demonstration of her new, courageous self, Arvay, "fierce with anger," pulls him off when he clutches Jim's leg, a scene obviously meant to contrast with her paralyzed state when Jim handled the rattlesnake. "The boat gave another shudder and then a leap, and glided out onto the calm waters of the Atlantic. The contrast was utterly startling. . . . She felt herself stretching and extending with her surroundings. . . . The fear that she had experienced while crossing the bar was like a birthpain. It was already forgotten and gone" (291). Obviously, the feelings Arvay experiences here are analogous to what Freud calls the "oceanic feeling," a sensation "of 'eternity,' a feeling as of something limitless, unbounded—as it were, 'oceanic'" (*Civilization* 11). Freud was disturbed by this concept, described to him by a friend, since it seemed to be a common experience, yet he himself never felt it. He linked it, however, to the only state in nonpathological consciousness where the ego does not draw sharp lines of separation between itself and the outside, the "height of being in love" (13), which these scenes represent, finally, for Arvay. Moreover, such a moment of loving embrace with the outside world expresses (and Arvay's case confirms it) a reexpansion of the ego back toward what it once was, for "originally the ego includes everything" (15). Now, years later, it leaps out from its narrowed parameters in an empowering embrace, presumably a feeling that brings exhilaration and laughter. Freud sees our joy in this moment as that of finding the "survival of something that was originally there, alongside of what was later derived from it" (15).

Arvay tells Jim she knows he took this risk over rough passage so that she could see the sunrise on her first trip out; he responds that "'Once I had seen and been on the sea, it got inside me, and I ever longed for it like a drop of water. . . . Don't you realize that the sea is the home of water? All water is off on a journey unlessen it's in the sea, and it's homesick, and bound to make its way home some day.' 'That's something to think about, Jim. It's never entered my mind before. Maybe it's like that with everything and everybody. If it's in there, it will return to its real self at last'" (294). Clearly, this echoes Freud's concept of the oceanic feeling as a "survival" of something feared lost. "Homecoming" was in Arvay's mind when she returned to Sawley; now the real homecoming seems to be not just to Jim but to her self, as the cosmic imagery Jim employs here suggests, and as the ship named for her, because of her saving action, passes through the last barrier into freedom.

Earlier, Hurston added some seemingly gratuitous, but humorous, folklore about shrimp in a conversation between the Third Man and Captain Jim: "'You suppose that there's some underground, or undersea, passage across under Florida that connects the ocean and the Gulf and some of them know it and go that way?' 'Could be. Then, too, they travel at night sometimes. When you see 'em with red feet, they been travelling at night'" (199). This seemingly innocuous story leads into a later, more serious exchange between Jim and Arvay. He elaborates with a more earth-bound simile, describing the water in the underground caves at Silver Springs breaking through into the "crystal air" after centuries, a cosmic expansion of the comic journey of the shrimp noted earlier. In human terms, "'Some folks are surface water and are easily seen and known about. Others get caught underground, and have to cut and gnaw their way out if they ever get seen by human eyes'" (294–95). Jim's poetic formulation here has something in common with Rebecca's well and Hagar's imagery, for as Savina J. Teubal has reminded us, "springs, fountains, ponds, and wells were female symbols in archaic religions, and were often considered water-passages to the underground womb" (25).

These convolutions of imagery thus fuse Florida localisms, on land and at sea, with psychological metaphors for the unconscious; we should remember, though, the basic metaphor of "crossing the bar," where the ship—significantly named the *Arvay Henson* and not the *Arvay Meserve*—finally breaks free from the enclosing shell of death-in-life into the teeming world of the sea, a watery rebirth. The phrase "crossing the bar" of course appears in Tennyson's poem about death, a work Hurston no doubt knew. His last lines, in fact, speak well of Arvay's feeling here, if one sees Jim, rather than God, as the pilot: "I hope to see my Pilot face to face / When I have crossed the bar." Jim in this sense would be functioning like Tea Cake in *Their Eyes*, "piloting" a woman to a rebirth; but again, as Hurston makes clear with her reference to Arvay's "birth-pangs," ultimately only Arvay can perform the "birthing." Now, and only now, can Arvay also become Arvay Meserve, serving others by honoring herself.

The bawdy, sly humor accompanies these cosmic scenes; observe the names of two comic sailors always with Jim: "Cup and Titty followed him laughing. By the time that Arvay descended to the galley, they were laughing and cleaning the shrimp, and indulging in horseplay. Arvay looked on and noted how like little boys they acted. Didn't men ever get grown? Arvay asked herself indulgently. It was nice to see how they could play like that. It made her feel good and like taking care of them. She fixed the dinner in a warm family atmosphere and was glad when they all praised her and said how good it was. . . . Arvay could hear the three men laughing and joking over their work on the after deck as she came up from the galley. . . . They sounded so happy and free of care together" (301).

Although dead serious about getting her marriage back on track, she conceptualizes the endeavor comically: "She was going to deal with things. Oh, yes she was! And she was not going to fool around with a try-net. She was going overboard with the drag and sweep the very bottom" (303). We notice here Arvay has uncharacteristically adopted the language people like Cup and Titty might use, an indication of her companionship with other people.

She's also filled with courage; she imagines a possible female rival, "maybe . . . young and ever so pretty, and of high family and learned in books and ways. Arvay crimped her mouth and . . . grimmed herself to go up against her. . . . If and when she got hold of Jim, it was not going to be as a gracious gift from Arvay" (304). While we admire her newfound courage and her realization that she can conquer problems of class and education, we see that she directs it here at mythical other women rather than at specific problems in the relationship. Similarly, when she rejects the paradigm of Isaac and Rebecca at the well for that of Ruth and Naomi, she's still stuck in typological modes of representation, but she's at least abandoned Hagar.

She prepares a formal speech for Jim, but in the big showdown in her cabin, she can't remember it. Jim gives her a start by joking, pretending her sass constitutes mutiny in the face of the ship's captain: "'You must think that you've found some weapon to your hand since I seen you last.'" In comic and markedly physical words redolent of the black church of *Jonah*, "she mounted to the pulpit and took her text from that. 'Do I need any more weapon than I already got? Did I ever need any different?' Arvay shot an impudent and challenging look at Jim. 'Maybe the reason you never see no bear-cat with hip-pockets is because he don't have no need to tote no pistol with him. I was born with all I ever needed to handle your case.'" (306). Clearly, Arvay has found the lost keys of the kingdom that she misplaced sometime earlier, and her confident joking offers an accurate barometer.[29] Jim's subsequent remarks indicate he's been nervous about others stealing her love, and he's feared approaching her too. Arvay thinks, "This was a wonderful and powerful thing to know, but she must not let him know what she had perceived" (307). This ironically echoes Jim's thought years before that he mustn't let Arvay know her power. Now, he covers his surprise by the bravado of macho rhetoric:

> "You took long enough to stumble round the tea-cup to get to the handle. . . . Never no more in this world, nor even in Georgia, will I act the goddamn fool for your benefit like that again. . . . So you're planted here now forever. You're going to do just what I say do, and you had better not let me hear you part your lips in a grumble. Do you hear me, Arvay?"
>
> "Yes, Jim, I hear you." . . . Jim was gripping her shoulders so hard until it hurt her, and trembling all over his body like a child trying to keep from crying. Like a little boy who had fled in out of the dark to the comfort of his mother. After a while, Jim sighed deeply, and his head slid down and snuggled on her breast. From long habit, Arvay's fingers began to play through his hair in a gentle way. Almost immediately, Jim sighed and went off into a deep and peaceful sleep. (309)

Obviously, in this return to the sea, the great mother, and Jim's return to Arvay's bosom, his actions belie his words.

And Arvay at last has realized this. In a revealing assertion, Arvay tells Jim, "'I ain't near so dumb as I used to be. I can read your writing. Actions speak louder than words'" (307). This once again points to Hurston's formulation of the "inaudible voice of it all," the difficulty of human communication—especially, perhaps, between men and women—and the need we all have to look for meaning beyond mere words. Humor plays a vital role in finding this new hieroglyphics.

Hurston lets the boat itself stand for our heroine: "The *Arvay Henson* rode gently on the bosom of the Atlantic. It lifted and bowed with the wind and the sea. It was acting in submission to the infinite, and Arvay felt its peace. For the first time in her life, she acknowledged that that was the only way." Full of acceptance now, she sees Earl's birth as predestined and purging. Earl seems to function as a sacred scapegoat: "Somebody had to pay off the debt so that the rest of the pages could be clean." God elects her to bear the burden and pain but rewards her with Angeline and Kenny. "Then it was like the Resurrection. The good that was in her flesh. . . . Kenny had come bringing the music part inside her that she had never had a chance to show herself. He represented those beautiful sounds that she used to hear from nowhere as she played around with her doll under the mulberry tree. But give credit where credit was due. Jim was the other part. Joined together, they had made these wonders. Human flesh was full of mysteries and a wonderful and unknown thing" (310). Taking a new look at Jim as he lies helplessly sleeping in her arms, "what she had considered her cross, she now saw as her glory. Her father and Larraine had taken from her because they felt that she had something to take from and to give out of her fullness. Her mother had looked to her for dependence. Her children, and Jim and all. Her job was mothering. What more could any woman want and need? . . . Holy Mary, who had been blessed to mother Jesus had been no better off than she was. She had been poor and unlearnt too" (310–11).

This scene completes a typological metamorphosis of some complexity. Arvay, alternating between self-imposed and self-pitying exile and a semisecure place in her family, finally throws off the Hagar identification, finds her identity and a matching/resultant sense of humor, and becomes Sarah, whose rejuvenation is signified by laughter. But Hurston takes it further. Both women are progenitors of nations and thus are types for the antitype of the Virgin Mary; paradoxically, the suffering Hagar rather than the happy Sarah fits even better here. As Phillis Trible points out, Hagar is the first woman in Israel's historical sequence to bear a child; she hears an annunciation, receives a divine promise of descendants, and is the first mother to weep for her dying child. She thus not only provides a prototype for all Hebrew mothers, as Trible claims (28), but the type for the Blessed Virgin as well. The translation to the Madonna here fits well, for it underlines both Arvay's new birth and the pieta-like pose we last see her in. "The sunlight rose higher, climbed the rail and came on board. Arvay sat up as best she could without disturbing Jim and switched off the artificial light overhead, and met the look of the sun with confidence. Yes, she was doing what the big light had told her to do. She was serving and meant to serve. She made the sun welcome to come on in, then snuggled down again beside her husband" (311).

We need to twist our critical lens yet again to properly understand this conclusion. Arvay here comes to a point Janie reaches in her final marriage, for as the latter cradles the dead Tea Cake's head in her lap near the conclusion of *Their Eyes*, she thanks him wordlessly "for giving her the chance for loving service" (273). Furthermore, both books combine a pair of lovers with cosmic elements in spiritual union; on the last page of *Their Eyes*, Tea Cake seems to come "prancing around" Janie with "the sun for a shawl," and Janie, in turn, adorns herself with a matching shawl, the "net of the horizon" which she pulls in like a fishnet and drapes over her shoulder. Both scenes properly belong to the "oceanic" milieu Freud describes but mistrusts and conjoins memory/horizon with the eternal/cosmic. Such a dissolving moment necessarily erases boundaries between humans and nature, man and woman, time and eternity, the cosmic and the comic. Freud, preoccupied with his masculinist oedipal configuration, no doubt saw the oceanic as a threat to his psychoanalytical construct. Hurston, who seems to agree with Freud about mourning and melancholia, would seem to differ from him here. I make the distinction because a failure to probe the psychological dimensions of Hurston's two powerful endings might suggest that both her heroines are what feminists call "man-defined" women and that Hurston approves. Conversely, following Freud's mistaken dismissal of the oceanic as "regressive," one could read Jim as "regressing" back to the mother's womb, with Arvay falling back into "mere" maternity. Conflating the conclusions of the two novels, however, and reading their implications as boundary-erasing and therefore empowering for all four figures aligns the oceanic with the Afrocentric. The African view of the cosmos assumes the interrelatedness of all things and argues for community and union rather than for difference, hierarchy, and individual dominance.

The final scene of *Seraph* becomes more personal when we compare it with a powerful concluding passage that was not included in the original version of *Dust Tracks*. There Hurston states, "I have given myself more harrowing pain than anyone else has ever been capable of giving me. No one else can inflict the hurt of faith unkept. I have had the corroding insight at times, of recognizing that I am a bundle of sham and tinsel, honest metal and sincerity that cannot be untangled. . . . I have been correlated to the world. . . . I know that destruction and construction are but two faces of Dame Nature. . . . I have served and been served. . . . I have touched the four corners of the horizon, for from hard searching it seems to me that tears and laughter, love and hate, make up the sum of life" (348). Thus in her fiction and her life story itself, Hurston suggests fulfillment lies in service to oneself and others, service that leads to a transcendental oneness, where class, gender, race, and all other categories melt away.

On the other hand, we should remember Hurston's glory in her artistic achievements, which Arvay does not share: "My dross has given my other parts great sorrow. But, on the other hand, I have given myself the pleasures of sunrises blooming out of oceans, and sunsets drenching heaped-up clouds. I have walked in storms with a crown of clouds about my head and the zigzag lightning playing through my fingers. The gods of the upper air have uncovered their faces to my eyes. I have found out that my real home is in the water, that the earth is only my stepmother. My old man, the Sun, sired me out of the sea" (*Dust Tracks* 347).

Obviously, Hurston is willing to give Arvay only some of her own "cosmic" gifts. Only the artist has played with the lightning and worn the crown of clouds. For Hurston, this may have been a key difference between her and Arvay; both suffer from a pattern of rejection and self-inflicted wounds. As Melanie Klein observes, however, some people find release in "painting, writing, or other productive activities under the stress of frustrations and hardships. Others become more productive in a different way—more capable of appreciating people and things, more tolerant in their relation to others—they become wiser" (328). Hurston became not only an artist but one capable of harnessing her talents and venting her frustrations through a dynamic and innovative use of folk-based humor in both her life and her art. We should also remember, however, as Hurston obviously did, that the maternal function is by definition creative as well, and recognizing this lifts and inspires Arvay to a new assessment of personal worth, signified by a strengthened sense of play and laughter, creative concepts clearly linked in *Seraph* with the maternal. The cosmic force of comedy also erases boundaries, also creates intimacy, also throws up avenues of development for both the self and the community.

Hurston, who harnessed the gifts of humor and narrative together to pull her in her ride across the cosmos toward the sun, knew of this "other way" of people like Arvay. In writing of that road not taken, she created a workshop for her psychological history but also a fictional family that finds fulfillment and resolution in laughing, loving communion with each other and the cosmos.

Notes

1. Moreover, Hemenway ceaselessly links the plot to specifics of Hurston's own life, obviously an impossible goal since Hurston was only briefly married (albeit to two men), had no children, never had a really permanent home after childhood, and certainly didn't suffer the nagging familial problems that plague Arvay throughout the novel. Perhaps more pertinent, however, is his insistence on somehow making Arvay represent all the men who had failed Hurston, while Jim is the author herself. His working out of this scenario is quite ingenious, and to be fair, sounds plausible at several points. Ultimately, however, this argument is more relevant to his biographical patterns than to a sustained reading of the text itself. A more profitable approach might lie in a psychological comparison. It seems certain that elements of Hurston appear in both Jim and Arvay, but most profoundly in the latter. Finally, Hemenway quotes Zora herself to settle the case; writing to Marjorie Kinnan Rawlings, she said "I am not so sure that I have done my best, but I tried. I need not tell you that my goal still eludes me. I am in despair because it keeps ever ahead of me" (315). As we saw earlier, however, Hurston had said much the same about *Moses* to Edward Grover; authors are hardly the best judges of the strengths or weaknesses of their works, and Hurston was no exception. Indeed, Rawlings herself wrote to her editor at Scribner's, Maxwell Perkins, about her first novel, *South Moon Under,* which may have influenced Hurston: "Now that it is done, I realize that it is not the book I wanted to write—not the picture I wanted to give. Very possibly it is a better book—probably more readable—but somehow or other the emotion I intended to convey, has escaped me. Probably it is always so with any writer except a true genius. The thing that sweeps across you, clamoring for expression, is probably always more powerful than the flabby words and phrases you begin to trot out against it. The profound reality, the essence, of an idea or a feeling, manages to slip away in the shuffle. I wonder what proportion of books gives the thing the writer wanted so much to give" (Bigelow and Monti 14).

2. For a detailed and interesting survey of Hurston's use of precise local characteristics, see Morris and Dunn, who examine all of Hurston's Florida novels, but do especially well in showing the authenticity and realism of *Seraph* and how the natural symbols play important roles in the novel.

3. Zora Neale Hurston to Carl Van Vechten, Nov. 2, 1942, James Weldon Johnson Memorial Collection, Yale Collection of American Literature, Beinecke Rare Book and Manuscript Library, Yale University, New Haven, Conn.

4. Hurston's admiration for Rawlings may be found in a series of letters she wrote her, now in the Marjorie Kinnan Rawlings Papers, Rare Books and Manuscripts, University of Florida Library, Gainesville. I would caution against viewing the two writers as friends, however. Rawlings didn't mind spending all day with Zora, or even getting drunk with her, but when Hurston spent the night at Cross Creek she had to sleep in the maid's cabin. For

more details, consult Idella Parker's memoir. I am examining this relationship closely in my work-in-progress, "Native Sons and Daughters: Place, Self, and the Other in Southern Fiction."

5. My discussion of Arvay, mourning, and melancholy centers on Freud's essay because it seems obvious that that was the source of Hurston's understanding of the syndrome. I am well aware, however, of the sexist dimensions of Freud's thesis, which tends to valorize "melancholia" as a great man's affliction, while minimizing mourning as a lowly woman's disease. The way Freud has been used to read the works of the Renaissance in a slanted way has recently been brilliantly delineated by Juliana Schiesari, who employs the work of Luce Irigaray, Kaja Silverman, and Julia Kristeva to reveal the fallacies of Freud's approach and the ways in which his entrenchment in the manhood myths of the Renaissance shaped him and many of his theories. It is interesting, however, to note that Hurston, while largely operating within the parameters of Freud's thesis, nevertheless portrays Arvay as more melancholic than mourning and is quite imaginative in her horrific, but detailed, mental iconography.

6. This would seem to be Hurston's expurgated version of a popular rural southern joke: What's the noisiest thing in the world? Two skeletons screwing on a tin roof during a thunderstorm, using a tin can for a rubber.

7. This yoking of Robert E. Lee and Peter as comic figures has serious import, as Arvay's inferiority complex owes much to the antebellum totem pole of class; moreover, her lack of faith in Jim, which parallels Peter's, is reversed in the last scenes in the book when she joins her husband's triumphant voyage over the bar into the ocean.

8. The basic outlines of the research on the topic may be found in Fasold, McDavid and McDavid, and P. Nichols. For an indication of the importance of these issues in matters of ethnic boundaries, see Rickford.

9. Zora Neale Hurston to Marjorie Kinnan Rawlings, Dec. 1948, Hurston Collection, Rare Books and Manuscripts, University of Florida Library, Gainesville.

10. Richard Wright uses this identical technique at the beginning of "Big Boy Leaves Home," where the reader hears a quartet of young male voices rising out of the woods, singing snatches of the dozens, a clear signal that he will be working with folk motifs in the narrative. For a complete reading of this, see my article "Wright Writing Reading."

11. For two classic versions of the "Saturday Night" joke, see Dorson 79–80. Maya Angelou told a version of this joke to a large audience at Louisiana State University in 1992.

12. On the other hand, at many other junctures in the book Jim demonstrates the effect black modes of discourse and joking have had on him. In the last chapters, as captain of a fishing fleet, he curses the sharks a la Stubb in *Moby-Dick*, but using a black mode of address: "Arvay had always known that Jim was a cursing man, but she had never heard him to this extent as he called the sharks every kind of low, unprincipled thing that he could lay his tongue to, and plenty seemed to be available. He played the

dozens with them and went way back in their ancestry. Never had a shark's mother been married or begot a shark in a decent bed. And as for their pappies, they were thus-and-sos" (298).

13. The assertion that the "pet's" owner will defend him even from murder finds a grimly serious testimonial in Charles Chesnutt's *The Marrow of Tradition,* when an aged black retainer is falsely accused of murder and promptly defended by his elderly white employer.

14. This important distinction applies to many humorous conventions of oppressed peoples, as Roger Abraham's comment on trickster stories reveals: "Trickster functions primarily as a release valve for all of the anti-social desires repressed by the men who tell and listen to his stories. He behaves as the members of the society would behave if they were not constrained by fear from acting. Vicariously, sympathetically, through the acts of this egocentric sensualist, man expunges the pressures that might otherwise destroy both his ordered world and himself" ("Trickster" 172). Abrahams is talking here only of the folk world germane to the tale; if we change the words "his ordered world" to "the *controlling* order that controls *his* cultural world" we see the relevance of Coser's observation and the way humor can ironically lance the pressure that otherwise could lead to social action/revolution. We might thus find a greater understanding of Richard Wright's objection to Hurston's fiction, mentioned earlier.

15. Hagar's Egyptian ancestry, moreover, would make her black in Hurston's eyes. This suggests Hurston's awareness of the triple bind of race, class, and gender as a black woman and confirms that her subtraction of race from the formula in *Seraph* permits intense exploration of class and gender psychology.

16. Hurston was not above milking this very real and painful Christmas memory; in 1928 she wrote Godmother to thank her for providing her with "the happiest Christmas season of all my life . . . the kind of Christmas that my half-starved childhood painted" (n.d., Hurston Collection, Rare Books and Manuscripts, University of Florida Library, Gainesville). This scene and others that reveal Hurston's rejection by her father suggest the possibility that the ultimate "lost object" (to use Freud's term) for her, as far as she suffered Arvay's syndrome, was her father. Arvay/Hagar loses a minister/suitor to her sister; Hurston/Hagar lost a minister/father to her sister, who was actually *named* Sarah.

17. I am indebted to Veronica Makowsky for this insight.

18. Zora Neale Hurston to Carl Van Vechten, Dec. 10, 1944, James Weldon Johnson Memorial Collection, Yale Collection of American Literature, Beinecke Rare Book and Manuscript Library, Yale University, New Haven, Conn.

As always, however, Hurston could turn about and try a comic tack. In a letter written to Van Vechten seven months later, she seems to be flaunting her supposedly near love affair with an English-born sailor she plans to accompany to Honduras. Fred Irvine, she relates, is thirty-one and quite the ladies' man (Hurston was fifty-four at this time). She hasn't had sex with him yet because she thinks it would make the projected trip difficult, since Fred was already jealous of her conversations with other men. Irvine, in fact, sounds much like the man Jim Meserve is in the final scenes set on the sea. The letter is fiendishly clever in its construction, for it makes Fred sound attractive in a way she knew would appeal to Van Vechten, but it also paints him as a rival for her friendship, while suggesting that she likes him because he's so like Van Vechten. The latter seems highly unlikely—this "virile, manly" hunk Hurston describes doesn't sound like the effete Van Vechten at all, a man who would have hated even the poshest campground facilities outside of the Waldorf (July 1945, James Weldon Johnson Memorial Collection).

19. Some readers may believe this refers to Thompson's famous marriage to Sinclair Lewis, but she divorced him in 1942. She was very happily married to the Czech painter Maxim Kopf at the time Hurston wrote this and was "inconsolable" when he died in 1958 (Sheen 323ff.).

20. Her feeling for Belinda soon changes, moreover, for when a driver delivers goods, sees Kenny and Belinda, and asks whose kids they are, both say Arvay's. "Arvay saw Belinda about to cry and understood. Belinda valued her and counted on her care and wanted to be loved by her. Arvay knew that feeling. 'Yes indeed, Belinda is my little girl. . . . Born right here on the place, and I wouldn't take a play-pretty for her either, I'm a'telling you!' . . . With her head away up, Belinda marched around in a small circle with her soiled little skirt spread out on both sides" (102).

21. The introduction of "'shinin'" into the plot isn't really developed, but is part and parcel of Hurston's intention of taking the reader through the varieties of enterprise fabled in Florida. She may also have had in mind Marjorie Kinnan Rawlings's extensive use of this motif as an expression of times when people quite rightly take the "law" into their own hands in order to survive (here of course, by breaking it); Rawlings had actually lived with Cracker moonshiners and learned exactly how to make "'shine" (Silverthorne 72 ff.). Her first novel, which Hurston probably read, *South Moon Under* (1934), centers on a moonshining Cracker family, and *Cross Creek* (1942), which Hurston certainly read, uses it too.

22. "Fast Mary" seems to be based on a woman in Eatonville who had an affair with Hurston's Uncle Jim. The lady was notorious as one who "couldn't give the community anything but love, baby." Aunt Caroline finds out about her and knocks her off the church steps on her head; Hurston waggishly speculates she did it less to get revenge than to "satisfy her curiosity, since it was said that the lady felt that anything more than a petticoat under her dresses would be an encumbrance. . . . The way the lady tumbled, it left no doubt in the matter. . . . Evidently Aunt Caroline was put out about it, because she had to expectorate at that very moment, and it just happened to land where the lady was bare. Aunt Caroline evidently tried to correct her error in spitting on her rival, for she took her foot and tried to grind it in. She never said a word, as usual" (*Dust Tracks* 25). *Seraph's* reworking of this material significantly refigures it in that unlike her aunt, Arvay in fact finds a vibrantly new, signifying voice, which does the work Aunt Caroline did physically.

23. Hurston's concentration on Angeline's beauty and sexual desire suggests she chose the name from a blues lyric she cites in "Folklore and Music," where "when she walks . . . she rocks and reels behind. . . . You feel her legs, and you want to feel her thighs. . . . You feel her thighs then you want to go on high. . . . They you fade away and die. . . . Oh! Angeline!" (5).

24. Angie's use of the term "Diddy-Wah-Diddy" is interesting, as it refers to the largest and best known of the Negro mythical places cited by Hurston in her short Federal Writers' Project piece "Negro Mythical Places." Angie's use of it is apt, for it's the place that breeds lazy folk (which of course Hatton isn't), so much so that if you say you're hungry, a baked chicken with a knife and fork stuck in it comes by and says "Eat me!" (shades of Al Capp and L'il Abner's "Shmoos"). For a variant of this tale, see "The Promised Land" in Botkin (10).

25. As Hurston wryly commented in 1934: "Speaking of the use of Negro material by white performers, it is astonishing that so many are trying it, and I have never seen one yet entirely realistic. They often have all the elements of the song, dance, or expression, but they are misplaced or distorted by the accent falling on the wrong element. Every one seems to think that the Negro is easily imitated when nothing is further from the truth. . . . Gershwin and the other 'Negro' rhapsodists come under this same axe. Just about as Negro as caviar or Ann Pennington's athletic Black Bottom. When the Negroes who knew the Black Bottom in its cradle saw the Broadway version they asked each other, 'Is you learnt dat *new* Black Bottom yet?' Proof that it was not *their* dance. And God only knows what the world has suffered from the white damsels who try to sing Blues" ("Characteristics" 46). On the other hand, in her 1946 review of Rudi Blesh's history of jazz, Hurston took him to task for chastising big swing bands for stealing material from small jazz bands. Hurston argues that Blesh himself states jazz was synthetic and borrowed from white music in the first place, so his complaints "amount to something like that anecdote which was going the rounds some years ago: The wife complains to her husband that the maid is not honest. What is the proof? Why, all those towels which they took from the hotel, the maid had stolen" ("Jazz Regarded" 8).

26. As Hazel Carby notes (xiii), this phrase from the book was picked up by the black press after Hurston was falsely accused of molesting a boy, shortly after *Seraph* was published. Supposedly, this speech was autobiographical, a perverted reading that nonetheless suggests it's possible to see Jim, rather than Arvay, as Hurston's alter ego. She certainly identified with the male figure in *Moses*. The passage following that compares Arvay to a hog eating acorns under a tree was used before in *Dust Tracks* in Hurston's tribute to Ethel Waters, whose victimization as it is described by Hurston might be something like what she saw as Jim's: "People to whom she has given her love and trust have exploited it heartlessly, like hogs under an acorn tree—guzzling and grabbing with their ears hanging over their eyes, and never looking up to see the high tree that the acorns fell from" (246–47). This represents an insertion into the book of one of Hurston's most beloved friends.

27. This scene, which juxtaposes the tree and the cabin as signifiers of Arvay's unconscious, also fits with Freud's description of melancholics who work through their ambivalence through long struggle: "It is possible for the process in the unconscious to come to an end, either after the fury has spent itself or after the object has been abandoned as valueless. . . . The ego may enjoy in this the satisfaction of knowing itself as the better of the two, as superior to the object" ("Mourning" 257).

28. These scenes set on the sea follow, step by step, many of the details of the article "St. Augustine Shrimp Fleet" by an anonymous writer working for the WPA Writer's Program in 1940. The narrator dons the same items Jim buys for Arvay to wear; the boat, like Jim's, is a diesel; the captain of the *Fortuna* is Portuguese, just as Alfred, captain of Jim's *Angeline,* is, and so on. The most salient parallel passage is an extended description of the "crossing of the bar," which Hurston, in retelling, makes much more dramatic. Many other details of Hurston's Florida scene-setting were drawn from WPA files. I am indebted to Pam Bordelon for my copy of this particular essay.

29. To show that a character in a novel has changed for the better, Ernest Gaines has stated, a writer should show him or her joking: "Once he becomes more of a human being, he becomes more humorous" (Gaudet and Wooton 24).

Works Cited

Abrahams, Roger. *Deep Down in the Jungle: Negro Narrative Folklore from the Streets of Philadelphia.* Hatboro, Pa.: Folklore Associates, 1964.

——. "Joking: The Training of the Man of Words in Talking Broad." In *Rappin' and Stylin' Out: Communication in Urban Black America.* Ed. Thomas Kochman. Urbana: University of Illinois Press, 1972. 215–40.

——. "The Negro Stereotype." *Journal of American Folklore* 83 (1970): 229–49.

——. "Playing the Dozens." 1962. In *Mother Wit from the Laughing Barrel: Readings in the Interpretation of Afro-American Folklore.* Ed. Alan Dundes. Englewood Cliffs, N.J.: Prentice-Hall, 1973. 295–309.

——. *Positively Black.* Englewood Cliffs, N.J.: Prentice-Hall, 1970.

——. "Rapping and Capping: Black Talk as Art." In *Black America.* Ed. John F. Szwed. New York: Basic Books, 1970. 132–42.

——. "The Training of the Man of Words in Talking Sweet." *Language in Society* 1, no. 1 (1972): 15–29.

——. "Trickster, the Outrageous Hero." In *Our Living Tradition: An Introduction to American Folklore.* Ed. Tristram Potter Coffin. New York: Basic Books, 1968. 170–78.

Adams, Edward C. L. *Tales of the Congaree.* 1928. Ed. Robert G. O'Meally. Chapel Hill: University of North Carolina Press, 1987.

Adams, Harold E. "Minority Caricatures on the American Stage." In *Studies in the Science of Society.* Ed. George P. Murdock. New Haven: Yale University Press, 1937. 1–27.

Albee, Edward. *Who's Afraid of Virginia Woolf?* New York: Atheneum, 1962.

Anderson, Jervis. *This Was Harlem: A Cultural Portrait, 1900–1950.* New York: Farrar, Straus, Giroux, 1982.

Apte, Mahadev. *Humor and Laughter: An Anthropological Approach.* Ithaca, N.Y.: Cornell University Press, 1985.

Arewa, E. Ojo, and Alan Dundes. "Proverbs and the Ethnography of Speaking Folklore." *American Anthropologist* 66 (1964): 70, 85.

Arnez, Nancy Levi, and Clara B. Anthony. "Contemporary Negro Humor as Social Satire." *Phylon* 19 (1968): 339–46.

Awkward, Michael. "Introduction." In *New Essays on* Their Eyes Were Watching God. Ed. Michael Awkward. Cambridge: Cambridge University Press, 1991. 1–27.

Awoonor, Kofi. *The Breast of the Earth: A Survey of the History, Culture, and Literature of Africa South of the Sahara.* Garden City, N.Y.: Anchor Press, 1975.

Ba, A. H., and L. Kesteloot. "Da Monzon et Karta Thema." *Abbia* 14–15 (1966): 179–205.

Baker, Houston. *Blues, Ideology, and Afro-American Literature: A Vernacular Theory.* Chicago: University of Chicago Press, 1984.

———. *Modernism and the Harlem Renaissance.* Chicago: University of Chicago Press, 1987.

———. *Workings of the Spirit: The Poetics of Afro-American Women's Writing.* Chicago: University of Chicago Press, 1991.

Bakhtin, Mikhail. *The Dialogic Imagination: Four Essays by M. M. Bakhtin.* Ed. Michael Holquist. Trans. Caryl Emerson and Michael Holquist. Austin: University of Texas Press, 1981.

———. *Problems of Dostoyevsky's Poetics.* Ed. and Trans. Caryl Emerson. Minneapolis: University of Minnesota Press, 1984.

———. *Rabelais and His World.* Trans. Helene Iswolsky. Bloomington: Indiana University Press, 1984.

Baldwin, James. *Go Tell It on the Mountain.* 1953. New York: Dell, 1970.

Banks, Adelle M. "Bible Tales Zapped into Nintendo Land." *Baton Rouge Morning Advocate,* March 23, 1991, 4F.

Banks, Frank D., and Portia Smiley. "Old-Time Courtship Conversation." In *Mother Wit from the Laughing Barrel: Readings in the Interpretation of Afro-American Folklore.* Ed. Alan Dundes. Englewood Cliffs, N.J.: Prentice-Hall, 1973. 251–57.

Barber, Karin. *I Could Speak until Tomorrow: Oriki Women and the Past in a Yoruba Town.* Washington, D.C.: Smithsonian Institution Press, 1991.

Benesch, Klaus. "Oral Narrative and Literary Text: Afro-American Folklore in *Their Eyes Were Watching God.*" *Callaloo* 11 (Summer 1988): 627–35.

Benjamin, Walter. "The Task of the Translator." Trans. James Hynd and E. M. Valk. *Delos: A Journal of Translation* 1, no. 2 (1968): 76–99.

Bercovitch, Sacvan. *The American Jeremiad.* Madison: University of Wisconsin Press, 1978.

———. *The Puritan Origins of the American Self.* New Haven: Yale University Press, 1975.

Bergson, Henri. *Laughter: An Essay on the Meaning of the Comic.* Trans. Cloudesley Brereton and Fred Rothwell. New York: Macmillan, 1911.

Berube, Michael. *Marginal Forces/Cultural Centers: Tolson, Pynchon, and the Politics of the Canon.* Ithaca, N.Y.: Cornell University Press, 1992.

Bethel, Lorraine. "'This Infinity of Conscious Pain': Zora Neale Hurston and the Black Female Literary Tradition." In *But Some of Us Are Brave: Black Women's Studies.* Ed. Gloria T. Hull, Patricia Bell Scott, and Barbara Smith. Old Westbury, N.Y.: Feminist Press, 1982. 176–88.

Bigelow, Gordon E., and Laura V. Monti, eds. *Selected Letters of Marjorie Kinnan Rawlings.* Gainesville: University of Florida Press, 1983.

Blake, Emma. "Zora Neale Hurston: Author and Folklorist." *Negro History Bulletin* 29 (Apr. 1966): 149–50, 165.

Blassingame, John W. *The Slave Community: Plantation Life in the Antebellum South.* 2d ed. New York: Oxford University Press, 1979.

Boas, Franz, ed. *General Anthropology.* Boston: D. C. Heath, 1938.

Bogle, Donald. *Toms, Coons, Mulattoes, Mammies, and Bucks: An Interpretive History of Blacks in American Film.* New York: Viking, 1973.

Bordelon, Pamela. "New Tracks on *Dust Tracks:* Toward a Reassessment of the Life of Zora Neale Hurston." *African American Review,* forthcoming.

Boskin, Joseph. "'Black'/Black Humor: The Renaissance of Laughter." In *A Celebration of Laughter.* Ed. Werner M. Mendel. Los Angeles: Mara Books, 1970. 145–59.

———. "Sambo: The National Jester in the Popular Culture." In *The Great Fear: Race in the Mind of America.* Ed. Gary B. Nash and Richard Weiss. New York: Holt, Rinehart, and Winston, 1970. 165–85.

———. *Sambo: The Rise and Demise of an American Jester.* New York: Oxford University Press, 1986.

Botkin, B. A., ed. *Lay My Burden Down: A Folk History of Slavery.* Chicago: University of Chicago Press, 1945.

Braithwaite, William Stanley. "The Negro in Literature." *Crisis* 29 (Nov. 1924): 24.

Brawley, Benjamin. *The Negro Genius.* New York: Dodd, Mead, 1937.

Brearly, H. C. "Ba-ad Nigger." In *Mother Wit from the Laughing Barrel: Readings in the Interpretation of Afro-American Folklore.* Ed. Alan Dundes. Englewood Cliffs, N.J.: Prentice-Hall, 1973. 578–85.

Brewer, J. Mason. *American Negro Folklore.* Chicago: Quadrangle Books, 1968.

———. *Dog Ghosts and Other Texas Negro Folk Tales.* Austin: University of Texas Press, 1958.

———. *The Word on the Brazos: Negro Preacher Tales from the Brazos Bottoms of Texas.* Austin: University of Texas Press, 1953.

Brown, Lloyd W. "The West Indian as an Ethnic Stereotype in Black American Literature." *Negro American Literature Forum* 5, no. 1 (1971): 8–14.

Brown, Sterling. *The Collected Poems of Sterling A. Brown.* Selected by Michael S. Harper. Chicago: Triquarterly Books, 1989.

———. *The Negro in American Fiction.* Washington, D.C.: Associates in Negro Folk Education, 1937.

———. *Negro Poetry and Drama.* Washington, D.C.: Associates in Negro Folk Education, 1937.

Bus, Heiner. "The Establishment of Community in Zora Neale Hurston's 'The Eatonville Anthology' (1926) and Rolando Hinojosa's 'Estampas del Valle' (1973)." In *European Perspectives on Hispanic Literatures of the United States.* Ed. Genevieve Fabre. Houston: Arte Publico Press, 1988. 66–81.

Byron, George Gordon, Lord. *Selected Poetry and Letters.* Ed. Edward E. Bostetter. New York: Holt, Rinehart, and Winston, 1965.

Caldwell, Erskine. *Tobacco Road.* New York: Scribner's, 1932.

Callahan, John F. *In the African-American Grain: The Pursuit of Voice in Twenti-eth-Century Black Fiction.* Urbana: University of Illinois Press, 1988.

Campbell, Joseph. *The Hero with a Thousand Faces.* 1949. Princeton, N.J.: Princeton University Press, 1972.

Campbell, Richard H., and Michael R. Pitts. *The Bible on Film: A Checklist, 1897–1980.* Metuchen, N.J.: Scarecrow Press, 1981.

Carby, Hazel. Foreword to *Seraph on the Suwanee* by Zora Neale Hurston. 1948. New York: Harper, 1991.

———. "The Politics of Fiction, Anthropology, and the Folk: Zora Neale Hurston." In *New Essays on* Their Eyes Were Watching God. Ed. Michael Awkward. Cambridge: Cambridge University Press, 1991. 71–93.

Carr, Glynis. *"Storytelling* as *Bildung* in Zora Neale Hurston's *Their Eyes Were Watching God." College Language Association Journal* 31, no. 2 (Dec. 1987): 189–200.

Carter, Bill. "Forecast for 'Today': Cloudy." *New York Times Magazine,* June 10, 1990, 66.

Chodorow, Nancy. *The Reproduction of Mothering.* Berkeley: University of California Press, 1978.

Cobbs, Hamner. "Give Me the Black Belt!" *Alabama Review* 17 (1964): 163–80.

Cooke, Michael G. *Afro-American Literature in the Twentieth Century: The Achievement of Intimacy.* New Haven: Yale University Press, 1984.

Coser, Rose Laub. "Some Social Functions of Laughter: A Study of Humor in a Hospital Setting." *Human Relations* 12, no. 2 (1959): 171–82.

Cothran, Kay Lorraine. "Such Stuff as Dreams: A Folkloristic Sociology of Fantasy in the Okefenokee Rim, Georgia." Ph.D. diss., University of Pennsylvania, 1972.

Crabtree, Claire. "The Confluence of Folklore, Feminism, and Black Self-determination in Zora Neale Hurston's *Their Eyes Were Watching God." Southern Literary Journal* 17, no. 2 (Spring 1985): 54–66.

Creel, Margaret Washington. "Gullah Attitudes toward Life and Death." In *Africanisms in American Culture.* Ed. Joseph E. Holloway. Bloomington: Indiana University Press, 1990. 69–97.

Cripps, Thomas. "The Death of Rastus: The Negro in American Films since 1945." *Phylon* 28 (1967): 267–75.

Cromwell, Otelia, Lorenzo Dow Turner, and Eva B. Dykes, eds. *Readings from Negro Authors for Schools and Colleges with a Bibliography of Negro Literature.* New York: Harcourt Brace, 1931.

Crowley, Daniel J., ed. *African Folklore in the New World.* Austin: University of Texas Press, 1977.

Cullen, Countee. "Heritage." 1925. In *The New Negro.* Ed. Alain Locke. New York: Atheneum, 1968. 250–53.

Dance, Daryl Cumber. "Contemporary Militant Black Humor." *Negro American Literature Forum* 8, no. 2 (1974): 217–22.

———. *Long Gone: The Mecklenburg Six and the Theme of Escape in Black Folklore.* Knoxville: University of Tennessee Press, 1987.

———. *Shuckin' and Jivin': Folklore from Contemporary Black Americans*. Bloomington: Indiana University Press, 1978.

Daniel, Jack L., and Geneva Smitherman. "How I Got Over: Communication Dynamics in the Black Community." *Quarterly Journal of Speech* 62, no. 1 (Feb. 1976): 26–39.

Davies, Christie. *Ethnic Humor around the World: A Comparative Analysis*. Bloomington: Indiana University Press, 1990.

Davis, Gerald L. *I Got the Word in Me and I Can Sing It, You Know: A Study of the Performed African-American Sermon*. Philadelphia: University of Pennsylvania Press, 1985.

De Jongh, James. *Vicious Modernism: Black Harlem and the Literary Imagination*. New York: Cambridge University Press, 1990.

Delbanco, Andrew. *The Puritan Ordeal*. Cambridge, Mass.: Harvard University Press, 1989.

Dewey, John. *Art as Experience*. 1934. New York: Capricorn Books, 1959.

Dickinson, Emily. *Final Harvest: Emily Dickinson's Poems*. Ed. Thomas H. Johnson. Boston: Little, Brown, 1961.

Dillard, J. L. *Black English: Its History and Usage in the United States*. New York: Random House, 1972.

Dixon, Melvin. *Ride Out the Wilderness: Geography and Identity in Afro-American Literature*. Urbana: University of Illinois Press, 1987.

Dodge, N. S. "Negro Patois and Its Humor." *Appleton's Journal of Popular Literature, Science, and Art* 3 (1870): 161–62.

Dollard, John. "The Dozens: Dialectic of Insult." *American Imago* 1 (1939): 3–25.

Dormon, James. "Ethnic Stereotyping in American Popular Culture: The Depiction of American Ethnics in the Cartoon Periodicals of the Gilded Age." *Amerikastudien/American Studies* 30 (1986): 489–507.

———. "Shaping the Popular Image of Post-Reconstruction American Blacks: The 'Coon Song' Phenomenon of the Gilded Age." *American Quarterly* 40 (1988): 450–71.

———. "The Strange Career of Jim Crow Rice." *Journal of Social History* 3 (Winter 1969–70): 109–22.

Dorson, Richard M. *American Negro Folktales*. 1958. New York: Fawcett Publications, 1967.

Dorst, John. "Rereading *Mules and Men:* Toward the Death of the Ethnographer." *Cultural Anthropology* 2, no. 3 (1987): 305–18.

Douglas, Mary. "Jokes." In *Implicit Meanings: Essays in Anthropology*. London: Routledge, 1975. 90–114.

———. "The Social Control of Cognition: Some Factors in Joke Perception." *Man* 3 (1968): 361–76.

Douglass, Frederick. *Narrative of the Life of Frederick Douglass, an American Slave, Written by Himself.* 1845. New York: New American Library, 1968.

Du Bois, W. E. B. *The Souls of Black Folk*. 1903. In *Three Negro Classics*. Ed. John Hope Franklin. New York: Avon, 1963.

Dunbar, Paul Laurence. "We Wear the Mask." In *The Heath Anthology of Amer-*

ican Literature. Ed. Paul Lauter et al. 2 vols. Lexington, Mass.: Heath, 1990. 2:486.

Dunne, Finley Peter. *Mr. Dooley Remembers: The Informal Memoirs of Finley Peter Dunne*. Ed. Philip Dunne. Boston: Little, Brown, 1963.

DuPlessis, Rachel Blau. "Power, Judgment, and Narrative in a Work of Zora Neale Hurston: Feminist Cultural Studies." In *New Essays on* Their Eyes Were Watching God. Ed. Michael Awkward. Cambridge: Cambridge University Press, 1991. 95–122.

Edwards, Jay. "Structural Analysis of the Afro-American Trickster Tale." *Black American Literature Forum* 15, no. 4 (1981): 155–64.

Ehrenberg, Lewis A. *Steppin' Out: New York Nightlife and the Transformation of American Culture, 1890–1930*. Westport, Conn.: Greenwood Press, 1985.

Ellis, A. B. *The Yoruba Speaking Peoples of the Slave Coast of West Africa*. London: Chapman and Hall, 1894.

Ellison, Ralph. *Going to the Territory*. New York: Random House, 1986.

Ellison, Ralph. *Invisible Man*. 1952. New York: Vintage, 1989.

Emerson, Ralph Waldo. "Nature." In *Selections from Ralph Waldo Emerson*. Ed. Stephen E. Whicher. Boston: Houghton Mifflin, 1957. 21–56.

Fasold, Ralph W. "The Relation between Black and White Speech in the South." *American Speech* 56, no. 3 (1981): 163–89.

Faulkner, William. *As I Lay Dying*. New York: Random House, 1930.

———. *Go Down, Moses*. New York: Random House, 1942.

———. *Requiem for a Nun*. 1950. New York: Vintage, 1975.

Fauset, Jessie. "The Gift of Laughter." 1925. In *The New Negro*. Ed. Alain Locke. New York: Atheneum, 1968. 161–67.

Federal Writers' Project. *Florida: A Guide to the Southernmost State*. New York: Oxford University Press, 1939.

Ferguson, Sally Ann. "Folkloric Men and Female Growth in *Their Eyes Were Watching God*." *Black American Literature Forum* 21, nos. 1–2 (1987): 185–97.

Finnegan, Ruth. *Limba Stories and Story-Telling*. Oxford: Oxford University Press, 1967.

———. *Oral Literature in Africa*. Oxford: Oxford University Press, 1970.

Ford, Nick Aaron. *The Contemporary Negro Novel: A Study in Race Relations*. College Park, Md.: McGrath, 1968.

Forshey, Gerald E. *American Religious and Biblical Spectaculars*. Westport, Conn.: Praeger, 1992.

Fox, Greer Litton. "'Nice Girl': Social Control of Women through a Value Construct." *Signs* 2, no. 4 (Summer 1977): 805–17.

Frazer, Sir James George. *The Golden Bough: A Study in Magic and Religion*. 3d ed. Vol. 2. London: Macmillan, 1922.

Freud, Sigmund. *Civilization and Its Discontents*. Trans. and ed. James Strachey. New York: Norton, 1961.

———. "Humour." *International Journal of Psychoanalysis* 9, no. 1 (1928): 1–6.

———. *Jokes and Their Relation to the Unconscious*. Trans. and ed. James Strachey. New York: Norton, 1963.

————. *Moses and Monotheism.* Trans. Katherine Jones. 1939. New York: Vintage Books, 1967.

————. "Mourning and Melancholia." In *The Standard Edition of the Complete Psychological Works.* Trans. James Strachey. Vol. 14. London: Hogarth, 1957. 243–58.

————. "On Narcissism: An Introduction." In *The Freud Reader.* Ed. Peter Gay. New York: Norton, 1989. 545–62.

Frye, Northrop. *The Great Code: The Bible and Literature.* New York: Harcourt Brace Jovanovich, 1982.

Gaines, Ernest. *The Autobiography of Miss Jane Pittman.* New York: Dial Press, 1971.

Gates, Henry Louis, Jr. "Criticism in the Jungle." In *Black Literature and Literary Theory.* Ed. Henry Louis Gates, Jr. New York: Methuen, 1984. 1–24.

————. "A Negro Way of Saying." *New York Times Book Review,* Apr. 21, 1985, 1, 41.

————. *The Signifying Monkey: A Theory of Afro-American Literary Criticsm.* New York: Oxford University Press, 1988.

————. "Why the Debate over *Mule Bone* Persists." *New York Times Book Review,* Feb. 10, 1991, 5, 8.

Gaudet, Marica, and Carl Wooton. *Porch Talk with Ernest Gaines: Conversations on the Writer's Craft.* Baton Rouge: Louisiana State University Press, 1990.

Gayle, Addison, Jr. *The Way of the New World: The Black Novel in America.* Garden City, N.Y.: Anchor Press, 1975.

Gennep, Arnold Van. *The Rites of Passage.* 1909. Trans. Monika B. Vizedom and Barielle L. Caffee. Chicago: University of Chicago Press, 1960.

Genovese, Eugene D. *Roll, Jordan, Roll: The World the Slaves Made.* 1972. New York: Vintage, 1976.

Gwynn, Frederick L., and Joseph L. Blotner. *Faulkner in the University.* Charlottesville: University of Virginia Press, 1959.

Hallpike, C. R. "Is There a Primitive Mentality?" *Man* 11, no. 2 (June 1976): 253–70.

Hammond, Peter B. "Mossi Joking." *Ethnology* 3, no. 3 (1964): 259–67.

Hannerz, Ulf. *Soulside: Inquiries into Ghetto Culture and Community.* New York: Columbia University Press, 1969.

Harmon, Marion F. *Negro Wit and Humor.* Louisville: Harmon Publishing, 1914.

Harper, Frances Ellen Watkins. *Moses, a Story of the Nile.* In *Complete Poems of Frances E. W. Harper.* Ed. Maryemma Graham. New York: Oxford University Press, 1988. 34–66.

Harrison, Daphne Duval. *Black Pearls: Blues Queens of the 1920s.* New Brunswick, N.J.: Rutgers University Press, 1988.

Havron, Laurie. *Hurricane Hush.* New York: Greystone Press, 1941.

Heller, Joseph. *God Knows.* New York: Knopf, 1984.

Hemenway, Robert. "Are You a Flying Lark or a Setting Dove?" In *Afro-American Literature: The Reconstruction of Instruction.* Ed. Dexter Fisher and Robert B. Stepto. New York: MLA, 1979. 122–52.

———. "Introduction: Author, Teller, and Hero" to *Uncle Remus: His Songs and His Sayings* by Joel Chandler Harris. Ed. Robert Hemenway. New York: Penguin, 1982. 7–31.

———. Introduction to *Dust Tracks on a Road* by Zora Neale Hurston. 2d ed. Ed. Robert Hemenway. Urbana: University of Illinois Press, 1984. ix–xxxix.

———. "The Personal Dimension in *Their Eyes Were Watching God*." In *New Essays on* Their Eyes Were Watching God. Ed. Michael Awkward. Cambridge: Cambridge University Press, 1991. 29–49.

———. *Zora Neale Hurston: A Literary Biography*. Urbana: University of Illinois Press, 1977.

Herskovits, Melville J. *The Myth of the Negro Past*. 1941. Boston: Beacon Press, 1991.

Higginson, Thomas Wentworth. *Army Life in a Black Regiment*. 1869. Boston: Beacon Press, 1962.

Hobsbawm, Eric. *Bandits*. New York: Dell, 1969.

Holloway, Joseph E., ed. *Africanisms in American Culture*. Bloomington: Indiana University Press, 1990.

Holloway, Karla. *The Character of the Word: The Texts of Zora Neale Hurston*. New York: Greenwood Press, 1987.

Holt, Grace Smith. "Stylin' Outta the Black Pulpit." In *The Nacirema: Readings on American Culture*. Ed. James P. Spradley and Michael A. Rynkiewich. Boston: Little, Brown, 1975. 323–35.

Horton, R. "African Traditional Thought and Western Science." *Africa* 37 (1967): 50–73, 155–87.

Howard, Lillie P. "Marriage: Zora Neale Hurston's System of Values." *College Language Association Journal* 21, no. 2 (Dec. 1977): 256–68.

———. *Zora Neale Hurston*. Boston: Twayne, 1980.

Huggins, Nathan Irvin. *Harlem Renaissance*. New York: Oxford University Press, 1971.

Hughes, Langston. *The Big Sea*. New York: Hill and Wang, 1940.

———. *Fine Clothes to the Jew*. New York: Knopf, 1927.

———. "Jokes Negroes Tell on Themselves." *Negro Digest* 9, no. 8 (1951): 21–25.

Hughes, Langston, and Arna Bontemps, eds. *The Book of Negro Folklore*. New York: Dodd, Mead, 1958.

Hughes, Langston, and Zora Neale Hurston. *Mule Bone: A Comedy of Negro Life*. New York: HarperCollins, 1991.

Huizinga, Johan. *Homo Ludens: A Study of the Play-Element in Culture*. Boston: Beacon, 1970. Orig. published in Dutch in 1938; trans. from the German ed., 1944.

Hurst, Fannie. "A Personality Sketch." In *Zora Neale Hurston*. Ed. Harold Bloom. New York: Chelsea House, 1986. 21–24.

Hurston, Zora Neale. "Black Death." Unpublished manuscript. Charles S. Johnson Papers, Special Collections, Fisk University Library, Nashville, Tenn.

———. "Book of Harlem." Unpublished manuscript. James Weldon Johnson Memorial Collection, Yale Collection of American Literature, Beinecke Rare Book and Manuscript Library, Yale University, New Haven, Conn.

———. "The Bone of Contention." Unpublished manuscript. Moorland-Spingarn Research Center, Howard University Library, Washington, D.C.

———. "Characteristics of Negro Expression." In *Negro: An Anthology*. Ed. Nancy Cunard. London: Wishart, 1934. 39–46.

———. "The Chick with One Hen." Unpublished manuscript. James Weldon Johnson Memorial Collection, Yale Collection of American Literature, Beinecke Rare Book and Manuscript Library, Yale University, New Haven, Conn.

———. "The Conscience of the Court." In *The Saturday Evening Post Stories, 1950*. New York: Random House, 1950. 16–30.

———. "The Conversion of Sam." Unpublished manuscript. Manuscripts, Archives, and Rare Books Division, Schomburg Center for Research in Black Culture, the New York Public Library, Astor, Lenox, and Tilden Foundations.

———. "Crazy for This Democracy." *Negro Digest* 4 (Dec. 1945): 45–48.

———. "Dance Songs and Tales from the Bahamas." *Journal of American Folklore* 43, no. 167 (1930): 294–312.

———. "Drenched in Light." *Opportunity* 2 (Dec. 1924): 371–74.

———. *Dust Tracks on a Road*. 1942. 2d ed. Ed. Robert Hemenway. Urbana: University of Illinois Press, 1984.

———. "The Eatonville Anthology." 1926. In *I Love Myself When I Am Laughing: A Zora Neale Hurston Reader*. Ed. Alice Walker. Old Westbury, N.Y.: Feminist Press, 1979. 177–88.

———. "The Elusive Goal: Brotherhood of Mankind." Unpublished manuscript. Hurston Collection, Rare Books and Manuscripts, University of Florida Library, Gainesville.

———. "The Fire and the Cloud." *Challenge* 1 (Sept. 1934): 10–14.

———. "The Fiery Chariot." Unpublished manuscript. Hurston Collection, Rare Books and Manuscripts, University of Florida Library, Gainesville.

———. "Folklore and Music." Unpublished manuscript. Hurston Collection, Rare Books and Manuscripts, University of Florida Library, Gainesville.

———. "The Gilded Six-Bits." In *I Love Myself When I Am Laughing: A Zora Neale Hurston Reader*. Ed. Alice Walker. Old Westbury, N.Y.: Feminist Press, 1979. 208–18.

———. "Herod the Great." Unpublished manuscript. Hurston Collection, Rare Books and Manuscripts, University of Florida Library, Gainesville.

———. "High John de Conquer." *American Mercury* 57 (Oct. 1943): 450–58.

———. "Hoodoo in America." *Journal of American Folklore* 44, no. 174 (1931): 317–417.

———. "How It Feels to Be Colored Me." 1928. In *I Love Myself When I Am Laughing: A Zora Neale Hurston Reader*. Ed. Alice Walker. Old Westbury, N.Y.: Feminist Press, 1979. 152–55.

———. "Jazz Regarded as Social Achievement." Rev. of *Shining Trumpets: A History of Jazz* by Rudi Blesh. *New York Herald Tribune Weekly Book Review*, Dec. 22, 1946, 8.

———. "John Redding Goes to Sea." *Opportunity* 2 (Dec. 1924): 371–74.

——. *Jonah's Gourd Vine.* 1934. New York: Harper and Row, 1990.

——. "Jonah's Gourd Vine." Original manuscript. Manuscripts, Archives, and Rare Books Division, Schomburg Center for Research in Black Culture, the New York Public Library, Astor, Lenox, and Tilden Foundations.

——. "Lawrence of the River." *Saturday Evening Post,* Sept. 5, 1942, 18, 55–57. Condensed in *Negro Digest* 1 (Mar. 1943): 47–49.

——. "The Lost Keys of Glory." Unpublished manuscript. Helen Worden Erskine Papers, Rare Book and Manuscript Library, Columbia University, New York, N.Y.

——. "Magnolia Flower." *The Spokesman* (July 1925): 26–29.

——. *Moses: Man of the Mountain.* 1939. Urbana: University of Illinois Press, 1984.

——. *Mules and Men.* 1935. Bloomington: Indiana University Press, 1978.

——. "Muttsy." *Opportunity* 4 (Aug. 1926): 246–50, 267.

——. "My Most Humiliating Jim Crow Experience." *Negro Digest* 2 (June 1944): 25–26.

——. "Negro Mythical Places." Unpublished manuscript. Hurston Collection, Rare Books and Manuscripts, University of Florida Library, Gainesville.

——. "The 'Pet Negro' System." *American Mercury* 56 (1943): 593–600.

——. "Possum or Pig." *Forum* 76 (Sept. 1926): 465.

——. "Race Cannot Become Great until It Recognizes Its Talent." *Washington Tribune,* Dec. 29, 1934.

——. *Seraph on the Suwanee.* New York: Charles Scribner's Sons, 1948.

——. "Seraph on the Suwanee." Original manuscript. Hurston Collection, Rare Books and Manuscripts, University of Florida Library, Gainesville.

——. "Spunk." *Opportunity* 3 (June 1925): 171–73.

——. "Story in Harlem Slang." *American Mercury* 55 (July 1942): 84–96.

——. "Sweat." 1926. In *I Love Myself When I Am Laughing: A Zora Neale Hurston Reader.* Ed. Alice Walker. Old Westbury, N.Y.: Feminist Press, 1979. 197–207.

——. *Their Eyes Were Watching God.* Urbana: University of Illinois Press, 1978.

——. "You Don't Know Us Negroes." Unpublished manuscript. Lawrence E. Spivak Papers, Manuscript Division, Library of Congress.

Hyatt, Marshall. "Franz Boas and the Struggle for Black Equality: The Dynamics of Ethnicity." *Perspectives in American History* 2 (1985): 269–95.

Jackson, Bruce, ed. *The Negro and His Folklore in Nineteenth-Century Periodicals.* Austin: University of Texas Press, 1967.

Jackson, Joyce Marie. "The Black American Folk Preacher and the Chanted Sermon: Parallels with a West African Tradition." In *Discourse in Ethnomusicology II: A Tribute to Alan P. Merriam.* Ed. Caroline Card, John Hasse, Roberta L. Singer, and Ruth M. Stone. Bloomington: Indiana University Press, 1981. 205–22.

Jacobson-Widding, Anita. "Body Symbolism in Connection with Relationships of Joking, Respect, and Avoidance." *Working Papers in African Studies* 2 (1984): 1–18.

Johnson, Barbara. "Metaphor, Metonymy, and Voice in *Their Eyes Were Watching God*." In *Black Literature and Literary Theory*. Ed. Henry Louis Gates, Jr. New York: Methuen, 1984. 205–19.

Johnson, Charles S. *Growing Up in the Black Belt: Negro Youth in the Rural South*. 1941. New York: Schocken Books, 1967.

Johnson, James Weldon. *Along This Way: The Autobiography of James Weldon Johnson*. New York: Viking, 1933.

———. *The Autobiography of an Ex-Colored Man*. 1912. In *Three Negro Classics*. Ed. John Hope Franklin. New York: Avon, 1963.

———. *God's Trombones*. New York: Viking, 1927.

———, ed. *The Book of American Negro Poetry*. 1922. New York: Harcourt Brace, 1969.

Jones, Anne Goodwyn. "Southern Literary Women as Chroniclers of Southern Life." In *Sex, Race, and the Role of Women in the South*. Ed. Joanne V. Hawks and Sheila L. Skamp. Jackson: University Press of Mississippi, 1983. 75–93.

Jones, Kirland C. "Folk Humor as Comic Relief in Hurston's *Jonah's Gourd Vine*." *Zora Neale Hurston Forum* 1, no. 1 (Fall 1986): 26–31.

Jung, C. G. "On the Psychology of the Trickster Figure." 1956. In *The Trickster: A Study in American Indian Mythology*. Ed. Paul Radin. New York: Schocken, 1972. 193–211.

Kalcik, Susan. "'. . . Like Ann's Gynecologist; or, The Time I Was Almost Raped': Personal Narratives in Women's Rap Groups." *Journal of American Folklore* 88 (1975): 3–11.

Kellner, Bruce. *Carl Van Vechten and the Irreverent Decades*. Norman: University of Oklahoma Press, 1968.

———, ed. *Letters of Carl Van Vechten*. New Haven: Yale University Press, 1987.

Kerenyi, Karl. "The Trickster in Relation to Greek Mythology." 1956. *The Trickster: A Study in American Indian Mythology*. Ed. Paul Radin. New York: Schocken, 1972. 171–91.

Killens, John O. *Youngblood*. 1954. Athens: University of Georgia Press, 1982.

Klein, Melanie. *Contributions to Psychoanalysis, 1921–1945*. London: Hogarth Press, 1948.

Kobbe, Gustave. *The New Kobbe's Complete Opera Book*. 1919. Ed. and rev. by the Earl of Harewood. New York: Putnam, 1976.

Kochman, Thomas. *Black and White Performance Styles in Conflict*. Chicago: University of Chicago Press, 1981.

———. "Toward an Ethnography of Black American Speech Behavior." In *Afro-American Anthropology: Contemporary Perspectives*. Ed. Norman E. Whitten, Jr., and John F. Szwed. New York: Free Press, 1970. 145–62.

Koestler, Arthur. *The Act of Creation*. London: Hutchinson, 1964.

Krapp, George Philip. "The English of the Negro." *American Mercury* 2 (1924): 190–95.

———. "The Psychology of Dialect Writing." *Bookman* 60 (1926): 522–27.

Kubitschek, Missy Dehn. "'Tuh De Horizon and Back': The Female Quest in *Their Eyes Were Watching God*." *Black American Literature Forum* 17, no. 3 (Fall 1983): 109–14.

Kunitz, Stanley J., and Howard Haycraft, eds. *Twentieth-Century Authors: A Biographical Dictionary of Modern Literature.* New York: H. W. Wilson, 1942.

Labov, William. "The Art of Sounding and Signifying." In *Language in Its Social Setting.* Ed. William W. Gage. Washington, D.C.: Anthropological Society of Washington, 1974. 84–116.

Lakoff, Robin. *Language and Woman's Place.* New York: Harper and Row, 1975.

Larsen, Nella. *Quicksand* and *Passing.* 1928. Ed. Deborah E. McDowell. New Brunswick, N.J.: Rutgers University Press, 1986.

Leab, Daniel. *From Sambo to Superspade: The Black Experience in Motion Pictures.* Boston: Houghton Mifflin, 1976.

Lemann, Nicholas. *The Promised Land: The Great Black Migration and How It Changed America.* New York: Knopf, 1991.

Levine, Lawrence. *Black Culture and Black Consciousness: Afro-American Folk Thought from Slavery to Freedom.* New York: Oxford University Press, 1977.

Lincoln, C. Eric, and Lawrence H. Mamiya. *The Black Church in the African American Experience.* Durham, N.C.: Duke University Press, 1990.

Linton, Ralph. "Primitive Art." *Kenyon Review* 3, no. 1 (1946): 34–57.

Lippman, Walter. *Public Opinion.* New York: Harcourt Brace, 1922.

Locke, Alain. "Jingo, Counter-Jingo, and Us." *Opportunity* 16 (Jan. 1938): 8–11, 27.

———. "The Negro and the American Stage." *Theatre Arts Monthly* (Feb. 1926): 112–120.

———. "Negro Youth Speaks." 1925. In *The New Negro.* Ed. Alain Locke. New York: Atheneum, 1968. 45–53.

Lomax, Louis E. "The American Negro's New Comedy Act." *Harper's Magazine,* June 1961, 41–46.

Lott, Eric. "'The Seeming Counterfeit': Racial Politics and Early Blackface Minstrelsy." *American Quarterly* 43, no. 2 (June 1991): 223–54.

Lowe, John. "Wright Writing Reading: Narrative Strategies in *Uncle Tom's Children.*" *Journal of the Short Story in English* 10 (Autumn 1988): 49–74.

McDavid, Raven I., Jr., and Virginia Glenn McDavid. "The Relationship of the Speech of American Negroes to the Speech of Whites." *American Speech* 26 (1951): 3–17.

McGhee, Paul. *Humor: Its Origin and Development.* San Francisco: W. H. Freeman, 1979.

McKay, Claude. "Harlem Dancer." *Seven Arts* 2 (1917): 741.

McKay, Nellie. "'Crayon Englargements of Life': Zora Neale Hurston's *Their Eyes Were Watching God* as Autobiography." In *New Essays on Their Eyes Were Watching God.* Ed. Michael Awkward. Cambridge: Cambridge University Press, 1991. 51–70.

Marks, Carol. *Farewell—We're Good and Gone: The Great Black Migration.* Philadelphia: University of Pennsylvania Press, 1989.

Mason, Julian. "Some Thoughts on Literary Stereotyping." *Negro American Literature Forum* 6, no. 3 (1972): 63–70.

Mayer, Philip. "The Joking of 'Pals' in Gusii Age-Sets." *African Studies* 10 (1951): 27–41.

Mbiti, John S. *African Religions and Philosophy*. Garden City, N.Y.: Doubleday, 1970.

Melville, Herman. *Pierre; or, The Ambiguities*. 1852. Evanston: Northwestern University Press, 1971.

Middleton, Russell. "Negro and White Reactions to Racial Humor." *Sociometry* 22 (1959): 175–83.

Miller, Perry. *Errand into the Wilderness*. Cambridge, Mass.: Harvard University Press, 1956.

Mitchell, Juliet. *Psychoanalysis and Feminism: Freud, Reich, Laing, and Women*. New York: Vintage Books, 1974.

Mitchell-Kernan, Claudia. "Signifying and Marking: Two Afro-American Speech Acts." In *Directions in Social Linguistics*. Ed. John J. Gumperz and Dell Hymes. New York: Holt, Rinehart, and Winston, 1972. 161–79.

———. "Signifying, Loud-Talking, and Marking." In *Rappin' and Stylin' Out: Communication in Urban Black America*. Ed. Thomas Kochman. Urbana: University of Illinois Press, 1972. 315–35.

Morell, Karen L. *In Person: Achebe, Awoonor, and Soyinka at the University of Washington*. Seattle: Institute for Comparative and Foreign Area Studies, 1975.

Morris, Ann R., and Margaret M. Dunn. "Flora and Fauna in Hurston's Florida Novels." In *Zora in Florida*. Ed. Steve Glassman and Kathryn Lee Seidel. Orlando: University of Central Florida Press, 1991. 1–12.

Morrison, Toni. *Beloved*. New York: Knopf, 1987.

———. "Rootedness: the Ancestor as Foundation." In *Black Women Writers (1950–1980)*. Ed. Mari Evans. New York: Anchor, 1984. 339–445.

Moses, Wilson Jeremiah. *The Golden Age of Black Nationalism, 1850–1925*. Hamden, Conn.: Archon Books, 1978.

Murray, Albert. *The Hero and the Blues*. Jefferson: University of Missouri Press, 1985.

———. "Regional Particular and Universal Statement in Southern Writing." *Callaloo* 12, no. 1 (1989): 3–6.

Neal, Larry. "Eatonville's Zora Neale Hurston: A Profile." In *Black Review 2*. Ed. Mel Watkins. New York: William Morrow, 1972. 11–24.

Neverdon-Morton, Cynthia. *Afro-American Women of the South and the Advancement of the Race, 1895–1925*. Knoxville: University of Tennessee Press, 1989.

Nichols, Charles H. "Comic Modes in Black America (A Ramble through Afro-American Humor)." In *Comic Relief: Humor in Contemporary American Literature*. Ed. Sarah Blacher Cohen. Urbana: University of Illinois Press, 1978. 105–26.

Nichols, Patricia C. "Black and White Speaking in the Rural South: Difference in the Pronominal System." *American Speech* 58, no. 3 (1983): 201–15.

O'Brien, John, ed. "Alice Walker." In *Interviews with Black Writers*. New York: Liveright, 1973. 185–211.

Ogundipe, Ayodele. "Esu Elegbara, the Yoruba God of Chance and Uncertainty: A Study in Yoruba Mythology." Ph.D. diss., Indiana University, 1978.

Okpewho, Isidore. *The Epic in Africa: Toward a Poetics of Oral Performance.* New York: Columbia University Press, 1979.

Oliver, Paul. *Savannah Syncopators: African Retentions in the Blues.* New York: Stein and Day, 1970.

Opland, Jeff. *Xhosa Oral Poetry: Aspects of a Black African Tradition.* Cambridge: Cambridge University Press, 1983.

Oring, Elliott. *Jokes and Their Relations.* Lexington: University Press of Kentucky, 1992.

Osofsky, Gilbert. *Puttin' on Ole Massa: The Slave Narratives of Henry Bibb, William Wells Brown, and Solomon Northrup.* New York: Harper and Row, 1969.

Ostendorf, Berndt. *Black Literature in White America.* Totowa, N.J.: Barnes and Noble, 1982.

Otey, Frank M. *Eatonville, Florida: A Brief History of One of America's First Freedmen's Towns.* Winter Park, Fla.: Four-G Publishers, 1989.

Owens, Leslie Howard. *This Species of Property: Slave Life and Culture in the Old South.* New York: Oxford University Press, 1976.

Pardes, Ilana. *Countertraditions in the Bible: A Feminist Approach.* Cambridge, Mass.: Harvard University Press, 1992.

Parker, Idella, with Mary Keating. *Idella: Marjorie Rawlings' "Perfect Maid."* Gainesville: University of Florida Press, 1992.

Piersen, William D. "Puttin' Down Ole Massa: African Satire in the New World." In *African Folklore in the New World.* Ed. Daniel J. Crowley. Austin: University of Texas Press, 1977. 20–34.

Plant, Deborah. "African-American Folklore as Style, Theme, and Strategy." Paper presented at the first annual Zora Neale Hurston Festival of the Arts, Eatonville, Florida, January 1990.

Pondrom, Cyrena N. "The Role of Myth in Hurston's *Their Eyes Were Watching God.*" *American Literature* 58, no. 2 (May 1986): 181–202.

Powdermaker, Hortense. "The Channeling of Negro Aggression by the Cultural Process." *American Journal of Sociology* 48, no. 6 (1943): 750–58.

Prange, Arthur, Jr., and M. M. Vitols. "Jokes among Southern Negroes: The Revelation of Conflict." In *Mother Wit from the Laughing Barrel: Readings in the Interpretation of Afro-American Folklore.* Ed. Alan Dundes. Englewood Cliffs, N.J.: Prentice-Hall, 1973. 628–36.

Pratt, Theodore. *Big Blow.* Boston: Little, Brown, 1936.

———. "Zora Neale Hurston." *Florida Historical Quarterly* 40, no. 1 (July 1961): 35–40.

Raboteau, Albert J. *Slave Religion: The "Invisible Institution" in the Antebellum South.* New York: Oxford University Press, 1978.

Rabuzzi, Kathryn Allen. *Motherself: A Mythic Analysis of Motherhood.* Bloomington: Indiana University Press, 1988.

Radcliffe-Brown, A. R. "A Further Note on Joking Relationships." 1949. *Structure and Function in Primitive Society.* London: Cohen West, 1965. 105–16.

Radin, Paul. "The Literature of Primitive Peoples." *Diogenes* 12 (1955): 1–29.

———, ed. *The Trickster: A Study in American Indian Mythology.* 1956. New York: Schocken, 1972.

Raskin, Victor. *Semantic Mechanisms of Humor.* Dordrecht, the Netherlands: D. Reidel, 1985.

Reid, Ira DeA. "Mrs. Bailey Pays the Rent." 1927. In *Ebony and Topaz: A Collectanea.* Ed. Charles S. Johnson. Freeport, N.Y.: Books for Libraries Press, 1971. 144–48.

Reik, Theodor. *Jewish Wit.* New York: Gamut, 1962.

Rickford, John R. "Ethnicity as a Sociolinguistic Boundary." *American Speech* 60, no. 2 (1985): 99–125.

Ricoeur, Paul. *Freud and Philosophy: An Essay on Interpretation.* New Haven: Yale University Press, 1970.

Riesman, David. *The Lonely Crowd.* New York: Doubleday, 1956.

Roberts, John W. *From Trickster to Badman: The Black Folk Hero in Slavery and Freedom.* Philadelphia: University of Pennsylvania Press, 1989.

Rosenberg, Bruce A. *Can These Bones Live?: The Art of the American Folk Preacher.* Rev. ed. Urbana: University of Illinois Press, 1988.

Rosenblatt, Roger. *Black Fiction.* Cambridge, Mass.: Harvard University Press, 1974.

Rourke, Constance. *American Humor: A Study of the National Character.* New York: Harcourt Brace, 1931.

Schechter, William. *The History of Negro Humor in America.* New York: Fleet Press, 1970.

Schiesari, Juliana. *The Gendering of Melancholia: Feminism, Psychoanalysis, and the Symbolics of Loss in Renaissance Literature.* Ithaca, N.Y.: Cornell University Press, 1992.

Schuyler, George S. "Our Greatest Gift to America." 1927. In *Ebony and Topaz: A Collectanea.* Ed. Charles S. Johnson. Freeport, N.Y.: Books for Libraries Press, 1971. 122–24.

Seyffert, Oskar, Henry Nettleship, and J. E. Sandys. *Dictionary of Classical Antiquities.* New York: Meridian, 1956.

Sheen, Vincent. *Dorothy and Red.* Boston: Houghton Mifflin, 1963.

Sheffey, Ruth. *Trajectory: Fueling the Future and Preserving the African-American Literary Past.* Baltimore: Morgan State University Press, 1989.

Short, Randall. "Just Folks." *Mirabella,* Mar. 1991, 72.

Silverthorne, Elizabeth. *Marjorie Kinnan Rawlings: Sojourner at Cross Creek.* Woodstock, N.Y.: Overlook Press, 1988.

Sims, Walter Hines. *Baptist Hymnal.* Nashville: Convention Press, 1956.

Singal, Daniel Joseph. "Towards a Definition of American Modernism." *American Quarterly* 39, no. 1 (1987): 7–26.

Slaughter, Frank G. "Freud in Turpentine." *New York Times Book Review,* Oct. 31, 1948, 24.

Smith, Bessie. "Florida Bound Blues." Columbia Records 14109-D. Reissued on *Bessie Smith: The Complete Recordings.* Vol. 2. Columbia Records C2K4741.

Smitherman, Geneva. *Talkin' and Testifyin': The Language of Black America.* Boston: Houghton Mifflin, 1977.

Sollors, Werner. *Beyond Ethnicity: Consent and Descent in American Culture.* New York: Oxford University Press, 1986.

————. "Literature and Ethnicity." In *The Harvard Encyclopedia of American Ethnic Groups.* Ed. Stephan Thernstrom, Ann Orlov, and Oscar Handlin. Cambridge, Mass.: Harvard University Press, 1980. 647–65.

————. "Never Was Born: The Mulatto, an American Tragedy?" *Massachusetts Review* 27, no. 2 (Summer 1986): 293–316.

Spaulding, Henry D., comp. and ed. *Encyclopedia of Black Folklore and Humor.* 1972; rev. ed., Middle Village, N.Y.: Jonathan David, 1978.

Sperling, Samuel J. "On the Psychodynamics of Teasing." *Journal of the American Psychoanalytic Association* 1, no. 3 (1953): 458–83.

Steiner, George. *After Babel: Aspects of Language and Translation.* New York: Oxford University Press, 1975.

Stepto, Robert. *From behind the Veil: A Study of Afro-American Narrative.* Urbana: University of Illinois Press, 1979.

Sterling, Philip. *Laughing on the Outside: The Intelligent White Reader's Guide to Negro Tales and Humor.* New York: Grosset and Dunlap, 1965.

Stevens, George. "Negroes by Themselves." Rev. of *Their Eyes Were Watching God* by Zora Neale Hurston. *Saturday Review,* Sept. 18, 1937, 3.

Stewart, William A. "Acculturative Processes and the Language of the American Negro." In *Language in Its Social Setting.* Ed. William W. Gage. Washington, D.C.: Anthropological Association of Washington, 1974. 1–46.

————. "Understanding Black Language." In *Black America.* Ed. John F. Szwed. New York: Basic Books, 1970. 121–31.

Stowe, William F., and David Grimsted. "White-Black Humor." Rev. of *Blacking Up* by Robert Toll. *Ethnic Studies* 3 (1975–76): 78–96.

Swift, Jonathan. *Gulliver's Travels and Other Writings.* Ed. Louis A. Landa. Boston: Houghton Mifflin, 1960.

Szwed, John. "An American Anthropological Dilemma: The Politics of Afro-American Culture." In *Reinventing Anthropology.* Ed. Dell Hymes. New York: Vintage, 1974. 153–81.

Taft, Michael. *Blues Lyric Poetry: An Anthology.* New York: Garland, 1984.

Talley, Thomas W. *Negro Folk Rhymes, Wise and Otherwise, with a Study.* 1922. Port Washington, N.Y.: Kennikat Press, 1968.

Teubal, Savina J. *Hagar the Egyptian: The Lost Tradition of the Matriarchs.* New York: Harper and Row, 1990.

Thurman, Wallace. *Infants of the Spring.* New York: MacCaulay, 1932.

Toll, Robert. *Blacking Up: The Minstrel Show in Nineteenth-Century America.* New York: Oxford University Press, 1974.

Toohey, John L. *A History of the Pulitzer Prize Plays.* New York: Citadel Press, 1967.

Torgovnick, Marianna. *Gone Primitive: Savage Intellects, Modern Lives.* Chicago: University of Chicago Press, 1990.

Trible, Phyllis. "Hagar: The Desolation of Rejection." *Literary-Feminist Readings of Biblical Narratives.* Philadelphia: Fortress Press, 1984. 9–35.

Turner, Darwin. *In a Minor Chord: Three Afro-American Writers and Their Search for Identity.* Carbondale: Southern Illinois University Press, 1971.

Turner, Victor. *The Ritual Process.* Ithaca, N.Y.: Cornell University Press, 1969.

Untermeyer, Louis. *Moses: A Novel.* New York: Harcourt Brace, 1928.

———. "Old Testament Voodoo." Rev. of *Moses, Man of the Mountain* by Zora Neale Hurston. *Saturday Review,* Nov. 11, 1939, 11.

Varnedoe, Kirk. "Abstract Expressionism." In *"Primitivism" in Twentieth Century Art: Affinity of the Tribal and the Modern.* Ed. William Rubin. 2 vols. New York: Museum of Modern Art, 1984. 2:615–59.

Vinacke, W. E. "Stereotypes as Social Concepts." *Journal of Social Psychology* 46 (1957): 229–43.

Walker, Alice. *The Color Purple.* New York: Harcourt Brace Jovanovich, 1982.

———. "If the Present Looks like the Past, What Does the Future Look Like?" In *In Search of Our Mother's Gardens: Womanist Prose.* New York: Harcourt Brace, 1983. 290–312.

———. *Meridian.* New York: Harcourt Brace Jovanovich, 1976.

———. *In Search of Our Mothers' Gardens: Womanist Prose.* New York: Harcourt Brace, 1983.

Walker, Nancy. *A Very Serious Thing: Women's Humor and American Culture.* Minneapolis: University of Minnesota Press, 1988.

Wall, Cheryl. "Zora Neale Hurston: Changing Her Own Words." In *American Novelists Revisited: Essays in Feminist Criticism.* Ed. Fritz Fleishmann. Boston: G. K. Hall, 1982. 371–93.

———, ed. *Changing Our Own Words: Essays on Criticism, Theory, and Writing by Black Women.* New Brunswick, N.J.: Rutgers University Press, 1989.

Washington, Booker T. *Up from Slavery.* 1901. In *Three Negro Classics.* Ed. John Hope Franklin. New York: Avon, 1965.

Washington, Mary Helen. "Introduction." In *Black-Eyed Susans: Classic Stories by and about Black Women.* Ed. Mary Helen Washington. New York: Anchor, 1975. ix–xxxii.

———. "Introduction: Zora Neale Hurston: A Woman Half in Shadow." In *I Love Myself When I Am Laughing: A Zora Neale Hurston Reader.* Ed. Alice Walker. Old Westbury, N.Y.: Feminist Press, 1979. 7–25.

———. *Invented Lives: Narratives of Black Women, 1860–1960.* Garden City, N.Y.: Anchor Press, 1987.

———. "Zora Neale Hurston: The Black Woman's Search for Identity." *Black World* (Aug. 1974): 68–75.

Werner, Craig. "Recent Books on Modern Black Fiction: An Essay-Review." *Modern Fiction Studies* 34, no. 1 (Spring 1988): 125–35.

———. "Zora Neale Hurston." In *Modern American Women Writers.* Ed. Elaine Showalter, Lea Baechler, and A. Walton Litz. New York: Charles Scribner's Sons, 1991. 221–33.

Wideman, John. "Playing, Not Joking, with Language." Rev. of *The Signifying Monkey* by Henry Louis Gates, Jr. *New York Times Book Review,* Aug. 14, 1988, 3.

Wiggins, William H., Jr. "Jack Johnson as Bad Nigger: The Folklore of His Life." *Black Scholar* (Jan. 1971): 35–46.

Williams, Sherley Anne. Foreword to *Their Eyes Were Watching God* by Zora Neale Hurston. Urbana: University of Illinois Press, 1978. x–xv.

Wittke, Carl. *Tambo and Bones.* New York: Greenwood, 1968.

Woll, Allen. *Black Musical Theatre: From Coontown to Dreamgirls.* Baton Rouge: Louisiana State University Press, 1989.

Works Progress Administration. *Drums and Shadows: Survival Studies among the Georgia Coastal Negroes.* Athens: University of Georgia Press, 1940.

Wright, Richard. "Between Laughter and Tears." Rev. of *Their Eyes Were Watching God* by Zora Neale Hurston. *New Masses* 5 (Oct. 1937): 25–26.

———. *Black Boy.* 1945. New York: Harper and Row, 1966.

———. *The Long Dream.* New York: Harper and Row, 1958.

Index

Buissi people, 81*n*11
Bunker, Archie, 319
Burroughs, Edgar Rice, 27
Bus, Heiner, 67
Buzzards' "funeral," 173
Byron, George Gordon, 327

Cahan, Abraham, 71
Cain, 210, 250, 290
Caldwell, Erskine, 266, 269
Callahan, John, 162–63, 192
Call and response, 66, 95, 130, 133, 163, 244
Campbell, Joseph, 37, 198*n*3
Cane (Toomer), 32, 70, 132
Capp, Al, 339*n*24
Carby, Hazel, 80*n*7, 264, 280–81, 339*n*26
Caricatures, 12, 71, 110, 170, 230
Carnival, 37, 171–72. *See also* Carnivalization
Carnivalization, 38, 230; of language, 39
Carr, Glynis, 191
Cartoons, ethnic, 12
"Carve That Possum" (song), 19
Cather, Willa, 37
Cat on a Hot Tin Roof (Williams), 75
Chariot of Fire, 145
"Charston" (song), 29
Chesnutt, Charles, 18, 222, 236, 237
Chinese philosophers, 37
Chocolate Drops from the South, 16
Chodorow, Nancy, 296
Chopin, Kate, 178
Choral function of community, 167, 267–68
Cinderella, 278
Civilization and Its Discontents (Freud), 328
Civil War (American), 16
Clansman, The (Dixon), 19
Class, social, 100, 107, 109, 114, 140, 159, 168, 183, 211, 220, 230, 234, 236, 265, 270, 292, 318, 330
Clay eaters, 292
Clubwomen, African American, 240, 253*n*26
Cobb, Irvin S., 36
Codes: in drumming, 133; in folklore, 18, 111; "lying sessions," 58; in lyrics, 12

Code-switching, linguistic, 143
Coined words, 74
Collections of "Negro Humor," 16
Colman, George, 16
"Colored folks' time," 113
Color prejudice within African American society, 100, 108, 185–86, 187, 202*n*22, 237
Color Purple, The (Walker), 100, 201*n*19
Comedians, African American, 28
Comic tradition, African, 3–8
Communitas, 103, 190, 327
Conjure, 6, 62, 129, 170; and dreams, 271; during slavery, 254*n*31. *See also* Hoodoo
Conjure Woman, The (Chesnutt), 254*n*32
Connelly, Marc, 87, 215
Conrad, Joseph, 28
Cooke, Michael G., 201*n*16
"Coon Song," 19, 119
Cooper, James Fenimore, 18
Corregio family, 307
Coser, Rose, 43*n*16, 288, 337*n*14
Cosmic imagery, 34–35, 77–78, 91, 102, 110, 124, 129, 132, 138–39, 140, 157, 213, 219, 247, 329, 333, 334
Costain, Thomas, 217
Courlander, Harold, 40
Courtroom scenes, 137–38, 189–93
Courtship thematic, 69
Cox, Ida, 12
Crackers, 321; aesthetic taste, 276; equation with African Americans, 318–19; lack of cultural memory, 266; speech, 280, 318
Creation stories, 4, 9
Cripps, Thomas, 42*n*5
Cross Creek (Rawlings), 338*n*21
Cullen, Countee, 44*n*18
Currier and Ives, 19
"Cuttin' the monkey," 21

Damballah, 160
Dance, Daryl, 40, 81*n*13, 87, 112, 252*n*14
Dance of Death (Strindberg), 318
Dandy, Jim, 16
Dante, 255*n*35
Dartmouth, Thomas. *See* Rice, Jim Crow
Davenport, "Cow Cow," 13

JOHN LOWE has taught at Columbia University, Saint Mary's College (Notre Dame), and Harvard University, where he was the Andrew W. Mellon Fellow in African American Studies. He is currently an associate professor of English at Louisiana State University, where he teaches African American, Southern, and ethnic literature and theory.